Changing Literacies for Changing Times

Of
Ch
futu
of
ting
Far
res

bei
des
pra
spe
for
boc

Jar
Aus

Yet
Un

Changing Literacies for Changing Times

An Historical Perspective on the Future of Reading Research, Public Policy, and Classroom Practices

Edited by

James V. Hoffman
University of Texas at Austin

Yetta Goodman
University of Arizona

Routledge
Taylor & Francis Group
NEW YORK AND LONDON

Learning Resource Centre

13725998

First published 2009
by Routledge
270 Madison Ave, New York, NY 10016

Simultaneously published in the UK
by Routledge
2 Park Square, Milton Park, Abingdon, Oxon OX14 4RN

*Routledge is an imprint of the Taylor & Francis Group,
an informa business*

© 2009 Taylor & Francis

Typeset in Baskerville by RefineCatch Limited, Bungay, Suffolk
Printed and bound in the United States of America on acid-free paper by
Walsworth Publishing Company, Marceline, MO.

Library of Congress Cataloging-in-Publication Data
Changing literacies for changing times : an historical perspective on the future of reading research, public policy, and classroom practices / edited by Yetta Goodman, James V. Hoffman.
    p. cm.
  1. Literacy—United States. 2. Literacy—Government policy—United States. 3. Reading—Research—United States.
I. Goodman, Yetta M., 1931– II. Hoffman, James V.
  LC151.C43 2009
  302.2'2440973—dc22

                            2008055162

ISBN 10: 0–415–99502–7 (hbk)
ISBN 10: 0–415–99503–0 (pbk)
ISBN 10: 0–203–87518–4 (ebk)

ISBN 13: 978–0–415–99502–3 (hbk)
ISBN 13: 978–0–415–99503–0 (pbk)
ISBN 13: 978–0–203–87518–6 (ebk)

Those who cannot learn from history are doomed to repeat it.
Santayana

Contents

Preface

Yetta Goodman
University of Arizona

James V. Hoffman
University of Texas – Austin

History has a way of repeating itself. Education is no exception. Ideas, theories, the language we use, and the ways of working with students recycle over time. Literacy professionals who have worked in the fields of teaching and learning literacy for decades have witnessed continuous shifts in reading research, policy, and pedagogy. Sadly, not all shifts have been for the better. Critical voices can turn cynical, as in old timers' musing: "We've been there." "Done that." "Won't work." "This too shall pass." Such statements do little to inform the discussions that are taking place in our field at this time. In this volume the authors use their histories and scholarly work to frame the changes that have been taking place in our dynamic profession to inform the future.

We have seen profound change in literacy in general and in literacy research over the past five decades. The authors reflect on the changes to provide insights and understandings about contemporary literacy issues that include: concerns with the multimodal and multicultural literacies; knowledge about diverse literacy learners; understanding about literacy processes; the influence of such knowledge on the teaching of literacies; and changes in understanding the critical and political nature of literacy. These changes represent the growth of knowledge and understanding that the authors have experienced and that have influenced our shifts in research and theoretical understanding.

Through the individual and collective experiences of the authors, we have reorganized, reconstructed, and expanded our knowledge and the meanings of our experiences in order to direct the course of our subsequent inquiries. Although we appreciate reference to our early work, in the present volume the authors present their work in the current sociocultural and political contexts. Scholars who have been actively writing for three decades or more appreciate having the opportunity to present their most recent work in a volume that includes a focus on the historical. When a researcher's earliest work is only referenced, then the field misses the examination and modifications that take place throughout an academic career. In this volume, readers are able to establish for themselves the changes that have taken place over time.

The authors represent their diversity and unique positions in the fields of literacy learning and teaching. As each of us continues to transact with literacy practices our views, attitudes, and knowledge continue to change and influence our intellectual growth. As a result of our continuous transactions with literacy issues in our global society, we expand our ideas to inform each other and other literacy researchers and theorists.

The lead author and in some cases more than one of the authors, is a member of the Reading Hall of Fame and have years of significant literacy experiences. The authors are recognized for their continuous contributions to reading research, the professional literature, and support for teachers. They offer the wisdom that experience and expertise bring to literacy learning and teaching. The Reading Hall of Fame was established to recognize scholars throughout the world whose work has impacted the literacy field for more than 25 years. Although Reading Hall of Fame members often joke that the modal age of its membership is "deceased", the majority of members remain active in research and writing and are current about the controversies and debates in the field. They have lived the modern history of the field through the lenses of the twentieth century and are well aware that the knowledge and understanding that are integral to the history of teaching and learning literacy must continue to inform the field in the twenty-first century. They recognize a responsibility to share this sense of history with younger and newer scholars. This sense of responsibility led to this book.

As a diverse group of scholars, theorists and researchers, members of the Reading Hall of Fame do not take single positions on the issues that are explored here. Rather members are comfortable with their diversity and present their unique views and perspectives in order to invite other scholars to take part in the discussions and conclusions. It is the dynamic nature of growth and change that sustain the richness of any field and it is enriched by continuous debate and critique.

The fields of literacy teaching and learning must reflect its history or, as Santayana cautions, literacy theory and research will repeatedly face the same problems over and over again from decisions made that do not take into consideration what is already known and has been learned. There is a tendency to think that new ideas are better than the old but ignorance of the past causes researchers, policy professionals, and practitioners to repeat past mistakes and to think that what are considered new ideas have never been previously explored. The power of historical analysis rests in the opportunity to look at what may seem similar at the surface level in the complexity of variable contextual factors.

The present educational scene provides numerous instances of issues that would benefit from a historical perspective and analysis. Transmission models of teaching, for example, are more prevalent than in previous decades in many classrooms from preschool through universities and colleges. Students from all levels of education are frustrated and bored as a result of the focus on testing outcomes and the regurgitation of single correct answers. Students are not being energized to become invested in their own learning, searching for their own understanding in their transactions with the increasing number and kinds of texts that are now available in the world. Those who know history know we've lived through such periods of highly skills-oriented literacy instruction before with similar results.

This volume provides the opportunity to read about the work of a wide range of literacy scholars in the Reading Hall of Fame whose work has spanned decades. The changes that have influenced each researcher become visible as they discuss their explorations and developing knowledge. At the same time, they use their growth over the years to suggest future projects and research. Literacy is viewed as social as well as personal. It has taken on new meanings and represents reading researchers' understanding of the changing relationships between reading and writing and new understanding about the many ways in which literacy is used by people throughout the world in many venues, for a range of powerful and mundane purposes and with a range of materials. Although the term literacy is preferable at this historical moment to the term reading, the term reading has been retained in the name *Reading Hall of Fame* to make visible the changes in the concept of reading and literacy over the past decades.

The chapters in this volume are organized into sections. In Part I we offer chapters that stretch our understanding of the term *literacy* itself (i.e., what counts and what gets counted) and the expanding access to these ever changing forms of literacy. In Part II we offer consideration of literacy issues as related to development from early readers through adulthood. In Part III, the authors describe the dynamic shifts in literacy learning and teaching, including a focus on foundational issues that have been part of the discourse around literacy for over a century. These authors describe the understandings and possibilities that have promoted changes, perspectives, and views of literacy. The two chapters in Part IV focus on themes related to teaching, teacher preparation, and professional development in the field of reading. In Part V the authors explore the shifting policy contexts for literacy and their impact.

We have been guided by a fundamental belief in the editing of this book. Change is an inevitable part of the future of our society. As literacy educators, we can learn from our past and use this knowledge to help shape a future that is better—more just for all. With conscious effort, intelligence, inspiration, dedication, and vigilance, education can lead change and not become its victim. We can finally act on Paulo Freire's plea for education as the "practice of freedom" and be mindful of his words as we consider the challenges ahead:

> Education either functions as an instrument which is used to facilitate integration of the younger generation into the logic of the present system and bring about conformity or it becomes the practice of freedom, the means by which men and women deal critically and creatively with reality and discover how to participate in the transformation of their world.
>
> (*Pedagogy of the Oppressed*)

Contributors

Yetta M. Goodman is Regents Professor Emerita of Education at the University of Arizona – Tucson, College of Education, Department of Language, Reading, and Culture. During her career she has been researching miscue analysis, early literacy processes, and kid watching for many years. In addition to her leadership roles in many professional organizations, she has authored and co-authored many books and articles, including *Reading Miscue Inventory: Alternative Procedures, Retrospective Miscue Analysis: Revaluing Readers and Reading,* and *Reading Strategies: Focus on Comprehension.* Other recent books also include *Critical Issues in Early Literacy Development* (Routledge) and *Valuing Language Study for Elementary and Middle School Students.* She strongly advocates for the professionalism of teachers and their capability in the development of language across the curriculum.

James V. Hoffman is a Professor of Language and Literacy Studies at The University of Texas at Austin. Dr. Hoffman's research has focused on teaching and teacher education in the area of reading. He has published numerous books and research articles related to reading. Recent books include: *Balancing Principles for Elementary Reading Instruction* and *The Texts in Elementary Classrooms* and he has served as President of the National Reading Conference, President of The Reading Hall of Fame, and as a member of the Board of Directors of The International Reading Association. He has served as editor for both the Yearbook of the National Reading Conference and the Reading Research Quarterly. Dr. Hoffman has been active internationally in literacy development work with a particular focus on improving the qualities of books and teaching in South African rural schools.

Diane Lapp, Distinguished Professor of Education at San Diego State University directs and teaches school based preservice and graduate programs in literacy education. She has taught in elementary and middle school, and is currently teaching 11th & 12th grade English at an urban high school. Her major areas of research and instruction focus on issues related to struggling learners and their families who live and learn in low economic urban communities.

James Flood was a Distinguished Professor of Education at San Diego State University before his passing in 2007. In addition to teaching at SDSU he was also a high school English teacher. He served as President of the National Reading Conference from 1993 to 1994 and also on the Board of Directors of The International Reading Association from 2003 to 2006. His major areas of research broadly sampled multiple dimensions of literacy acquisition and utilization of learners of all ages.

Shirley Brice Heath, Professor at Large, Watson Institute for International Studies at Brown University, and Margery Bailey Professor of English and Dramatic Literature and Professor of Linguistics, Emerita, Stanford University, is a linguistic anthropologist whose work centers on the oral and written language socialization of children and youth.

Judith Langer, Distinguished Professor at the University at Albany, is the Director of the Albany Institute for Research in Education and Director of the Center on English Learning & Achievement. Her research focuses on the literate mind: how people become highly literate, how they use reading and writing to learn, the relationships among society, schooling and learning, and what teachers and schools can do to facilitate effective learning, particularly among urban and low performing youth.

Nancy L. Roser is Professor of Language and Literacy Studies, the Flawn Professor of Early Childhood, and Distinguished Teaching Professor at the University of Texas at Austin. A former elementary teacher, she now teaches undergraduate elementary reading and language arts, as well as graduate courses in teaching the English Language Arts and Children's Literature. She has been awarded the Outstanding Teacher Educator in Texas Award and Lifetime Service Award (Texas Council of Teachers of English), Indiana University School of Education Distinguished Alumni Award, the Dean's Distinguished Service Award, Texas Excellence Teaching Award, and Piper Professor.

Sam Weintraub is Professor Emeritus at SUNY at Buffalo. He has taught in public schools, the University of Chicago, Indiana University, and the University at Buffalo. He was a Visiting Professor at Texas Woman's University. He was editor and major author of the Annual Summary of Research Related to Reading from 1975 to 1995. He has been awarded the Special Service Award, International Reading Association and the William S. Gray Citation of Merit, International Reading Association.

Jerome C. Harste is an Emeritus Professor of Literacy, Culture & Language Education at Indiana University where he was the first person to hold the Martha Lee and Bill Armstrong Chair in Teacher Education. In addition to his work in multiple-ways-of-knowing, Dr. Harste is known for his work in early literacy, inquiry-based education, and teacher education reform. He is past president of the National Reading Conference, the National Conference on Research in Language and Literacy, the Whole Language Umbrella, and the National Council of Teachers of English. He also has served on the International Reading Association's Board of Directors and together with Dr. Carolyn Burke was named 2008 Language Arts Educator of the Year by the Elementary Section of NCTE.

Rudine Sims Bishop is the author of *Free Within Ourselves: The Development of African American Children's Literature*. Before retiring, she was Professor of Education at The Ohio State University, where she taught courses in children's literature. Currently she is working on a young people's biography of a 19th century African American educator and bishop.

Emilia Ferreiro received her doctorate in 1970 at the University of Geneva under the direction of Jean Piaget. She is currently Full Professor at the Center for Research and Advanced Studies of the National Polytechnic Institute in Mexico. As a psychogenetic psychologist she is recognized for having set up a new theoretical account about how young children develop literacy concepts. Her work has had great impact on literacy education throughout Mexico, Central and South America and Europe. She has published many books and articles in English, French, Italian, Spanish and Portuguese in the areas of literacy learning of a wide range of populations, dealing particularly with small children. She has received seven honorary doctorates and awards such as the National Order of Educational Merit by the government of Brazil in 2001. A recent book of essays on literacy Past and Present of the Verbs *To Read and to Write* is published in English by Groundwood Press.

William H. Teale is Professor of Education at the University of Illinois at Chicago. Author of over one hundred publications, his work has focused on early literacy learning, the intersection of technology and literacy education, and children's literature. He is a former editor of *Language Arts* and was elected to the Reading Hall of Fame in 2003. His current focal research involves two US Department of Education funded Early Reading First projects in urban, low-income schools in Chicago.

Jessica Hoffman is a doctoral student in Literacy, Language and Culture at the University of Illinois at Chicago. She is a former primary-grade teacher and presently working as a research assistant on two Early Reading First projects in Chicago. Her current research focuses on reading aloud and young children's responses to literature.

Katleen Paciga is a graduate research assistant working with UIC's Early Reading First projects. A former kindergarten teacher, she is focusing her research on young children's engagement with traditional and electronic print literacy, as well as the development of early literacy skills.

Jennifer Garrette Lisy is a Literacy, Language, and Culture doctoral student at the University of Illinois at Chicago and a research assistant on UIC's Early Reading First projects. Formerly, she taught kindergarten and first grade. She is now researching primary grade students' writing, creation of digital texts, and uses of technology in education.

Samantha Richardson is currently earning her master's degree in Literacy, Language and Culture at the University of Illinois at Chicago. Through this program she will be receiving her Reading Specialist certification and her English Language Learner endorsement. She is a former elementary school teacher and plans to return to the field upon graduation.

Charlise Berkel is currently a literacy coach for the Early Reading First projects at the University of Illinois at Chicago. She received a MAT in Elementary Education from National-Louis University and a Montessori elementary diploma from the Association Montessori Internationale. Formerly, she taught in a bilingual Montessori immersion language program at the elementary school level and was also a middle school teacher.

Donna E. Alvermann is University of Georgia Appointed Distinguished Research Professor of Language and Literacy Education. Formerly a classroom teacher in Texas and New York, her research focuses on adolescents' multiple literacies in and out of school. From 1992 to 1997 she co-directed the National Reading Research Center, funded by the U.S. Department of Education. Her co-authored and co-edited books include *Content Reading and Literacy: Succeeding in Today's Diverse Classrooms* (5th ed.), *Reconceptualizing the Literacies in Adolescents' Lives* (2nd ed.); *Bridging the Literacy Achievement Gap, Grades 4–12*, and *Adolescents and Literacies in a Digital World*. A past president of the National Reading Conference (NRC), co-chair of the International Reading Association's Commission on Adolescent Literacy (1997–2000), member of the 2009 NAEP Reading Framework, and editor of *Reading Research Quarterly*, she currently serves on the Adolescent Literacy Advisory Group of the Alliance for Excellent Education. She was elected to the Reading Hall of Fame in 1999, and is the recipient of NRC's Oscar Causey Award for Outstanding Contributions to Reading Research, the NRC and American Reading Forum's Service Awards, and the College Reading Association's Laureate Award and Herr Award for Contributions to Research in Reading Education. In 2006, she was awarded the International Reading Association's William S. Gray Citation of Merit.

Thomas Sticht is an international consultant in adult education. He has taught at Harvard University and the University of British Columbia. He has published over 170 books and articles on adult literacy. In 1997 researchers in the Reading Research Quarterly reported that his research and the work of Paulo Freire were the two most influential lines of adult literacy research in the last 30 years. In 2003 he was awarded UNESCO's Mahatma Gandhi medal for 25 years of volunteer work on the International Literacy Prize Jury that selects the annual winners of UNESCO literacy prizes.

Eric J. Paulson is Associate Professor of Literacy Education at the University of Cincinnati, where he is also Director of Graduate Studies for Teacher Education. His research interests include using combinations of eye movement analysis and miscue analysis to investigate social, psycholinguistic, and transactional reading processes.

Edward Fry was a professor of Education and Director of the Reading Center at Rutgers University for 26 years. Before that he taught at Loyola University in Los Angeles and public school classes of 6th grade, special education, and high school reading improvement. He is known to a wider audience of reading educators because of his readability formula, the Instant Words (a high frequency vocabulary), dozens of journal articles, and a dozen or so reading text books and curriculum materials, such as *The Reading Teacher's Book of Lists*. He is past president of the National Reading Conference and a member of IRA since its inception. He was elected to the Reading Hall of Fame in 1993 and has had two Fulbright Lectureships to Africa.

Richard E. Hodges is Professor Emeritus of the University of Puget Sound, Tacoma, Washington. He is the author and co-author of two books and nearly fifty journal articles and book chapters pertaining to current and historical practices in literacy and spelling. He has presented a similar number of papers at national and regional programs. He was editor of *The Elementary School Journal* while a faculty member of the University of Chicago. With Theodore Harris (deceased) he edited *The Literacy Dictionary* (1995) published by the International Reading Association. He is a member of The National Conference on Research in English (past president); The National Society for the Study of Education; and The International Reading Association. He was inducted into The Reading Hall of Fame in 1995.

Gerald G. Duffy is the William Moran Distinguished Professor of Literacy and Reading in the Curriculum and Instruction Department at the University of North Carolina at Greensboro and a Professor Emeritus at Michigan State University where he spent twenty-five years as a teacher educator and researcher. Sandra Webb and Stephanie Davis are both Clinical Professors in the Curriculum and Instruction Department at the University of North Carolina at Greensboro.

Sandra Webb is a Clinical Professor in the Curriculum and Instruction Department at the University of North Carolina at Greensboro.

Stephanie Davis is a doctoral student in the Curriculum and Instruction Department at the University of North Carolina at Greensboro.

Taffy Raphael, Ph.D., President of SchoolRise, is a professor in Literacy Education at the University of Illinois at Chicago (UIC). She also is Director of Partnership READ, a school-university partnership to improve literacy instruction through professional development. Prior to joining the UIC faculty, Taffy taught intermediate grade students in Illinois and North Carolina. In addition, she has taught and conducted research at the University of Utah, Michigan State University, and Oakland University. Taffy's research has focused on Question Answer Relationships and strategy instruction in writing, and for the past decade, Book Club, a literature-based reading program. Throughout these research projects, she has studied teacher learning and professional development through teacher study groups. Taffy coauthored and edited several books on literacy instruction, including *Book Club: A Literature-Based Curriculum* (Small Planet Communications, 2002) and, with Kathy Au, *Super QAR for Testwise Students* (Wright Group, 2002) and *QAR Now* (Scholastic, 2006). Taffy's work in teacher education was recognized by her receipt of the Outstanding Teacher Educator in Reading Award from the International Reading Association. She received Oakland University's Research Excellence Award and was designated as a University Scholar at UIC. In 2002, the International Reading Association elected her to the Reading Hall of Fame.

Kathryn Au, Ph.D., Chief Executive Officer of SchoolRise, is an internationally recognized literacy researcher and educator. She was a professor at the University of Hawaii and was the first person at that institution to hold an endowed chair in education. Kathy's research interest is the school literacy learning of students of diverse cultural and linguistic backgrounds. She is best known for her research on culturally responsive teaching. She has published about 80 articles and chapters, as well as three textbooks and two edited volumes, including *Multicultural Issues and Literacy Achievement* (Erlbaum, 2006). Kathy has been elected president of the National Reading Conference, vice president of the American Educational Research Association, and president of the International Reading Association. She has been recognized as a Distinguished Scholar by the AERA Standing Committee on the Role and Status of Minorities in Educational Research, was named a fellow of the National Conference on Research in Language and Literacy, and has been elected to the Reading Hall of Fame. She received the first National Scholar Award presented by the National Association for Asian and Pacific American Education and the Oscar Causey Award for outstanding contributions to reading research presented by the National Reading Conference.

Misty Sailors is an Associate Professor of Literacy Education in the department of Interdisciplinary Learning and Teaching in the College of Education and Human Development at the University of Texas at San Antonio. She currently teaches undergraduate and graduate literacy education courses. Her research agenda focuses on texts found in elementary classrooms and the instruction that surrounds these texts; teacher education; and language policies related to reading instruction in international settings. The primary investigator of a Teacher Quality Professional Development Reading grant, Sailors' research interests focuses on comprehension instruction, the professional development of teachers, and the importance of print-rich environments for literacy development. She has published in journals such as *Reading Research Quarterly* and the *Journal of Literacy Research*. She has worked in South Africa with classroom teachers for several years and is overseeing the development of 2 million supplementary reading and content integrated learning materials for elementary learners in conjunction with the Republic of South Africa Department of Education and the United States Agency for International Development. Sailors has received prestigious awards for her work, including the 2007 President's Distinguished Achievement Award for Teaching and the 2007 American Association of University Women's Emerging Scholar award. Collectively, Sailors' work is making local, national, and international contributions to literacy education.

Leketi Makalela is the English Studies Department chair, University of Limpopo, South Africa. His research interests are L2 writing, reading, language policy, and World Englishes.

Bertus Matthee is the Training Manager for READ Educational Trust. READ has worked closely with the Ministry of Education in various systemic programmes that involves the teaching of languages, improvement of reading skills and the evaluation of inservice teaching programmes.

Dr. Ortega received her PhD in Curriculum and Instruction from Penn State University in 2008. Her dissertation topic was focused on the conceptual frameworks associated with digital practices among pre-service English teachers and implications for the development of a critical literacy curriculum. Her research interests include: language diversity, literacy technologies, and teacher inquiry. Currently, she teaches Spanish K-8 at the R.J. Hendley Community School in Riviera Beach, Florida.

Susan Pitcher is Associate Professor in the Education Department at Elizabethtown College. She teaches language and literacy courses. Interests include urban education and reading policy.

Dick Allington is Professor of Education at the University of Tennessee. He has previously held the positions of the Irving and Rose Fien Professor of Education at the University of Florida and chair of the Department of Reading at the University at Albany – SUNY. He is a past President of the International Reading Association and the National Reading Conference. He was co-recipient of the Albert J. Harris Award with Anne McGill-Franzen for contributions to the understanding of reading and learning disabilities, a recipient of the Outstanding Reading Educator Award from the New York State Reading Association, and has been elected to the IRA Reading Hall of Fame. Dick serves on the editorial boards of *Language Arts, Remedial and Special Education, Reading Research Quarterly*, the *Journal of Literacy Research*, and the *Elementary School Journal*. He has previously served on the editorial boards of the *Reading Research Quarterly, Review of Educational Research* and the *Journal of Educational Psychology*.

Ken Goodman's theory and model of the reading process is widely studied throughout the world. This psycho-socio-linguistic model is based on oral reading miscue research, a method of studying construction of meaning he developed by analyzing unexpected responses (miscues) in oral reading. He is also known as a major contributor to whole language pedagogy. His book, *What's Whole in Whole Language* sold 250,000 copies in several languages between 1986 and 1995. During the period of imposition of federal and state mandates of reading methods and curriculum, Ken Goodman has been an advocate for teachers and students. *In Defense of Good Teachers, Saving Our Schools* and *The Truth About DIbels* are books he has edited to expose the attacks on public education. He is professor emeritus in Language, Reading and Culture, College of Education, University of Arizona. He is past President of the International Reading Association, the National Conference of Research in Language Arts, the Center for Expansion of Language and Thinking, and the Whole Language Umbrella. He served as secretary of the Reading Hall of Fame.

Susan R. Goldman, PhD, is Distinguished Professor of Psychology and Education at the University of Illinois at Chicago and Codirector of the Learning Sciences Research Institute. Her interests are in learning and assessment in subject matter domains such as literacy, mathematics, history, and science and roles for technologies in supporting assessment, instruction, and learning. For the past fifteen years she has been collaborating with educational practitioners to bridge research and practice. Dr. Goldman is widely published in discourse, psychology, and education journals and is presently Associate Editor for *Cognition & Instruction, Discourse Processes*, and *Journal of Educational Psychology* and is a consulting editor for *Reading Research Quarterly*.

Patrick Shannon is a professor of education at Penn State University. He studies educational policy and its impact on schools, teachers, and children. His most recent book is *Reading Against Democracy* (Heinemann, 2007). He's a member of the Reading Hall of Fame since 2002.

Jacqueline Edmondson is currently Associate Dean for Teacher Education and Undergraduate Programs and Associate Professor of Education in Curriculum and Instruction (Language & Literacy Education). Her research focuses on education policy, critical theory, teacher education, rural schools and communities, and biography for adolescent readers. Jackie's books include: *America Reads: A Critical Policy Analysis (2000)*, *Prairie Town: Redefining Rural Life in an Age of Globalization (2003)*, *Understanding and Applying Critical Policy Study: Reading Educators Advocating for Change (2004)*, *Venus and Serena Williams: A Biography (2005)*, *Reading Education Policy (2005 – co-edited with Patrick Shannon)*, *Condoleezza Rice: A Biography (2006)*, and *Jesse Owens: A Biography* (forthcoming, Greenwood Press). Her research has been published in a variety of academic journals.

Robert J. Tierney is currently Dean of the Faculty of Education at the University of British Columbia. Prior to moving to Canada, Rob was on the faculty at several US universities. He has been engaged in a number of international projects in Australia, Europe, Asia and Africa with the support of funding from groups such as UNESCO, international government agencies and foundations. In the early eighties, Rob Tierney was probably best known for his scholarly contributions in the area of teaching reading comprehension. In the late eighties, Rob contributed to a major shift in reading & writing research, theory and practice with his writings on the reading–writing relationship. In the nineties, he turned his attention to "assessing assessment" and has written various articles and books on literacy assessment principles and practices. Rob has also made contributions to the research and theory on the acquisition of digitally based literacy skills. His more recent writings have focused upon discussions of professionalism in the current political climate of accountability, evidence-based practices and meeting student needs. He has held a number of key leadership roles in professional organizations such as the NCTE Assembly on Research as its first Chair, the National Reading Conference as President and as active participant in other groups. He is the Past-President of the Canadian Deans of Education. In 2000, he was inducted into the Reading Hall of Fame for his contributions to literacy education. In 2002, he was the recipient of the William S. Gray Citation of Merit for outstanding contributions to literacy education internationally. He is past editor of the *Reading Research Quarterly* and has been a board member of a number of international and national advisory boards.

Brian Cambourne is a member of the faculty at the University of Wollongong in the Department of Education. His expertise, research and many publications are in the fields of teaching and learning, literacy birth to adult, critical analysis of misinformation by politicians, journalists and lobby groups, Australian literacy standards and teacher education with a special focus on teachers teaching literacy. He is sought after throughout the world for consultations, workshops and conference presentations. His prestigious awards include the Garth Boomer Award by Australian Literacy Educators in 1995, the National Council of Teachers of English Outstanding Educator in Language Arts Award, and the Australian College of Education Outstanding Educational Achievement Award in 2008. He was inducted into the Reading Hall of Fame in 1998.

Part I

Expanding Views of Literacy

Chapter 1

The Communicative, Visual, and Performative Arts
Core Components of Literacy Education

Diane Lapp and James Flood
San Diego State University

Shirley Brice Heath
Brown University and Stanford University

Judith Langer
State University of New York at Albany

Recognition of the communicative, visual, and performing arts as integral components of literacy instruction is rich in its history and evocative of a new phenomenon that is radically changing literacy education. The long, full history includes the uses of technologies such as radio, television, films and videos (Baines, 1997; Trier, 2008); the use of illustrations and graphics in texts (Lapp, Flood, Brock, and Fisher, 2007); the use of trade books that often work equally well as reading materials and pieces of art (Kiefer, 1997); and Amazon's new reading machine, *Kindle*, which changes the way we can store and read print materials. We should add to these material forms of technology the longstanding complements to the written word of drama, dance, and instrumental music. All these both evoke powerful tales of their own but also deepen and extend meanings of written texts as well as notational systems, such as that used for music and choreography (Heathcote, 1980; Heathcote and Bolton, 1995; Wagner, 1999). Important, too, are the growing and widespread uses of multimedia and mixed media in music and the performing arts as well as in other aspects of life, work, and play.

Much confusion has arisen over terms such as *multiliteracies, visual literacies*, and the like, and when definitions accompany these terms, the arts—visual, communicative, and performative—rarely figure significantly. Though we make no claim to an absolute definition, our perspective is that *literacies* involve all media forms that combine iconic images, symbol systems, and conventions of presentation. Western societies have, since the Middle Ages, generally allowed for all of these identifications of the author (whether single individual or collaborative company).

Critical in the history of visual literacies/arts has been their retrievability—i.e., they have some kind of permanent or quasi-permanent form. This kind of broad definition covers *visual* literacies/arts back to Stone Age narrative paintings through illuminated manuscripts to contemporary print matter, films, and many kinds of exhibitions. *Communicative arts* refers to those forms that generate meaning through their primary reliance on oral language, alive or recorded in audio or visual transmission (as in the case of sign language representation). Also dependent on the communicative arts are print representations of language usually (though not always) associated with paper.

The performing arts rely largely on the human body or its extension (cf. puppetry) as a means to convey meaning through both communicative and visual arts (through costume, etc.). Such art forms may be visually recorded (and have long been rendered in paintings or for well over a century in photographs as well). Yet, the performing arts are generally not fully retrievable. Live dance, musical, and dramatic performances always carry a one-time-only quality. Even though the same play or dance is performed again and again, each performance (and script, if one is present), will become the unique presentation of the individual, group, or company performing. Technology has entered the visual, dramatic, musical, and performative arts to complement, reproduce, and supplement each of these individually and in new combinations.

In this chapter we focus on the past few years where visual, communicative, and performing arts have rapidly become core components and essential companions of print literacy. As Goodman and Hoffman, the editors of this volume, suggest in their introduction, we attempt to stretch your definition of what counts as literacy. As yet, little recognition and response to the arts within the print medium have influenced behaviors or values surrounding formal schooling. This statement stands out especially when we compare the role of the arts in schools with their centrality in the worlds of medicine, commerce, recreation, and, indeed, most occupations. Teacher education and preparation as school teachers have always relied firmly on the idea of teaching and of formal instruction within specified times and places by authorized agents. In sharp contrast, both historically and in today's world, learning in the arts goes on before, within, and well beyond (and sometimes largely without) formal instruction.

Few ever speak of pedagogy as established or fixed in the arts. In the Middle Ages and the Renaissance, studios or *schools* that produced dozens of "original" Rembrandt paintings were viewed not as factories of sameness, but as climates supporting particular styles of production and generative of innovative works as well. In today's world, the idiosyncratic teaching and creative styles of arts directors, choreographers, or drama directors often find their way to center place in critical reviews as well as within the marketplace of competition for the work of certain artists.

In the first volume of the *Handbook of Research on Teaching Literacy through the Visual and Communicative Arts* (hereafter HRTLVC, 1997), Flood, Heath, and

Lapp urged educators to consider an expanded view of literacy that would embrace changes in literacy certain to increase rapidly with advances in electronic and digital technologies and graphic design. The HRTLVC, in a host of ways and through the voices of authors and artists, readers, and writers, pointed out how advances in the arts were sure to continue to convey, complement, and sometimes supplant printed texts. The volume predicted that most print forms would decline in significance, and most would increasingly incorporate the graphic arts, iconic representations, and abbreviated language. The HRTLVC 1997 plea to educators was for openness to the kinds of learning desperately needed and sure to be embraced by the young whose lives were already largely shaped by the *information economy*. By 2005, young television viewers turned less and less to sitcoms, films, and dramas produced by strangers. Instead they created their own, blending fact, fiction, mystical, and fantasy. They looked to comedians and talk-show hosts as their new sources. Certain to come were paper-free and nearly print-free representations of information and persuasion within the worlds of commerce, medicine, and entertainment. Instructors in formal education settings would surely have to do much more than simply think about a few clever ways to insert electronically transmitted representations in their classrooms as mere add-ons for "ordinary" print materials.

Prescient as these points may seem from today's backward glance over the past decade, no amount of foresight in 1997 could have fully predicted the pace or direction of the radical, swirling changes of what would come within only a few years. These changes have manifested themselves as innovations, disappearances, reappearances, mutations, and innovations.

Disappearances, Comebacks, and Innovations

Video reigned throughout the 1990s; by 2010, its extinction may very well be complete. High definition DVD (HDDVD) is disappearing. Newspapers, which have long linked visual representations to print, face rapidly dwindling circulation rates throughout the world. The Internet offers minute-by-minute updates of world events, and newspapers scramble to morph into new functions and forms.

On the other hand, comic books, near extinction by the end of the 1990s, made a quick comeback no more than a decade later. Graphic novels, seemingly a heftier version of comics, jumped into prominence, and both media forms stepped to the forefront in innovative designs, strong character development, and narratives with "legs." In 2007 *The Invention of Hugo Cabret* by Brian Selznick, a thick, sober-looking volume ostensibly for pre-adolescent readers of children's literature, combined text and large bold visual images. The work earned the Caldecott Award for picture books, perhaps suggesting a move toward honoring images rather than words. Consumers of both graphic novels and comic books generate network forms, such as blogs, zines, and chatrooms, replacing traditional print reviews and critiques. Both comic books and graphic novels bear close kinship with film animation designs and innovative trends in storylines.

Also pushing hard on any narrow conception of either *literacy* or *literacies* have been other advances in interpretive forms of play or games. After less than a decade of prominence, hand-held video games almost entirely gave way to online games. Telephones quickly accelerated possibilities for linking verbal and visual communication, recording photographic images, giving immediate Internet access, and storing data for later transfer to computers.

As the end of the first decade of the twenty-first century approaches, visual images serve as primary introductions to products, organizations, and candidates. In the world of food and restaurants, images including flowers, prints, pictures, and ice sculptures have replaced menus as the first encounter with consumers. Museums use multimedia kaleidoscopic productions to lure patrons into viewing collections. Installation art, street performance, and interactive art make aesthetic traditions framed or fixed in form or space seem outdated. Exhibition and performance continue to merge; artists and reviewers, producers and engineers now seem inseparable.

As electronic and digital technologies continue to expand, traditional processes, agents, and materials of formal schooling no longer figure as the primary transmitting site of learning. Every occupation in contemporary society demands continual learning to handle ever-changing requirements in skills, information, and ability to interpret regulations and directives. Taxi cab drivers, stock clerks, and factory workers need to keep up with recent software required in their workplaces. Many professional service jobs (e.g. health workers, hygienists, physical therapists, bank tellers, and fiber optic technicians) stay current through workshops supported by manuals filled with elaborate illustrations and accompanied with interactive DVDs. In the health field, patients learn about drug procedures and medical routines through these same technologies with accompanying written materials that often seem optional or supplementary at best. All professions from law to medicine to health care are bombarded with new areas of specialization inextricably tied to visual and performative arts.

For example, as the legal field of intellectual property expands, key documentation in patent requests and specifications, as well as high-tech applications, comes in visual and interactive forms through digital means. Every field depends on an array of visual literacies. Consumers of all goods, products, and services have to respond to marketing in which visual displays and even interactive DVDs of the product do the selling. In fact, the demand for more visuals to replace the written word is illustrated by the significant increase in the production of instructional DVDs for a wide array of products and services (e.g. refrigerators, ovens, tools, or window upgrades).

Roles beyond K–16 Schooling

Only those beyond their early twenties would speak of any of the above as changes; these phenomena are the expected or normal way to know or go (Prensky, 2001, 2005). Consider, for example, how rare it is in many communities for anyone under 30 years of age to look up a number in a telephone book; instead the choice is to go to the Internet or call a friend. (For more on the *normalcy* of technology in seeking, confirming, communicating, and representing, see Hobbs, 1997, 1998; Moje, 2007; Semali, 2000, 2003). A favorite form of entertainment for young people comes in visits to specialty stores filled with new technologies. There highly specialized young salespeople, many of whom have had little or no advanced education, engage the young visitors in animated conversations in which they exchange knowledge and predict the success or failure of specific products or means of communication (Goodson and Norton-Meier, 2003). The knowledge of the young emanates from their fascination with technology and is honed through experience gained from observations and conversations with friends who have similar interests.

Icons such as Steven Spielberg, George Lucas, and Steven Jobs all grew up with a fascination for visual technology. All shared their interests with their friends during their teen years and into their twenties when they began to convert their hobbies, inventions, artistic creations, and business leadership into business organizations. From their own experiences, based in neither higher education nor extensive dependence on print media, leaders such as these used their own learning lives as models for hiring their employees. Apple, Google, and many other new companies depend on selecting employees who are creative, experienced, self-directed learners who willingly experiment and work in teams. In the high-tech world, features such as flexibility, risk-taking, and "wild dreaming" are seen as critical to staying ahead of competitors.

Visual, experiential, and interactional means of learning have taken primacy in the lives of most young people in post-industrial societies (Heath, 2004b; Luke and Elkins, 1998). Their learning parallels what happens in on-the-job training or refresher workshops and certification courses. Some think of such learning as moving well beyond the information age to the create-experience-communicate age that will mark the "post-post industrial." The information economy of the end of the twentieth century has a critical dependence on an imagine-it, do-it, change-it economy.

Access is perhaps the most critical issue in predicting and considering the implications of these realities of learning for what we have thought of as *literacy education* (Flood and Lapp, 1995). Problems stem from both school and home opportunities. Some homes do not have up-to-date equipment for students that allow graphic design, multimedia editing, and mergers of forms of entertainment or communications. Additional problems for many young people come from the lack of availability of experts at home or among friends. Many young people lack the material resources for obtaining the latest technologies or the accessories they require. Materials may not be available in the home language; adults in the home may object to techno-communications because they worry about not having enough control to protect their children from predators or pornographic materials. Many parents fear that their religious beliefs are being violated in the content of entertainment forms. Access is not a simple phenomenon and it is not merely a matter of economics.

Through and with and behind all of the media or art forms noted above is oral language. Conversation, conferencing, instructional detailing, coaching, and many other channels of oral expression both support and are supported by the introduction and spread of all of these visual and performative innovations. Visual demonstrations almost always call for some kind of oral language; dreams and experiments have to find their way into oral expression, especially since their transfer to invention and production depends so intimately on collaborative work.

Yet it is critical to remember that at some point along the way—from inception to marketing and usage—visual and performative innovations will surely rely in a variety of degrees and manners on written materials. But information in print is often regarded by the young as elective, a last resort, or easily outdated. (Note the evolution in cellphone instructions from printed manuals to CD format to the caution [given early on the CD for the new user] to go to such-and-such website for the latest update on instructions.) In medicine, the pattern for new prescriptions or regimens of exercise or therapy is often a circular routine from oral instructions to oral counseling to oral referencing to print and/or DVD or CD, and back again to oral advice. For example, in cases of a new regimen of injections for a chronic condition, the physician will recommend the product and then instruct the patient on use, possible outcomes, etc. In life-threatening or new-product cases, a counselor or nurse practitioner or social worker will meet with the patient to answer questions and to provide a call-in line number should difficulties arise. The pharmacist will fill the prescription, talk to the patient, and provide the patient package insert and possibly recommend a website or other sources of further information on possible side effects. Patient package inserts (PPIs) purport to "tell all" in small print, often with diagrams of the chemistry that support and process the production of the drug. Yet for most patients, comprehension comes only through talking and listening, asking questions about processes and implications, and determining ways to check in their own words just how they should act from the information provided.

Those who used to think of themselves as instructors of reading and writing now have students who will live in a world of rapid-fire multiparty oral communication, supported by visual and performance demonstrations that require relatively little use of print in extended texts. Today's "just-do-it" mantra of learning means that all learners, regardless of age, have to take on new roles that extend far beyond anything associated in past centuries with the role of student. Becoming a speaker, panelist, actor, interviewer, or member of a conversation group who talks about printed materials allows multiple roles for talking, drawing, demonstrating, and charting. The art of self-presentation, as well as that of role-shifting with layers of media as props, defines success (Paul, 2000). Print enters in and often supports verification and validation for the performance of various roles.

The value of role-playing has long been known to language teachers whose focus has been conversation, oral fluency, and oral comprehension (Flood, Lapp, Jensen, and Squire, 2003). English language learners learn most quickly and most competently when their roles as speakers and listeners shift and their models of language remain consistent (Lapp et al. 2005).

Learners with a wide range of special needs also require consistency in their instruction. In some parts of the post-post-industrial world, artistic directors create transformations for students with cerebral palsy, Down's syndrome, and visual and hearing impairments. Children who are diagnosed along the autism disorder spectrum or with attention deficits find that following dance routines helps them sustain visual and social focus. Evidence from numerous arenas of research makes clear the power of performance based on "see-it, do-it" opportunities. Through all these circumstances, oral language is critical to gaining experience, skills, and strategies to advance to higher levels of achievement.

Teacher Education

Where does all of this situate literacy teachers within formal educational systems (K–16), especially those in schools of education who are responsible for preparing future teachers? The foundations (cognitive, social, economic, anthropological, psychological, and pedagogical) of visual, dramatic, oral, and interactive performance are constant companions to written forms (Flood and Salús, 2004). Many neuroscience researchers who are involved in studies of emotion, memory, or *transfer* point to the values of learning in meaningful roles through visual representation and layers of symbol systems (Heath, 2006, 2004a, 2004b, 2000, 1999; Heath and Wolf, 2005a, 2005b, 2004). These systems include the sound and grammatical systems of verbal language and those linked to electronic and digital transmission as well as to embodied performance (mime, dance, and other gestural systems). From text messaging to graphic design to dramatic role-playing, symbol systems of various kinds work alongside oral and written language.

Teacher education must accept the challenge of enabling instructors to feel at ease with a multitude of symbol systems. This is done most effectively when students and teachers are full partners in learning. Since the Middle Ages, those who *profess* (instruct) have been active hand-it-on transmitters; learners have been expected to assume the generally passive and silent role of students or individual receptacles of information. None of these conditions can any longer be considered appropriate to what we know from learning theories, the human condition in post-industrial societies, or the continuities of change in technologies

Schools of education have to accept the responsibility for making drastic changes that include professors learning not only the substance of visual and communicative arts but also their effects on cognitive and linguistic learning. If formal education is truly to be preparation for entering the world of employment, citizenship, and family, vast changes in roles, materials, times, and spaces of learning have to take place. K–16 education has to undergo major transformations if its professional members and institutions are to retain respect and saliency in post-post-industrial societies. Learners now respect and open themselves to learning from adults who "get it, see it, and just do it."

Just as the discipline of history in the 1960s and 1970s had to undergo radical change when American society reshaped its view of African Americans and other "minorities" in the history of the nation, so today must education remake itself. In the field of history, this reshaping was termed *revisionist*, and many critics argue that *revising* did not go nearly far enough. The same will certainly be the case for literacy studies.

Lying deep within the institution of education, literacy studies is perhaps least likely to change very much within formal schooling. Change will come, if at all, only with considerable difficulty. All constituents within education hold firmly to their values surrounding language and its uses, and they cling most fiercely to the centrality of the teaching of reading to ensure the continuity of the importance of reading and writing. In spite of all these barriers to change, the authors of this piece plead for at least a revision of literacy studies.

Simply put, definitions fundamental to literacy and to what it means to be *literate* have to change (Alvermann and Hagood, 2000; Bearne, 2003; Flood and Lapp, 1995; Hobbs, 2004, 2005). A revisionist literacy involves, at the very least, figuring out what it will take to bring about for teachers and students together the multiple abilities needed to manipulate and understand the array of signs, symbols, sounds, and movements (those that exist and those not yet imagined) associated with the visual, communicative, and performing arts. Each art form needs to be understood as a phenomenon carrying within itself a representational system that contains and imparts meaning. Associated signs, sounds, symbols, and movements have to be recognized as representations of meaning essential to an engaged learning approach to bridging classrooms and everyday life (Bakhtin, 1981, 1986; Langer 1987; Vygotsky, 1987). Bringing about a sense of learning across and through these representations of meaning as created and drawn upon in a wide array of learning contexts speaks to future vocational learning and organizational changes (Brown, 1998; New London Group, 1987; Meyrowitz, 1998).

Revisionist literacy must give weight to oral, visual, gestural, and graphic performances as well as semiotic and sign presentations. All these aim to develop the mindset and skills that learners—young and old—need in order to keep on adapting their abilities and methods used to create, use, and critique information. Revising what we mean by all the terms connected with literacy will come with greatest difficulty for institutions of formal schooling and their core constituents: administrators, teachers, textbook publishers, and those in the testing industry.

Students will have no problem with revising past ideas of literacy. Most beyond the age of 10 have already mastered more knowledge and skills related to technologies than have the adults in their everyday lives. Since 1995, in particular, the young in post-post-industrial societies have grown up in the world of inventive media, performance, and communication. They have not only skills of manipulation, but many even have some familiarity with the kinds of planning, organizational structures, and relationships between hardware design and market forces that figure in making films, recording music, and transferring art forms across technologies (Bearne, 2003; Heath, 2005, 2006; Langer, 1987, 1995; Luke and Elkins, 1998).

The challenge for formal school institutions is to interact more productively with students' environments of learning that lie outside formal instruction. To do so will mean bringing teachers and teacher educators into creative hands-on learning experiences as creators (and not just passive participants in professional development) of new technologies and the visual, communicative, and performative arts. In doing so, the skill base of all will expand so that teachers, in particular, know how to seek and value the kinds of learning partners who complement their own strengths.

Currently, formal educational systems, whether kindergartens or universities, have found this challenge unrealistic in economic and intellectual terms. As a consequence, classrooms at the K–16 levels suffer in terms of their inability to keep up either with what the broader society provides or what students know and expect in terms of the visual, communicative, and performing arts to support their learning of print-based or orally transmitted information. The learning worlds of students—for life-wide as well as life-long learning—must become unified, connecting activities and materials available in classrooms with sources, skills, agents, and supplementary/contradictory information beyond the classroom. This will mean rethinking instruction, materials, curricula, and, most especially, testing.

Independent learning, as well as collaborative work within families, friendship groups, and community organizations now generally outpace schools and classrooms in their normative inclusion of multiliteracies and all the arts. Youth in peer groups or in self-motivated individual leisure time create videofilms, DVDs, zines, blogs, and dialogues in chatrooms. They share their expertise with one another, yet these roles and bases of knowledge and skills rarely come into play within classroom assignments and standard assessment instruments (Goodson and Norton-Meier, 2003; Heath, 2005; Hull and Schultz, 2002; Maira and Soep, 2005; Moje, 2007).

Many teachers feel inadequate to judge the quality of performance in art forms other than written language. Some teachers do not know the genres or the standards of dance, drama, visual, or video arts well enough to help children support their attempts at learning and displaying information through these means. However, teachers do feel comfortable and generally confident assessing written essays, question-and-answer tests, and research papers. These were the means by which they learned as they prepared to become teachers. But teachers can—and often want to—learn the standards of production for video, dramatic, and graphic production, and they often relish partnering with experts in these art forms in order to do so.

University schools and departments of education have to work hand in hand with artists and others to ensure that critique, standards, and forms of evaluation take center stage within teacher education. Teacher education can no longer be a mismatch with the skills and attitudes toward learning across media that teachers must have in order to keep up with both what their students know and what they will need as they mature into adulthood and the worlds of medical, consumer, and business decision-making. Moreover, teachers and the systems in which they work have to find ways to partner meaningfully with young learners' friendship groupings, community organizations, and the public media.

Educators need the distributed expertise of all learners and of specializations typically not considered within "education." The interdependence of all the art forms in multiliteracies calls for radical alterations in the ways that classroom instruction, materials, pacing, and layering of media work with learners as they meet the continuous challenges of learning throughout life.

The HRTLVC (Flood, Heath, and Lapp, 1997) noted: "We know of human beings that their changes in beliefs, attitudes, and theories come most easily after they have been entrained by certain actions; hence, ideology and belief often follow from rather than precede action" (p. xvii). This statement reminds us that change comes slowly and in small increments. Those who already know the powers and range of visual and communicative arts need to be at the vanguard of the radical changes that must occur within revisionist literacy. These individuals have to take responsibility for bringing colleagues—students and teachers—into the realization that the prior dichotomous roles of transmitter and receptacle can no longer hold. Expressions such as *learning together, performance-based learning, embodied learning, communities of practice,* and *working knowledge* have to become more than catchphrases associated with this or that reform move in education. A passion for what is possible should motivate a proactive approach to the future.

In 2006, the Congress of the United States gave approval for learners to "attend" higher education exclusively through the Internet. Even before this legislative approval, many individuals were already taking advantage of the Internet to gain higher education degrees. Tens of thousands of K–12 students receive homeschooling that blends face-to-face, experiential with Internet resources. Many more young learners leave school and go directly to the places where they can find Internet access to gain information, try out new ideas, and converse with others—near and very far. If these trends continue, it may well be that our research will be devoted almost entirely to learning beyond the expected sites of schooling that we have taken for granted as the keystone of education. In the new version of HRTLVC (2008), this research direction is firmly evident. Most of the articles there detail the layered and multiply shaped arrays of visual symbols, gestures, oral and written texts, and performance that take place in the everyday lives of learners. Many of the learning environments detailed in these accounts stress the critical importance of social networking and social capital that learners gain through becoming expert in several forms of representation of their ideas. Extended periods of meaningful practice, along with access to professional experts, determine possibilities of moving from beginning level to advanced in various forms of representation that include music, dance, graphic design, and collaborative production and exhibition. Almost all the accounts in the 2008 volume of HRTLVC highlight the value of extended learning opportunities that stretch far beyond classrooms and into meaningful and productive uses in families, peer groups, communities, and religious institutions.

In the past, we have expected to find most literacy researchers and educators at work within schools. Today scholars who study literacy and wish to spread its forms, uses, and effectiveness look outside K–16 institutions to understand families, communities, public media, and training and development programs where learning goes on with multiple roles and symbol systems to accelerate motivation and achievement.

At the end of the second decade of the twenty-first century, primary and secondary schools as we know them today will have decreased significantly in number and influence. Homeschooling and other alternatives and combinations of community organizations, formal education, Internet resourcing, and experiential learning will be more and more the norm for families with resources, connections, ideology, and will. If schools remain caught in the serious *cultural lag* that omits the visual, communicative, and performative arts from their learning environments, the academic and class divide will continue to increase. In some regions of the United States, much of schooling will change shape, modes of operating, and physical locations so extensively as to be unrecognizable to those educated in the final decades of the twentieth century. Turning this historical corner will present unforeseen choices, and we can be sure that scholars, higher education institutions, and certification agencies will face challenges not now imagined. Researchers in literacy studies have the enticing possibility of taking on leadership to revise in substantial and inclusive ways our notions of literacies, arts, and communication. Doing this means first and foremost documenting rigorously and honestly the world that young learners populate and the contexts that draw them in, foster their creativity, and enable them to take on meaningful roles throughout their lives.

References

Alvermann, D.E. and Hagood, M.C. (2000). Critical media literacy: Research, theory, and practice in new times. *Journal of Educational Research 93*(3), 193–205.

Baines, L. (1997). Film, video and books: Some considerations for teaching and learning. In Flood J., Heath, S.B., and Lapp, D. (Eds.). *Handbook of research on teaching the communicative and visual arts* (Vol. 1) (pp. 545–558). New York: Macmillan Publishing Co., Inc.

Bakhtin, M.M. (1981). *The dialogic imagination: Four essays.* (C. Emerson and M. Holquist Trans.) Austin, TX: University of Texas Press.

Bakhtin, M.M. (1986). *Speech genres and other late essays.* Austin, TX: University of Texas Press.

Bearne, E. (2003). Rethinking literacy. *Reading, Literacy, Language.* November 37(8): 98–103.

Brown, James. (1998). Media literacy perspectives. *The Journal of Communication.* Winter: 48(1): 44–57.

Flood J., Heath, S.B. and Lapp, D. (Eds.), (1997). Preface to *Handbook of research on teaching literacy through the communicative and visual arts.* New York: Macmillan Publishing Co., Inc. xv–xvii.

Flood, J., Heath, S. and Lapp, D. (Eds.), (2008). *Handbook of literacy research: Communicative, visual, and performative arts.* Mahweh, NJ: Lawrence Erlbaum Press.

Flood, J. and Lapp, D. (1995). Broadening the lens: Towards an expanded conceptualization of literacy. In K. Hinchman, D. Leu and D. Kinzer (Eds.), *Perspectives on literacy research and practice* (pp. 1–6). Chicago, IL: 44th Yearbook of the National Reading Conference.

Flood, J., Lapp, D., Jensen, J., and Squire, J. (2003). Preface to *Handbook of research in teaching the English language arts* (2nd ed.). Mahweh, NJ: Erlbaum.

Flood, J. and Salus, P. (2004). *Language: A user's guide.* San Diego: Academic Professional Development (APD).

Goodson, T. and Norton-Meier, L. (2003). Motor oil, civil disobedience, and media literacy. *Journal of Adolescent and Adult Literacy, 47*(3), 258–262.

Heath, S.B. (1999). Dimensions of language development. In A.S. Masten (Ed.), *Cultural Processes of Child Development* (Vol. 29) (pp. 59–75). Hillsdale, NJ: Lawrence Erlbaum Publishers.

Heath, S.B. (2000). Seeing our way into learning. *Cambridge Journal of Education, 30*(1), 121–132.

Heath, S. (2004a). Learning language and strategic thinking through the arts. *Reading Research Quarterly, 39*(3), 8–12.

Heath, S. (2004b). Risks, rules, and roles: Youth perspectives on the work of learning for community development. In A.N. Perret-Clermont, C. Pontecorvo, L.B. Resnick, T. Zittoun, and B. Burge (Eds.), *Joining society: Social interaction and learning in adolescence and youth* (pp. 41–70). New York: Cambridge University Press.

Heath, S. (2005). *Artshow 2 Grow.* DVD production. [Available through Partners for Livable Communities, Washington, DC.]

Heath, S. (2006). Dynamics of completion: Gaps, blanks, and improvision. In M. Turner (Ed.), *The artful mind* (pp. 133–150). New York: Oxford University Press.

Heath, S. and Wolf, S. (2004). *Visual learning in the community school. [A series of five booklets.]* London: Creative Partnerships.

Heath, S. and Wolf, S. (2005a). Focus in creative learning: Drawing on art for language development. *Literacy, 39*(1), 38–45.

Heath, S. and Wolf, S. (2005b). *Dramatic learning in the primary school. [A series of four booklets.]* London: Creative Partnerships.

Heathcote, D. (1980). *Drama as context.* Aberdeen, Scotland: Aberdeen University Press.

Heathcote, D. and Bolton, G. (1995). *Drama for learning: Dorothy Heathcote's mantle of the expert approach in education.* Portsmouth, NH: Heinemann.

Hobbs, R. (1997). Literacy for the information age. In J. Flood, S.B. Heath, and D. Lapp (Eds.), *Handbook of research on teaching literacy through the communicative and visual arts* (pp. 7–14). New York: Macmillan.

Hobbs, R. (1998). The seven great debates in the media literacy movement. *Journal of Communication, 48*(1), 16–31.

Hobbs, R. (2004). Media literacy, general semantics, and K-12 education. *Et Cetera, 61*(1), 24–28.

Hobbs, R. (2005). Strengthening media education in the twenty-first century: Opportunities for the state of Pennsylvania. *Arts Education Policy Review, 106*(4), 13–45.

Hull, G. and Schultz, K. (2002). *School's out: Bridging out-of-school literacies with classroom practice.* New York: Teachers College Press.

Kiefer, B. (1997). The visual arts made accessible through picture books. In J. Flood, S. Heath, and D. Lapp (Eds.), *Handbook of research on teaching literacy through the communicative, visual and performing arts* (Vol. 1) (pp. 820–822). New York: Macmillan.

Langer, J.A. (1987). A sociocognitive perspective on literacy. In *Language, literacy and culture: Issues of society and schooling.* Norwood, NJ: Ablex.

Langer, J.A. (1995). *Envisioning literature.* New York: Teachers College Press.

Lapp, D., Flood, J., Moore, K. and Nichols, M. (2005). *Teaching literacy in first grade.* New York: Guilford Press.

Lapp, D., Flood, J. Bock, C. and Fisher, D. (2007). *Teaching reading to every child* (4th ed.). Mahweh, NJ: Lawrence Erlbaum.

Luke, A. and Elkins, J. (1998). Reinventing literacy in new times. *Journal of adolescent and adult literacy, 42,* 4–7.

Maira, S. and Soep, E. (Eds.) (2005). *Youthscapes: The popular, the national, the global.* Philadelphia: University of Pennsylvania Press.

Meyrowitz J. (1998). Multiple media literacies. *Journal of Communication, 48*(1), 96–108.

Moje, E.B. (2008). Youth cultures, literacies, and identities in and out of school. In J. Flood, S.B. Heath, and D. Lapp (Eds.), *Handbook of research on teaching literacy through the communicative and visual arts* (Vol. II) (pp. 207–220). Mahweh, NJ: Lawrence Erlbaum.

New London Group (1987). A pedagogy of multiliteracies: Designing social futures. *Harvard Educational Review, 66*(1), 60–92.

Paul, D.G. (2000). Rap and orality: Critical media literacy, pedagogy, and cultural synchronization. *Journal of Adolescent and Adult Literacy, 44*(3), 246–251.

Prensky, M. (2001). Digital natives, digital immigrants [Electronic version]. *On the Horizon, 9*(5), 1–6. Available at: http://www.marcprensky.com/writing/Prensky%20-%20Digital%20Natives,%20Digital%20Immigrants%20-%20Part1.pdf

Prensky, M. (2005). Listen to the natives. *Educational Leadership, 63*(4), 8–11.

Semali, L. (2000). *Literacy in multimedia America: Integrating media education across the curriculum.* New York: Falmer Press.

Semali, L. (2003). Ways with visual language: Making the case for critical media literacy. *The Clearinghouse.* July/August. 76:6, 271–277.

Trier, J. (2008). Media over the decades: From radio (fast-forward) to podcasting and the iPod. In J. Flood, S.B. Heath, and D. Lapp (Eds.), *Handbook of research on teaching literacy through the communicative and visual arts* (Vol. II) (pp. 513–520). Mahweh, NJ: Lawrence Erlbaum.

Vygotsky, L.S. (1987). Thinking and speech. In R. Rieber and A. Carton (Eds.), *The collected works of L.S. Vygotsky.* New York: Plenum.

Wagner, B.J. (Ed.) (1999). *Building moral communities through educational drama.* Stamford, CN: Ablex.

Chapter 2

From Gray to Google
Learning within a Profession

Nancy L. Roser
University of Texas at Austin

Sam Weintraub
State University of New York at Buffalo

In 1893, the first author's grandfather wrote a little book with a big name: *How to Teach Reading*. The book cost 2 cents, postpaid, cheaper if you bought in quantities. Inside, this Illinois prairie teacher/principal/grandpa offered his two cents' worth:

> I have heard pupils read an entire selection and not have the vaguest idea of the theme—there was no mental picture imprinted in their minds, no idea, no moral, nothing elevating, in fact nothing gained except a slight drill in articulation.

And Grandpa wrote this:

> Pupils cannot afford to waste their entire time pronouncing words, as it has little to do with developing thought—the end and object of school life.

At the end of his little book with the big title, Grandpa spoke directly to his reader:

> But you say I have uttered nothing new on teaching—a fact I candidly admit. Educationally speaking of this secular age, we believe the old proverb "there is nothing new under the sun" is certainly true.

When Grandpa wrote, the first psychological laboratory in Germany was just over a decade old, eye movement studies flourished in Europe, and William S. Gray was in third grade.

When that same William S. Gray produced the first *Summary of Investigations Relating to Reading* in 1925, a table of studies (see Figure 2.2) would show that if Grandpa could have "Googled" or located the extant research in the library, the possible length of his 1893 bibliography would have been three studies: one on the hygiene of reading; the second, a co-relational analysis of rate

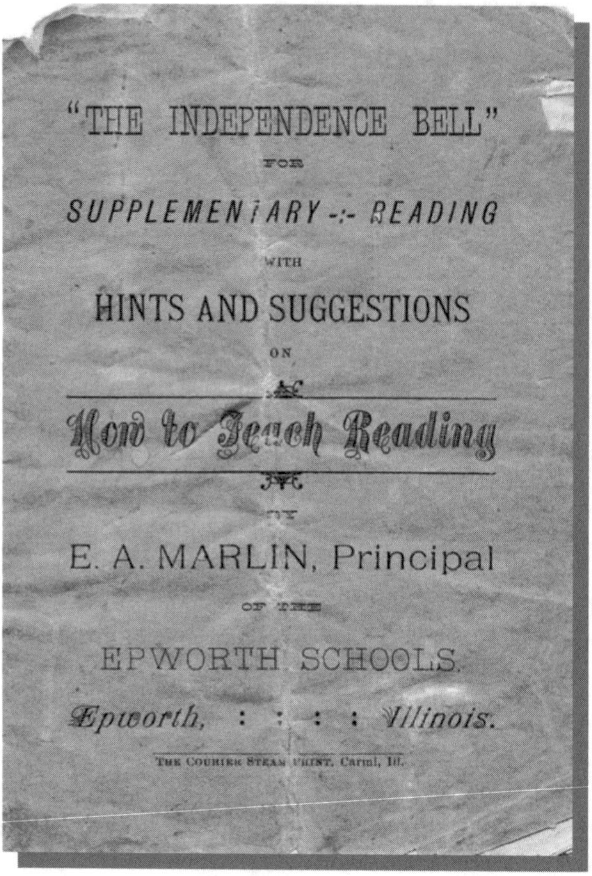
"THE INDEPENDENCE BELL"
FOR
SUPPLEMENTARY -:- READING
WITH
HINTS AND SUGGESTIONS
ON
How to Teach Reading
BY
E. A. MARLIN, Principal
OF THE
EPWORTH SCHOOLS.
Epworth, : : : : Illinois.
THE COURIER STEAM PRINT, Carmi, Ill.

Figure 2.1 How to teach reading (when the research base was smaller).

and comprehension; and the third, an investigation into the legibility of small letters.

Perhaps there really was not *much* new under the sun.

Our Focus

The topic of this chapter represents not just our own concerns but those of all researchers in the field—that of collecting, reviewing, and situating our scholarship and professional activities within the work that has come before—while adding new understandings. All of us want to inform our practices, even as knowledge proliferates and the ways of learning within a profession shift. Our title, "From Gray to Google: Learning within a Profession," was intended to raise and examine the remarkable shifts over time in the ways we search and

TABLE I

NUMBER OF SCIENTIFIC STUDIES OF READING MADE IN ENGLAND AND AMERICA SINCE 1880

Period	Number of Studies
1884–85	1
1886–90	1
1891–95	2
1896–1900	10
1901–05	6
1906–10	14
1911–15	49
1916–20	151
1921–24	201
Total	435

Figure 2.2 The table of studies from the U.S. and England in the first *Summary of Research Related to Reading.*

compile scholarship to inform our learning, our teaching, our research, and our policy.

On one end, Gray represents the farsightedness of a pioneering scholar who first went in search of the research evidence in reading. He collected and abstracted studies, and found a way, beginning in 1925, to disseminate the results. It was Gray's hope that the *Summary* would aid current and future researchers to build on accruing scholarship as they expanded a field's knowledge base.

At the contemporary end, Google serves metaphorically to represent the powerful search engines and databases through which Gray's heirs (our students and colleagues) reach for the grounding upon which *their* scholarship sits. It is because of the "way it was" and the "way it is" that we offer three contentions for consideration: *First*, we are students of a field with a long and worthy history of collecting its scholarship; *second*, in an era of powerful search engines and databases, we are duty bound to understand the limitations of our own and others' scholarly searches; and *third*, when the selection/collection procedures belong to others, so, too, do the decisions for preservation, interpretation, and dissemination of the scholarship. We are attempting to lift some of the issues that surround locating and learning from studies across time, with a focus on comprehensiveness, accessibility, relevance, and intent of sources.

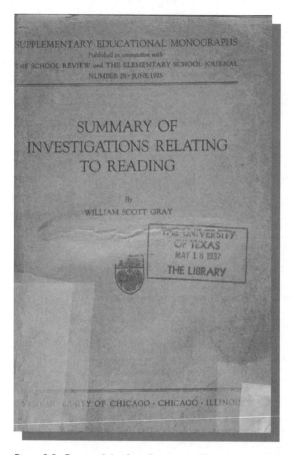

Figure 2.3 Cover of the first *Summary of Investigations Relating to Reading.*

We chose the topic not only because we, too, reach for the research of colleagues and face the task of situating our work within a perspective of precedence, but because we are both a part of Gray's heritage of research summary (one of us playing a major and the other a minor role in the published *Summaries*). Finally, we chose the topic because it allowed us to explore a growing sense that we cannot yet, in these days, Google our way to scholarship (Sadeh, 2004, 2006). Somehow, we must find time to understand better the ways contemporary scholarship is selected, amassed, and made public. In an age of scientifically based reading research, we need to be paying close attention to reviews and syntheses of scholarship that dramatically affect policies and mandates.

A Worthy History

First, some of our history. Gray's first compilation, *Summary of Investigations Relating to Reading*, published in 1925, offered citations and abstracts for 436 investigations (the number of studies in his bibliography) conducted between 1880 and 1924 in the U.S. and England, along with reference to earlier studies conducted in Germany and France. This early effort meant that the field of literacy studies, more than any curriculum-related field, made the most systematic and long-term effort to collect its scholarship. (Guy Buswell (1926) simultaneously published the research in mathematics, but those summaries were not continued.)

Figure 2.4 offers a sample abstract from Gray's first *Summary*, a 1923 investigation by Clifford Woody focusing on the variation in amount of first grade children's reading. Each of Gray's abstracts dependably described the study's *purpose, participants, findings*, and *implications*. At least one of Gray's contemporaries, literacy researcher C.T. Gray (1926), lauded this step toward systematic

Number of pages read in the first grade in ten school systems of Michigan. —Woody reports the results of a study to determine the numbers of pages read during the first five months and the second five months of the first grade in ten school systems of Michigan. Table XIX (427: 18-19) presents a summary of his findings. This table shows that the median number of pages read was 157 for the first five months and 371 for the second five months. Other tables showed that individual classrooms varied in the amount read from a very small number of pages (0–24) to a very large number of pages (800–899). The widest variations and the largest numbers of pages read were in the schools having "two groups" and in the "undifferentiated" classes. On the basis of these findings, Woody suggests that from 175 to 200 pages is a reasonable requirement for the first five months and that from 140 to 250 pages represents reasonable limits of a "zone of safety"; for the second five months he suggests 375 pages as a

reasonable requirement. These recommendations are based on current practice. There is need for additional studies to determine the causes of the wide differences in the amount that is read and to determine the amount which should be read under favorable conditions.

TABLE XIX*

NUMBER OF PAGES OF READING MATERIAL READ IN THE FIRST GRADE OF TEN SCHOOL SYSTEMS

	Three Groups			Two Groups		Single Group	Total
	Fast	Average	Slow	Fast	Slow		
First five months:							
First quartile	144	129	53	153	73	135	112
Median	219	158	77	216	132	152	157
Third quartile	300	213	113	298	197	254	244
Number of teachers reporting	24	24	24	69	69	49	259
Second five months:							
First quartile	238	119	38	336	204	353	218
Median	375	250	100	607	322	374	371
Third quartile	494	321	219	792	531	695	680
Number of teachers reporting	18	18	18	55	55	57	221

* Rearranged from author's data.

Figure 2.4 An abstract from the first summary.

collection, praising the collection for its organization and clarity, and then adding this prescient phrase: ". . . the extensive development in the field of reading demands such a summary" (p. 298). Because the production of a research summary seemed an idea worthy enough to continue, every year from 1925 until his death in 1960, Professor Gray collected the studies that contributed to the knowledge base in reading, including published and unpublished reports, dissertations, theses, books, monographs, and journal articles. Of course, he admitted missing some, and those works, once identified, were included the following year.

Under Gray's impetus and later his financial subsidy, the collection and dissemination continued, and became the *Annual Summary*. It appeared from 1926 to 1932 in *The Elementary School Journal*, and then until 1960 in the *Journal of Educational Research*. By that time, the "Gray Collection," as the physical papers came to be called, comprised nearly 3,900 studies (n=3,895). Following Gray's death, the work was capably continued by his student and then colleague, Helen M. Robinson, Director of the University of Chicago's Reading Center. Under her direction, the Summary appeared in *The Reading Teacher* for four years, and then moved to the *Reading Research Quarterly*. For its remaining years, it appeared as a stand-alone volume (see Table 2.1).

For almost a decade, Robinson served first as the sole author and then as chief editor when she was joined by her colleague, Sam Weintraub (as well as Helen K. Smith and Carol Hostetter). Under Robinson, the number of journals monitored and the number of studies identified increased substantially. It was Helen Robinson who stabilized and refined the categorization system for the abstracts into six consistent divisions: *Research Summaries, Teacher Preparation, Sociology of Reading, Physiology and Psychology of Reading, Teaching of Reading,* and *Reading of Atypical Learners.* Within those heads, Dr. Robinson worked to systematize the procedures for abstracting, to generate and fine-tune subheadings, and to continue to *describe* the burgeoning world of reading research without critique.

Upon Robinson's retirement, and when Weintraub moved to Indiana University from the University of Chicago, the *Summary* came as well, to be partially sponsored by the new clearinghouse on reading research (the

Table 2.1 Outlets for the annual summary of research related to reading across time

Location of the Summary	Dates
The Elementary School Journal	1926–1932
Journal of Education	1933–1960
The Reading Teacher	1961–1965
Reading Research Quarterly	1965–1979
Stand-Alone Volume (IRA)	1980–1997

Clearinghouse on Retrieval of Information and Evaluation on Reading), part of the ERIC system being established in Indiana. With Weintraub as lead editor, the 1970 *Summary* included 416 abstracts representing 111 different journals, monographs, proceedings, and book-length reviews. With the final issue (in 1997), 285 journals were being monitored for research related to reading. According to Summers (1983), research activity in a field naturally expands the sources in which the studies appear:

> Disciplines which experience rapid expansion in their published literature present problems in information retrieval because as interest in a topic becomes more wide-spread, the scatter of items across sources increases.
>
> (p. 103)

Weintraub continued the practices of carefully collecting, categorizing, abstracting, and offering a field its inquiry—first in the *Reading Research Quarterly* and then as a separate, stand-alone publication published by the International Reading Association. Under Weintraub's invitation, Roser, a doctoral student, became the second reader on some of the abstracts for the *Annual Summary of Investigations Related to Reading*. With the 1974 issue, Roser became an official contributor to the Gray/Robinson/Weintraub legacy and continued to serve as a contributing author.

Across the 72 years in which there *was* an *Annual Summary of Investigations Relating to Reading*, approximately 25,000 studies (Weintraub, 1997, p. viii) were collected and offered to the profession (and the public)—all under the guidance of only three editors. The record year seems to have been 1985, in which 1,150 studies were collected and summarized. In its latest editions, the *Summary* continued to include book-length research, articles in journals, conference proceedings, and published monographs, but no longer included dissertations, theses, or unpublished reports. Foreign language journals were monitored as well, and included if accompanied by an extensive English summary.

Procedures for Collecting Studies

The production of each Summary was systematic: The editors or their university libraries subscribed to likely journals, were sent them without charge, or borrowed them from other libraries. In addition, the editors identified and collected book-length research, again relying on libraries. From the journals, relevant studies were identified, copied, and at times (when the copy was owned) physically extracted for indexing and coding. Each piece of research was then read closely, followed by the preparation of the abstract. Consistently, studies were identified, gathered, cataloged, closely read, and abstracted. The abstract was reread and compared with the original study for accuracy and clarity before dissemination. Although there were changes in subtopics and

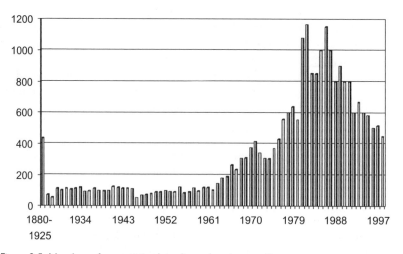

Figure 2.5 Number of summarized studies related to reading across years.

sources, the procedures for the preparation of the summary in the mid-1990s would have seemed familiar to Gray.

According to Weintraub, Gray wrote the abstracts himself, and kept a copy of each article in his office. Helen Robinson did the same. In addition, there was a complete set of non-circulating copies, cataloged by topic, housed in the University of Chicago education library to serve faculty, students, and visiting scholars. Although graduate students were hired to help locate, identify, and verify entries, they were rarely invited to produce abstracts.

Weintraub (1997) explains that it was Gray's intent to offer dependable abstracts with consistent features, reported without evaluating the quality of the published study: "Indeed, beginning in the 1930s, Gray prefaced each *Summary* with a statement to that effect" (p. vii). (See, for example, Gray, 1933, p. 401.) In her dissertation on Gray, Mavrogenes (1985) noted that critical discussions had been planned, but were eliminated because of "space limitations" (p. 162). At the one-hundredth anniversary of Gray's birth, Robinson (1985) wrote that although critical reviews to help school officers and teachers improve practice were "one of the original purposes of the *Annual Summary*," they were not continued due to the growth in quantity of research (p. 31). Consumers of research were constantly reminded to use the *Summary* as a starting point, and to determine the relevance and adequacy of the study for their own work or practice. Weintraub (1981) indicated that the responsibilities for ensuring quality of the research lay with (among other factors) editors, review boards, and a more critical educational community. Further, he argued it was the responsibility of scholars to read and judge a work's relevance and worth. The intended strengths of the *Summary* included comprehensiveness, consistency, accuracy, leavened reporting, and longevity. Further, the studies were identified and their abstracts produced by professionals with expertise within the field. Finally, each study was predictably categorized, arrayed by topic and subtopic, and included in an index of researchers' names. Investigators searching for studies related to their own work had a relatively straightforward procedure: Users found relevant studies by browsing within sections, or by relying on familiarity with names of researchers with similar interests.

Changes in Collection and Dissemination

Despite a long history of collecting our scholarship in a scholarly way, innovations in technology made some of the work with the *Summary* seem more akin to a scriptorium than an information age. Searches of the *Summaries*, other than by the major topic, were by hand. Because each study was placed in only one category, a researcher needed to skim all possible related subheadings to identify relevant research.

In 1966, the U.S. Office of Education established ERIC, the Educational Resources Information Center, including a clearinghouse for reading research (ERIC/CRIER, the Clearinghouse on Retrieval of Information and Evaluation on Reading) at Indiana University. Subject matter specialists in each of 18 ERIC sites became responsible for collecting, storing, reducing, and disseminating information that could be readily retrieved by audiences of users (Harris & Laffey, 1968). Photocopies of the Gray Collection from 1950 to 1965 were sent from the Reading Center at the University of Chicago to become the core of ERIC/CRIER (Robinson, Weintraub, & Smith, 1968). ERIC offered for purchase regularly published indexes (*Research in Education*) and microfiche copies of studies (for nine cents per card). By 1968, Summers and his colleagues were describing an effort to produce a magnetic tape of *Summary* abstracts (dating from 1884 to 1966), making over 5,000 studies available for computer storage and retrieval. By 1984, approximately 12,000 pieces of research identified for the Annual Summary were on microfiche, and available through the Alvina Treut Burrows Institute (Summers, 1984).

In the time period that has lapsed since the cessation of the systematic compilation of the research in reading into only one volume, much has changed in the way we gain access to scholarship: electronic "key word" and full text searches have become our expectation. Although there was conceptual logic in the organization in each *Annual Summary*, its print boundaries limited navigation and search. In an electronic age, "browsability" means more than turning the pages of a print index. Access has been redefined.

Describing the ERIC Clearinghouse on reading established at Indiana University, Larry Harris and James Laffey (1968) predicted the future of searches: "An approach using electronic data processing equipment to handle the material and produce the printout is envisioned" (p. 429). As the *Annual Summary* ceased publication, the top search engines were already indexing hundreds of millions of webpages (Brin & Page, n.d.). An information age means ready access to increasingly powerful searches of databases and indexes that tap more (and more interdisciplinary) journals. Our field is already acclimatized to metasearches. Having learned, though, that cyberspace, unlike libraries, is not always free, we rely on libraries for access to new, unindexed, remote, and sometimes costly online sources.

The Cautious Researcher

But there are drawbacks. First, abstracts (the materials from which search terms were selected and assigned) vary in quality and in the kind and amount of information, depending upon the abstracting service providers. Writers with professional backgrounds in other fields may not necessarily file consistently dependable descriptions in education (personal communication, Janelle Hedstrom, Educational Librarian, U. of Texas), contributing to inconsistent searches. With the *Summary*, the scholar could depend that the abstract was written by an insider who had read the study thoroughly, written to its essence, and had the representation checked by others. Farr (1997) wrote that the *Summary* ". . . was accomplished with standards and quality control that can be applied to few, if any . . . computer-based collections" (p. v). The *Summary*'s abstractors were informed (a strength), but the resource was print-bound (a limitation).

In spite of their scope, electronic searches are sometimes made more difficult by restrictions placed by publishers, including embargos and moving walls. Embargos serve to protect the economic viability of print journal subscriptions by limiting access to issues; moving walls indicate the range of months or years a journal's most recent issues or years are restricted. In addition, because vendors (suppliers of services to libraries) provide access to scholarly sources and because vendors aren't free, libraries must make decisions about which services and searches to provide. Yet, even budget-rich libraries and powerful databases might not necessarily yield the *grey* literature. Grey literature is the term used by librarians for materials that are hard to retrieve either because they are not commercially published or they are not indexed—technical reports, conference papers, and even some proceedings (e.g., the Yearbook of the National Reading Conference). Further, the lexicon of professions change and as terms are replaced, redefined, or added as knowledge advances, lack of familiarity with older search terms may impede searches.

Finally, we who search may be at fault. Like our students, we may be habitual users of a single, favorite database. Although we may clearly understand that Google's findings are arrayed by a page rank algorithm that displays webpages by the frequency of hits rather than the relevance or worth of data (Sadeh, 2004), we may understand less about the limitations of our academic search engines.

Just a year ago, for example, we couldn't retrieve a full-text copy of Kenneth Goodman's 1965 study, "A Linguistic Study of Cues and Miscues in Reading," a study that has been reprinted, replicated, and repeatedly cited. Searching by title, Google Scholar got us to an ERIC number and the message that the study was "not available from ERIC." We added Goodman's name to the search, then the journal title, and finally the keywords *miscue* and *oral reading*. Entering data in the same way, we next tried various databases, including ERIC, PsychInfo, and Academic Search Premier. We found references to the work, but were unable to get to the full-text article itself. ERIC didn't yet go back as far as 1965, and PsychINFO and other databases did not include the journal in which Goodman published (see Table 2.2 for a comparison of databases). Ulrich's, a source that tracks publisher information for academic and professional journals, informed us that the journal (*Elementary English*) changed its name to *Language Arts*.

Even so, we still couldn't retrieve the study online. To get to the complete article, it was necessary to enter the bowels of the library, thumb through the box of author/subject filecards, and then locate the microfiche from the Gray Collection file using the document's official ED (Education Document) number. To read the full text, readers must drop the microfiche into a waiting (and somewhat dusty) reader.

But that was last year. Today, even a non-expert searcher can Google a full-text copy of Goodman's miscue study through ERIC (updated monthly, and now containing over 1.2 million citations). The digitized copy sits askew on the page, is edged with markings, and stamped with warnings: "This document has been reproduced exactly as received from the person or organization originating it. Points of view or opinions stated do not necessarily represent official Office of Education position or policy."

The full-text ERIC collection is growing because authors and other copyright holders are being urged by the Clearinghouse to grant permissions for digitizing and uploading research published between 1966 and 1992, a project that may add 340,000 manuscripts to the database. Even so, the argument is still to be made: When we choose and use databases and search engines, we need to be aware of the scope and coverage of the sources (Mayr & Walter, 2007). Today, for example, it is not yet possible to Google a full text of the

Table 2.2 Sources coverage of selected databases

Databases	Date	Coverage
ERIC	1966–	560 journals
Education Full Text	1983; full text since 1996	650 periodicals
Education Index	1929–1983	500 periodicals and yearbooks
Academic Search Premier	1990–	3,180 journals in all fields
PsychINFO	1887–coverage varies	1,700 sources plus chapter books
Linguistics and Language Behavior Abstracts	1973–	244,000 citations

Figure 2.6 Locating a source using Microfiche.

Annual Summary of Investigations Relating to Reading in its stand-alone volumes. As Peter Morville (2005) contends, "Ambient findability describes a fast emerging world where we can find anyone or anything from anywhere at anytime. We're not there yet, but we're headed in the right direction" (p. 6).

In *The Reading Teacher*, Gray (1957) wrote that to prepare one manuscript for publication, [he] "reviewed the findings of scores of pertinent studies published during the *last five decades.*" Given the scope of our collected body of research mid-century, we can conclude that Gray's review was a comprehensive one. Today's scholars, perhaps because of access, journal limitations, research proliferation, and/or the complex, innovative, and interdisciplinary nature of contemporary literacy study, don't appear to produce such deep core samples of relevant literature. Deciding how much to report seems to be one issue (Gilgun, 2005). Deciding how much to locate and read seems another.

In a highly unsystematic sampling, Roser stacked all the 2006 issues of four professional journals (*Reading Research Quarterly, American Educational Research Journal, Journal of Literacy Research,* and *Research in the Teaching of English*), and then randomly selected one journal from each stack. She tallied each reference in those four issues, categorizing each citation by year and source. Altogether, there were 1,425 references in these four journals, with 77% of the citations published in 1990 or later, and 93% of the references published since 1980. This array may say very little except that researchers may tend to read and cite studies published within their own life spans (with the noted exception of the citations of Rosenblatt and Vygotsky).

There are other explanations for "citations light," as well, including the challenges of bringing together voluminous research, preserving space to stake claims for our own findings, and to make original forays into theory (Gilgun, 2005). Nevertheless, Jeanne Chall (1984) boldly asserted that a "common misconception among some researchers [is] that only the research of the last 5, or at most 10 years, needs to be searched and read" (p. x). By contrast, contemporary researchers may claim to have sifted thousands of reports (electronically) without clarifying how *a priori* categories of relevance operated to focus the review.

Making Informed Decisions About Retrieval

In the infancy of research collection undertaken by clearinghouses and centers (ERIC), Harris and Laffey (1968) admitted that the "collection of potentially useful materials had been somewhat shotgun" in approach, suggesting plans were under way to "develop a system to insure that the published journal literature is systematically covered" and announced (p. 427). Our last contention is that all of us should know more about the systematic procedures through which research evidence is selected and arrayed to scaffold further work. One potential place for learning more is ERIC itself. Currently, on the ERIC website, decisions for acceptance of documents into the ERIC database are described as based on the quality of *utility/importance*, marked by these words: "The materials must be relevant to current priorities in education . . ." (www.eric.ed.gov). One wonders: Whose current priorities? And what if, as they will, priorities shift? Collections of scholarship, it seems certain, should not be held to mainstream positions or "official" stances.

Further, a recent structured abstract initiative on the ERIC website

Table 2.3 Citation sampling

Sources	RTE	JLR	AERJ	RRQ	Totals (%)
Before 1920	0	0	0	4	4 (0%)
1920–1929	0	0	0	5	5 (0%)
1930–1939	0	0	0	4	4 (0%)
1940–1949	0	0	0	1	1 (0%)
1950–1959	4	0	1	1	6 (0.5%)
1960–1969	4	5	6	7	22 (2%)
1970–1979	4	13	19	23	59 (4%)
1980–1989	31	44	75	72	222 (16%)
1990–1999	105	111	198	217	631 (44%)
2000–2006	104	85	90	192	471 (33%)
Total	252	258	389	526	1425 (99.5%)

announces itself to be voluntary, but to encourage its use, the webpage explains that decision-makers and researchers want to see "at a glance" such key elements as research design and outcomes. Those preparing a structured abstract for ERIC are asked to complete a checklist indicating whether the work is quantitative, what hypotheses were tested, what interventions were installed, and so forth. Could it be that the nature of categories help to readily sort for research that doesn't "count" in particular case building? The ERIC website—and others as well—tells you less than you might like to know about how decisions are made.

Whether carefully building on the work of others, constructing new theories, or both, we depend on and learn from the work that precedes us. As learners and leaders in a field, we need to remember that scholarship is being collected by a host of houses, vendors, analysts, and organizations. The results and recommendations ("research says") are being offered to us through portals of various dimensions, the domains of which are not always easy to discern. But far from William S. Gray's university office overstuffed with paper copies, the world of literacy research lies almost, but not quite, at our fingertips. We are a burgeoning democracy of researchers and consumers of research. And in the interval, we need to apply due diligence:

- to know how to navigate libraries
- to understand the coverage time frames of our favorite databases
- to understand what is included and excluded from databases
- to understand the scope and function of popular search engines, and (even)
- to understand how our colleagues select and include sources when they prepare research reviews and policy reports.

Scholars continue to remind one another of the critical nature of the literature review (Boote & Beile, 2005). When research is pulled together to make sense of a field, to influence direction, policy, curriculum, and instruction, how much more do we need to understand about the nature and scope and assumptions of the scholarly searches that underlie the distillation of research? The sheer number of studies is staggering. In his own lifetime as a researcher, Gray produced more studies and books (over 500) than the totality of studies he abstracted for the 41 years covered by his first *Summary* (Guthrie, 1984). A contemporary report may indicate that tens of thousands of studies were identified through electronic searches, but Gray might ask, "But was that all?" "Did you read closely?" "Did you show how and why *a priori* decisions affected inclusion/exclusion?" In her Foreword to the reprint edition of Gray's review of research from the 1941 *Encyclopedia of Education Research*, Jeanne Chall (1984) asked:

Have we perhaps tended to pay too little attention to the research richness of our past? Do we do so in our eagerness to make our own discoveries? . . . Are we aware of what has already been learned?

(p. xii)

We who investigate and try to make sense of things have yet another challenge. It could be called the Adam Complex—meaning that we are all the children of a desire to name. For example, Roser's work examines children's literary meaning making in the presence of good books and good teachers. Across reviews of related literature, similar phenomena are named and renamed, making the synthesis of understanding more difficult, even given the power of full text searches. It is yet another challenge to the plowers of new furrows in old fields: to connect with adjacent acreage.

Pulling It Together

And as for the discovery and systematizing of knowledge, in retirement, William S. Gray (1958) wrote that he believed we have "explored at least in some preliminary way practically all known reading problems that arise from birth to old age" (p. 75). In the sunset of our lives, do we imagine that we have seen all the day has to offer? Well . . . not Grandpa. He left a caveat at the end of the book:

> Things can be new to you or to me, and they can be new to the pupils when strictly speaking, they are not new.

From a text costing two cents to a microfiche card for nine cents to a "free" and unimaginably extensive electronic library, the economics for responsible scholarship are in our favor. Our students (and their students) will no doubt continue to decide that we have much to learn. They should also be prepared to acknowledge that much has been learned. It is incumbent upon us, as well as those who follow, not simply to cover in some superficial manner that which is relevant, but to uncover that which is significant and to note the strengths and weakness of the research we are building upon. Thorough searches are one step; close reading another; responsible compilations a third—toward a merging of the power and meticulousness of Google and Gray.

Gray ended some of the issues of the *Annual Summary* with "to be continued," and so shall we.

References

Boote, D.N. & Beile, P. (2005). Scholars before researchers: On the centrality of the dissertation literature review in research preparation. *Educational Researcher, 34,* 6, 3–15.

Brin, S. & Page, L. (n.d.). *The anatomy of a large-scale hypertextual web search engine*. Retrieved April 6, 2008, from http://infolab.stanford.edu/~backrub/google.html

Buswell, G. (1926). Summary of arithmetic investigations. *Supplementary Educational Monographs*. Chicago, IL: University of Chicago.

Chall, J. (1984). Foreword. In J.T. Guthrie (Ed.), *Reading: William S. Gray: A Research Retrospective, 1881–1941* (pp. viii–xii). Newark, DE: International Reading Association.

Farr, R. & Weintraub, S. (1970). Using the annual summary. *Reading Research Quarterly*, 5, 2, 127–128.

Farr, R. (1997). Foreword. In S. Weintraub (Ed.), *Annual Summary of Investigations Related to Reading, July 1, 1995–June 30, 1996* (p. v). Newark, DE: International Reading Association.

Gilgun, J.F. (2005). Lighten up: The citation dilemma in qualitative research. *Qualitative Health Research*, 15, 5, 721–724.

Goodman, K. (1965). A linguistic study of cues and miscues in reading. *Elementary English*, 42, 639–643.

Gray, C.T. (1926). Reviews and abstracts. *Journal of Educational Research*, 13, 4, 297–298.

Gray, W.S. (1925). Summary of investigations relating to reading. *Supplementary Educational Monograph*. Chicago, IL: University of Chicago.

Gray, W.S. (1933). Summary of reading investigations. *Journal of Educational Research*, 26, 6, 401–424.

Gray, W.S. (1957). Role of group and individualized teaching in a sound reading program. *The Reading Teacher*, 11, 2, 99–104.

Gray, W.S. (1958). Research in reading marches on. *The Reading Teacher*, 12, 2, 4–82,

Guthrie, J. (Ed.) (1984). Preface. *Reading: William S. Gray: A Research Retrospective, 1881–1941* (pp. viii–xii). Newark, DE: International Reading Association.

Harris, L. & Laffey, J. (1968). ERIC/CRIER, *Reading Research Quarterly*, 3, 3, 424–429.

Marlin, E.A. (1893). *How to teach reading*. Carmi, IL: Courier Steam Print.

Mavrogenes, N.A. (1985). *William Scott Gray: Leader of teachers and shaper of American reading instruction*. Doctoral dissertational, University of Chicago, 1985.

Mayr, P. & Walter, A-K. (2007). An exploratory study of Google Scholar. *Online Information Review*, 31, 6, 814–830. Retrieved October 24, 2007, from www.emeraldinsight.com/1468-4527.htm

Morville, P. (2005). *Ambient findability*. Cambridge, MA: O'Reilly.

Robinson, H.M. (1985). William S. Gray: The scholar. In J. Stephenson (Ed.), *William S. Gray: Teacher, scholar, leader* (pp. 24–36). Newark, DE: International Reading Association.

Robinson, H.M., Weintraub, S. & Smith, H.K. (1968). The Summary and the Gray Collection. *Reading Research Quarterly*, 3, 2, 147–148.

Sadeh, T. (2004). *To Google or not to Google: Metasearch design in the quest for the ideal user experience*. A paper presented at the 28th Library Systems Seminar, Trondheim, Norway. Retrieved February 1, 2007, from www.elag2004.no/papers/Sadeh.pdf

Sadeh, T. (2006, March). Google scholar versus metasearch systems. *High Energy Physics Libraries Webzine*, 12, 16 pp. Retrieved April 6, 2008 from http://library.cern.ch/HEPLW/12/papers/1/

Summers, E.G. (1968). Reading research literature: Identification and retrieval. *Reading Research Quarterly*, 4, 1, 5–48.

Summers, E.G. (1983). Bradford's Law and the retrieval of reading research journal literature. *Reading Research Quarterly, 19*, 1, 102–109.

Summers, E.G. (1984). A review and application of citation analysis methodology to reading research journal literature. *Journal of the American Society for Information Science, 35*, 6, 332–343.

Weintraub, S. (Ed.), (1981). *Annual Summary of Investigations related to reading, July 1, 1979– June 30, 1980*. Newark, DE: International Reading Association.

Weintraub, S. (Ed.), (1997). *Annual summary of investigations related to reading*. Newark, DE: International Reading Association.

Chapter 3

Multimodality

In Perspective

Jerome C. Harste
Indiana University

We observed young children move from written language to art, mathematics, and even drama when asked to write (Harste, Woodward, & Burke, 1984). Megan, age 3, for example, when asked to tell us a story, turned her pencil into a pretend bunny that went hip-hopping across the page. The marks left on the paper were merely the residue of her dramatic activity.

Alison, age 6, had a telephone conversation with her friend Jennifer (Berghoff et al., 2000). Afterwards, she immediately recorded the conversation on a piece of paper. When asked to read what she had written, Alison read Figure 3.1 as saying, "After church on Sunday, Jennifer [J.T.] will come over to play ballet. She will bring her hair ribbon, tutu, and ballet slippers with her [in a bag]. I [A.H.] will get my hair ribbon, tutu, and ballet slippers from my dresser, and together we will play balleting!" One has to be impressed with the elegance of Alison's note. This, after all, was a fairly complicated phone

Figure 3.1 Alison, Age 6, uninterrupted writing (Berghoff et al., 2000).

conversation. As can be noted, Alison used symbols from language, art, and mathematics to record her message.

Adults would have a hard time recording the phone conversation Alison had with Jennifer as succinctly as did Alison. That may be true because as we have gotten older we have lost our ability to move freely between and among sign systems in an effort to mean. Despite the fact that as people age they become more and more conventional (through experience they come to know that *writing* means *writing letters* and not *writing art* or *writing math*), all language events are multimodal to some sense. Oral language, for example, is filled with gesture. Writers often use pictures or figures (as I did above) to complement their writing. Website designers take multimodal texts to new heights, with some researchers even claiming that the Internet changes the basic nature of both the reading process and the writing process (Leu et al., 2004).

Intentionality, or the desire to use written language multimodally to mean, seemed to be a given in our studies of 3–6-year-olds (Harste et al., 1984). Although we never directly said it, we wrote as if we assumed intentionality was something children were born knowing. It took Deborah Wells Rowe (2008) studying 1–2-year-old preschoolers to show that intentionality is learned socially as children interact with adults who assume intentionality, and in so assuming convince children to adopt this standard. *Multimodality* may be learned the same way, as the lines between sign systems do not seem to be marked as tightly in the everyday world as they often are in school settings. One of the problems with talking about literacy as multimodality is that it proliferates the notion of literacy. All of a sudden each channel of communication or one's level of competency in a sign system becomes a literacy (*oral literacy, visual literacy, gestural literacy*). Because literacy is a complex event, I have been trying to focus my thinking about multimodality on social practices and how the multiple use of sign systems to mean is used to do particular kinds of work. Like Brian Street (2003) I prefer thinking of multiple sign systems as a semiotic resource involving language (broadly defined), vision, and action. These are the semiotic resources which simultaneously are taken up and enacted in culturally valued social practices that communicate meaning. Seeing multimodality in this way focuses attention on the definition of literacy which is in operation, the social practices which sustain that definition, and the pragmatic effects of that definition as "read" by others.

A Psychological Perspective

Having entertained the notion that all language events are multimodal in nature, Carolyn Burke, Marjorie Siegel, Kathy Short, Karen Feathers and I initially became interested in multimodality as a cognitive or psychological strategy for learning. By this I mean we noticed that the move across sign systems seemed to be generative (Siegel, 1995), to invite new ideas and new ways of thinking. One of the instructional strategies we developed to explore this phenomenon was *Sketch-to-Stretch* (Harste, Short, w/Burke, 1986). Marjorie Siegel used Sketch-to-Stretch in her dissertation to study reading comprehension (Siegel, 1983). *Ira Sleeps Over* (Waber, 1975) is the story of a young boy on his first sleepover. His sister teases him unmercifully because he sleeps with a teddy bear, which she assures him is going to seem babyish to his friend. He comes to find out, however, that his friend sleeps with a teddy bear too. Figure 3.2 is Matt's sketch of what *Ira Sleeps Over* meant to him. His picture is a bedroom scene in which a boy is getting something out of his dresser. Matt read the markings on the top of the sketch as a formula: "One boy plus a teddy bear plus another boy plus a teddy bear equals two good friends." If one knows this book, one immediately notices that this is a great retelling. There can be no doubt that Matt understood the story. He even captured the unstated bigger message. The second thing one notices is that Matt's summation has the same sort of succinct elegance as was present in Alison's transcription of her telephone conversation.

Phyllis Whitin (1996) used Sketch-to-Stretch with her 7th graders over the course of a year. These were a group of reluctant readers. While initially she asked students to sketch what it was they thought their book meant, she later challenged them to represent what they were reading into other sign systems such as mathematics. Toward the end of the year she asked students to identify pieces of art that they thought reflected one of the stories they had read. Whitin argues that by using Sketch-to-Stretch she literally transformed a group of non-readers into readers. Transcripts of the conversations they had about

Figure 3.2 A sketch from *Ira Sleeps Over* (Waber, 1975); Matt, Age 10 (Siegel, 1983).

their books using the sketches they created prove her point. Whitin's students sound more like a group of English majors talking about books than a group of middle-school readers. Even further, Whitin reported that on average the students in her classroom read more books in one year than they had read during their entire first six years of school.

What these studies demonstrate is the power of *transmediation* (Sebeok, 1970; Suhor, 1992). Students were asked to take the sense that they made in language and recast it into another sign system. Because each sign system has its own semantics, syntax and graphic forms, there is no one-to-one correspondence between language and art, for example. *Love* can be expressed in language, but it can also be expressed by sending a bouquet of roses, or by suggestively grouping the four letters which make up the word into a warm, cozy bundle as Robert Indiana has shown (1976). Importantly, taking what one knows in language and moving it to art (or clay, or music, or mathematics, or drama) "wiggles" the system by augmenting the semiotic resources which are available as well as what can be afforded. While some affordances may be lost, new meanings become available, and it is this opening up of meaning that gives Sketch-to-Stretch its generative qualities.

Vera John-Steiner (1985) studied scholars in a wide variety of disciplines in an attempt to understand the basis of their brilliance. What she found is that almost all moved very freely across multiple sign systems in an effort to mean. Kirby and Kuykendall's text, *Mind Matters* (1991), moves these ideas to instruction by inviting teachers and students to think about thinking. Students are invited to think like an artist, an inventor, an anthropologist, and more. In our own work on inquiry-based learning we often begin the year by studying what it means to learn (Short, Harste, w/Burke, 1996). We also invite community members and experts to offer workshops on what it means to think like a psychologist, an anthropologist, a musician, a gardener, a carpenter, and so on. As part of these workshops community members and experts introduce the tools which they find particularly beneficial, like in the case of the historian, a time line. Students then used these workshops as resources when pursuing their own inquiry questions.

A Sociological Perspective

Back in the late 1970s I was invited to do an evaluation of the Wingate language arts program on the Navajo Reservation (Harste, 1978). While the Bureau of Indian Affairs was concerned about the students' academic progress in reading, speaking, and writing English, I was completely awed by the quality of the artwork that graced the classroom walls. Much of the artwork looked as if it were done by professional artists rather than elementary and middle school students. As a result of this experience I joined Elliot Eisner (1982), Maxine Greene (1988), and a host of sociolinguists in hypothesizing that different cultural groups may have different ways of knowing. While linguistics may be the dominant way of knowing for children of a European heritage, art or music or dance may be a dominant way of knowing for children raised in other cultural traditions.

There is more and more research to support this hypothesis. The Key School in Indianapolis is built on Gardner's seven intelligences (1993) and claims to reach a much wider group of students than does traditional instruction (Balanos, 1994). The Arts Education Partnership (2005) released its study of an arts-integrated approach to learning in 10 urban schools and found significant gains in achievement, especially among struggling learners. The Center for Inquiry in Indianapolis, a public school with which I am closely associated, advocates inquiry-based instruction, multiple ways of knowing, and critical literacy. While it is hard to know how much of its success with African-American children is attributable to multiple ways of knowing per se, the fact remains that consistently the school has outscored other schools serving a similar inner-city population. Scores on Indiana State Test of Education Progress (ISTEP), in fact, suggest that students at the Center do as well as students attending suburban schools around Indianapolis (Harste, Vasquez, Leland, Schmidt, & Ociepka, 2004). Carger (2004) recently reported on the positive influence that the visual arts have on learning for bilingual children. Karen Grady (2002) and Peter Cowan (2004) have studied the role that lowrider art plays in allowing Hispanic students to maintain a cultural sense of self and identity even while their home cultures are seemingly systematically being ignored in the schools they attend.

Even different linguistic or discourse styles make a difference. Shirley Brice Heath (1983) showed that communities have different "ways with words." Tracton parents talked differently than did Roadville parents and they inducted their children into literacy quite differently. Kathryn Au (1979) showed that Hawaiian children learned better through a *talk story* form of instruction than through instructional approaches that ignored their cultural ways of knowing. Lewis, Thompson, Celious, & Brown (2002) have used hip-hop to support African-American students find relevance in life as well as their school subjects, including philosophy. Scollon and Scollon (1981) have pointed out that school-based discourses that incorporate essayist practices and values conflict with the values, attitudes, and ways with words embedded in some Athabascan home and community-based discourses. Their work, to some degree, spawned a culturally responsive school movement, the effects of which can be seen in the work of a host of scholars. McCarty and Watahomigie (1999) have shown, for example, that when indigenous students and teachers share the same cultural values, learning is enhanced.

These research studies suggest that sign systems position people differently. To return to Wingate as an example, art positioned the Navajo child as an expert whereas language positioned the Navajo child as failing. Which sign system dominates determines how the Navajo child is perceived and what identities he or she is permitted to take on.

It is important to understand, however, that sign systems are not necessarily in competition with one another. Each affords a particular type of meaning. I like to think about literacy broadly as all of the ways that humankind has for mediating their world. A language arts program by this way of thinking ought to expand our communication potential not just in language but in all the ways there are to know and mean. Like Halliday (1975) I assume that each of the sign systems has something unique to contribute to meaning making or it would cease to exist. This stance positions me as a *social semiotician*, or someone interested in signs and how humankind uses sign systems—art, music, language, mathematics, dance, and drama—to mediate and transmediate themselves and their world.

A Critical Perspective

From the perspective of identity, sign systems have a critical edge. While critical theorists are interested in what counts as literacy in a society, they are even more interested in what social practices are in place (Luke & Freebody, 1997). They argue that in order to change what counts as literacy, the social practices—the practices that give certain sign systems more clout than other sign systems—need to change. While individual schools might institute a set of social practices that give priority to multiple ways of knowing, the systems of meaning that operate in the larger system are still in place. Students might do well at the Center for Inquiry, for example, but they still need to survive in a world where linguistics, rather than art, rules.

The Internet is a good example of how the use of multiple sign systems has transformed ourselves and our ways of being in the world. Gunther Kress (2003) says, "In this 'New Media Age' the screen has replaced the book as the dominant medium of communication. This dramatic change has made the image, rather than writing, the center of communication" (p. 1). James Gee (1996) argues that children are learning more about what it means to be literate outside of school than they are learning inside of school. I won't argue that I see all these changes as good. They are nonetheless reality as we know it today.

I get worried about children being manipulated by media. I want to create students who are agents of text rather than victims of text, regardless of the sign systems involved. From my perspective it is not sensible to ignore the everyday literacies that students encounter nor the everyday literacies that children bring with them to school and upon which a viable literacy curriculum should be built (Lewison, Leland, & Harste, 2008a). While a lot of this work still needs to be done, some of us (Harste et al., 2007; Albers et al., 2008) have begun by looking closely at art as a sign system in an effort to help students both read art and create texts which use art to *talk back*, what scholars call *counter-narrative texts* (Giroux et al., 1996).

The Grammar of Visual Design

One of the assumptions social semioticians make about art is that all signs are motivated. By this they mean that there is nothing random in art; what is there was done for a purpose. Kress and van Leeuwen (1996/2006) say that we often think of art as abstract and language as concrete. Using a very young child's rendering of an elephant (in this case I've used my own daughter's elephant, which she made at age 3, see Figure 3.3), Kress and van Leeuwen make clear that a child saying, "This is an elephant" is a lot more abstract than is a picture of an elephant drawn by the same child. Typically we think of language as concrete and art as abstract. Said the other way around, we know a lot more about what the child thinks an elephant is from the picture than we do from her statement.

Visual discourse analysis (Albers, 2007) builds on Kress and van Leeuwen's framework for unpacking visual images by inviting the user to analyze a "text" systematically whether that text is all art or a mixture of various semiotic systems, like language, music, art, etc.

Top and Bottom

The top of a picture is *the ideal*; the bottom, *the real*. In Figure 3.4 the top of the picture is a blue sky, which metaphorically we might read as *open* or *full of unlimited possibilities*. The bottom is green grass, which metaphorically we read as a stabilizing force, an *anchor*.

Figure 3.3 Alison, Age 3. Uninterrupted drawing elephant (Lewison, Leland, & Harste, 2008b).

Figure 3.4 Literacy as counter narrative (Student work done in the style of Jacob Lawrence).

Left and Right

The left side of the picture is *the given* or what I prefer to call the *here and now*; the right side, *the new*. In Figure 3.4 the two sides are pretty much the same, with the exception of the top right-hand corner. What is new here is the figure expressing herself in multiple literacies.

Center

The center of the picture provides a focus. In this case we have an African-American girl sitting in a chair rather rigidly (hands at her side, feet squarely on the ground) while her voice rises to the heavens. Since her chair and feet fall in the bottom part of the picture (the real), we read the figure as fixed, immobile, trapped. What is new and ideal is her voice and the multiple forms of expression that are symbolized in the wedge of her voice rising.

Vectors

Kress and van Leeuwen argue that vectors are important. One vector in this picture is the line separating the grass from the sky, the real from the ideal. Another vector is created by the speech bubble, from the girl's head to the top right corner of the page, which we read as positive, or in the direction from the real to the ideal and the here and now to the new. It is these vectors that give us confidence in our reading of the picture. They, in a sense, confirm our other interpretations.

Colors

Although the colors are not shown, there is something fairly optimistic about the use of blues, greens, and yellows in this picture. The colors themselves suggest something positive or hopeful.

Gaze

The character in the picture is looking away from the viewer. In this instance her head is up and off the page, in the direction of the new and the ideal. Her gaze suggests she is focused on the future rather than on the here and now.

Exaggeration

Peggy Albers (2007) is particularly interested in exaggeration and the use of iconic images. Jacob Lawrence, for example, often exaggerates the hands in his paintings to honor hard labor and to remind us of the hard work that African-Americans performed in serving their masters and in building this society. In this picture, the artist has drawn the hands out of proportion to the rest of the figure. They are weak hands adding credence to our reading of her as being trapped, a bit helpless and/or weak.

Interpretation

Both Albers and Kress and van Leeuwen see understanding as a search for unity across all available signs. Any of the following statements seem to capture what message this picture conveys. While there clearly are differences in these messages, the similarities in meaning across the statements made by four "readers" of this "text" is striking:

- We need an expanded definition of literacy that includes multiple ways of knowing.
- In order for literacy to give voice to all learners, multiple ways of knowing need to be advocated.
- Individuals are trapped with old notions of literacy rather than with multiple ways of knowing.
- Multiple sign systems provide access to literacy for minority learners.

To confirm what the author/artist had in mind, I asked participants to write a reflection on their experience. Here is what this artist/author had to say about her work and what she was hoping to say:

> This is a representation of a Jacob Lawrence postcard. The girl here is representing all learners and all sign systems: dance, language, drama, science, visual art, and movement. I hope this work demonstrates how educators can honor all learners and multiple ways of knowing. As I was painting, I was remembering a line of poetry, "I'll tear those words from your throat and shout them into the hot night for all the world to hear."

The readings that four readers gave to this picture as well as the author's reflection on what it was she was attempting to say adds credence to visual discourse analysis for raising consciousness as well as interrogating new forms of literacy. My argument is that for the twenty-first century we need to help children develop not only visual literacy but the language of visual literacy critique.

While work in studying the grammar of visual design is just beginning, I have found the frameworks presented by Kress and van Leeuwen (1996/2006) and Albers (2007) to work surprisingly well for studying cereal boxes, advertisements, public sculptures, scenes in movies as well as some forms of graffiti. Art, like language, is a semiotic (or meaning-centered) system. According to Halliday (1975), and regardless of the complexity of the form, in order to interpret that message one simultaneously has to attend to the field (the setting, the content of the message, as well as what is happening), the mode (the various sign systems involved and what messages each carry), and the tenor (the relationship depicted between and among people, including how you as the reader of this text are positioned and what identity you are asked to take on).

An Instructional Perspective

One of the hard things about creating a critical as well as a multimodal curriculum is that few of us have had the opportunity actually to live such a curriculum. For the most part we have been taught *consumer literacy* rather than *critical literacy*; the skills needed to acquire goods or services for direct use or ownership rather than the skills needed to critique what is being sold in terms of how such goods position us and who is or is not being served by our consumerism.

We recently reported on a study of how 5th graders and preservice teachers read advertisements (Albers et al., 2008). We purposefully selected advertisements that we thought would generate critique. While we found that 5th graders were more critical than were preservice teachers, both groups tended to describe isolated signs rather than explicate and critique underlying messages. One of the ads, for example, advertised Wal-Mart's new line of Barbie clothing by showing young girls parading down a fashion show runway. The whole ad was done in pink, of course. Preservice teachers showed no concerns for how girls were being positioned. They saw the ad as showing: "Beautiful little girls . . ." who were "stylish . . . walking down the runway like models . . ." suggesting ". . . you could be a model too." Rather than talk back to these ads, participants bought into the lifestyle presented in these ads without so much as raising a question.

We clearly have our work cut out. There is some research which shows that having students produce multimedia ads is more effective in teaching them to read ads critically than is just teaching them to unpack visual images by themselves (Burns & Duran, 2007). Using the same ads as those we used in the study cited above, our next research project is to teach students both to read ads critically and to create a multimedia ad which speaks back. We'll study how their creation of one critical ad affects their critique of the other ads being used in the study.

These research projects are our attempt to put in place a new set of social practices. Importantly these social practices value various ways of knowing as well as social critique. Equally significant from a historical perspective, these social practices once again redefine literacy and what it means to be literate. The good news is that there are lots of places to begin and that we do not need to start from scratch. The key, we believe, is to focus on social practices rather than worry about which particular forms of literacy are being highlighted.

We began in our school in Indianapolis, for example, with picture books that raise important social issues (for an annotated list of picture books we used, see Harste et al., 2000; Leland, Harste et al., 2002; Lewison et al., 2008b). Semiotically, we defined a picture book as one in which the message is conveyed by both the print and the picture. Because the social issues which the books address coincided with social issues which the students themselves were facing, we simply read these books aloud to open up the conversation. Once students began to make personal connections they began to unpack issues and offer suggestions for how things should be. Many of the books we read led to social action projects which students took to the community. Importantly, the reading of social issue picture books put a new set of social practices in place. These social practices redefined what it meant to be literate in this classroom.

Vivian Vasquez (2004) turned the walls of her pre-kindergarten classroom into a *learning wall* (what researchers would call *an audit trail*) of the social issues and social action which her students took over the course of a year as a result of the books they were reading and the classroom conversations which ensued. What her study shows is that critical literacy is enhanced when addressed multimodaly and both are stances even very young children are capable of taking.

Dorothy Heathcote has been a long-time advocate of process drama. While process drama (Wagner, 1999) is not a new literacy, one of its strengths is that it allows students to try on a new way of being in the world. Michelle Knobel and Colin Lankshear (2007) talk about the new literacies as having two components: a technical component and an *ethos* component. By ethos they mean a new way of belonging in the world. They argue that too often we as educators worry about the technical component, when what is really important is the ethos component, as it is this component that allows children to try on new identities and new ways to position themselves in the world. In similar fashion, rather than worry about whether the literacy is a new one or an old one like drama, what is important is that it allows children to explore a new ethos, to try it on for size, to orient themselves in the world differently. There is, after all, nothing sacrosanct about how the new literacies position people. There are, as Carole Edelsky (2006) has pointed out, lots of people using the new literacies to position themselves and us in very unsavory ways: "Neo-liberalism is capitalism run amok. 'Symptoms' . . . include: corporate domin-ation, infinite concessions to transnational corporations, use of state force to protect markets, intensified surveillance, cheapened labor (a race to the bottom), commodification, and privatization of the public sphere" (p. 2).

Conclusion

While this is clearly not the first time we, as a society, have changed our minds as to what constitutes literacy (Myers, 1996), today's new literacies herald new times for English language arts teachers. This is so even though Andrew Manning (2004) would argue that by bringing any of the new literacies into school we ruin them. By changing the context we change the ethos, or the way of being and interacting this semiotic resource affords. Bringing the new litera-cies into school, then, is a catch-22. Yet, I don't see the answer as backing away from the new literacies nor failing to address the issues which surround their use. Because so many schools block their students' use of various Internet sites (rather than talk about the moral and ethical issues these sites raise), part of the answer may lie in using the old literacies in new ways, to serve new purposes. What students learn from process drama they can apply to how they position themselves in a world with or without iPods, iPhones, and YouTube. What is key, I think, is making this agenda—to think curriculum—explicit. *To think curriculum*, by my view, is to keep perspective of the big picture. It is not enough that only teachers think curriculum; children need to be invited to think curriculum too.

I see the key to instruction in this multimedia era, like it has been all along, as using the child as your curricular informant. Cynthia Lewis (2007) argues that what the *New Literacies* researchers are essentially doing is watching children work on the computer or with new literacies much like those of us who were early literacy researchers watched young children write with paper and pen (Harste et al., 1984). By "kidwatching" (Goodman, 1978) we teachers and researchers can attend to the new literacies which children bring with them to school as well as with their ways of knowing. Instructionally we educators need to start from that base as we learn to be critically literate ourselves in this multimedia era. Like everything else, we can't as teachers do for children what we cannot first do ourselves. But this is not bad news. Like all good instruction, critical multimodal literacy is an ongoing inquiry, one in which the children in our classroom and we can simultaneously engage.

References

Albers, P. (2007). *Finding the artist within: Creating and reading visual text in the English language arts classroom.* Newark, DE: International Reading Association.

Albers, P., Harste, J.C., Vander Zaden, S., & Felderman, C. (2008). Using popular culture to promote critical literacy practices. Presentation at the annual meeting of the National Reading Conference, Austin, TX.

Arts Education Partnership. (2005). *Third space: When learning matters.* Washington, DC: Arts Education Partnership.

Au, K.H. (1979). Using the experience-text relationship method with minority children. *The Reading Teacher, 32*:1, 677–679.

Balanos, P.J. (1994). From theory to practice: Indianapolis' Key School applies Howard Gardner's multiple intelligences theory to classrooms. *The School Administrator, 51*:1, 30–31.

Berghoff, B., Egawa, K., Harste, J.C., & Hoonan, B. (2000). *Beyond reading and writing: Inquiry, curriculum, and multiple ways of knowing.* Urbana, IL: National Council of Teachers of English.

Burns, A. & Duran, J. (2007). *Media literacy in schools: Practice, production, and progression.* London: Paul Chapman.

Carger, C.L. (2004). Art and literacy with bilingual children. *Language Arts, 81*:4, 283–292.

Cowan, P. (2004). Devils and angels: Literacy and discourse in lowrider culture (pp. 47–74). In J. Mahiri (Ed.), *What they don't learn in school: Literacy in the lives of urban youth.* New York: Peter Lang.

Edelsky, C. (2006). *What's resisted, who's resisting, and other questions* (mimeographed). Ethnography Forum, University of Pennsylvania, Philadelphia.

Eisner, E.W. (1982). *Cognition and curriculum*. New York: Longman.

Gardner, H. (1993). *Frames of mind: The theory of multiple intelligences*. New York: Basic Books.

Gee, J. (1996). *Social linguistics and literacy: Ideology in discourse* (2nd ed.). New York: Taylor & Francis.

Giroux, H., Lankshear, C., McLaren, P., & Peters, M. (1996). *Counternarratives: Cultural study and critical pedagogies in postmodern spaces*. London: Routledge.

Goodman, Y.M. (1978). Kidwatching: An alternative to testing. *Journal of the National School Principals, 57*:4, 22–27.

Grady, K. (2002). Lowrider art and Latino students in the Midwest. In S. Wortham, E.G. Murillo, & E.T. Hamann (Eds.), *Education in the new Latino diaspora: Policy and the politics of identity*. Westport, CT: Ablex.

Greene, M. (1988). *The dialectic of freedom*. New York: Teachers College Press.

Halliday, M.A.K. (1975). *Learning to mean: Explorations in the development of language*. London: Edward Arnold.

Harste, J.C. (1978). *Navajo school evaluation report: Wingate language arts program—grades 5–8* (mimeographed). Bloomington, IN: Division of Teacher Education, Indiana University.

Harste, J.C., Breau, A., Leland, C., Lewison, M., Ociepka, A., & Vasquez, V. (2000). Supporting critical conversations in classrooms. In K.M. Pierce (Ed.), *Adventuring with books* (12th ed., pp. 506–554). Urbana, IL: National Council of Teachers of English.

Harste, J.C., Leland, C.H., Grant, S., Chung, M., & Enyeart, J. (2007). Analyzing art in the language arts. In D. Rowe, R.T. Jimenez, D.L. Compton, D.K. Dickerson, Y. Kim, K.M. Leander, & V.U. Risko (Eds.), *56th Yearbook of the National Reading Conference* (pp. 254–280). Oak Creek, WI: National Reading Conference.

Harste, J.C., Vasquez, V., Leland, C., Schmidt, K., & Ociepka, A. (2004). Practice makes perfect: Or does it? *Reading Today, 7*:4, 44 pages (http://readingonline.org).

Harste, J.C., Short, K.G., w/Burke, C.L. (1986). *Creating classrooms for authors*. Portsmouth, NH: Heinemann.

Harste, J.C., Woodward, V.A., & Burke, C.L. (1984). *Language stories & literacy lessons*. Portsmouth, NH: Heinemann.

Heath, S.B. (1983). *Ways with words*. New York: Cambridge University Press.

Indiana, R. (1976). *Love sculpture*. Philadelphia: Philadelphia Museum of Art.

John-Steiner, V. (1985). *Notebooks of the mind: Explorations of thinking*. Albuquerque: University of New Mexico Press.

Kirby, D. & Kuykendall, C. (1991). *Mind matters: Teaching for thinking*. Portsmouth, NH: Heinemann.

Knobel, M. & Lankshear, C. (Eds.) (2007). *A new literacies sampler*. New York: Peter Lang.

Kress, G. (2003). *Literacy in a new media age*. London: Routledge.

Kress, G. & van Leeuwen, T. (1996). *Reading images: The grammar of visual design*. London: Routledge.

Kress, G. & van Leeuwen, T. (2006). *Reading images: The grammar of visual design* (2nd ed.). London: Routledge.

Leland, C., Harste, J., Berghoff, B., Bomer, R., Flint, A., & Lewison, M. (2002). Critical literacy. In J. Kristo and A. McClure (Eds.), *Adventuring with books* (13th ed., pp. 465–487). Urbana, IL: National Council of Teachers of English.

Leu, D.J., Kinzer, C.K., Coiro, J.L., & Cammack, D.W. (2004). Toward a theory of new literacies emerging from the internet and other information and communication technologies (pp. 1570–1613). In R.B. Ruddell & N.J. Unra (Eds.), *Theoretical models and processes of reading* (5ᵗʰ ed.). Newark, DE: International Reading Association.

Lewis, C. (2007). New literacies (pp. 253–274). In M. Knobel & C. Lankshear (Eds.), *A new literacies sampler*. New York: Peter Lang.

Lewis, L., Thompson, M.E., Celious, A.K., & Brown, R.K. (2002). Rap music, is it really all bad? Why hip-hop scholarship is important. *Perspectives, 8:*2, 68–74.

Lewison, M., Leland, C., & Harste, J.C. (2008a). *Creating critical classrooms*. New York: Erlbaum

Lewison, M., Leland, C., & Harste, J.C. (2008b). An annotated list of picture books, chapter books, videos, songs, and websites. *Creating critical classrooms*. New York: Erlbaum.

Luke, A., & Freebody, P. (1997). Shaping the social practices of reading. In S. Muspratt, A. Luke, & P. Freebody (Eds.), *Constructing critical literacies* (pp. 185–223). Creskill, NH: Hampton Press.

Manning, A. (2004). *How teachers sanitize the new literacies.* Presentation given at the annual meeting of the National Council of Teachers of English, Atlanta, GA.

McCarty, T.L. & Watahomigie, L.J. (1999). Indigenous community-based language education in the USA. In S. May (Ed.), *Indigenous community-based education* (pp. 74–94). Great Britain: Multilingual Matters Ltd.

Myers, M. (1996). *Changing our minds: Negotiating English and literacy*. Urbana, IL: National Council of Teachers of English.

Rowe, D.W. (2008). Social contracts for writing: Negotiated shared understandings about text in preschool years. *Reading Research Quarterly, 43:*1, 66–95.

Scollon, R. & Scollon, S.W. (1981). *Narrative literacy, and face in interethnic communications*. Norwood, NJ: Ablex.

Sebeok, C. (1970). *A theory of semiotics*. Bloomington, IN: Indiana University Press.

Short, K.G., Harste, J.C., w/Burke, C.L. (1996). *Creating classrooms for authors and inquirers*. Portsmouth, NH: Heinemann.

Siegel, M. (1983). *Reading as signification*. Doctoral Dissertation, Language Education, Indiana University.

Siegel, M. (1995). More than words: The generative power of transmediation for learning. *Canadian Journal of Education, 20:*4, 455–475.

Street, B.V. (2003). What's "new" in new literacy studies? Critical approaches to literacy in theory and practice. *Current Issues in Comparative Education, 5:*2, [online]. http//www.tc.columbia.edu/cice/articles/bs152.htm

Suhor, C. (1992). Semiotics and the English language arts. *Language Arts, 69:*1, 228–230.

Vasquez, V.M. (2004). *Negotiating critical literacy with young children*. New York: Erlbaum.

Waber, B. (1975). *Ira sleeps over*. Boston, MA: Houghton Mifflin.

Wagner, B.J. (1999). *Dorothy Heathcote: Drama as a learning medium*. Portsmouth, NH: Heinemann.

Whitin, P. (1996). *Sketching stories, stretching minds: Responding visually to literature*. Portsmouth, NH: Heinemann.

Chapter 4

Surveying the Hopescape

Rudine Sims Bishop
Ohio State University

Editors' note: This chapter features the acceptance speech given by Rudine Sims Bishop at the NCTE Elementary Section Get-Together on November 15, 2007, where she received the 2007 Outstanding Educator in the English Language Arts Award. It has been slightly adapted for print.

This year marks the twenty-fifth anniversary of the publication of my first book, *Shadow and Substance: Afro-American Experience in Contemporary Children's Fiction* (1982). Published by NCTE, it was a survey of black-centered children's books that had been published between 1965 and 1980. That study was seeded in part in my own history as an African-American child reader. Once I learned to read, I was hooked, and once I was old enough to walk downtown alone, I spent many hours in the children's section of the public library browsing and reading whatever caught my attention. From that experience, I learned that the world of children's books was an all-white world; I found not one child's book in that library that featured characters who looked and lived like me. In a town full of unwritten but well-understood restrictions on jobs and housing for black people, and taken-for-granted power and privilege for whites, that was not surprising to me; that was just the way things were. It didn't stop me from reading, but I did feel the absence. I remember devouring fairy tales, and enjoying them, but still feeling the same way as Faith Ringgold's granddaughter, another fairy tale reader who, decades later, asked her grandmother, "Where are the African-American princesses?"

Then, when I was a freshman in college, one of my four roommates—Patricia Grasty Gaines, who would later become an active NCTE member—introduced me to Marguerite De Angeli's *Bright April* (1946). It was the first fictional children's book I had ever encountered that featured an attractive, realistic black family. *Bright April* was the story of an African-American Brownie Scout and her first encounters with racial prejudice. April is the youngest child in a middle-class family living in a racially integrated neighborhood in Philadelphia. Pat loved the book because she saw in it reflections of the child she had been, having herself grown up in a middle-class African-American family in Philadelphia. I had grown up miles from the big city, and in much less privileged circumstances than either Pat or April, and even though now I can see its imperfections, back then I loved the book for much the same reason as Pat did—it reflected something of the physical me and my experiences and my aspirations. So *Bright April* was a revelation—evidence that the way things were was not the way they had to be. There was room in the world of children's books for people like me.

Nevertheless, *Bright April*, which had been published in 1946, several years before our freshman year, was one of a very few books of its kind available when I was in college. It was not until the early 1970s, when I was in graduate school at Wayne State University, that I came across anything like a substantial number of children's books featuring African-Americans. They were a compilation of review books assembled by the late Prof. Donald J. Bissett and labeled "The Darker Brother Collection" after a Langston Hughes poem: "I, too, sing America. I am the darker brother." That there were—finally— enough books to highlight a set about African-Americans was a sign of hope and an indication of progress on the journey to a world of children's books that is reflective of American society—multicolored, multivoiced, and multicultural.

I followed the progress of the African-American component of that new world of children's books for another decade or so, and while I was teaching at the University of Massachusetts at the end of the 1970s, I undertook the work that became *Shadow and Substance* (Sim, 1982). It was an examination of the body of black-centered fiction that had appeared since the mid-1960s, with a view to discovering how that literature was developing. I was looking at questions such as: What sorts of images and representations of African-Americans were being presented in books for children? From what perspective? How were African-American cultural values and practices being reflected or ignored? And to whom did these books seem to be addressed primarily? From that survey, I concluded that three main sociocultural perspectives or stances appeared to motivate the creation of the black-centered children's fiction of that period: 1) a view of books as a means to foster a social conscience among children of privilege; 2) a view of books as a means to figuratively assimilate African-Americans into the American melting pot; 3) a view of books as a means to share stories derived from or grounded in the experience of growing up black in America. *Shadow and Substance* was a snapshot of the landscape at one point on the journey to a holistic American children's literature.

In the 25 years since *Shadow and Substance*, I have continued to follow the progress of the African-American component of American children's literature. My mission has been to document its history, to describe its distinguishing characteristics, and to emphasize its importance to *all* American children, but especially to black children, or in the words of W.E.B. DuBois, "the children of the sun." This is the work that has resulted in my most recent book, *Free Within Ourselves: The Development of African American Children's Literature* (Bishop, 2007).

The title comes from Langston Hughes (1926/1984). When he was 24 years old and already one of the stars of the Harlem Renaissance, he published what I think of as a manifesto for African-American authors and artists. He wrote:

> We younger Negroes who create now intend to express our individual dark-skinned selves without fear or shame. If White people are pleased we are glad. If they are not, it doesn't matter. We know we are beautiful. And ugly too . . . If colored people are pleased we are glad. If not, their pleasure doesn't matter either. We build our temples for tomorrow, strong as we know how, and we stand on top of the mountain, free within ourselves.
>
> (p. 202)

That notion of building temples for tomorrow and feeling free to express their own truths as they see it is a spirit that pervades the creation of African-American children's literature. My book chronicles the development of this literature from its early seeds and roots through the end of the twentieth century and a little beyond. It describes some nineteenth-century precursors to African-American children's literature. It also looks at the contributions of important twentieth-century African-American authors and artists, particularly in relation to poetry, picture books, and contemporary and historical fiction. And it connects the literature with the historical, political, and sociocultural contexts out of which it emerged.

My purpose here is to share some of the observations I have made about the African-American children's literature published in the 25 years since *Shadow and Substance*, and then to point out why I think African-American children's literature matters to all of us.

Threaded through African-American children's literature—across time, across writers, and across genres—are a few thematic strands that help to characterize the literature as a cultural expression. One of the most potent is the importance of family and family relationships. Some of the premier contemporary African-American writers were very clear about the value they placed on the importance of family. (By contemporary, I mean post-1967, when the modern era of African-American children's literature was launched.) For example, through the 1970s and 1980s, Lucille Clifton acknowledged that all her children's books are about love in a family (Clifton, 1981). Eloise Greenfield (1975) likewise said that one of the paramount goals of her writing was to "reflect the strength of the Black family." What is noteworthy about the African-American *family* books of the past 25 years, however, is the strong focus on honoring the elders in black families. The 1980s book that was the landmark in honoring elders was Valerie Flournoy's *The Patchwork Quilt* (1985, illustrated by Jerry Pinkney), in which Tanya's grandmother makes a quilt out of scraps of family clothing and household fabrics. The quilt, of course, becomes a family heirloom, with contributions from all the family, but especially Tanya. Tanya's grandmother is matriarch, teacher, family historian, and loving companion to her young granddaughter.

That characterization is echoed in almost all the African-American inter-generational books. And the elders don't have to be grandparents. They can be great-aunts or great-uncles, as in *Aunt Flossie's Hats—and Crab Cakes Later* (Howard, 1991), in which each of Aunt Flossie's hats has a story to tell. Or *Uncle Jed's Barbershop* (Mitchell, 1993), in which Great Uncle Jed postpones fulfilling his dream in order to pay for medical care for his grandniece. In her author's note for *Things I Like about Grandma*, Francine Haskins (1992) captures the essence of the relationships between these children and their elders as portrayed in these books. She writes:

> It's a special relationship. It's teaching, telling, giving, and bonding. It's learning family histories and traditions, things that have been passed from generation to generation. It's building the foundation—giving the child a basis to grow on and come back to. It's love shared.

Although books about family are not unique to African-Americans, I would argue that this strong emphasis on family love and this respect for and celebra-tion of elders is a cultural value forged in the fires of black history and offered by a couple of generations of African-American writers as an ideal to be passed on to the young.

A second observation about the African-American children's books of the last 25 years is the strong focus on fostering a positive self-image in black children. Again, the overarching theme isn't new. As far back as the 1920s, W.E.B. Du Bois was asserting the need to encourage black children to see themselves as normal and beautiful. And another of the goals Eloise Greenfield identified for her work was to encourage black children to love themselves. What is interesting to me about the books with those themes of the last decade or so is the focus on black children's physical selves. It shows up in picture books such as Sandra and Myles Pinkney's *Shades of Black* (2000), which celebrates the great variety of physical features to be found among black chil-dren, as well as the uniqueness of each individual child. The theme appears in novels such as Eleanora Tate's *Thank You, Dr. Martin Luther King, Jr.* (1990) and Sharon Flake's *The Skin I'm In* (1998), both of which are concerned with young women who have absorbed negative attitudes towards their dark skin color. And it shows up in all those recent picture books about black hair—*Nappy Hair* (Herron, 1997), *Happy to Be Nappy* (hooks, 1999), *Crowning Glory* (Thomas, 2002), *Catching the Wild Waiyuzee* (Williams-Garcia, 2000), *I Love My Hair* (Tarpley, 1998).

Why, in this supposedly enlightened time, are we still getting books that deal with those issues? The answer could be a dissertation, but one of the reasons African-American children's literature exists is to counter or contradict the negative messages that black children have been receiving for years and years about themselves and their physical features. If you think it's not relevant anymore, think about the Rutgers' women's basketball team. Don Imus didn't just call them an offensive name, he called them "nappy-headed." In 2005, a New York high school student did a research study based on the famous doll study conducted by Dr. Kenneth Clark in the 1950s (http://www.mediathatmattersfest.org/6/#). The Clark study was part of the basis for the 1954 Brown vs. Board of Education Supreme Court school desegregation decision. This young woman placed two dolls—one white, one black, otherwise identical—in front of individual young black children and asked questions such as, "Show me the nice doll." Most of the children chose the white doll. "Why is it nice?" *"Because it's White."* "Show me which doll you would like to play with." Again, most chose the white doll. "Which one is the bad doll?" *"The Black one."* "Why is it bad?" *"It's Black."* It's heartbreaking, but it helps to answer the question of why some African-American authors and artists still feel compelled to create books that offer black children a mirror in which they can see themselves as normal and beautiful.

A third observation is that many African-American writers have been concentrating on history, reclaiming the past. It shows up in stories of ordinary children from past times and their courage and determination. Elizabeth Fitzgerald Howard, for example, published a number of stories based on her family history, such as *Virgie Goes to School with Us Boys* (2000). It also appears in Pat McKissack's stories out of her family history—from Mirandy and her pursuit of Brother Wind to be her partner in the cakewalk in *Mirandy and Brother Wind* (McKissack, 1988), to Tricia Ann's courageous trip through a segregated city to the sanctuary of a free and open public library in *Goin' Someplace Special* (McKissack, 2001). Even though Tricia Ann must confront discrimination and racism, for the most part these books are not centered on responses to racism, but on the everyday lives of black people making their way in the world, doing the best they can, loving each other, supporting each other, and trying to be decent human beings.

What is striking, however, is the number of recent books that are set in the era of slavery. These stories are told from the perspective of those who had been enslaved, but the authors take special pains not to paint them as passive victims of oppression. The stress is on representing enslaved Africans as complex human beings, experiencing the full range of human emotions—including love and joy—and responding to slavery in whatever ways enable them to survive. There is also an emphasis on destigmatizing slave ancestry by placing the responsibility for slavery outside the enslaved, and by focusing on the ways enslaved people actively sought to liberate themselves, if not physically, then psychologically. For the most part, these books are driven by three main themes: the pursuit of freedom; the importance of family, especially in the context of the cruel buying and selling of loved ones; and the importance of literacy as a liberating force and a threat to the institution of slavery. These books are related to, if not examples of, Virginia Hamilton's concept of *liberation literature*, in which the reader becomes witness to the struggle and is liberated along with the protagonist. They offer a way to reinterpret American history and gain a deeper understanding of the ways the past is still present.

My fourth observation is that a new era in children's literature is emerging, marked by both continuity and change. One obvious sign of continuity is the ongoing productivity of writers and artists who started publishing in the late 1960s or early 1970s and are still going strong, winning awards almost 40 years later—writers like Walter Dean Myers and Eloise Greenfield, and artists such as Ashley Brian, Jerry Pinkney, and Leo and Diane Dillon. The most obvious change is the emergence of a new generation of African-American artists and writers, some of whom are or will be among the "stars" of twenty-first-century American children's literature. We now have a cadre of second-generation African-American writers and artists, the sons and daughters of the premier creators of modern African-American children's literature—among them Brian Pinkney, Christopher Myers, Javaka Steptoe, Nina Crews, and Jaime Adoff. All except Jaime are illustrators and, along with other newer artists such as Brian Collier, Gregory Christie, and Kadir Nelson, have won well-deserved recognition and awards, such as Caldecott Honor citations and Coretta Scott King Awards. And while they bring to children's books their own innovative and original styles, there is also a sense of continuity with the past in some of their choices. Christopher Myers, Javaka Steptoe, Nina Crews, and Brian Collier, for example, all use collage, which, according to Christopher, is "one of the central metaphors of the African diaspora . . . It's about making do . . . about taking those little pieces of something and putting them together" (personal communication, 1976). Or as Javaka notes, it's about "taking the scraps of life and transforming them into art" (personal communication, 1997). In both their comments are echoes of Tom Feelings's concept of "improvising within a restricted form" (1985), which he was talking about in the early 1970s, a sign of continuity from one generation to the next.

We also have a cadre of African-American *writers* who entered the field in the 1990s. Some of them have also received well-deserved recognition and awards: Christopher Paul Curtis, who was the first African-American male and third African-American writer to win the Newbery; Angela Johnson, who was awarded a MacArthur Fellowship; also Jacqueline Woodson, Sharon Flake, Sharon Draper, Rita Williams-Garcia, Marilyn Nelson, and others. And while some of them are telling new stories in new ways, many are also exploring themes that have become traditional in African-American children's literature, such as family love and intergenerational relationships. As Lucille Clifton (1976) put it at the end of her memoir *Generations*, "Things don't fall apart. Lines connect in thin ways that last and last and lives become generations made out of pictures and words just kept" (pp. 78–79).

The good news about the last 25 years of African-American children's literature is that it has become a substantial component of American children's literature. The news would be even better if there were more evidence that this literature is an essential component of libraries in American homes and classrooms. Why is that important? First, like all good literature, African-American children's literature offers enrichment and often soul-satisfying literary artistry. It nurtures the imagination, an extremely important but often-neglected purpose of education. African-American writers offer stories about all kinds of experiences that are familiar to children around the world, and they explore themes that are found in many children's books—children confronting their fears, figuring out how to fit into their peer groups, dealing with tensions within the family, getting into and out of trouble with a group of buddies, laughing at the funny things that happen in life, following the adventures of bigger-than-life characters, solving life problems, resolving life's dilemmas. Stories set in an African-American cultural context that reflect some African-American cultural practices are not alien to readers from other cultures. They are no more closed to people who are not African-American than *Bridge to Terabithia* (Patterson, 1977) is closed to children who are not white. African-American children's literature is at the same time culturally specific and universal.

Second, African-American children's literature can function not only as a vehicle for teaching literacy, but as a means to inspire children to understand and question who we are as a nation, how we came to the place we are now, and how we might move forward as a democratic society. Historically based African-American children's literature lends itself especially well to such critical inquiry because we cannot understand, let alone begin to change, American society without knowing the history of black people's journey across the American hopescape. It is a critical part of American history, as is the story of other parallel culture people. Story is one way of knowing, and also a way of teaching. This is the argument for diversity in children's books. If we are to foster a truly democratic and equitable society, we must develop a respect for multiple perspectives and multiple approaches to solving the problems we as humans encounter on life's journeys. A body of literature that is multivoiced, multicolored, and multicultural fosters the attitude that "all God's children have a voice in the choir," and every voice counts.

Finally, I want to place African-American children's literature in the larger context of children's literature in general, and assert that in times like these, literature is particularly crucial in children's lives. I know that literature in and of itself won't solve many of today's big problems—it won't stop war; it won't stop hunger; it won't eliminate poverty. But it can make a difference in children's lives. The right book at the right time may be a blessing to a story-starved child who is feeling all alone. And literature can prompt children to recognize the existence of terrible inequities in our society, and inspire them to be a part of making things better. Maybe, just maybe, if those high school boys in Jena, Louisiana, had had the opportunity to be a literary witness to history, to experience—through story—suffering, sorrow, and injustice, they would not have been so quick to hang nooses from a tree. And the right books at the right time could have kept me, when I was a little black girl, from feeling that people like me had no place in literature—except as readers—because I saw no reflections of my physical being either in the books I was given in school or the ones I found on my own in the library.

Literature reaches the heart, as well as the head. It teaches us what it means to be a decent human being in our society. But sadly, too many of our political and educational leaders are more concerned with measuring our children on high-stakes tests than nurturing them with high-quality texts. We all need to be reminded of Einstein's statement, "Not everything that can be counted counts, and not everything that counts can be counted." The experience of engaging with good literature cannot be reduced to something that can be counted and measured on a computer-scored, standardized test. Too many of our children are faced today with schooling that threatens to numb their minds and drain their souls. In an article published in 1932, Langston Hughes wrote a powerful statement about the vital role that literature can play in children's lives. He was talking about African-American children, but his point is relevant to all American children today: America's children now are in pressing need of literature that will give them back their own souls.

References

Bishop, R.S. (2007). *Free within ourselves: The development of African American children's literature.* Portsmouth, NH: Heinemann.

Clifton, L. (1976). *Generations: A memoir.* New York: Random House.

Clifton, L. (1981). Writing for black children. *The Advocate, 1,* 32–37.

De Angeli, M. (1946). *Bright April.* Garden City, NY: Junior Literary Guild/Doubleday.

Feelings, T. (1985). Illustration is my form, the black experience, my story and my content. *The Advocate, 4,* 73–82.

Flake, S. (1998). *The skin I'm in.* New York: Jump at the Sun.

Flournoy, V. (1985). *The patchwork quilt* (J. Pinkney, Illus.). New York: Dial.

Greenfield, E. (1975, December). Something to shout about. *The Horn Book Magazine, 51,* 624–626.

Hamilton, V. (1989, March/April). Anthony Burns. *The Hornbook Magazine, 65,* 183–185.

Haskins, F. (1992). *Things I like about Grandma.* San Francisco: Children's Book Press.

Herron, C. (1997). *Nappy hair* (J. Cepeda, Illus.). New York: Knopf.

hooks, b. (1999). *Happy to be nappy* (C. Raschka, Illus.). New York: Jump at the Sun.

Howard, E.F. (1991). *Aunt Flossie's hats—and crab cakes later* (J. Ransome, Illus.). New York: Clarion.

Howard, E.F. (2000). *Virgie goes to school with us boys* (E.B. Lewis, Illus.). New York: Simon & Schuster.

Hughes, L. (1926/1984). Free within ourselves. In M. Meltzer (Ed.), *The black Americans: A history in their own words, 1619–1983* (pp. 198–202). New York: Thomas Y. Crowell.

Hughes, L. (1932). Books and the Negro child. In *Children's Library Yearbook, No. 4* (pp. 108–110). Chicago: American Library Association.

McKissack, P. (1988). *Mirandy and Brother Wind* (J. Pinkney, Illus.). New York: Knopf.

McKissack, P. (2001). *Goin' someplace special* (J. Pinkney, Illus.). New York: Atheneum.

Mitchell, M.K. (1993). *Uncle Jed's barbershop* (J. Ransome, Illus.). New York: Simon & Schuster.

Patterson, K. (1977). *Bridge to Terabithia*. New York: HarperCollins.

Pinkney, S. (2000). *Shades of black* (M. Pinkney, Photog.). New York: Scholastic.

Sims, R. (1982). *Shadow and substance: Afro-American experience in contemporary children's fiction*. Urbana, IL: National Council of Teachers of English.

Tarpley, N. (1998). *I love my hair* (E.B. Lewis, Illus.). New York: Little, Brown.

Tate, E. (1990). *Thank you, Dr. Martin Luther King, Jr.!* London: Watts.

Thomas, J.C. (2002). *Crowning glory* (B. Joysmith, Illus.). New York: Joanna Cotler Books.

Williams-Garcia, R. (2000). *Catching the wild waiyuzee* (M. Reed, Illus.). New York: Simon & Shuster.

Part II

Literacy Development

The Transformation of Children's Knowledge of Language Units During Beginning and Initial Literacy

Emilia Ferreiro
CINVESTAV-Instituto Politécnico Nacional de México

The relationships between oral language and written language, in terms of similarities and differences, have been the matter of concern of philosophers, linguists, educators, psycholinguists, and other disciplines. The differences are evident at the pragmatic, syntactic, and lexical levels. But this chapter deals with another problem. Any writing system (historically developed) is an analytical representation of a given oral language. Among the multiple oral units that can be identified in oral discourses, what are the ones that are marked in writing? How do children develop awareness of those units?

Alphabetic writing systems seem to focus on phonemes since letters correspond (roughly) to the smallest speech units. However, strings of letters separated by blanks correspond to another unit: the word. Between the word and the phoneme are the syllable and many possible intrasyllabic units that may have psychological reality even if the writing system does not mark them.

The dominant position in English-speaking countries follows a sequential view, in which an analysis of oral emissions into the minimum units (phonemes) is a precondition for learners to understand an alphabetic writing system. Such a view is a single-directional conception that moves from orality toward the written material. Writing is not considered to be a source of information that stimulates or provokes an analysis of orality (Vernon & Ferreiro, 1999). In addition, this position divorces reading from writing. Such a separation is surprising, taking into account that the English language has a word— literacy—that covers both activities. Without having an equivalent inclusive term, other traditions (especially the languages of Latin origin) have historically had a more integrating perspective, particularly in teaching approaches.

My main interest as a researcher has been to understand children's early cognitive efforts when dealing with an alphabetical writing system (Ferreiro & Teberosky, 1982; Ferreiro, 2003). The terms *emergent literacy* (Clay, 1972; Teale & Sulzby, 1986) and *beginning literacy* have been applied with certain success to designate a period of development (ages three to six, approximately) when we can observe children making exploratory attempts to understand the social uses of writing as well as the functioning of the writing system as a system of symbols. These explorations take place before children are obligated to learn literacy at school. I use the term *initial literacy* to deal with problems children face at the beginning of the first grade of elementary school, when children are required to show learning results.

Little attention has been paid to children's efforts to understand the writing system as a system (Ferreiro, 1984). Grapho-phonic relations are only one of the problems children face, and they are neither the first nor the main problem at the beginning. Some primer books isolate letters but in the environmental print letters do not appear in isolation. The importance of environmental print has been enhanced by some authors, among them Goodman (1986). Letters appear in texts and are organized according to the specific rules of each language. For instance, many written languages share the Greco-Latin alphabet, but have specific rules for letter combinations (particularly, possible or impossible sequences of letters at the beginning or end of graphic words). Written languages also differ in the length of the strings of letters separated by blank spaces. All languages have short and long strings, but the average length of graphic strings varies noticeably from one written language to another. In addition to letters, many of those languages have diacritical marks that noticeably modify the appearance of the letters. In fact, the use of diacritical marks is a resource for creating "new letters" without moving away from the historically defined set of graphemes. The location of diacritical marks (above or below letters), the frequency of their use, and the variants in diacritical marks are indicators that permit identifying a given language practically at first glance (Ferreiro, 2002a).

If we think only about grapho-phonic relations, we are unable to understand the efforts children make to grasp the complex relations between orality and writing. The fundamental question that guides these efforts is of an epistemological nature. When children understand that writing is a *substitute object* (an object that represents something else), the question that guides their interpretative efforts can be formulated as: What does writing represent and how does it represent it? (Ferreiro, 1986, 1991).

As literate adults, we know that historically constituted alphabetical writing systems do not represent speech; they represent that abstract entity called *language*. But can children make the distinction between speech and language? In all cases—and this is a central point for my argument—writing cannot represent language without analyzing it. All writing systems are analytical representations. Writing is a representation that analyzes the object, looking for units to be represented. Writing systems differ in the main unit that is chosen at the level of characters (or letters) and in the units that correspond to strings of written characters. Even if we restrict ourselves to alphabetical writing systems, several units need to be considered.

The Word as a Conceptual Unit and as a Graphic Unit

Let us begin with the units that are easiest to understand: *words*. "We write the words that we say" is such a common expression that it seems to be an evident truth. Yet how do we know if something produced by the vocal organs is or is not a word? After many unsuccessful attempts, most schools of linguistics refused to consider the word as a technical term:

> Twentieth-century linguists almost unanimously eliminated the "word" from their theoretical arsenal. The International Congress of Linguists in 1948 buried the "word". (. . .) It is a concept whose definition has always been entirely linked to the practice of writing.
>
> (Pergnier, 1986, p. 16)

Other terms, such as *morphemes*, were created to designate *minimum units of meaning*. But we already know that only a partial overlapping exists between the intuitive notion of word and the technical concept of morpheme. The term *word* corresponds to everyday language; it is not a technical term.

Do preliterate children have a notion of *word*? Of course they do. But their notion of word does not coincide with ours, as literate adults. Romina, aged five, believes that when we say and write "the girl bought a candy", there are only three words: "girl/bought/candy". "The" and "a" are not words, as Romina is able to explain in an extraordinary manner: "Es lo que decimos para juntar las palabras que decimos, pero no son palabras" ("It's what we say to join the words we say, but they're not words"). Romina distinguishes clearly among words with a full meaning and nexus words, functors or functional words. Why call all of them words? Why combine into a single category the parts of a sentence that are clearly distinguishable?

Let us not be tempted to say: Children have not yet grasped the notion of word, they have little *metalinguistic awareness*. False: Children have a notion of word that corresponds to an illiterate speaker, while our adult notion of word derives from writing, not from our previous intuitions. To be more precise: Our notion of word derives from writing in its current condition, because words have not always been segmented in the same manner. For instance, in Spanish handwritten texts from the sixteenth century, it is frequent to observe: clitic pronouns in pre-verbal position attached to the verb; prepositions attached to the near content word; articles attached to the noun; the adverb of negation *no* attached to the verb, and so on.

It is useful to look at the history of written practices (Ferreiro, 1994) because when Spanish-speaking children begin to write alphabetically, they use segmentations that are quite similar to those of the sixteenth century. In just a few months they progress from *scriptio continua*, that is writing without segmenting words, as in classic Latin (Desbordes, 1990), to sixteenth-century segmentations, and finally to the standard segmentations of the present time. Does this process mean that children recapitulate the history of the segmentations of writing? Of course not. What it means is that the notion of graphic words used in sixteenth-century writing is closer to a speaker's intuitions than the standard segmentations imposed by philologists, printers, and the Spanish authority of the Real Academia de la Lengua Española.

In summary, the intuitive notion of preliterate speakers is very reasonable and can be enunciated as follows: A word is something that can be detached from the flow of speech; this sequence of sounds must be a good candidate for the "What does it mean?" question. Articles, prepositions, and functional particles are not good candidates for this question (Ferreiro, 1978).

This very reasonable definition must be replaced by another, which is purely practical: Words are all sequences of letters separated by blank spaces. This practical definition is, in fact, everyone's definition even if examples of inconsistencies exist in every language, including English: *Cowboy* is one word. *Ice cream* is two words. *Himself* is one word, although composed of two words, as *cowboy* is. And so on.

Many psychological evaluations include word counting tests, and answers are considered as good or bad by comparison with the written model. The problem is that the written model is used without analysis, because the assumption is that writing indicates the *natural* frontiers that exist in the speaker's mind before any written attempt.

David Olson (1994, p. 68) is one of the few researchers who sustains the importance of the written → oral path. He states that "writing systems provide the concepts and categories for thinking about the structure of spoken language rather than the reverse. Awareness of linguistic structure is a product of a writing system, not a precondition for its development."

I would add, although not mentioned by Olson, that such awareness is suggested since writing offers an analytical representation. However, understanding the different types of analysis involved in the written representation of language implies considerable cognitive effort.

In the case of the word unit, the writing that exists in the cultural world generates serious conflicts for children. These conflicts are not automatically resolved when children learn to write alphabetically. One research example is necessary in order to explain what happens and why it happens that way.

We proposed to second grade children, at the beginning of the school year, a word counting task to be performed both orally and in writing. We selected 40 children (boys and girls, 7 years old) that present instability in graphic segmentation, leaving aside those who segmented conventionally as well as those who made too many hypo-segmentations (closer to the *scriptio continua*). We chose six well-known traditional proverbs that use words from everyday language. Proverbs, like poetry, are fixed expressions that need to be repeated *verbatim*.

To carry out the study, a research student in linguistics made a recording of the six proverbs, taking care to say each one in a single breath, with normal intonation, and without stress on any word. The children were interviewed one by one. Each child was asked to repeat the first proverb and count the words by saying each word aloud. Then the child was asked to write the proverb and count the written words (by underlining them if necessary). If the two forms of counting did not lead to the same result, the researcher mentioned the disparity to the child. For the second proverb, the order of the tasks was inverted: The child wrote the proverb first and counted the written words; then the sheet of paper was removed and the child counted the words orally. Each interview covered six proverbs, alternating the oral/written counting with written/oral counting. Half of the children started the interview with an oral task, and the other half with a written task. A very important point is that the adult used the term *word* exclusively throughout the interviews, and repeated the term several times during each task (Ferreiro, 1999).

The most striking result was that only five children out of 40 obtained the same number, without difficulty, when counting the proverbs' words in the oral and written forms. All of the children counted and wrote everything that was said, but their totals did not usually coincide.

The differences between the types of counting could be quite large: for example, 15 words in the oral task versus seven or eight in the written task. Why were the differences so large? Because many children count oral syllables while saying that they are counting words. And how did the children react to the differences?

1. Some children showed no indication of disturbance. The different results obtained do not constitute a problem for them. The oral and written units, both called words, seemed to be heterogeneous for these children. Rodolfo is an example. The proverb is: *el pez por la boca muere* (rough equivalent in meaning of "every bird loves to hear itself sing").

Rodolfo counts the proverb in syllables: *el-pez-por-la-bo-ca-,mu-e-re. There are nine*. Then he writes in a near conventional way [*el pes porla boca muere*]. He counts on his own writing; *there are five*. The adult comments: "This time you said five words and the last time you counted nine words. Is that possible?" Rodolfo checks his writing saying: *aha*.

The second proverb is *el que tiene más saliva traga más pinole* (rough equivalent in meaning of "the squeaky wheel gets the grease"). Rodolfo starts writing it and his writing is near conventional: [*el que tiene mas saliba traja maspinole*]. Then he counts the written words: *There are eight*. The piece of paper is removed and the child says the proverb and counts the words, but in fact he counts the syllables: *el-que-ti-e-ne-mas-sa-li-va-tra-ga-mas-pi-no-le. There are 15*. The adult comments: "You wrote eight words and then you said them and you counted fifteen." Rodolfo repeats: *Aha*. The adult asks: "You wrote and said the same thing, right?" The child accepts. The adult insists: "Can there be 15 words and eight words?" Rodolfo says: *Yes*

2. Some children were surprised by the difference between the results of the two types of counting. Even though the results for each proverb represented new amazement, the children had often accepted the difference as a matter of fact by the end of the task. Salvador is an example of a child who found the situation strange, yet could not change the results. The first proverb is: *el pez por la boca muere*. Salvador's writing is conventional; he counts six words in the written text and anticipates six in the oral counting. However, he counts in a syllabic way: *el-pez-por-la-bo-ca-mu-e-re*, showing great surprise. The adult asks: "Is it possible that you wrote six and when you counted them, there were nine?" Salvador says: *No*. The adult stimulates the child: "Count them again!" Salvador repeats the same way of counting and looks confused: *I thought that there were six, and there are nine!* The same happens with the following proverb.

3. Other children reacted to the Difference in results by saying that something was wrong. They assumed that reaching the same number was a requirement and looked for a solution, not always successfully. Jorge is an example of this case. He is working with the proverb: *ojos que no ven corazón que no siente* (equivalent in meaning to "out of sight, out of mind."). He writes: [*ojos quccno ven corason que nosiente*], and says: *There are six*. His oral counting is a mixture of units: *ojos-que-no-ven-corazón,cora-zon-que-nosiente. There are eight.* The adult asks: "Is it possible to get eight and six?" Jorge says: *No. Because if there are six there cannot be eight.* He repeats the proverb, without finding a solution.

Oral syllabic segmentation was responsible for the higher numbers the children obtained from counting. When writing, on the other hand, the children tended to show a tendency towards hypo-segmentation. Sometimes, the researcher shows a proverb written in syllabic pieces. Children strongly rejected it. As Salvador remarked, *Está mal, está todo separado, no se le entiende nada. Van a pensar que es abecedario* ("That's wrong. Everything is broken apart and you can't understand it. It looks like the ABCs").

These children have heard their teacher dictate traditional sentences that start with a definite article. To prevent spurious segmentation, teachers usually say: "*el*, leave one space" or "*la*, skip a square." Children follow the instructions, without understanding the underlying reason. To separate *el* or *la* (definite articles) from the rest of the sentence is one thing, but to understand that such short strings of letters are separated because they are words, is another. A very expressive example follows. The proverb is: *la ropa sucia se lava en casa* (equivalent in meaning to "don't air your dirty laundry"). Daniela's writing is conventional. The adult comments: "I see that you leave spaces when you write. What are they for?" Daniela answers: *To keep it from being all together and to make it look pretty*. Adult: "To keep what from being all together?" Daniela: *Things, words*. Adult: "But how do you know where to leave spaces?" Daniela: *When a word is finished I leave a space and I start with another word*. Adult: "OK, but how do you know which ones are words?" Daniela: *By reading them.* The adult asks if the definite article (*la*) is a word. Daniela answers: *No.* Adult: "It's not a word?" Daniela: *Well . . . it is . . . but it's too short [Bueno, sí . . . pero es que es muy cortita].* The adult repeats the same question about the clitic pronoun (*se*). Daniela: *"Se"? Yes, it's a word . . . Well, "la" is a word but it's very short like "se". ["Se"sí es una palabra . . . Bueno, "la"es una palabra pero cortita como la "se"].* The adult asks for the difference between these "small words" and a common noun (*ropa*) or a verb (*lava*). Daniela answers, referring to the small words: *They aren't like "house." They're not things, they're just letters. [Es que no son así como casa, no son así cosas, son letras nada más.]*

We can see that conventional alphabetical writing does not guarantee that the child who produces it has automatically modified his preliterate notion of word. (The complete results of this study are in Ferreiro, 2000.)

Writing resists children's desires to change it. People are capable of negotiation. However, writing as a material object of the social world does not permit negotiation. As children develop notions that are crucial in the literacy process, they face multiple situations of conflict. Such conflicts are not interpersonal; they are cognitive conflicts between psychological constructions and the object "as it is" that resists assimilation. Therefore, in the case of the unit word we state that the evolution is as follows: Small children attempt to apply their intuitive notion of *word* to the written material. Children expect that only words of full content should be written (as in Romina's example). Writing as it is generates a conflict with the children's conceptualizations of *word*. It is, in a certain sense, an oral → written path. However, we need to take into account that these small children have already established certain formal restrictions about writing material: they have understood that letters are elements used to build meaningful totalities (words). Although they may not yet understand the value of each letter, they know that letters, by themselves, do not have a meaning. Only sequences of letters have meaning. How many letters are necessary to form a written word? More than one and at least two. The ideal is three letters. Since preliterate speakers believe that one letter cannot be a word, they reject, for graphic reasons, writing that isolates prepositions, articles, conjunctions, and clitic pronouns (in Spanish, *a, en, de* (prepositions); *y, o* (conjunctions); *el, la, un* (articles); *me, te, se, la lo* (clitic pronouns)) (Ferreiro, 1978).

Children in the process of becoming literate produce texts that obey their own conceptions, but sooner or later they discover that established writing (printed books and adults' writing) resists their attempts to modify it. Finally, after numerous conflicts, children renounce their conceptual definition of *word* and adopt the practical definition proposed by writing. But even at the beginning of the alphabetic writing period we find the preliterate conception at work, as in Daniela's example. There is really no transformation of previous ideas, only clear substitution. Writing *imposes* its own definition of words, and that practical definition (a series of letters separated by blank spaces) impresses speakers' awareness to such a degree that literate adults, with years of practice in the craft of reading and writing, find it absurd to think about any other definition. If these adults are teachers, they tell their students, "Separate the words when you write!" implicitly assuming that words—as they know them—existed before writing.

We are in the presence, therefore, of a case of interaction between both paths (oral → written as well as written → oral paths), with two clearly defined developmental moments.

The Syllable as a Psycholinguistic Unit

Let us now consider the syllable, the most natural unit when breaking up a word. An English-speaking linguist, Daniels (2006), posits: "The shortest bits of speech that people recognize 'automatically' are syllables." Almost all romance languages are characterized by clear syllabic borders. Research data with Spanish, Portuguese (Silva & Alves-Martins, 2002, 2003), Italian, and Catalan children show that the early phonetization period of writing is guided by a syllabic idea: one letter per syllable. Children writing in these languages prefer to write with vowels, and often select the vowel that corresponds to the vocalic nucleus of the syllable. For example, in a kindergarten classroom (children aged five), four groups of children are asked to write "sopa de fideos" ("noodle soup") for the next day's menu. The resulting writing is syllabic, yet each sample is unique:

- *O A I E O*
- *O A E I E O*
- *SA I D O*
- *O P E I D O*

Vowels dominate, and all the vowels are pertinent. The children who wrote *OAIEO* or *OAEIEO* use only vowels. The difference is that the first writing sample contains only the representation of the vowels for the words "sopa (so-pa)" and "fideos (fi-de-os)", while the second sample includes a vowel representation for the preposition "de". Did these children write "de" because they accept prepositions as words? There is no reason to believe they did. We analyzed "sopadefideos" as three words, but the children actually alternated between two solutions: either "sopadefideos" as a name with six part-syllables ("de" is a part-syllable that is repeated in that name); or as two names ("sopa" and "fideos") with their respective syllables giving a total of five part-syllables.

The children who wrote *SAIDO* or *OPEIDO* use two consonants. One of those consonants has a unique status since its name coincides with one of the syllables the children are attempting to write (D = "de"). When the name of the letter coincides with the desired syllable, it is a happy coincidence that favors the appearance of a pertinent consonant. Yet this occurrence is not imperative. The name of the letter S is "ese," but it works for the syllable, "so:" the name of the letter P is "pe," but it works for the syllable "pa." It is important to take into account that the Hispanic and Anglophonic traditions differ markedly regarding the social value of knowing how to spell. Spanish has no equivalent of the songs and rhymes for teaching children the names of the letters, so appreciated in the English cultural tradition. The hypothesis sustained by other authors (for instance, Treiman, 2006) that the names of the letters drive development is very improbable outside English traditions.

In Romance languages syllabic writings are of greatest evolutional importance. Syllabic writing is not limited to word lists. We have examples of texts written almost entirely in a syllabic system.

In English, syllabic productions may appear when children are asked to write words of three or more syllables. For instance:

- Erika (5;9) writes *eFPOR* (re-fri-ge-ra-tor), *LAVR* (e-le-va-tor), *RBK* (gar-bage-can) and *ICTB* (I see a bee) (reported by Vernon, 1993).
- Michael (4;9) writes *HNB* (ham-bur-ger) and Ben (5;3) writes *BBQ* (bar-be-cue) (reported by Mills, 1998).

Five-year-old children write *VKn* (vacation), *pnmt* (punishment), *Oen* (ocean), *cmnt* (cement) (reported by Kamii & Manning, 1999). The same authors (2002) reported pairs of words written by five-year-old children: *Hn* (ham), *HnT* (hamster); *Bn* (butter), *BnF* (butterfly); *BR* (butter), *BTF* (butterfly); *KE* (key), *ME* (monkey); *KE* (key), *MKE* (monkey); *GM* (gum), *BLGM* (bubblegum). The use of the letters' names is much more frequent in English than in Spanish, at times for writing a complete sentence. (*ICTB* = I see a bee). Consonants predominate in the English examples, perhaps due to the low reliability of written vowels. (The great number of one-syllable words with full content in English generates a conflict with the requirement of a minimum of two letters in order to have a written word.)

In a recent study (Molinari & Ferreiro, 2007), we were able to show the extraordinary force of the syllabic hypothesis. The research has the aim to analyze the stability of writing produced by five-year-olds. We asked the children, individually, to write a grocery list, first on paper and then, immediately after, on a computer (without having access to their previous writing). Santiago wrote "lechuga" (in syllables, "le-chu-ga", i.e. lettuce) on paper as *LUG*; then, on computer, as *LUA*. He wrote "raviolis" ("ra-vio-les") on paper as *RVL*; then, on computer, as *ROL*. The same happens with the rest of the list. All of Santiago's productions are syllabic. All the letters are pertinent (i.e., they belong to the syllable), but the child usually does not repeat the same sequence of letters. Two written words are of particular interest. Santiago wrote "soda" on paper as *SA*; then, on computer, as *OD*. He wrote "salami" on paper as *SAM* and then, on computer, as *ALE*. These two written versions produced for the same word show that Santiago has identified all of the word's letters, but he continues using one letter per syllable. He cannot use two letters simultaneously for a single syllable. One orally identified unit (syllable) must correspond to one unit of writing (one letter). However, Santiago's writing reveals the possibility of centering successively on the two elements of a CV syllable: either at the consonant onset or at the vocalic nucleus. Yet these cognitive centrations are successive without coordination. Writing two letters for a single syllable seems unacceptable for Santiago. We propose using the term *grapho-phonic alternations* to refer to letters that alternate in a child's successive productions of a single syllabic segment.

Intra-syllabic Segmentations

Do children go directly, without intermediaries, from an oral syllabic analysis into a sequential phonemic analysis? There is now a renewed linguistic interest in the syllable—that "forgotten" unit, overshadowed by linguists' fascination for the phoneme (Bell & Hooper, 1978; Goldsmith, 1995). This renewed interest leads psycholinguists to pay attention to *intra-syllabic units*. Following the hierarchical model of analyzing the syllable, psycholinguists try to consider the onset/rime distinction as a possible level of analysis that perhaps precedes the analysis of phonemes.

In Spanish, when children begin to write two letters per syllable, are they doing an analysis into phonemes? Are they doing an onset/rime analysis? CV syllables, i.e. consonant plus vocalic syllables, are the most frequent in Spanish (Lara, 2007). Even in the case of CV syllables, it is rather frequent to observe strange results. For example, María (5-year-old) writes "sopa" as *OASP*. She begins by writing the vowels from the two syllables "so-pa"; the result does not satisfy her because there are only two letters. Then she reanalyzes both syllables and is able to center on the consonant onsets (S and P). The result appears to be total confusion, but the situation is about double syllabic writing: first the vowels and then the consonants. Upon trying to read the writing, María is unable to recuperate her own production process. Vanesa (6-year-old) writes the same word as *OPAS*. After writing *OPA*, she discovers a letter is missing; instead of putting it at the beginning, she adds it to the end. She is not able to interpret that S in her reading, but neither does she erase it because she knows that the S is needed.

So, we observe that even with CV syllables the construction process does not follow the order of the phonemes. These syllables are the most frequent ones, but many other syllables appear in frequently used words: syllables with a diphthong (CVV), syllables with a consonant in the coda position (CVC), syllables with a cluster in the onset position (CCV). Let us look at some data that show how difficult it is for children to go from syllables to phonemes. We asked 38 first grade children (average age 6 years 9 months) to write 20 bi-syllable words, of which 10 have one CVC syllable (for instance, "per-") and the other 10, one CCV syllable (for instance, "pre-"). In the CCV syllables, the second consonant is necessarily R or L; therefore, in this study we used the same consonants in a coda position (CVC syllables). We always ensured that the children identified the dictated word as a known word in the language (Ferreiro & Zamudio, 2008). The children wrote 20 words, but in terms of syllables, each child wrote 40 CV syllables, plus 10 CVC and 10 CCV syllables. The total sample has 760 CV syllables, 380 CVC syllables, and 380 CCV syllables. The correct answers show a clear progression:

- 97.5% for the CV syllables
- 57% for the CVC syllables
- 25.5% for the CCV syllables.

Most of the deviating responses by the children consist of omitting the coda from the CVC syllables, or omitting one of the cluster consonants from the CCV syllables. Omissions lead to writings such as *PELA* instead of "perla", *PESO* instead of "preso". However, other deviating responses are extremely instructive. The most striking ones are those that, instead of omitting letters, add letters: *PERELA* instead of "perla", *PERESO* instead of "preso", *FIRIMA* instead of "firma" and so on.

Omitted letters are generally interpreted as the result of insufficient oral analysis. The problem is that omissions coexist with responses that have all of the necessary letters ... plus something more. The children who write *PERELA/FIRIMA/PERESO* have identified all the phonemes, but the graphic result is a CV+CV+CV sequence. In addition, when they omit a letter, the graphic result is also a CV+CV sequence. It is perhaps a case of over-generalizing a graphic pattern that is derived from a way of writing rather than from breaking down the syllable into phonemes. The teacher teaches words with CV syllables as a *facilitator* but the children may learn it as the graphic way of representing any syllabic segment.

Students' early books for learning Spanish have an abundance of words with CV syllables. The tradition of teaching *families of syllables* in school is kept alive in a somewhat underground fashion in spite of the fact that these *syllabic families* (*ma, me, mi, mo, mu; sa, se, si, so, su* and so on) are no longer promoted by official authorities in most Latin American countries. For this reason, we began another study, this time in Argentina, with five-year-old children who have been surrounded in preschool by books and writing since age three. The preschool setting favors social uses of written language (reading and writing for specific purposes), offers children a diversity of written texts, and does not establish graduated difficulty levels for instructional purposes. These children should not present the restrictions of a graphic model, although they write words with CV syllables quite often, simply because they are more frequent in the language. The longitudinal data obtained from the children are currently undergoing analysis. Here I present a single example of writing a very complex syllable.

Camila (5;5) attempted to write an invitation card. She needs a very difficult word: *fiesta* (party), whose first syllable is CVVC. (In addition to a diphthong, it had a consonant in the coda position.) Camila says: *Con efe* (with F). She writes *FETA*. Then she controls by reading her own writing: *fi-es* . . . (she says *fi* pointing to F and *es* pointing to E). She comments: *Me falta la ese* (the S is missing). She inserts the S but not in the right position, resulting in *FETSA*. She begins reading again: *fi* . . . *me falta la i* (the I is missing). She inserts the I but not in the right position, resulting in *FEITSA*. Once again, she controls if the result is right: *fi* . . . *Tengo que sacar la E* (I have to take out the E). This time she rewrites the word as *FITA*. She begins to say the word, pointing to the first letters: *fies* . . . *Me falta la ese* (the S is missing). Camila inserts an S but not in the right position. The result is *FITSA*. Camila, now tired, renounces an analytical reading and reads *fiesta*, without segmentations, sliding her finger over all of the letters in a continuous gesture.

What does Camila show us? On one hand, that she continues trusting the syllable as a unit of analysis and tries to find, within the syllable, the letters that must be used. One thing is to realize that the syllable "fies-" has an I and an S, and another thing is to know exactly where to put those letters. Going from "it's inside of" to "it goes before" or "it goes after" is as difficult in writing as in other aspects of cognitive development. Camila inserts letters, a sign of great progress. Her productions indicate that the syllabic-alphabetic period is beginning. Other children who are less evolved add letters as they reanalyze the word, even if they are dealing with CV syllables.

It seems that children do not proceed from syllables to a sequence of phonemes. They are doing intra-syllabic analysis, but not exactly in the order foreseen by the hierarchical theory of the syllable. Linguistic models can be a source of inspiration for psycholinguists, but linguistic models are what they are: not psychological models of adult behavior and even less so for children becoming literate.

Concluding Remarks

We have seen that children try to interpret the units they see in written material. In this sense, it is true that "writing systems provide the concepts and categories for thinking about the structure of spoken language rather than the reverse," as Olson (1994) said. However, Olson seems to believe that this model is easy to interpret. Yet for the developing child, it is neither easy nor immediate to recognize such "categories for thinking."

Recognition is hindered, in the first place, because the categories are implicit and far from systematic (as we saw with respect to the representation of the unit, word); and in second place, because alphabetic writing does not represent the syllable, a unit that is of great prominence for the speaker. The syllable has all the conditions for being a homogeneous unit, as it has articulatory, acoustic, and especially, rhythmic and accentual properties.

I shall try to delineate the main points of my argument. Understanding an alphabetical writing system requires an initial level of reflection on language. Language was used first as an instrument of communication. Now, the child needs to transform language in order to make it an object of thinking. The possibilities of segmenting speech are at the core of this process of transformation. Oral emissions can be segmented, and the four- or five-year-old child already has practical experiences in speech segmentation. The units of linguistic analysis, however, are not the child's, since such units are theoretical units that do not pre-exist the efforts of conceptualization.

The levels of language analysis are multiple and only partially coordinated in the adult speaker (non-linguist). Oral emissions can be segmented but several levels of segmentation exist. Units must be constituted in order to gain stability at each level of analysis. Oral emissions can be segmented but there are still no *units* in a strict sense. They can be segmented in the same sense that Piaget said that objects are "countable" before being "ones" that can be added to other "ones." What is needed is a certain mental activity that "makes them equal," in spite of their differences (Piaget & Szeminska, 1941/1952). I have already mentioned the difficulties of transforming graphic words into fully comparable units. These difficulties grow when levels lower than the syllable are considered (Ferreiro, 2002b).

The very expression *phonological awareness* assumes that phonemes exist at an unconscious level, before the speaker is aware of them. What is implied is that the very unit is already there, that the same unit moves from the unconscious level to the level of voluntary "manipulation;" or, in other terms, from an unconscious to a conscious module, without transformations. However, it may not be the same unit. I want to suggest that the phoneme does not pre-exist phonological awareness, that the phoneme is the result of a new level of reorganization of speech units, that is permitted (suggested, or even imposed) by writing. I am suggesting that, indeed, we should use another term to refer to the practical distinctions that allow us to distinguish, in the communicative uses of language, between two neighborhood oral words of different meanings. I am suggesting that we should reserve the term *phoneme* to designate conceptual entities that put all pertinent sound features on equal footing. (It matters little if they are nasal sounds, glottal stops, trilled consonants, long or short vowels and so on.) After all, twentieth-century linguistics taught us that phonemes are conceptual entities that should not be confused with particular speech sounds. A phoneme is not a sound; it is a position in a system of oppositions created by the other phonemes. It is to say that a phoneme is what the others are not (Ferdinand de Saussure, 1917/1966). There is a necessary distinction between what is distinguishable at the level of experience, and what becomes equal at the conceptual level.

It may be that neither phonemes nor language as conceptual objects exist for small children. That object—language—must be constructed in a process of objectification, a process in which writing provides the starting point for thinking. I will suggest that writing units and language units are constructed at the same time through an interactive process (probably a dialectic one). Therefore, it seems to me out of the question to consider a perspective that goes from oral language to written language, as if writing were a simple mapping of speech units.

These are topics full of theoretical interest. In addition, theoretical discussions impact the educational field. The old and persistent slogan of "going from the simple to the complex" reappears once and again, with new expressions but old ideas. Confusion is permanent between "beginning teaching with what is simple" (from the viewpoint of linguistic analysis) and assuming that the subject matter is "simple" for the learning child. Let us place the psychological subject in the center of the learning process. This has been my contribution to literacy debates, and continues to be my primary concern.

References

Alves-Martins, M. & Silva, C. (2001). Letter names, phonological awareness and the phonetization of writing. *European Journal of Psychology of Education, XVI*(4), 605–617.

Bell, A. & Hooper, J. (1978). *Syllables and Segments*. Amsterdam: North Holland.

Clay, M. (1972). *Reading: The patterning of complex behaviour*. Auckland, New Zealand: Heinemann.

Daniels, P. (2006). On beyond alphabets. *Writing Language & Literacy, 9*(1), 7–24.

Desbordes, F. (1990). *Idées Romaines sur l'écriture*. Lille, France: Presses Universitaries. (Spanish translation: *Concepciones sobre la escritura en Antigüedad Romana*. Barcelona: Gedisa, 1995.)

Ferreiro, E. (1978). What is written in a written sentence? A developmental answer. *Journal of Education, 160*(4), 25–39.

Ferreiro, E. (1984). The underlying logic of literacy development. In H. Goelman, A. Oberg, & F. Smith (Eds.), *Awakening to Literacy* (pp. 154–173). Exeter, NH: Heinemann.

Ferreiro, E. (1986). The interplay between information and assimilation in beginning literacy. In W. Teale & E. Sulzby (Eds.), *Emergent Literacy* (pp. 15–49). Norwood, NJ: Ablex.

Ferreiro, E. (1991). Psychological and epistemological problems on written representation of language. In M. Carretero, M. Pope, R. Simons, & J. Pozo (Eds.), *Learning and Instruction. European research in an international context* (pp. 157–173). Oxford: Pergamon Press.

Ferreiro, E. (1994). Two literacy histories: A possible dialogue between children and their ancestors. In D. Keller-Cohen (Ed.), *Literacy: Interdisciplinary conversations* (pp. 115–128). Cresskill, NJ: Hampton Press.

Ferreiro, E. (1999). Oral and written words. Are they the same units? In T. Nunes (Ed.), *Learning to read: An integrated view from research and practice* (pp. 65–76). Dordrecht: Kluwer.

Ferreiro, E. (2000). Entre la sílaba oral y la palabra escrita. *Infancia y Aprendizaje, 89*, 25–37.

Ferreiro, E. (2002a). The disctinction between graphic and ortographic knowledge. Its relevance for understanding literacy development. In J. Brockmeier, M. Wang, & D. Olson (Eds.), *Literacy, narratives and culture* (pp. 215–228). London: Curzon.

Ferreiro, E. (2002b). Escritura y oralidad: unidades, niveles de análisis y conciencia metalingüística. In E. Ferreiro (Ed.), *Relaciones de (in)dependencia entre oralidad y escritura* (pp. 151–171). Barcelona: Gedisa.

Ferreiro, E. (2003). *Past and present of the verbs to read and to write* (M. Fried, Trans.). Toronto: Groundwood. (Original work in Spanish published 2001.)

Ferreiro, E. & Teberosky, A. (1982). *Literacy before schooling* (K. Goodman, Trans.). Exeter, NH and London: Heinemann. (Original work in Spanish published 1979.)

Ferreiro, E. & Zamudio, C. (2008). La escritura de sílabas CVC y CCV en los inicios de la alfabetización escolar. ¿Es la omisión de consonantes prueba de incapacidad para analizar la secuencia fónica? *Revista di Psicolinguistica Applicata*, *VIII*(1–2), 37–53.

Goldsmith, J. (Ed.), (1995). *The Handbook of Phonological Theory*. London: Blackwell.

Goodman, Y. (1986). Children coming to know literacy. In W. Teale & E. Sulzby (Eds.), *Emergent Literacy* (pp. 1–14). Norwood, NJ: Ablex.

Kamii, C. & Manning, M. (1999). Before "invented" spelling: Kindergartners' awareness that writing is related to the sounds of speech. *Journal of Research in Childhood Education*, *14*(1), 16–25.

Kamii, C. & Manning, M. (2002). Phonemic awareness and beginning reading and writing. *Journal of Research in Childhood Education*, *17*(1), 38–46.

Lara, L.F. (2007). *Resultados numéricos del vocabulario fundamental del Español de México*. México: El Colegio de México.

Mills, L. (1998). Syllabic stage of English speaking preschoolers. *Reading Research and Instruction*, *37*(4), 297–317.

Molinari, C. & Ferreiro, E. (2007). Identidades y diferencias en las primeras etapas del proceso de alfabetización. Escrituras realizadas en papel y en computadora. *Revista Latinoamericana de Lectura. Lectura y Vida*, *28*(4), 18–30.

Olson, D. (1994). *The world on paper*. Cambridge: Cambridge University Press.

Pergnier, M. (1986). *Le mot*. Paris: Presses Universitaires de France.

Piaget, J. & Szeminska, A. (1952). *The child's conception of number*. New York: The Humanities Press. (Original work in French published 1941.)

Saussure, F. de (1966). *Course in General Linguistics* (W. Baskin, Trans.). New York: McGraw-Hill. (Original work in French published 1917.)

Silva, C. & Alves-Martins, M. (2002). Phonological skills and writing of presyllabic children. *Reading Research Quarterly*, *37*(4), 466–483.

Silva, C. & Alves-Martins, M. (2003). Relations between children's invented spelling and the development of phonological awareness. *Educational Psychology*, *23*(1), 3–16.

Teale, W. & Sulzby, E. (Eds.), (1986). *Emergent literacy*. Norwood, NJ: Ablex.

Treiman, R. (2006). Knowledge about letters as a foundation for reading and spelling. In R.M. Joshi & P.G. Aaron (Eds.), *Handbook of orthography and literacy* (pp. 581–599). Mahwak, NJ: Erlbaum.

Vernon, S. (1993). Initial sound/letter correspondences in children's early written productions. *Journal of Research in Childhood Education*. *8*(1), 12–22.

Vernon, S. & Ferreiro, E. (1999). Writing development: A neglected variable in the consideration of phonological awareness. *Harvard Educational Review*, *69*(4), 395–415. (Reprinted in *Perspectives on language and literacy. Harvard Educational Review Reprint Series No. 35*, pp. 309–327, by S. Beck & L. Nabors (Eds.), 2001, Cambridge, MA: Harvard University Press).

Chapter 6

Early Literacy
Then and Now

*William H. Teale, Jessica Hoffman, Kathleen Paciga,
Jennifer Garrette Lisy, Samantha Richardson, and
Charlise Berkel*
University of Illinois at Chicago

This chapter is authored by six people, only the first of whom is anywhere near old enough to be considered as Reading Hall of Fame age. This may seem a strange way to write about one's "history and scholarly work to frame the changes that have been taking place in our dynamic profession" in order to "inform the future" (see p. x of the introduction to this volume). But we chose this approach because we represent the voices of the different generations, or eras, of scholar-practitioners that this book is intended to address. We currently work closely together on two Early Reading First projects in which we are attempting to put into practice research-based early literacy theory, instruction, and assessment (http://education.uic.edu/erf). Through these projects and varied professional activities in elementary schools, we have been fortunate to gain inside perspectives on an array of contemporary early literacy practices and policies—at the classroom, school, and school district levels; in relation to state and federal government initiatives; in the world of foundations and other non-governmental organizations involved with early childhood education, and in the community of scholars in the United States and internationally.

Despite being deeply involved on a daily basis in early literacy research and practice, we struggled mightily with the question of what to say in this chapter and how to say it. Early literacy—development and instruction during both the preschool period and the first few years of formal schooling—is certainly the most studied and arguably the most theoretically and politically contentious area of literacy research and practice. That made it not easy to "reflect on the changes to provide insights and understandings about contemporary literacy issues" (see p. x in this volume). It's a lot to get one's mind around. In the end, we chose to focus our analysis in two ways: (a) on children from ages 3–8 (rather than from birth–8); and (b) on factors related to classroom/school environments (rather than home environment also).

As a starting point, we decided to go back approximately a quarter century as a time frame for contextualizing the situation today because that period, like the current time, was an era of intense excitement and robust research and development in early childhood literacy. We also decided to be selective; from among the myriad topics related to early literacy, we focused on what we find to be key issues that have most affected the lives of young children and their teachers. Specifically, we highlight the current instructional scene in preschool and primary grade classrooms in the United States in light of what scholarship indicates are better and not so great ways to foster children's growth in language, reading, and writing in the school setting.

Our remarks are organized under the following three general headings:

- Where Were We Then? A New Day for Young Children and Literacy
- Where Are We Now? "That's Good! That's Bad!"
- Curriculum and Early Literacy in the Preschool and Primary Grades: The Intersection of Research, Educational Wisdom, and Policy

Where Were We Then? A New Day for Young Children and Literacy

Looking back a quarter century seems especially appropriate because the mid-1980s was a time of great activity, energy, and transformation in early literacy. The winds of change, begun in the late 1970s, had, by the mid-1980s, grown to a category 3 in hurricane terms. They would be a full-force category 5 by the end of the decade.

Understandings from Research

Thirty years earlier, Chomsky (1959) ravaged behaviorist/empiricist theories of language development. In the succeeding years, scholars in various disciplines adopted new psycholinguistic (e.g., Slobin, 1971) and social interactionist (e.g., Snow & Ferguson, 1977) looks at language development. By the mid-1980s, these new perspectives on language learning made it clear that:

- children learn things about language that they were not taught
- at points in development children use language features and structures that they had never heard but generalized (constructed) based on the language they experienced, and
- the language environment around children is enormously important in guiding them to construct their oral language.

One spin-off of the scholarly energy and insights generated by these ideas was that reading once again became a hot topic for research. Virtually ignored since the 1930s in psychology, reading blossomed as research focused on understanding reading processes and the development of reading in children. By the mid-1980s, the Center for the Study of Reading (CSR), which had brought together psychologists and educational researchers employing a variety of cognitive perspectives, produced a wealth of studies indicating that reading is an interactive, constructive, and strategic process and stressing the centrality of schema theory, metacognition, and various comprehension factors.

Early literacy, in particular, was studied widely. Preschoolers' literacy development began to be researched as intently as their early oral language development, and five especially robust areas of research activity developed:

- Intensive observational studies that yielded detailed portraits of preschool children's home and community literacy environments (e.g., Heath, 1983; Taylor, 1983; Teale, 1986), including case studies of individual children's language and literacy development (e.g., Bissex, 1980; Miller, 1982). This work provided a descriptive base suggesting that early literacy learning was fundamentally a social process intimately connected with the daily activities of families and young children.
- Print awareness studies (e.g., Goodman & Altwerger, 1981; Harste, Woodward & Burke, 1984), together with the observational work, indicated that the roots of the reading and writing processes are established very early in life.
- Invented spelling studies (e.g., Henderson & Beers, 1980), spurred by the earlier work of Charles Read (1975), showed that children constructed logical and developmental solutions to the language puzzle they faced in learning about written words.
- Read aloud research, both in the context of the family and early childhood classrooms, provided insights into the language and social interactions between adults and children that give rise to early literacy learning (see Teale, 1984, for a review of research of the time).
- Studies of young children's metalinguistic awareness showed how emerging readers and writers thought about language, words, and print—concepts important in becoming literate (e.g., Yaden & Templeton, 1986)—both in English and other languages (e.g., Ferreiro, 1986; Tolchinsky-Landsman & Levin, 1985).

Teale and Sulzby (1986) concluded that these bodies of data and theoretical perspectives had become legitimized as a field. Building on Marie Clay's (1966) use of the term *emergent reading*, they proposed that *emergent literacy* be recognized as a new paradigm for conceptualizing young children's written language development. Sulzby (1991) defined emergent literacy as the reading and writing concepts, behaviors, and dispositions that precede and develop into conventional literacy. This paradigm shift became widely accepted among researchers.

At the same time, with respect to *beginning reading* in the primary grades, numerous researchers were exploring insights emanating from the cognitive revolution in general and the CSR in particular as they pertained to the reading comprehension of first and second graders. No longer was research on beginning readers focused centrally on word recognition and perceptual processes. The lens expanded to examine the cognitive, social, and cultural factors related to primary grade children's literacy development.

Policy

Currently, when federal and state policies are so much in the face of educators, it may seem hard to believe, but the vigorous activity and intellectual shift in language/literacy research and theory of the 1980s was not mirrored in the arena of early childhood education policy. There were certainly hot policy issues related to early childhood. For example, scholars and activists used data coming from longitudinal studies of the time (e.g., research on Head Start or the High/Scope project [Barnett, 1985; Consortium for Longitudinal Studies, 1983; McKey, Smith, & Aitken, 1985; Schweinhart, Weikart, & Larner, 1986]) showing positive, long-term effects of high-quality early childhood programs to advocate for more universal funding for preschool.

However, early literacy was not much in evidence when it came to relating such research findings to policy addressing the focus or content of preschool education. The notable exception was in the area of beginning reading instruction in elementary school. The policy that did have a huge ripple effect was the *California Literature Framework* (California State Department of Education, 1987), which adopted the emerging ideas about schema theory, comprehension, a composing model of reading, and the need for explicit instruction in comprehension hook, line, and sinker, mandating the use of literature as the core of the language arts curriculum. Because basal reader programs were *the* beginning reading program in the vast majority of primary grade classrooms and because California represented a huge chunk of the market, mainstream publishing companies reacted to this policy in a way that caused perhaps the most significant, abrupt shift in beginning reading materials ever.

Curriculum and Instruction

The shift in early reading curriculum and instruction during this period in history was monumental, both in preschool/kindergarten settings and in the primary grades. We group preschool and kindergarten together because, until this time, it was not commonplace to begin actual reading instruction in kindergarten. But a profound change in K began gathering full force in the mid-1980s. Emergent literacy as a concept took hold in a variety of ways: it was adopted by ERIC as a descriptor and also was recognized as a distinct area of work by organizations like the National Association for the Education of Young Children, the National Reading Conference, and the International Reading Association. In classrooms, curriculum materials took on an emergent literacy perspective. The upshot? The reading readiness approach that for decades had held sway in kindergarten and the first half of first grade was replaced. In retrospect, five specific features of this early literacy curriculum and instruction shift were especially noteworthy:

- Kindergarten (rather than first grade) came to be regarded as the place where real literacy instruction begins.
- Reading aloud was established as an instructional activity, not merely a fun time for children (Teale, 1984).
- Phonological awareness made its way into the consciousness and curriculum of kindergarten (and first grade) teachers (Juel, Griffith & Gough, 1986).
- Writing became accepted as a valuable part of the K curriculum (Martinez & Teale, 1987).
- The notion of creating a print-rich environment in the classroom was established (Neuman & Roskos, 1990).

Overall, written language came to be viewed as a functional and central part of the kindergarten classroom, and the emergent literacy classroom later described by Labbo and Teale (1997) became a model widely accepted among early childhood educators.

In the primary grades, the change was equally profound. CSR and related work changed the face of instructional materials designed to teach beginning reading. Holistic, comprehension-centered, integrated approaches began taking hold, and considerable attention was paid to using children's literature as a central vehicle for literacy instruction. *Whole language*, a philosophy of language and literacy development espousing that reading and writing are learned best by reading and writing (not through reading and writing exercises), that instruction should be rich in content, and that children's interests and purposes need to be paramount in teaching reading and writing (see, e.g., Goodman, 1986), came into its own by the mid-1980s and would continue to influence early literacy instruction for a number of years.

The changes in instruction initiated statewide by the *California Literature Framework* dovetailed with a whole language philosophy, but while whole language advocates eschewed basal reader programs, the state of California was a "state adoption" state that provided all public school teachers language arts with instructional materials that satisfied the criteria specified in the *Framework*. Other big-market state adoption sites like Texas and Florida followed in the footsteps of California's criteria, and the basal reader materials for K–2 that resulted took on the new, comprehension/literature-centered approach to primary grades reading instruction. As a result, these materials and the instructional model that accompanied them looked different from anything publishers had produced for teachers before. Appearing first in the late 1980s and hitting their real stride in the 1990s, the materials for first grade, had, as Hoffman et al. (1994) found in their content analysis:

- significantly less vocabulary control and repetition
- literature that was more engaging and less adapted
- texts that were substantially more predictable in their language and design features
- texts that were more demanding in terms of decoding
- considerably fewer words for children to read.

Instructional recommendations accompanying the materials placed less emphasis on phonics than in the past, with teachers being encouraged to teach phonics to individual and small groups of children as the need arose, rather than systematically for all children.

One final aspect related to this period's classroom literacy practice bears commenting on: assessment. Traditional standardized reading tests had long been in use, but their utility for the classroom teacher was constantly called into question. The standards movement was yet to come with any force; at this time most schools and states examined elementary students' literacy achievement more in terms of minimal competencies. Few states *required* that reading be tested in the early grades (most assessments started in grade 3), but standardized testing of first and second graders did take place in various districts. There was virtually no required formal testing of reading in kindergarten, no assessment of writing at any of the early grades, and preschool literacy assessment was nonexistent.

By the same token, there was considerable activity focused on reconceptualizing large-scale standardized reading assessment, most notably in Illinois and Michigan (Valencia & Pearson, 1987; Valencia et al., 1989), where there were efforts to incorporate comprehension and authentic reading activities into the state tests. The new assessments also downplayed the testing of individual reading skills in favor of assessing skills as they apply in actual reading. At the early childhood level, educators put considerable effort into developing assessments for K–1 that would reflect the new emergent literacy paradigm and also be useable by classroom teachers in planning day-to-day instruction (see, e.g., Teale, 1988; Teale, Hiebert, & Chittenden, 1987). In short, one might say that assessment of early literacy was a topic of central importance, but standardized testing did not yet have the major impact on teachers' and children's day-to-day classroom lives that it does today.

Where Are We Now? "That's Good! That's Bad!"

For all but the ideologically minded, the "reading wars" (Lemann, 1997; Pearson, 2004) related to beginning reading that were played out during the 1990s are over. As has been increasingly realized over the past decade, deliberate instruction in the alphabetic code, in reading comprehension, and in writing are all part of high-quality early literacy instruction, both in the regular language arts curriculum (e.g., Pressley et al., 2001; Pressley et al., 2001) and in early intervention programs focused on literacy (e.g., Taylor et al., 2000). Although differences of opinion about early literacy have by no means disappeared, there is currently considerably more shared vision about early literacy learning, the nature of children's early reading and writing processes, and what constitutes good early literacy instruction.

As Teale stated in his foreword to the book *Achieving Excellence in Preschool Literacy Instruction* (Justice & Vukelich, 2007): "In many respects, in the United States today, it is the best of times for preschool literacy" (p. xv). The same could also be said about literacy education in the primary grades. Consider the following:

Scholarship

- Beginning reading instruction (K–grade 3) remains the most studied aspect of all areas of educational research. We recently conducted an informal content analysis of selected research journals (*Reading Research Quarterly, Journal of Literacy Research, Early Childhood Research Quarterly*), examining publications from 1990 to 2007. Nearly one-quarter of all articles (23%) focused on some aspect of early literacy.
- That same content analysis found that early literacy is also widely featured in journals focused on classroom practice (*The Reading Teacher, Language Arts, Young Children*), with 26% of their articles addressing literacy instruction, preK–grade 3.
- Two editions of the *Handbook of Early Literacy Research* have been published (Neuman & Dickinson, 2002; Dickinson & Neuman, 2006), and a third is in the works. With multiple chapters focused on beginning reading and writing, the fourth *Handbook of Reading Research* appears in 2009. Research on early literacy also occupies a central place in the *Handbook of Research on Teaching* (Richardson, 2001), the *International Handbook of Literacy and Technology* (McKenna et al., 2006), and other widely read research review sources such as the *Review of Education Research*.

Policy

- Since 2002, the U.S. federal government has put significant funding into early literacy—over US$1 billion per year into Reading First to "put proven methods of early reading instruction in classrooms" during the primary grade years (http://www.ed.gov/programs/reading first/index.html) and approximately US$100 million per year into creating preschool centers of literacy excellence through Early Reading First (http://www.ed.gov/programs/early reading/index.html).
- Professional organizations such as the International Reading Association, the National Association for the Education of Young

Children, and the American Library Association have been very actively engaged in awareness campaigns, position statements, and professional materials related to preschool and primary grades reading and writing (e.g., IRA's preschool literacy series or position statement on phonemic awareness; ALA's Born to Read (http://www.ala.org/ala/alsc/alscresources/borntoread/bornread.cfm).

- Current guidelines for federally funded Head Start and most state preschool programs explicitly incorporate early literacy standards or benchmarks.
- A National Early Literacy Panel was formed to "conduct a synthesis of scientific research on the development of early literacy in young children" in order to "identify interventions and practices that promote positive outcomes in literacy for preschool children" (www.nifl.gov/nifl/NELP/NELP09.html).

Curriculum and instruction

- Never before have there been as many materials on the market focused on reading and writing instruction for preschool–grade 3 children.
- Sales of instructional materials in the El-Hi (elementary-high school) area have remained strong for a number of years, with beginning reading representing one of the largest segments of the market (http://www.bisg.org/news/press.php?pressid=49). At the same time, children's hardback trade book sales also have been strong over recent years (e.g., http://www.publishers.org/main/IndustryStats/indStats_02.htm).

Despite indicators like these, as we considered how to frame this discussion of where we are now, we felt that although this *is* an exciting time for early literacy, rather than being characterized by outright optimism, Dickens' (1859) analysis of the situation in eighteenth-century France and England, depicted in his opening of *A Tale of Two Cities*, more accurately captures the end of the first decade of the twenty-first century with respect to early literacy. In a Reading Hall of Fame address at the 49th Annual Convention of the International Reading Association, Teale (2004) took the liberty of rewriting Dickens' words, applying them to his analysis of the state of early literacy:

It is the best of times, it is the worst of times, it is the age of available wisdom, it is the age of too much applied foolishness, it is the epoch of belief, it is the epoch of incredulity, it is the season of Light, it is the season of Darkness, it is the spring of hope, it is the winter of despair, we have everything before us, we have nothing before us, we are all going direct to heaven for our attention to children's early literacy, we are all going direct the other way because of what we are doing in the name of early literacy—in short, this is a period that worries me severely.

(Teale, 2004)

In addition to Dickens' novel, we find the motif of another literary classic perhaps even more fitting as a frame for our analysis of what has occurred in early literacy over the past several years in many U.S. preschools and primary grades. That motif is the one employed by Marjorie Cuyler and David Catrow in their picture book *That's Good! That's Bad!* (Cuyler, 1991). In this book a young boy experiences a series of incidents involving a balloon, a wide variety of animals, and even quicksand that appear to be positive but turn out to be negative (and vice versa). This fits the current situation in early literacy: There have been considerable positive strides such as those noted above ("That's good"); on the other hand, in almost every area where progress has taken place, there are reasons for grave concern ("That's bad"). These concerns are critical to address in order to insure the continued health of early literacy in the United States. We found five "what's good/what's bad" issues particularly salient.

Early Literacy: A Central Part of Early Childhood Education

There can be no doubt that both preschool literacy and beginning reading in K–3 are hot topics these days. As was noted above, more research continues to be conducted in early literacy than any other specific area of educational study, and during the past decade more federal money has gone into early literacy implementation and research than at any time in history.

In addition, early childhood education has come into its own as a cause célèbre in recent years. Research showing that:

- quality early childhood education programs result in positive short-term effects on children's cognitive functioning, school readiness, and social behavior
- model early interventions are associated with positive long-term effects
- crucial brain development takes place during the early years and the environmental/educational stimulation young children receive from preschool teachers relates positively to subsequent learning and intellectual growth

has received considerable attention from local, state, and federal policymakers. As a result, 38 states currently fund pre-kindergarten programs for three- and four-year-old children so that now almost one-quarter of 4-year-olds in the U.S. are served through public funding (over 50% more children than five years earlier) (Barnett et al., 2008).

Many foundations and community organizations, as well as federal departments and the White House, have championed the need for high-quality early education (e.g., the White House Summit on Early Childhood Cognitive Development [http://www.whitehouse.gov/firstlady/initiatives/education/earlychildhood.html]) and the importance of getting off to the right start in reading (e.g., see U.S. Department of Education resources for parents like *Helping Your Preschool Child*, *Put Reading First*, or *Helping Your Child Become a Reader* [http://www.ed.gov/parents/read/resources/edpicks.jhtml]).

Such developments are good because they have elevated the importance of early childhood education in the eyes of the public, one result being increased funding that enables more children to experience the benefits of a preschool educational program. These studies and policy initiatives have also highlighted the critical importance of deliberately infusing literacy into all early childhood programs. It is no longer enough to place books in the classroom, display the alphabet and trust that children will discover literacy when they are ready. Preschool literacy instruction has significantly more impact if it is intentional and systematic.

But this perspective has also been bad. These days, when terms such as *intentional, deliberate, systematic*, and *direct* are applied to teaching 3- and 4-year-olds, there are frequently unintended, unplanned for—and highly negative—consequences. The mid-1980s saw considerable concern related to the "push down" of the first-grade literacy curriculum into kindergarten (International Reading Association, 1985). That issue is now applicable to prekindergarten. Three- to five-year-old children can learn plenty about reading and writing, including a range of specific skills. We, as authors of this chapter, are all for intentional literacy instruction in preK and K. We are currently implementing two Early Reading First projects in Chicago-area preschool classrooms (http://education.uic.edu/erf), and in both of these projects we *teach* children vocabulary, listening comprehension, oral language, phonological awareness, alphabet, and other early literacy skills. But that does not mean implementing worksheets, workbooks, and skill-and-drill computer programs, or having young children sit through 25-, 30-, or 45-minute teacher-centered or, worse, scripted literacy lessons.

In too many early childhood classrooms, and especially classrooms where children are considered at risk and therefore in need of as much intervention as possible as soon as possible to prevent their reading difficulties, intentional instruction has been confused with *direct instruction*. Dramatic play designed to teach foundational literacy skills (Roskos & Christie, 2007) has disappeared from the majority of kindergarten classrooms that we observe these days and is even being viewed with skepticism by parents and school administrators in many preK situations. The approach to assessment taken in these situations can reinforce a focus on discrete skills when the only indicator of children's early literacy learning that really counts in many classrooms is how the children did on the test. Thus, although the war fought to establish the importance of infusing literacy into early childhood education may have been won, it has come at the cost of developmentally appropriate literacy instruction in far too many classrooms.

What Research Tells Us about Early Literacy Development and Instruction

Early literacy research activity today is perhaps even more robust than it was 25 years ago. Current scholars and practitioners continue to draw upon the insights provided from quality research of the past in developing theory and implementing early literacy instruction in preschool and primary grade programs, but what we have learned in the intervening years has resulted in a much richer understanding of early literacy development and effective literacy instructional practices in a variety of areas, such as the:

- centrality of oral language and vocabulary for young children's overall learning and literacy learning in particular (e.g., Hart & Risley, 1995)
- role that phonological awareness plays in early literacy learning and the necessity for emphasizing it instructionally in preK, K, and grade 1 (e.g., Ehri et al., 2001)
- nature of reading fluency and instructional strategies for building primary grade students' skill in this area (e.g., Kuhn & Stahl, 2003)
- kinds of early literacy intervention programs that succeed (e.g., Taylor et al., 2000).

In addition, research of the past quarter century has deepened understanding of the role of phonics instruction in beginning reading, showing it as a necessary but not sufficient instruction component of a beginning reading program, supporting the conclusion that systematic phonics instruction for K–2 children is better than opportunistic phonics instruction, and clearly showing that no one phonics program is superior (National Institute of Child Health and Human Development, 2000).

It is certainly good that we have accumulated much more research-based knowledge about early literacy. So, what could be bad about more knowledge? We see concerns on two intertwined fronts. First, recent years have witnessed the rise of the concept of scientifically based research (Shavelson, 2001) and, in particular for our concerns in this chapter, scientifically based reading research (SBRR) (McCardle & Chhabra, 2004). The idea behind SBRR is laudable in many respects—the characteristics of high-quality scientific research should be recognized, and literacy policy and instruction should be based on SBRR rather than on trendy ideas that may have good marketing but lack substance. The characteristics of SBRR have our full support, but the specific ways in which SBRR has been applied in early literacy since the concept was introduced leave much to be desired.

The story of what's bad with SBRR begins with the *Report of the National Reading Panel* (NRP) (National Institute of Child Health and Human Development, 2000). The NRP conducted a meta-analysis designed to answer a central question:

- What scientific assessments have been made of the effectiveness of common instructional approaches to teach children to read?

To answer such a question requires that one employ empirical data gathered from experimental and quasi-experimental research. That was the research the NRP used, and the answers the Panel came up with to this question were quite reasonable. But the Panel was also charged to address the following questions:

- Based on answers to the preceding question, what does the Panel conclude about the readiness for implementation in the classroom of these research results?
- What practical findings from the Panel can be used immediately by parents, teachers, and other educational audiences to help children learn to read?

This is where the bad comes in: The ways in which the NRP findings have been applied to the practical questions have resulted in severely restricting the research evidence that is viewed as contributing to current knowledge about early literacy. Information from rigorous, systematic, objective ethnographies, case studies, correlational research, and observational studies that have been accepted by peer-reviewed journals contribute substantive research knowledge that should also be used to draw policy and instructional implications in the field of early literacy. In reality, however, studies grounded in observational, qualitative methodologies have largely been shut out of the decisions. For all intents and purposes, research that is not some form of a randomized control design has received a condescending pat on the head at the highest levels of policy formation: "That's nice, dear, but run out and play while the grown-ups use the real data and make the real decisions about good early literacy practice."

The NRP did not intend this, for the full report clearly states that other forms of research in addition to experimental and quasi-experimental studies should absolutely be used to make decisions about effective reading instruction. But that is the way the world of early literacy research data has played itself out in recent years, largely, we suspect, because the most influential policy decisions about early literacy have increasingly been controlled at the federal level, and the forces in charge of early literacy educational policy there have exhibited a narrow view of about what constitutes legitimate research. In other words, scientifically based reading research is not by definition a narrow concept, but it has certainly been realized narrowly in terms of the reality it has imposed on preK–grade 3 classroom literacy practices.

The second research-related "that's bad" concerns the larger issue of the relationship between research findings and practical implications for early literacy. It is crucial that early literacy policy and instruction be research-based. But, the link between research and practice must be seen as more nuanced than has been the case in recent years. That is to say, even multiple sources of research evidence should not be the *sole* basis for decisions about early literacy instruction. A number of well-reasoned explications of the literacy research-practice relationship have appeared in the past few years (e.g., Pearson, 2007; Shanahan, 2002); we wish to make only two related points. One, just because an early literacy instructional practice or program is research-proven in one context does not mean it will have the same results if the conditions for its implementation differ from the original context. That program Q or policy R worked in setting S does not mean that they will work with T children in U school. For example, if a phonics program significantly raised the decoding skills of first and second graders in 30 suburban classrooms as compared with 30 similar classrooms not using the program, it does not necessarily follow that the same results will be realized in an urban classroom with a majority of children who come from extremely low-income homes.

We raise this point in reference to the federal initiatives the What Works Clearinghouse (WWC) (http://ies.ed.gov/ncee/wwc/) and Doing What Works (DWW) (http://dww.ed.gov/). WWC "assesses the rigor of research evidence on the effectiveness of . . . programs, products, practices, and policies, giving educators the tools to make informed decisions." A program reviewed by WWC under "Beginning Reading" might receive a ++ rating (Positive Effects: strong evidence of a positive effect with no overriding contrary evidence) or even a "+" (Potentially Positive Effects: evidence of a positive effect with no overriding contrary evidence). Most educators would assume that such a review indicates a program that works. But, it is our contention that educational research results of this kind are not universal—they must be understood in terms of the conditions under which the results were obtained.

DWW is even more prone to criticism in this respect. It is based on WWC and "help(s) educators identify and make use of effective teaching practices" by "provid(ing) examples of possible ways educators might apply research findings." Notice that DWW does rightly qualify ("might", "possible") the relationship between the research found on WWC and how to make use of such findings, but it still operates under the guise of SBRR, in essence recommending "examples of . . . research-based instructional practices (that make it) more likely (to) affect an increase in student achievement." DWW also provides professional development materials and planning templates on the website, none of which, as far as we can see, have scientifically based research that indicate their effectiveness in helping teachers implement such instructional practices.

We bring up this example to show how claims to scientific rigor can get fuzzy in a range of circumstances. Our concern is that decision-makers—school boards, administrators, curriculum directors, teachers, even parents—may look to a source like WWC or DWW without fully understanding how such ratings or recommendations should be understood.

Thus, even though research—and especially scientifically based research—stresses that it is objective and based strictly on evidence, those who purchase or implement early literacy programs, practices, or curricula should be educated consumers to avoid being misled as to what *research-based* actually means in publishers' and others' claims and to not fall victim to scoundrels who masquerade under the guise of research purists (see Teale & Shanahan, 1999, for a discussion of this issue).

The recent debacle involving Reading First (RF) stands as an example of what can happen when researchers who are convinced that they are right (based on what they consider quality research) pursue their ends in the extreme. The U.S. Department of Education Inspector General's six audit and investigation reports into RF and the related report of the Chairman of the Health, Education, Labor, and Pensions Committee clearly revealed, at best, serious conflict of interest and bad judgment and, at worst, outright criminal activity in administering Reading First (e.g., Kennedy, 2007). Here is a quote from an email written by former RF director Chris Doherty, discussing certain programs that were attempting to qualify to be used in RF classrooms: "They are trying to crash our party and we need to beat the [expletive] out of them in front of all the other would-be party crashers who are standing on the front lawn waiting to see how we welcome these dirtbags" (Grunwald, 2006). Not quite what one thinks of as a discussion about scientifically based reading research. In 1995, writing about the ongoing debates about good beginning reading instruction, Teale noted, "never has the debate been more strident. Each side is fighting hard—and sometimes fighting nasty—for its position" (p. 121). What was then an emerging mean-spiritedness from segments of the reading research and policy communities has only escalated during the intervening years. Our hope is that this approach to matters of early literacy research and applications of that research will change profoundly and as soon as possible.

Curriculum and Early Literacy in the Preschool and Primary Grades: The Intersection of Research, Educational Wisdom, and Policy

Much of what we have discussed in the previous two sections about the current *good/bad* in early literacy directly affects instruction in U.S. preK–grade 3 classrooms. Virtually all schools today begin literacy instruction with 3- and 4-year-olds. In addition, research findings, especially the findings synthesized by the National Reading Panel (NICHD, 2000) have had a major impact on K–3 instruction.

A number of aspects of this impact have been positive. Reading instruction is no longer delayed until children are deemed ready based on the results of a standardized assessment or by virtue of their age. The importance of a literacy-rich environment in all early childhood classrooms is widely recognized. Young children are given experience writing. Literacy is woven into a wide variety of contexts and activities. Engaging phonological awareness and read aloud activities are now a central part of preK and K instruction in the vast majority of early childhood classrooms. That's all good.

But, as Teale, Paciga, and Hoffman (2007) recently pointed out, there are causes for concern about current trends in preschool and primary grade classrooms, especially in many urban schools where the narrow implementation of Reading First and a correspondingly narrow interpretation of the NRP findings has created a curriculum gap. The result in many K–3 classrooms is a literacy curriculum that emphasizes instruction in phonological awareness (PA), phonics, and reading fluency at the expense of three critically important areas: (1) comprehension instruction; (2) developing children's knowledge (of the world in general and of core concepts in content domains like science and social studies); and (3) writing instruction. Teale et al. (2007) called for rethinking the foundational skills of literacy to include not only PA, phonics, and fluency but also the three aforementioned areas, saying that "lack of sustained instructional attention to comprehension, content knowledge, and writing in the early grades is rather like expecting children to grow up to be healthy teenagers with a childhood diet of meat and potatoes but no fruits or vegetables" (p. 347). The grave danger is that without such an emphasis, although many children who attend Reading First schools (primarily children who qualify for free or reduced-price lunch) may actually not suffer severely in their reading achievement in grades 1 or 2; they will very likely experience profound difficulties in reaching the literacy levels necessary for success in the intermediate grades and beyond—but by then it will be too late to help most of them read and write well.

Assessment in Early Literacy

Assessment—gathering data about children's reading and writing knowledge and skill—is central to young children's literacy education. However, as Glasswell and Teale (2007) remind us, assessment should be "an integral part of what we teach (curriculum) and how we teach it (pedagogy) rather than a process that is conducted in addition to—and apart from—instruction" (p. 262). In other words, the ultimate purpose of early literacy assessment should be using assessment data to enhance children's achievement and engagement as readers/writers.

Early childhood literacy instruction has become increasingly data-driven in recent years. This is good—good for teachers, children, and parents. When teachers use class profiles and information on individual children to differentiate instruction, the result is usually higher achievement for children and greater confidence by teachers that they are meeting student needs.

However, an incident involving the first author of this chapter illustrates the bad associated with current trends in early literacy assessment:

> I was at a reading conference and came upon the director of literacy for a large school district in the U.S. I hadn't seen her in quite a while, and after exchanging felicitous greetings, I asked, "How's it going?" Her answer: "We'll see when the test results come out next week." I must admit that I was flabbergasted. It taught me a disconcerting lesson: Of all the things she could have mentioned that affect the life of someone with such a large responsibility—the literacy education of thousands of students—the only thing that really counted is how well the students do on the yearly standardized reading assessment.

Assessment, in particular formal literacy testing, has become the single most important force affecting early literacy curriculum and instruction in many, many schools. This has happened in large part because a cornerstone of the Bush administration's educational plan for all eight years in office has been testing (and accountability). The first component listed of the No Child Left Behind (NCLB) Act of 2001 was "annual testing of . . . students in reading . . . every year in grades 3–8." Earlier grades have felt the impact of this policy, even if NCLB does not mandate it until grade 3.

Assessment that functions to inform instruction is good; however, the direction that early literacy assessment has taken in recent years is perilously close to being so far down the wrong path that it will be difficult to reverse. The type of early literacy assessment increasingly seen today is driving curriculum more and more toward teaching early reading and writing skills in isolation—that is, in ways that resemble how they will be formally tested. And even assessments that were theoretically designed to be quick, rather informal measures that would aid instructional planning have ended up restricting instruction or being ends unto themselves rather than means to a larger end. The prime example is, of course, DIBELS, the Dynamic Indicators of Basic Early Literacy Skills (http://www.dibels.uoregon.edu). In 2006, P. David Pearson, known for his balanced approach to early literacy, called DIBELS "the worst thing to happen to the teaching of reading since the development of flash cards" (p. v). He goes on to say that in K–grade 3, the use of DIBELS:

> . . . shapes instruction in ways that are bad for students (they end up engaging in curricular activities that do not promote their progress as readers) and bad for teachers (it requires them to judge student progress and shape instruction based on criteria that are not consistent with our best knowledge about the nature of reading development).
>
> (p. v)

His analysis points out that DIBELS has, in essence, become a blueprint for primary grades reading curriculum in thousands of schools, thus effectively reducing what is taught to what is measured on the test.

The direction that many early literacy assessment efforts have taken in recent years is disheartening because the potential for productive, developmentally appropriate assessment to improve instruction and, ultimately, early literacy achievement, is enormous. We have seen firsthand in our Early Reading First projects (http://education.uic.edu/erf) the realization of that assessment potential. We involve children in quite a bit of literacy assessment—and follow up with professional development that helps teachers understand (a) how to conduct useful assessments in the context of ongoing instruction, (b) what particular assessments can and cannot tell one about children's learning, (c) how to interpret assessment data on each child in the classroom as well as what group patterns suggest about children's instructional needs, and (d) implications for daily literacy instruction. The evaluation data clearly show positive changes in teachers' instruction and significantly higher early literacy learning for the children in relation to the comparison group (DeStefano et al., 2008). Teachers clearly indicate that the work in assessment has contributed integrally to these changes.

The lesson we take from these contrasting situations—where child measures function merely as tests that are ends unto themselves and where they serve as an integral part of classroom planning, teaching, and differentiating—is that assessment always makes a difference. In so many instances these days, the difference is turning out to be a bad one. What's good is that there are numerous examples to draw on around the country of the educative power of early literacy assessment.

Educating Teachers for Early Literacy Instruction

The final area we address in talking about where we are now in early literacy is teacher education, or more specifically teacher professional development (PD). The need for ongoing, high-quality professional development for teachers has long been recognized, but one of the most promising trends in recent years has been the enhanced commitment to and support for substantive early literacy PD by local schools and districts, state departments of education, university-school district collaboratives, and even federal initiatives.

These efforts have relied heavily on the concept of literacy coaching—ongoing, job-embedded professional development in which the coach (lead literacy teacher, reading specialist) works side by side with the teacher in the classroom, modeling, co-teaching, supporting in other ways as a prime means of enhancing the quality of early literacy instruction. Our own Early Reading First projects (http://education.uic.edu/erf) in Chicago preschool classrooms involve children who traditionally do not fare well with literacy in school. Independent, external evaluations of this work showed that we have been able to significantly raise teachers' early literacy knowledge and classroom teaching skill and, more importantly, the children's early literacy achievement in a range of areas (see, e.g., DeStefano et al., 2008). What our literacy coaches did in the classrooms was key to achieving these results. Coaches worked across the school year with teachers to help them set specific goals for enhancing literacy instruction in their classrooms, based on areas research has shown that make a difference: classroom literacy environment, embedding early literacy experiences in children's dramatic play, interactive read alouds, intentional and embedded phonological awareness instruction, and so forth.

That's good indeed, and we have been encouraged about what we have seen with respect to the effects of coaching on early literacy practice and achievement. The bad news on the coaching/PD front is that many places are rushing headlong into putting early literacy coaches in classrooms with little regard for what background and training coaches need to be effective or what coaches should actually be doing in classrooms that will make a difference. In these situations it is as if the use or presence of coaches will change things rather than realizing that it is what coaches do that will change things.

Research on the effects of literacy coaching is only now emerging, so many unanswered questions remain, including the big issue of whether or not coaching as a large-scale practice works and under what conditions (how much coaching, what is the coaching content, etc.), as well as its cost-effectiveness. The Literacy Coaching Clearinghouse (http://www.literacycoachingonline.org/) reports considerable research activity in this area, some of which will hopefully soon provide answers to such questions. Initial findings suggest that when coaches spend significant amounts of time conferring individually with teachers and working in their classrooms, there is a payoff for both teachers and students, but that it may require two to three years of quality coaching to realize such benefits.

Furthermore, we believe that although coaching can be a powerful ingredient, it is only one factor in the complex of professional development that can make a positive difference in early literacy instruction and children's achievement. Building capacity that results in sustainable improvement in early literacy requires PD at the individual teacher, building, and district levels. We suggest, therefore, that schools pay close attention to the work of Au, Goldman, Raphael, and colleagues, which has provided important insight into the complexity of factors and the developmental trajectories that characterize models of school literacy change (e.g., Advanced Reading Development Demonstration Project, 2008; Au, 2005; Au, Raphael, & Mooney, 2008; Raphael, Au, & Goldman, this volume).

The Coming Decade: A Pivotal Period for Early Literacy

We *have* come a long way in early literacy. There will always be positives and negatives associated with developments in education, but we felt that a *That's*

Good / That's Bad frame was especially helpful for characterizing early literacy education and policy right now. Overall, we believe that the goods currently have the upper hand on the bads. Our educational systems are providing more young children with better access to the wonders and power of reading and writing in their many forms than ever before. Many successful programs and intervention efforts have paid off for children who have traditionally been disenfranchised in our society. But also, the field and the public should not be content with the current state of early literacy. We believe that, on all the fronts discussed above, things are currently on a kind of tightrope, poised to slip into the bad misapplication of research and judgment of just the kind that has befallen Reading First unless scholars, teachers, policymakers, and the public keep their heads up and their eyes open. We believe also that the next decade will prove as pivotal to where early literacy research, policy, and instructional practice head as the 1980s were. We have attempted to offer in this chapter information that will guide early literacy in a positive direction over the coming years and hope that in 2019, when we write our next review of the state of early literacy education in the United States, we can end the way Marjorie Cuyler (1991) did: "Oh, that's good. No, *that's GREAT.*"

References

Advanced Reading Development Demonstration Project. (2008). Partnerships for improving literacy in urban schools. *The Reading Teacher, 61*, 674–680.

Au, K.H. (2005). Negotiating the slippery slope: School change and literacy achievement. *Journal of Literacy Research 37*:3, 267–288.

Au, K.H., Raphael, T.E., & Mooney, K. (2008). What we have learned about teacher education to improve literacy achievement in urban schools. In V. Chou, L. Morrow, & L. Wilkinson (Eds.), *Improving literacy achievement in urban schools: Critical elements in teacher preparation.* Newark, DE: International Reading Association (www.reading.org).

Barnett, W.S. (1985). Benefit–cost analysis of the Perry Preschool Program and its policy implications. *Educational Evaluation and Policy Analysis, 7*(4), 333–342.

Barnett, W.S., Hustedt, J.T., Friedman, A.H., Boyd, J.S., & Ainsworth, P. (2008). *The state of preschool 2007.* New Brunswick, NJ: National Institute for Early Education Research.

Bissex, G.L. (1980). *Gnys at wrk: A child learns to write and read.* Cambridge, MA: Harvard University Press.

California State Department of Education. (1987). *The California literature framework.* Sacramento, CA: Author.

Chomsky, N. (1959). A review of B.F. Skinner's *Verbal Behavior. Language, 35*, 26–58.

Clay, M.M. (1966). *Emergent reading behaviour.* Unpublished doctoral dissertation, University of Auckland, New Zealand.

Consortium for Longitudinal Studies. (1983). *As the twig is bent . . . Lasting effects of preschool programs.* Hillsdale, NJ: Erlbaum.

Cuyler, M. (1991). *That's good! That's bad!* Illustrated by D. Catrow. New York: Henry Holt and Co.

DeStefano, L., Rempert, T., O'Dell, L., & Innes, E. (2008). *Charting a Course to Literacy: Early Reading First in Chicago charter schools—External evaluation, year two report.* Urbana, IL: University of Illinois at Urbana-Champaign.

Dickens, C. (1859). *A tale of two cities.* London: Chapman and Hall.

Dickinson, D. & Neumann, S. (2006). *Handbook of early literacy research. Volume 2.* New York: Guilford Publications.

Ehri, L.C., Nunes, S.R., Willows, D.M., Schuster, B., Yaghoub-Zadeh, Z., & Shanahan, T. (2001). Phonemic awareness instruction helps children learn to read: Evidence from the National Reading Panel's meta-analysis. *Reading Research Quarterly, 36*(3), 250–287.

Ferreiro, E. (1986). The interplay between information and assimilation in beginning literacy. In W.H. Teale & E. Sulzby (Eds.), *Emergent literacy: Writing and reading* (pp.15–49). Norwood, NJ: Ablex.

Glasswell, K. & Teale, W.H. (2007). Authentic assessment of authentic student work in urban classrooms. In J.R. Paratore & R.L. McCormack (Eds.), *Classroom literacy assessment: Making sense of what students know and do* (pp. 262–279). New York: Guilford.

Goodman, K.S. (1986). *What's whole in whole language?* Portsmouth, NH: Heinemann.

Goodman, Y.M. & Altwerger, B. (1981). *A study of literacy in preschool children (Research Report No. 4).* Tucson: University of Arizona.

Grunwald, M. (2006, October 1). Billions for an inside game on reading. *Washington Post,* p. B01.

Harste, J., Woodward, V., & Burke, C. (1984). *Language stories and literacy lessons.* Portsmouth, NH: Heinemann.

Hart, B. & Risley, T.R. (1995). *Meaningful differences in the everyday experiences of young American children.* Baltimore: Paul H. Brookes.

Heath, S.B. (1983). *Ways with words: Language, life, and work in communities and classrooms.* New York: Cambridge University Press.

Henderson, E.H. & Beers, J. (Eds.), (1980). *Developmental and cognitive aspects of learning to spell: A reflection of word knowledge.* Newark, DE: International Reading Association.

Hoffman, J.V., McCarthey, S.J., Abbott, J., Christian, C., Corman, L., Curry, C., Dressman, M., Elliott, B., Matherne, D., & Stahle, D. (1994). So what's new in the new basals? A focus on first grade. *Journal of Reading Behavior, 26,* 47–73.

International Reading Association. (1985). *Literacy development and pre-first grade: A joint statement of concerns about present practices in pre-first grade reading instruction and recommendations for improvement.* Newark, DE: International Reading Association.

Juel, C., Griffith, P., & Gough, P. (1986). Acquisition of literacy: A longitudinal study of children in first and second grade. *Journal of Educational Psychology, 78,* 243–255.

Justice, L.M. & Vukelich, C. (2007). *Achieving Excellence in Preschool Literacy Instruction.* New York: Guilford Publications.

Kennedy, E.M. (Chairman) (2007, May 9). *The chairman's report on the conflicts of interest found in the implementation of the Reading First program at three regional technical assistance centers.* Washington, DC: United States Senate Health, Education, Labor and Pensions Committee.

Kuhn, M.R. & Stahl, S.A. (2003). Fluency: A review of developmental and remedial practices. *Journal of Educational Psychology, 95*(1), 3–21.

Labbo, L.D. & Teale, W.H. (1997). Emergent literacy as a model of reading instruction. In S.A. Stahl & D.A. Hayes (Eds.), *Instructional models in reading* (pp. 249–281). Mahwah, NJ: Lawrence Erlbaum Publishers.

Lemann, N. (1997). The reading wars. *The Atlantic Monthly, 280*(5), 128–133.

McCardle, P. & Chhabra, V. (Eds.) (2004). *The voice of evidence in reading research.* Baltimore, MD: Paul Brookes.

McKenna, M.C, Labbo, L.D., Kiefer, R.D., & Reinking, D. (Eds.) (2006). *International handbook of literacy and technology.* Mahwah, NJ: Lawrence Erlbaum Associates.

McKey, R.H., Smith, A.N., & Aitken, S.S. (1985). *The impact of Head Start on children, families, and communities.* Washington, DC: The Bureau.

Martinez, M.G. & Teale, W.H. (1987). The ins and outs of a kindergarten writing program. *The Reading Teacher, 40,* 444–451.

Miller, P. (1982). *Amy, Wendy, and Beth: Learning language in South Baltimore.* Austin, TX: University of Texas Press.

National Institute of Child Health and Human Development. (2000). *Report of the National Reading Panel. Teaching children to read: An evidence-based assessment of the scientific research literature on reading and its implications for reading instruction* (NIH Publication No. 00-4769). Washington, DC: U.S. Government Printing Office.

Neuman, S.B. & Dickinson, D. (2002). *Handbook of early literacy research.* New York: Guilford Publications.

Neuman, S. & Roskos, K. (1990). The influence on literacy-enriched pay settings on preschoolers' engagement with written language. *Annual Yearbook of the National Reading Conference, 39,* 179–187.

Pearson, P.D. (2004). The reading wars. *Educational Policy, 18*(1), 216–252.

Pearson, P.D. (2006). Foreword. In K.S. Goodman (Ed.), *The truth about DIBELS: What it is, what it does* (pp. v–xix). Portsmouth, NH: Heinemann.

Pearson, P.D. (2007). An historical analysis of the impact of educational research on policy and practice: Reading as an illustrative case. *Annual Yearbook of the National Reading Conference, 55,* 15–39.

Pressley, M., Allington, R., Wharton-McDonald, R., Block, C.C., & Morrow, L.M. (2001). *Learning to read: Lessons from exemplary first grades.* New York: Guilford.

Pressley, M., Wharton-McDonald, R., Allington, R., Block, C.C., Morrow, L., Tracey, D., et al. (2001). A study of effective grade-1 literacy instruction. *Scientific Studies of Reading, 5,* 35–58.

Read, C. (1975). *Children's categorization of speech sounds in English.* Urbana, IL: National Council of Teachers of English.

Richardson, V. (2001). *Handbook of research on teaching.* Washington, DC: American Educational Research Association.

Roskos, K. & Christie, J.F. (2007). *Play and literacy in early childhood: Research from multiple perspectives.* Mahwah, NJ: Lawrence Erlbaum.

Schweinhart, L.L., Weikart, D.P., & Larner, M.B. (1986). Consequences of Three Preschool Curriculum Models through Age 15. *Early Childhood Research Quarterly, 1,* 15–45.

Shanahan, T. (2002). What reading research says: The promises and limitations of applying research to reading education. In A. Farstrup & S.J. Samuels (Eds.), *What research has to say about reading instruction* (pp. 8–24). Newark, DE: International Reading Association.

Shavelson, R. (2001). *Scientific research in education.* Washington, DC: National Academies Press.

Slobin, D. (1971). *Psycholinguistics.* Glenview, IL: Scott Foresman.

Snow, C.E. & Ferguson, C.A. (Eds.), (1977). *Talking to children: Language input and acquisition*. Cambridge: Cambridge University Press.

Sulzby, E. (1991). The development of the young child and the emergence of literacy. In J. Flood, J.M. Jensen, D. Lapp, & J.R. Squire (Eds.), *Handbook of research on teaching the English language arts* (pp. 273–285). New York: Macmillan.

Taylor, D. (1983). *Family literacy: Young children learning to read and write*. Exeter, NH: Heinemann.

Taylor, B.M., Pearson, P.D., Clark, K., & Walpole, S. (2000). Effective schools and accomplished teachers: Lessons about primary grade reading instruction in low-income schools. *Elementary School Journal, 101*(2), 121–166.

Teale, W.H. (1984). Reading to young children: Its significance in the process of literacy development. In H. Goelman, A. Oberg, & F. Smith (Eds.), *Awakening to literacy* (pp. 110–121). Exeter, NH: Heinemann Educational Books.

Teale, W.H. (1986). Home background and young children's literacy development. In W.H. Teale & E. Sulzby (Eds.), *Emergent literacy: Writing and reading* (pp. 173–206). Norwood, NJ: Ablex Publishing Corporation.

Teale, W.H. (1988). Developmentally appropriate assessment of reading and writing in the early childhood classroom. *The Elementary School Journal, 89*, 173–183.

Teale, W.H. (1995). Young children and reading: Trends across the 20th century. *Journal of Education, 177*, 95–125.

Teale, W.H. (2004, May). *Past, present, and future of early literacy*. Paper presented at the 49th Annual Convention of the International Reading Association, Reno, NV.

Teale, W.H., Hiebert, E.H., & Chittenden, E.A. (1987). Assessing young children's literacy development. *The Reading Teacher, 40*, 772–777.

Teale, W.H., Paciga, K.A., & Hoffman, J.L. (2007). Beginning reading instruction in urban schools: The curriculum gap insures a continuing achievement gap. *The Reading Teacher, 61*, 344–348.

Teale, W.H. & Shanahan, T. (1999). What is research-based reading instruction? *Illinois Reading Council Journal, 27*(1), 5–6.

Teale, W.H. & Sulzby, E. (Eds.), (1986). *Emergent literacy: Writing and reading*. Norwood, NJ: Ablex Publishing Corporation.

Tolchinsky-Landsman, L. & Levin, I. (1985). Writing in preschoolers: An age-related analysis. *Applied Psycholinguistics, 6*, 319–339.

Valencia, S. & Pearson, P.D. (1987). Reading assessment: Time for a change. *The Reading Teacher, 40*, 726–733.

Valencia, S., Pearson, P.D., Peters, C.W., & Wixson, K.K. (1989). Theory and practice in statewide reading assessment: Closing the gap. *Educational Leadership, 46*, 57–63.

Yaden, D., Jr. & Templeton, S. (Eds.), (1986). *Metalinguistic awareness and beginning literacy: Conceptualizing what it means to read and write*. Portsmouth, NH: Heinemann.

Chapter 7

Reaching/Teaching Adolescents

Literacies with a History

Donna E. Alvermann
University of Georgia

American author and editor George William Curtis is quoted in Bartlett (1919) as saying "while we read history we make history." I would venture the same could be claimed for what we write. This chapter, written from my perspective on adolescents' changing literacies in currently changing times, will one day be history, but for the present at least, it frames possibilities for reaching/ teaching young people in a way that attempts to make sense of who they are, where we've been as a field, and where we might be headed if we take them and their changing literacies into account. Toward addressing this purpose, I have divided the chapter into three sections:

- a brief description of adolescent literacy as it is presently reflected in major research reports, practitioner journals, and policy mandates
- an equally brief tracing of the social and cultural constructions of adolescence and adolescents that have played a role in bringing us to the point we are at, pedagogically speaking
- a more extended look at what is missing or taken for granted in those constructions that might serve as guideposts in how we reach/teach adolescents as literate beings with their own agendas for learning and communicating.

Adolescent Literacy: Year 2009

I am hard pressed to name another time in my four decades as a teacher, teacher educator, and researcher when so much attention has been focused on the field of adolescent literacy. Although not referred to as *adolescent literacy* when I was a classroom teacher in the mid-1960s to mid-1970s in Texas and upstate New York—Hal Herber's (1970) *teaching reading in content areas* was the phrase used then—adolescent literacy in 2009 refers to a vast array of reading, writing, and communicative practices in which young people engage:

> Adolescents today live in a world characterized by a vast array of media available at their fingertips and by unprecedented migration between

places and peoples, qualities of the modern age made possible by advances in technology. Consequently, an adolescent may speak a heritage language at home, converse in English with friends, receive text messages on a cellular phone, write an analytical essay in school, and peruse multimodal websites, all in the same day.

(Alvermann & Wilson, 2007, p. 3)

Adolescent literacy is also a rallying cry for disparate groups, including those that call for legislative action, curriculum reform, and high-stakes testing. Within a year's time in 2007, no fewer than eight major reports on adolescent literacy, commissioned by highly respected professional organizations and private foundations, were distributed to state departments of education and local school districts across the United States (Alvermann, 2009). Most of these reports are based on credible research findings in the field, although how well they generalize to an increasingly diverse school population is largely unknown. Nonetheless, they are used to drive policy decisions and introduce bills into the legislature (e.g., the Striving Readers Initiative), and to support curriculum reform movements aimed at ensuring literacy instruction does not stop at the elementary school level. Often these same reports are used in conjunction with overhauled state standards that have professional organizations' backing. In turn, the standards find their way into secondary teacher education programs certified by the state.

But policy- and curriculum-driven groups are not the only players in today's adolescent literacy scene. The results of high-stakes testing in reading/language arts and math are used to determine if individually identified schools have made adequate yearly progress (AYP) under the federal government's No Child Left Behind Act (2001). If not, parents of adolescents in "failing" schools that do not improve over a specified number of years are given options to transfer their child to another school or obtain free, supplemental tutoring services. In the meantime, large-scale media coverage of Title I (low-income) schools that fail to make AYP places adolescent literacy in a none too positive light.

Given all of this top-down attention to adolescent literacy, I have to wonder when the high profile that the field is presently experiencing will have a major impact on classroom instruction at the secondary level, or for that matter, at the postsecondary/tertiary level. Although the literacy journals in our field offer more research and practical advice on teaching content-area and disciplinary literacy to adolescents than ever before in my memory, the ideas contained in that literature are sometimes slow to make their way into actual classroom practice for any number of legitimate reasons. It is easy to become distracted by myriad calls for change; plus, changing one's pedagogy is not a simple lock-step process. Moreover, I question the wisdom of calls for changing instructional practices without first making sure that teachers and teacher educators acquire a better understanding of how learners are changing. Young people and their literacies in 2009 are a composite of past and present discursive practices that need careful consideration and study.

Social and Cultural Constructions of Adolescence and Adolescents

A contested term in some quarters due to pejorative connotations that relegate young people to marginalized positions on the periphery of adulthood and limit their options for engaging with society, *adolescence* has been described as "a kind of purgatory between childhood and adulthood" (Appleman, 2001, p. 1). By most accounts, adolescence as a term did not come into use until after the nineteenth century; before then, the teen years were not treated as separate from adulthood.

Scholars who view the concept of adolescence as being socially and culturally constructed point to certain historical, societal, economic, and political conditions that seek to normalize and regulate youth. For example, Lesko (2001) critiqued the notion that adolescence is a period in young people's lives marked by turmoil thought to consume most of their waking moments—a still prevalent assumption steeped in psychological and developmental theories dating back to the turn of the twentieth century (Hall, 1904). Others, myself included, have questioned the validity of sociocultural constructions that relegate youth to a marginalized position on the periphery of adulthood—a discursive practice that offers young people but a limited set of options for engaging with society and learning in general (Alvermann & Eakle, 2007; Harper & Bean, 2006).

Conceiving of young people *not* as lacking in adult knowledge and experience, but rather as knowing things that have relevance for them and their particular situations argues for exploring how all of us, adults and youth alike, act provisionally at times given particular circumstances and within particular discourses (Morgan, 1997). It also argues for viewing adolescents as having at least some degree of agency within a larger collective of social practices (Mac an Ghaill, 1994; Marsh & Stolle, 2006). Although this particular construction of youth, along with one that points to generational interdependency (Cintron, 1991; Hagood, Patel Stevens, & Reinking, 2002), have helped to move the conversation about sameness (all adolescents are alike) and hierarchical positioning (adolescents are not yet adults) to a new level of inquiry, they have had relatively little direct pedagogical impact to date in the United States. With this country's fairly monolithic view of youth and a narrowly defined sense of literacy still in place, it is not surprising that with few exceptions (e.g., Leander, 2007; Miller & Borowicz, 2006), classroom teachers have been reluctant to incorporate various aspects of adolescents' online literacies into their instruction (Alvermann, 2008), even on a trial basis, and especially in districts where high-stakes testing and AYP are the *sine qua non*. All this may be about to change, however, especially if the conditions described next remain in effect long enough for teachers, teacher educators, and the students they teach to get their footing.

Missing Pieces: Guideposts for Reaching/Teaching Adolescents

Undoubtedly, the potential for young people to exercise agency over their own reading and writing practices is at least theoretically enabled by their access to the Internet and by researchers' growing doubts about the stability of an age hierarchy when communicating online (Alvermann, 2006; Hagood et al., 2002). Findings from contemporary research on young people's multiliteracies, for instance, have revealed some underlying issues of power that complicate the very notion of adolescence (Hinchman & Chandler-Olcott, 2006; Vadeboncoeur & Patel Stevens, 2005). Also, acknowledging that young people are not in constant turmoil and that they do not comprise a homogeneous group challenges certain assumptions about how adolescents learn and what they find motivating. It is these two challenges in the current literature on sociocultural constructions of adolescents and their literacies that suggest possible openings and new directions for reaching/teaching adolescents as literate beings with their own agendas for learning and communicating.

Challenges to the Age Hierarchy Assumption

New information communication technologies have produced some profound changes in how adolescents use literacy, at least among those fortunate to have consistent and ready access to the Internet. In part, these changes represent full-blown challenges to assumptions about an age hierarchy, a social dynamic that traditionally has seen youth take a back seat to their elders. Unlike in face-to-face communication, interactions in a virtual world need not reveal age differences. Thus, upstaging or disagreeing with an expert, conduct typically discouraged in real life, can become somewhat of a non-issue for adolescents when interactions are mediated by various communication technologies. In a sense, virtual world interactions could be said to democratize the expert/ novice relationship between teacher and student.

When young people take responsibility for their own learning, we say they are self-motivated. When they produce content on the Web, the establishment takes note. For instance, according to a report released in December 2007 as part of the PEW Internet & American Life Project (Lenhart et al., 2007):

> The use of social media—blogging; working on a webpage for school or for personal use; sharing original content such as artwork, photos, stories, or videos; and remixing online content to create new texts—is central to the lives of many young people living in the continental United States. Of

the 935 adolescents between the ages of 12–17 who were interviewed by phone in a nationally representative sample (with the results weighted to correct for known sociodemographic discrepancies), 93% treated the Internet as a venue for social interaction. Of those young people who identified as having online access, 64% reported participating "in one or more . . . content-creating activities on the internet . . . up from 57% of online teens in a similar survey at the end of 2004."

(p. i)

In response to the PEW Internet & American Life Project's report, I commented elsewhere that:

As impressive as these numbers are, they do not represent all adolescents and certainly not all their literate activities. Neither do they agree completely with findings from studies conducted in the United Kingdom (Livingstone & Bober, 2005) and in the United States with Latino/a youths (Moje, Overby, Tysvaer, & Morris, 2008). Nonetheless, the PEW Report does raise questions about what we may have overlooked, or failed to consider relevant, in young people's penchant for creating online content that could have a bearing on how we teach and research adolescent literacy both now and in the future.

(Alvermann, 2008, p. 9)

That all of this activity is going on in a space largely devoid of direct adult supervision is further indication, in my opinion, that earlier assumptions about hierarchical positioning in sociocultural constructions of adolescents need revisiting—if for no other reason than to document the ways in which changing learners in changing times may eventually alter how we, as teachers and teacher educators, view the expert/novice relationship.

A cyberspatial mindset does not assume that adolescents are the same kind of learners they once were, and it is not only because new communication technologies are changing the environment in which they learn. Instead, as Lankshear and Knobel (2007) explain, such a mindset supports an ethos that is in synch with a certain kind of discourse on adolescence—one that rewards collaboration and participation in disseminating online content. It also supports a learning environment in which young people can experience how authority and expertise are distributed across age, as well as race, class, and gender lines. The new ethos does not ration literacy success, as in the case of the older, scarcity-oriented paradigm where high-stakes tests are typically re-normed once the pass rate rises to an unacceptable level. Nor does it sanction the dominance of the book over other forms of text, such as fan fiction, manga, 'zines, anime, and online gaming in which multiple players perform multiple (and often changing) roles in response to a particular game's multiple (and often changing) storylines.

In virtual learning spaces, literacy practices that require collaboration and participation in disseminating knowledge are but two factors in indexing achievement and communicative competence. Others include the opportunity for dialogue, the gratification that comes with virtually immediate feedback, and the lure of a literacy community in which writers can see how many people visit their sites and ostensibly read what they have written. As Lankshear and Knobel (2007) have pointed out, however, there are still norms for publishing one's work in cyberspace, but they are "less fixed . . . and less controlled by 'centralized' authorities and experts" (p. 14). And, I would add, the texts to which such norms apply are less likely to have been written by individuals who assume all readers will respond in similar fashion. This sense of the uniqueness and importance of one's audience in creating online content extends to identity formation in role-playing cyber communities as well.

Cyberspace is said to be both culture and cultural artifact (e.g., an everyday literacy practice, or a multimodal text) (Bell, 2001; Hine, 2000). Working within this theoretical frame, Thomas (2007) showed how young people "sustain communities, explore, play, resist, and tinker with their identities [while simultaneously engaging] in sophisticated and multiple forms of literacy practices" (p. 671). For example, her research on 30 adolescent girls' choices of avatars in an online role-playing community made visible how the girls were able to manipulate words in socially constructing alternate identities, and how those verbal manipulations were every bit as important as the changes the girls made in their avatars' physical features. Thomas concluded, among other things, that the storylines through which adolescents exist in online spaces are highly social, as are the literacy skills they employ. This finding, in my opinion, stands in sharp contrast to how real-life schooling is conducted, especially in instances where the demarcation between teacher and learner is more firmly drawn.

Challenges to the Sameness Assumption

Adolescents are not a monolithic group; nor are they cut from the same fabric. Although some young people would readily claim citizenship in a literate cyberspace (Thomas, 2008), others would just as soon remain aloof. And still others, largely because of the digital divide, have few options but to remain on the outside. This, despite the claim made by Danah Boyd, a fellow at the Berman Center for Internet and Society at Harvard Law School, that the current generation of young people views online culture as not a separate place "but as just a sort of continuation of their existence" (Boyd cited in Lee, 2008, n.p.) Although Boyd's assumed nexus may be the case for young people who have access to the Internet at home, I doubt seriously that it applies to those who must depend on rationed, or even metered, time on a public computer. Such disparity has tangible effects educationally, for as Jenkins (2006) has cogently pointed out, "What a person can accomplish with an outdated machine in a public library with mandatory filtering software and no opportunity for storage . . . pales in comparison to what [that same individual can accomplish] with a home computer with unfettered Internet access, high bandwidth, and continuous connectivity" (n.p.).

It is also useful to point out, I think, that Web 2.0, while it offers powerful and intellectually engaging spaces in which to create online content, is not the only site of adolescents' text-making activities. Just as adolescents are not all alike, neither are the texts they create all that similar. Young people have demonstrated many times over their ability and versatility in making use of available resources to generate equally engaging offline content. Whether in classrooms (Hinchman & Chandler-Olcott, 2006; Moje, Dillon, & O'Brien, 2000) or in deregulated spaces of learning, such as after-school media clubs and museums (Alvermann & Eakle, 2007), young people generate content that is unique to their own individual set of circumstances.

Changing times (and changing adolescents) can be understood more fully, perhaps, when contextualized historically—at a time in which *sameness* was taken for granted, at least as it applied to the type of learner who was the intended beneficiary of content area reading instruction. More than 25 years ago, in tracing the history of such instruction, Moore, Readence, and Rickelman (1983) identified five issues that occupied educators' thinking at the time; interestingly, none of them pertained directly to students' motivations for learning. The five included:

- locus of instruction, that is, whether or not content area reading skills would be taught separate from the subject matter in which they were embedded
- reading demands of various subjects
- instructional approaches for helping students acquire information
- types of reading material, and
- age level at which content area reading instruction should be the focus.

Also absent, although not surprisingly so, was any mention of technology in relation to learning in the content areas.

However, some 25 years later the link between technology and adolescent literacy instruction is clear, as indicated in a document titled "Toward a Definition of 21st-Century Literacies," which the Executive Committee of the National Council of Teachers of English (NCTE) issued on February 15, 2008:

Literacy has always been a collection of cultural and communicative practices shared among members of particular groups. As society and technology change, so does literacy. Because technology has increased the intensity and complexity of literate environments, the twenty-first century demands that a literate person possess a wide range of abilities and competencies, [thus] many literacies. These literacies—from reading online newspapers to participating in virtual classrooms—are multiple, dynamic, and malleable. As in the past, they are inextricably linked with particular histories, life possibilities and social trajectories of individuals and groups. Twenty-first century readers and writers need to:

- Develop proficiency with the tools of technology
- Build relationships with others to pose and solve problems collaboratively and cross-culturally
- Design and share information for global communities to meet a variety of purposes
- Manage, analyze and synthesize multiple streams of simultaneous information
- Create, critique, analyze, and evaluate multi-media texts
- Attend to the ethical responsibilities required by these complex environments.

(NCTE, 2008, n.p.)

In sum, this NCTE document, which shares many of the same goals outlined in the *Framework for 21st Century Learning*, a publication of the Partnership for 21st Century Skills (2007), is focused clearly on the needs of young people in changing times. Whether they learn in what I have heard loosely referred to as "the bricks versus the clicks"—that is, in traditional school settings versus online spaces—their literacies are historically grounded but ever evolving. Thus, reaching and teaching adolescents in currently changing times will require a healthy respect for their past, present, and future literacies. This is the challenge for literacy teaching and learning in changing times.

References

Alvermann, D.E. (2006). Ned and Kevin: An online discussion that challenges the "not-yet-adult" cultural model. In K. Pahl & J. Rowsell (Eds.), *Travel Notes from the New Literacy Studies* (pp. 39–56). Clevedon, UK: Multilingual Matters.

Alvermann, D.E. (2008). Why bother theorizing adolescents' online literacies for classroom practice and research? *Journal of Adolescent & Adult Literacy, 52,* 8–19.

Alvermann, D.E. (2009). Sociocultural constructions of adolescence and young people's literacies. In L. Christenbury, R. Bomer, & P. Smagorinsky (Eds.), *Handbook of Adolescent Literacy Research* (pp. 14–28). New York: Guilford.

Alvermann, D.E. & Eakle, A.J. (2007). Dissolving learning boundaries: The doing, re-doing, and undoing of school. In D. Thiessen & A. Cook-Sather (Eds.), *International handbook of student experience in elementary and secondary school* (pp. 143–166). Dordrecht, The Netherlands: Springer.

Alvermann, D.E. & Wilson, A.A. (2007). Redefining adolescent literacy instruction. In B.J. Guzzetti (Ed.), *Literacy for the new millennium* (Vol. 3, pp. 3–20). Westport, CT: Praeger/Greenwood Publishing Group.

Appleman, D. (2001, April). *Unintended betrayal: Dilemmas of representation and power in research with youth*. Paper presented at the meeting of the American Educational Research Association, Seattle, WA.

Bartlett, J.B. (1919). *Familiar quotations* (10th ed., Quote No. 7521). Boston, MA: Little, Brown & Co. Retrieved July 22, 2008, from http://www.bartleby.com/100/524.2. html

Bell, D. (2001). *An introduction to cybercultures*. London: Routledge.

Cintron, R. (1991). Reading and writing graffiti: A reading. *The Quarterly Newsletter of the Laboratory of Comparative Human Cognition, 13*, 21–24.

Guzzetti, B.J. & Gamboa, M. (2004). Zines for social justice: Adolescent girls writing on their own. *Reading Research Quarterly, 39*, 408–436.

Hagood, M.C., Patel Stevens, L.P., & Reinking, D. (2002). What do *they* have to teach *us*? Talkin' 'cross generations! In D.E. Alvermann (Ed.), *Adolescents and literacies in a digital world* (pp. 68–83). Mahwah, NJ: Lawrence Erlbaum Associates.

Hall, G.S. (1904). *Adolescence: Its psychology and its relations to physiology, anthropology, sociology, sex, crime, religion, and education* (2 vols.). New York: D. Appleton.

Harper, H.J. & Bean, T.W. (2006). Fallen angels: Finding adolescents and adolescent literacy in a renewed project of democratic citizenship. In D.E. Alvermann, K.A. Hinchman, D.W. Moore, S.F. Phelps, & D.R. Waff (Eds.), *Reconceptualizing the literacies in adolescents' lives* (2nd ed., pp. 147–160). Mahwah, NJ: Lawrence Erlbaum.

Herber, H.L. (1970). *Teaching reading in content areas*. Englewood Cliffs, NJ: Prentice-Hall.

Hinchman, K.A. & Chandler-Olcott, K. (2006). Literacies through youth's eyes: Lessons in representation and hybridity. In D.E. Alvermann, K.A. Hinchman, D.W. Moore, S.F. Phelps, & D.R. Waff (Eds.), *Reconceptualizing the literacies in adolescents' lives* (2nd ed., pp. 231–251). Mahwah, NJ: Lawrence Erlbaum.

Hine, C. (2000). *Virtual ethnography*. London: Sage Publications.

Jenkins, H. (2006). Confronting the challenges of participatory culture: Media education for the 21st century (part two). Retrieved February 20, 2008 from http://henryjenkins.org/2006/10/confronting_the_challenges_of_1.html

Kress, G. (2003). *Literacy in the new media age*. London: Routledge.

Lankshear, C. & Knobel, M. (2007). Sampling the "new" in new literacies. In M. Knobel & C. Lankshear (Eds.), *A new literacies sampler* (pp. 1–24). New York: Peter Lang.

Leander, K.M. (2007). "You won't be needing your laptops today": Wired bodies in the wireless classroom. *A new literacies sampler* (pp. 25–48). New York: Peter Lang.

Lee, F.R. (2008, January 22). The rough-and-tumble online universe traversed by young cybernauts. *The New York Times Online*. Retrieved February 22, 2008 from http://www.nytimes.com/2008/01/22/arts/television/22front.html?pagewanted=all

Lenhart, A., Madden, M., Macgill, A.R., & Smith, A. (2007, December). Teens and social media. *PEW Internet & American Life Project*. Washington, DC: Pew Charitable Trusts. Retrieved July 21, 2008 from http://www.pewinternet.org/PPF/r/230/report_display.asp

Lesko, N. (2001). *Act your age! A cultural construction of adolescence*. New York: Routledge Falmer.

Livingstone, S. & Bober, M. (2005). *UK children go online: Final report of project findings*. Retrieved March 16, 2008, from http://www.children-go-online.net/

Mac an Ghaill, M. (1994). *The making of men: Masculinities, sexualities, and schooling*. Buckingham, UK: Open University Press.

Marsh, J.P. & Stolle, E. (2006). Re/constructing identities: A tale of two adolescents. In

D.E. Alvermann, K.A. Hinchman, D.W. Moore, S.F. Phelps, & D.R. Waff (Eds.), *Reconceptualizing the literacies in adolescents' lives* (2nd ed., pp. 47–63). Mahwah, NJ: Lawrence Erlbaum.

Miller, S.M. & Borowicz, S. (2006). *Why multimodal literacies? Designing digital bridges to 21st century teaching and learning.* GSE Publications & SUNY Press.

Moje, E.B., Dillon, D.R., & O'Brien, D.G. (2000). Reexamining the role of learner, text, and context in secondary literacy. *Journal of Educational Research*, *93*, 165–180.

Moje, E.B., Overby, M., Tysvaer, N., & Morris, K. (2008). The complex world of adolescent literacy: Myths, motivations, and mysteries. *Harvard Educational Review*, *78*, 107–154.

Moore, D.W., Readence, J.E., & Rickelman, R.J. (1983). An historical exploration of content area reading instruction. *Reading Research Quarterly*, *18*, 419–438.

Morgan, W. (1997). *Critical literacy in the classroom.* London: Routledge.

National Council of Teachers of English Executive Committee. (2008). Toward a definition of 21st-century literacies. Retrieved July 20, 2008, from http://www.ncte.org/announce/129117.htm

No Child Left Behind Act of 2001. PL 107–110, 115 Stat.1425, 20 U.S.C. 6301 *et. seq.*

Partnership for 21st Century Skills. (2007). *Framework for 21st-century learning.* Retrieved July 22, 2008, from (http://www.21stcenturyskills.org/index.php?Itemid=120&id=254&option=com_content&task=view

Thomas, A. (2007). *Youth online: Identity and literacy in the digital age.* New York: Peter Lang.

Thomas, A. (2008). Community, culture, and citizenship in cyberspace. In J. Coiro, M. Knobel, C. Lankshear, & D.J. Leu (Eds.), *The handbook of new literacies research* (pp. 671–697). New York: Lawrence Erlbaum Associates.

Vadeboncoeur, J.A. & Stevens, L.P. (Eds.), (2005). *Re/constructing "the adolescent."* New York: Peter Lang.

Chapter 8

The Lamplighters
Pioneers of Adult Literacy Education in the United States

Thomas Sticht
International Consultant in Adult Education

Adult literacy education as a government activity in the United States can be traced back to 1778 when General George Washington and troops were encamped at Valley Forge during the Revolutionary War. Following the drastic winter at Valley Forge, when spring arrived, the health of men improved to the point that a hospital was turned into a camp school and illiterate troops were taught the basics of reading, writing, and arithmetic. The school continued to operate until the end of the Valley Forge encampment (Wildes, 1938, p. 257).

Since these beginnings in the Revolutionary War, adult literacy education has been a recurring activity, sometimes as a sporadic activity based on the work of individuals or charitable organizations, and since 1966, when the federal Adult Education Act was passed, by the federal and state governments of the United States. Today, in addition to an unknown number of charitable programs, some 3,000–4,000 programs operate with state and federal funds across the nation, with enrollments averaging between 2.5 and 3 million adults a year (Sticht, 2002).

Between the programs of Valley Forge and those of today a number of individuals have distinguished themselves as adult literacy educators. Their work went a long way to bringing the present system of adult literacy education into being. Indeed, as will be discussed below, there is evidence that through their activities adult literacy educators helped to preserve the unity of our nation during and after the Civil War, they protected the freedom of our nation during World Wars I and II, and they stimulated the Civil Rights movement of the 1950s and 1960s.

They also introduced many innovations in teaching adult literacy, including the use of functional contexts, newspapers for adult literacy learners, film strips, photo novels, and other tools that today would be included within the concept of multiple *literacies* as discussed in other chapters of this volume.

These are the lamplighters who lit the lamp of literacy for the social and political empowerment of millions of undereducated and disadvantaged adults in the richest and most powerful nation the world has ever known.

Methods of Teaching Reading in Adult Literacy Education

In this chapter I discuss the contributions of six lamplighters of adult literacy upon whose shoulders the present field of adult literacy educators stand. I point out the general approach to reading taken by five of these six pioneers of adult literacy education as I draw upon the work of two other pioneers in the field of reading: E.B. Huey and Paul Klapper.

Shortly after the turn of the century, Huey (1968/1908) published his classic volume, *Psychology and Pedagogy of Reading*. In it he pointed out that "he methods of learning to read that are in common use to-day may be classed as alphabetic, phonic, phonetic, word, sentence, and combination methods" (p. 265). Six years later, Klapper (1914) published a book in which he developed a new classification system for methods of teaching reading. In his system he created two divisions, one for the *synthetic methods* and the other for the *analytic methods*.

As synthetic methods, Klapper included the *alphabetic, phonic,* and *phonetic* methods. In the classification system that Jeanne Chall (1967) developed, these methods were called a *code emphasis* and some contemporary scholars use the term *alphabetics*. These methods consider the teaching of reading as essentially a means of decoding the written text to recover a spoken message which is then comprehended as usual. In these methods parts of speech sounds are associated with the letters of the alphabet, and then with written syllables and then with words in a synthesis of parts into wholes.

As analytic methods, Klapper included the *word basis* and *thought basis*. Under the thought basis method he included the *sentence unit* and the *story unit*. In Jeanne Chall's classification system, the analytic methods would be called *meaning emphasis* and the contemporary term would be *whole language*. These methods consider the teaching of reading as essentially a process of *meaning making* and consider the written text as a guide for the learner to use in constructing the meaning the author has in mind. The meaning-making process serves as an aid to learning to decode the written language in a whole-to-part analysis process.

Throughout the twentieth century, both synthetic and analytic methods of teaching reading have been favored by different adult literacy educators. Among the adult literacy educators favoring the synthetic or *code* methods are Harriet A. Jacobs (2005/1861) and J. Duncan Spaeth (1919). Those favoring the analytic or meaning making methods include Cora Wilson Stewart (1922), Paul Witty (1947, 1943), and Septima Poinsette Clark (1962, 1986).

In addition to illustrating one or the other of the two major subdivisions of reading teaching methods, each of these five educators have introduced innovations in teaching adult literacy beyond their emphasis upon either the code or the meaning methods. Each of these educators is discussed below in chronological order of their work. Before this, however, I introduce the work of Susie King Taylor, whose approach to teaching adults to read I have not found. I introduce her to illustrate the deplorable conditions under which adult literacy educators have too often worked in the past, and which still persist to the present in many cases. These are the lamplighters of adult literacy education in the United States.

Lamplighters of the Civil War Era

Susie King Taylor (1848–1912)

During the Civil War, the Union Army initiated the practice of enlisting freed African-Americans. But it was soon apparent that there were problems in using these men as soldiers. Among other problems, it was difficult for officers to communicate with illiterate former slaves. So promotion and advancement in the Army was difficult for the African-American soldiers. Many of them blamed this situation on their lack of education. In response to these needs, some officers initiated programs of education for the former slaves. One officer, Colonel Thomas W. Higginson of the 33rd U.S. Colored Troops, appointed the chaplain as the regimental teacher. Higginson reportedly saw men at night gathered around a campfire, "spelling slow monosyllables out of a primer, a feat which always commands all ears," and he observed that:

> Their love of the spelling book is perfectly inexhaustible, they stumbling on by themselves, or the blind leading the blind, with the same pathetic patience which they carry into everything. The chaplain is getting up a schoolhouse, where he will soon teach them as regularly as he can. But the alphabet must always be a very incidental business in a camp.
>
> (Cornish, 1952, p. 370)

One of the people whom the chaplain engaged in teaching soldiers of the 33rd to read and write was Susie King Taylor (Blassingame, 1965), who was born a slave in Savannah, Georgia, in 1848. She was raised by her grandmother, who sent her and one of her brothers to the home of a free woman to learn to read and write. As she explained in her 1902 book, "We went every day with our books wrapped in paper to prevent the police or white persons from seeing them" (Taylor, 1902, p. 5). Later, as a freed woman traveling with the 33rd Colored Regiment, Taylor (1902) described some of the macabre conditions under which she taught:

> Outside of the Fort were many skulls lying about; I have often moved them one side out of the path. The comrades and I would have wondered a bit as to which side of the war the men fought on, some said they were the skulls of our boys; some said they were the enemies; but as there was no definite way to know, it was never decided which could lay claim to them. They were a gruesome sight, those fleshless heads and grinning

jaws, but by this time I had become used to worse things and did not feel as I would have earlier in my camp life.

(p.31)

I taught a great many of the comrades in Company E to read and write when they were off duty, nearly all were anxious to learn. My husband taught some also when it was convenient for him. I was very happy to know my efforts were successful in camp also very grateful for the appreciation of my services. I gave my services willingly for four years and three months without receiving a dollar.

(Taylor, 1902, p. 21)

Here Taylor reports her voluntary work in the Civil War, and this use of volunteers in adult literacy education is a mainstay in the programs offered across the nation today. In the programs funded by the U.S. Department of Education and the States, of the 144,169 adult education personnel in Program Year 2004–05, some 51,091, over 35%, were volunteers (U.S. Department of Education, 2005).

Harriet A. Jacobs (1813–1897)

One of the earliest accounts of teaching an adult to read that I have found comes from the work of the slave Harriet A. Jacobs. Even though it was unlawful to teach slaves to read, Jacob's owner's daughter taught her to read and write. In 1861, after she became a free woman, Jacobs wrote a book entitled, "Incidents in the life of a slave girl written by herself" (Jacobs, 2005/1861). In it she tells the story of how she helped an older black man, a slave like her, learn to read. She said:

I knew an old black man, whose piety and childlike trust in God were beautiful to witness. At fifty-three years old he joined the Baptist church. He had a most earnest desire to learn to read. He thought he should know how to serve God better if he could only read the Bible. He came to me, and begged me to teach him. . . . I asked him if he didn't know it was contrary to law; and that slaves were whipped and imprisoned for teaching each other to read. This brought the tears into his eyes. "Don't be troubled, Uncle Fred," said I. "I have no thoughts of refusing to teach you. I only told you of the law, that you might know the danger, and be on your guard." . . . I taught him his A, B, C. Considering his age, his progress was astonishing. As soon as he could spell in two syllables he wanted to spell out words in the Bible. The happy smile that illuminated his face put joy into my heart. After spelling out a few words he paused, and said, "Honey, it 'pears when I can read dis good book I shall be nearer to God. White man is got all de sense. He can larn easy. It ain't easy for ole black man like me. I only want to read dis book, dat I may know how to live; den I hab no fear 'bout dying." I tried to encourage him by speaking of the rapid progress he had made. "Hab patience, child," he replied. "I larns slow." At the end of six months he had read through the New Testament, and could find any text in it.

(Jacobs, 2005, pp. 83–84)

Following the Civil War, after achieving her freedom, Jacobs taught school for former slaves in the Freedmen's Schools. These schools were set up after the Civil War when the U.S. Congress created the Bureau of Refugees, Freedmen, and Abandoned Lands as the primary agency for reconstruction (Morris, 1981). In the Freedmen's Schools it was not unusual for both children and their parents to be taught reading, writing, spelling, and arithmetic in the same classroom at the same time. This was an early form of *family literacy* education.

Special textbooks were developed for the Freedmen's Schools that emphasized practical affairs of life and the instilling of positive values. For instance, a lesson from *The Freedman's Second Reader*, published by the Boston wing of the American Tract Society in 1865, first presents a list of words for sight reading instruction, but with some attention to phonics (e.g., What letter is silent in hoe?). It shows a drawing of an African-American family gathered around a table listening while the father reads. Beneath the drawing the text says:

The Freedman's Home

See this home! How neat, how warm,
how full of cheer it looks! It seems as
if the sun shone in there all the day long.
But it takes more that the light of the sun
to make a home bright all the time. Do
you know what it is? It is love.

(Morris, 1981, p. 9)

Developing positive self-image and promoting religious faith was also a purpose of many of the Freedmen's Schools educators. As an example of how self-concept development and religious beliefs were approached, *The Freedman's Third Reader* includes a story about the African-American poet Phyllis Wheatley. Like the example above, the lesson begins with a list of sight words. Then below that is a drawing of Phyllis Wheatley and this is followed by a brief story that tells how Wheatley was brought to the United States from Africa in 1761, who bought her as a slave, and her appearance when purchased. The story concludes:

The life of Phillis Wheatley gives most interesting proof of the power of talents and virtues, crowned with "the pearl of great price,"—the love of

Christ,—to raise one from the lowest position to the notice and the esteem of the wise and good.

The work of Harriet Jacobs both before the Civil War in teaching the slave Uncle Fred and after the Civil War teaching former slaves in the Freedmen's Schools illustrates two aspects of teaching reading with adults during the nineteenth century. First, Jacob's used what she called the "A, B, C" method, which others have referred to as the *alphabetic* method. Second, with Uncle Fred who wanted to learn to read the Bible, Jacobs used the Bible as the functional context for teaching reading. This illustrates the practice of using materials that are relevant to the needs and desires of adult learners when teaching them literacy. This was illustrated again in the use of specially written Freedman's readers which oriented their lessons to the types of things that the authors thought would be of interest and relevance to former slaves, both children and adults, and they included illustrations with African-American children and adults in them. This use of materials of relevance to and with which adults can relate is an early form of what I call *functional context education* in teaching adults to read.

Lamplighters of the World Wars I and II

Cora Wilson Stewart (1875–1958)

A leading pioneer of adult literacy education, Cora Wilson Stewart, Superintendent of Instruction in Rowan County, Kentucky, initiated the first campaign in the nation aimed specifically at eradicating adult illiteracy in a given area. She mobilized a group of teachers who volunteered to teach adults to read and write. The adults would be taught in the same schools as used by children but at night, after the children went home. But because there were no street lights in the hills and hollows of Rowan County in those days, classes could only be held on moonlit nights, when adults could see their way to school. For this reason, the literacy program became known as the Moonlight Schools of Kentucky, and they operated from 1911 to the 1930s (Nelms, 1997).

Striking out in a crusade against adult illiteracy in Rowan County, Kentucky, Stewart later went on to convince President Hoover to create the first National Advisory Committee on Illiteracy, she initiated a National Illiteracy Crusade, chaired for five times the Illiteracy Section of the international World Conference of Education Associations, spoke before the national Democratic Party convention in 1920, spoke at numerous meetings across the United States, reached hundreds of thousands of listeners through radio broadcasts, and inspired numerous other states to initiate campaigns to combat adult illiteracy (Nelms, 1997).

Starting the Moonlight Schools for adult illiterates was the first of a long list of innovations for adult literacy education that Stewart introduced, including the first newspaper designed especially for adult literacy students, called the

Rowan County Messenger, the first reading series for rural adults comprising three *Country Life Readers*; the *Soldier's First Book* used during World War I, and the *Mother's First Book: A First Reader for Home Women*.

Stewart was devoted to the analytic, meaning making, method of teaching reading. This is clearly indicated in the *Soldier's First Book*. In the "Instructions to Teachers" at the front of the book, she states:

> The reading lessons in this book are to be taught by the word and sentence method combined. It is as easy to teach "I go" as it is to teach I "g" "o"— "go". The first lesson should be learned at one recitation. After teaching the pupil the sentence, drill him on words by pointing out and having him point out each word as many times as it occurs in the lesson, and by other drills.
> (Stewart, 1917, p. 1)

Stewart was the first to produce reading materials especially for adults learning to read in the context of country living. In her approach to teaching adult literacy, she explicitly recognized the importance of not using materials for adults that were designed for children. She prepared a special newspaper, the *Rowan County Messenger*, to keep new learners up to date with local and national events. She wrote three *Country Readers* with contents that were related directly to the lives of adults outside the classroom. All of her materials integrated the teaching of literacy with the teaching of important knowledge content in farming, healthy living, civics, home economics, financial management, parenting, and other functional contexts. As Stewart (1922) stated, ". . . each lesson accomplished a double purpose, the primary one of teaching the pupil to read, and at the same time that of imparting instruction in the things that vitally affected him (sic) in his daily life" (p. 71). This use of functional context education helped adults learn to read *real life* materials and transfer their new learning to contexts outside the classroom.

Cora Wilson Stewart was profoundly aware of the importance that learning to sign their names had for the illiterate adults of the Moonlight Schools. It was their means of escaping the stigma and humiliation of making their mark. To teach adults to write their names she introduced the practice of taking a soft sheet of ink blotting paper and carving the person's name in it. Students then traced over the indented name until they could write it without any guide from the blotter paper. With her understanding of the importance of being able to write one's name, it is no surprise that in her older age, and blind in both eyes, Stewart clung to the power of the pen and insisted on signing her own name on letters and important documents up to the end of her life. Willie Nelms, Stewart's biographer, wrote:

> The elderly lady gently took the letter that she had just dictated. Because she was blind, she had to be shown where to begin her signature. Her hands trembled so that her writing, which had been so graceful earlier in life,

seemed shaky and uneven. Determined to complete the task, she doggedly persevered; after carefully completing the signature, she rested her pen.

(Nelms, 1997, p. 3)

Only a few years later, in December 1958, blind and infirm, Cora Wilson Stewart, founder of the Moonlight Schools of Kentucky "for the emancipation of adult illiterates," passed away. Her death came just shy of half a century after she had started the Moonlight Schools, which historian Wanda Dauksza Cook (1977) said ". . . might well be classified as the official beginning of [adult] literacy education in the United States" (p. 13).

J. Duncan Spaeth (1868–1954)

During World War I, it was discovered that large numbers of men being called for military service were illiterate, or of very limited literacy, or non-English speaking. Because of this, the teaching of English language, reading, and writing became a necessary element of military training. As mentioned above, Cora Wilson Stewart quickly moved to help the illiterate young men being called to military service to learn to read and write and wrote the *Soldier's First Book* (Stewart, 1917).

In World War I, the task of delivering education and morale services to military personnel fell to the Young Men's Christian Association (YMCA). To deliver adult literacy education, one of the key people that the YMCA engaged was John Duncan Spaeth, a Professor of English at Princeton University. He was assigned to be the Educational Director of the YMCA's educational efforts at Camp Wheeler, Georgia and Camp Jackson, South Carolina. In 1918, the Southwestern Department of the National War Work Department of the YMCA in Atlanta, Georgia published the *Camp Reader for American Soldiers*, written by Spaeth. In this book Spaeth wrote:

> The Country Life Readers of Mrs. Cora Wilson Stewart have furnished valuable suggestions as to form of presentation, and the writer wishes to acknowledge the debt that all who have worked in the Southern camps owe to Mrs. Stewart.
>
> (Spaeth, 1918, p. 8)

But in a revised edition (Spaeth, 1919) there was no recognition of Stewart's influence. In fact, Spaeth rejected the analytic method of teaching reading that Stewart favored and instead became the first person to prepare an extensive theoretical introduction to the synthetic, phonics method of teaching literacy written especially for teachers of adults.

In the preface to the 1918 edition of the *Camp Reader*, Spaeth devoted just three paragraphs to introducing the principles underlying the lessons and explained that:

The "Camp Reader for American Soldiers" is more than a mere reader. It combines exercises in reading, writing, phonics, and spelling in each lesson. The essence of the method here advocated lies in the simultaneous acquisition of the ability to read words, to recognize and differentiate articulate sounds and sound groups, to associate them with visual symbols, and to write these symbols. The three types of association must go hand in hand, and it is therefore essential that in each hour part of the time be devoted to reading, part to phonic drill, and part to exercises in writing.

In the 1919 revision of the *Camp Reader*, Spaeth expanded his discussion of the instructional principles of the lessons from three paragraphs to six pages. In these pages, he produced the first teacher training materials I have found for adult literacy educators, which discussed relationships among the four communication processes of listening, speaking, reading, and writing, and he provided an explanation of the phonetic system of reading (phonics) and its relevance to writing. Throughout the book, extensive footnotes further instruct the teacher in the teaching of phonics, and extensive drills are provided on decoding lists of words. In this book, Spaeth showed clearly that he was a proponent of the methods of teaching reading and writing that rely heavily upon the understanding of the written language as a substitution code for the spoken language, and he advised considerable attention to the teaching of the decoding and encoding of the written language through phonics. He also presented in an appendix the first teacher training materials I have found for teaching literacy and English as a second language for foreign-speaking adult students. In these lessons, instruction moves from listening and speaking to reading and writing.

The first lesson in the 1919 revision of the *Camp Reader for American Soldiers* included a list of sight words at the top of the page: I, yes, A mer I can, am, an, man. These were followed by six sentences:

1   I am an American.
2   Am I an American?
3   Yes, I am an American.
4   I am a man.
5   Am I a man?
6   Yes, I am a man.

These sentences were followed by a *sound drill* showing how to pronounce: am (a m), (a), man (m an), (an), and (a). The page ends with 16 sentences of a "Note to Teacher" that discusses how to use the sound drill. Clearly this places Spaeth well within the category of those espousing the synthetic, phonics approach to teaching reading.

Though he eschewed the analytic method of teaching reading favored by

Stewart, Spaeth used the same functional context education approach in the *Camp Reader for American Soldiers* as used by Stewart in the *Country Life Readers* and the *Soldier's First Book*. Both versions of Spaeth's *Camp Reader for American Soldiers* were illustrated with pictures of Army situations with which men could identify, it included much of the vocabulary and concepts used in training in soldiering that the Army expected new recruits to learn, and it provided spiritual and morale-building readings as well.

Paul A. Witty (1898–1976)

During World War II, just as in World War I, the armed services once again faced the need to utilize hundreds of thousands of men who were illiterate or poorly literate. Paul Andrew Witty, with an M.A. (1923) and Ph.D. (1931) from Columbia University in Psychology, specialized in understanding the process of learning to read and in developing methods for helping students who were having difficulties in learning to read. With this background, he was called upon to serve as an education officer in the War Department. In his work for the Army's Special Training Units for literacy instruction, Witty directed the production of numerous adult literacy education materials which today would be known as developing multiple literacies (Witty, 1947; Witty & Goldberg, 1943).

- He directed the production of the first film media materials for teaching adults to read, including a 1943 film strip entitled *Meet Private Pete*, which introduced 40 sight words. In this film strip, soldiers were introduced to Private Pete, a fictional fellow member of a Special Training Unit who was also learning reading, writing, and arithmetic. The idea was that soldiers would be able to identify with Private Pete and understand what they were reading about him because they shared common experiences, such as living in the camp, sleeping in the barracks, eating in the mess hall, and so forth. Witty was apparently the first adult literacy educator to use this approach of trying to motivate adults learning to read by providing a fictional counterpart with whom they could identify.
- In May 1943 the War Department published TM 21–500, entitled the *Army Reader*. In this book, which was produced under Witty's direction, soldiers in the Army's Special Training Units for literacy instruction once again read about Private Pete just as they had done earlier in working with the film strip. In the *Army Reader* the fictional Private Pete did the kinds of things that the real soldiers did in their daily lives in camp, just as in the film strips.
- The first *instructional systems* approach to assessing progress in learning to read by adult learners was introduced by Witty in the *Army Reader* by the use of pre- and post-unit tests for each part of the four-part manual to

determine if the soldier was ready to progress from one part to the next, more difficult part of the reading program.

- Like Cora Wilson Stewart's special newspaper, the *Rowan County Messenger* for country folk learning to read, a special newspaper called *Our War* was produced for the men in the literacy programs of World War II. In another innovation, a comic strip was incorporated into the newspaper featuring Private Pete and a buddy, Daffy, in various activities that were frequently aligned with major holidays such as Thanksgiving, Christmas, New Year's Day, Valentine's Day and so forth.

- In yet another innovation, Witty introduced the first photo novel for teaching adults to read, which used real people as models for Private Pete, Daffy, and other fictional soldiers. These characters were portrayed in materials for soldiers who were getting ready to be discharged from the Army who had missed entry literacy education in the Special Training Units.

Witty was a follower of the meaning emphasis approach to teaching reading, known at the time as the *word* method. In this method students first developed readiness to read by discussing illustrations from the film strips or readers. Then they learned a basic store of sight words used in the readiness training. Then they moved on to simple sentences made up of the sight words. In this approach, phonics instruction was postponed until the student could do quite a bit of reading based upon discussion and whole word recognition training. Witty continued his work on reading teaching following World War II and is a deceased member of the Reading Hall of Fame.

Though not much is known to me about those who served as teachers in the Special Training Units for literacy learners, I made a rough estimate of the numbers of teachers involved based on data for various Army camps given in Goldberg (1951) and came up with a figure of some 5,291 teachers in the Special Training Units. Interestingly, one of these teachers was the famous Cuban musician and actor Desi Arnaz, the real-life and TV husband of Lucile Ball in the TV series *I Love Lucy*. He was drafted in May 1943. But he suffered a torn knee cartilage, so instead of reporting to a regular camp for training, he was assigned as a *limited service* soldier to one of the Special Training Units where illiterate enlisted men were assigned. In his autobiography he states:

> I wound up in another camp as an instructor of illiterates. I was there for about six months. I didn't know how many illiterates were drafted into the Army. I really didn't think there were that many illiterates in the whole country.
>
> (Arnaz, 1976, p. 146)

But through the endeavors of Arnaz and thousands of other teachers, over a quarter million illiterate, semi-literate, and non-English-speaking men were taught the rudiments of the English language and literacy (Goldberg, 1951).

Lamplighter of the Civil Rights Movement

Septima Poinsette Clark (1898–1987)

Septima Poinsette Clark, the great civil rights teacher from the Highlander Folk School in Tennessee, was an innovator in teaching adult reading and writing within the functional context of the civil rights movement to free African-Americans from the oppression of those wanting to deny them full citizenship. In this regard, she predated the Brazilian educator, Paulo Freire, in developing a *pedagogy of the oppressed* (Freire, 1970). Clark followed the analytic, meaning making method in teaching word recognition and followed functional context education methods in using real-life materials for teaching adults to read (Clark, 1986). On January 7, 1957, Clark and her teachers started the first Citizenship School serving adult African-Americans on Johns Island in South Carolina. Clark (1962) recalled that when the teachers asked the students what they wanted to learn, the answer was that, "First, they wanted to learn how to write their names. That was a matter of pride as well as practical need" (p. 147).

In teaching students to write their names, Clark used what she said was the *kinesthetic* method, which she had learned from Wil Lou Gray, State Super-intendent of Adult Education in South Carolina in the middle of the twentieth century. Gray was familiar with the work of Cora Wilson Stewart, and had used Stewart's *Country Life Readers* in South Carolina. It seems likely that she had learned the method of teaching adults to write their name from Stewart and used it as part of an anti-illiteracy campaign across South Carolina called the "Sign-Your-Own-Name" campaign in one county and "I'll Write My Own Name" campaign elsewhere in the state. The Write-Your-Name Crusade aimed to get adults into literacy programs to learn to sign their names when voting and in other important situations.

According to Ayres (1988), Gray recommended to teachers that they ". . . use a thorn or hairpin to trace letters on copy papers prepared so students could practice at home" (p. 101). Ayres suggests that this may have been an early use of what she calls the kinesthetic method of teaching reading and writing and that Gray may have been the first proponent of this method for adults. But the fact that Gray was acquainted with Stewart, her methods, and books suggests that Gray may have learned the method from Stewart. Following Gray's lead, Clark instructed teachers to write students' names on cardboard. Then, according to Clark (1962):

> What the student does is trace with his pencil over and over his signature until he gets the feel of writing his name. I suppose his fingers memorize it

by doing it over and over; he gets into the habit by repeating the tracing time after time.

(p. 148)

She went on to say:

And perhaps the single greatest thing it accomplishes is the enabling of a man to raise his head a little higher; knowing how to sign their names, many of those men and women told me after they had learned, made them FEEL different. Suddenly they had become a part of the community; they were on their way toward first-class citizenship.

(p. 149)

Brown-Nagin (1999) reported that:

The most critical elements of the citizenship program were the curricula Clark used and the type of teachers she chose to lead the citizenship effort. In regard to curricula, the guiding principle was that it was to be functional: It was to be determined by what students wanted to know and what pragmatism dictated they needed to know about the civic system . . . [adult learners] would prepare for citizenship and voting using curricula logically related to their needs. They learned to read using state and federal constitutions, codes of law, sample ballots, and other legal documents as "texts." . . . at each step, the students were asked to participate in the process, through demonstrative classes, role-playing and small group sessions where they formulated their own plans and educational programs . . . citizenship school instructors taught practical matters such as how to: make purchases from mail order catalogues; utilize bank accounts; compute income tax; utilize social security and disability benefits; and take care of the many other affairs involved in functional adulthood.

(p. 94)

Working with the Southern Christian Leadership Conference (SCLC) and other civil rights groups from 1962 to 1966, Clark led the Voter Registration Project, which subsequently prepared 10,000 teachers for citizenship schools where they taught literacy within the functional context of voter registration, and eventually led some 700,000 African-Americans to vote. By the time Clark retired from her SCLC work in 1970, over a million African-Americans had registered to vote in the south (Clark, 1986, p. 70). Speaking of a cleaning woman who asked to be taught to read and write in the Citizenship School on Johns Island, South Carolina, Clark (1962) wrote:

This woman is but one of those whose stories I could tell. One will never be able, I maintain, to measure or even to approximate the good that this work among the adult illiterates on this one island has accomplished. How can anybody estimate the worth of pride achieved, hope accomplished, faith affirmed, citizenship won? These are intangible things but real nevertheless, solid and of inestimable value.

(p. 154)

Conclusion

It is astonishing to realize that across half a century, Cora Wilson Stewart, Wil Lou Gray, and Septima Poinsette Clark all used the same simple instructional technique to teach adults to write their names, that this technique was used by Clark in the development of the citizenship schools of the Southern Christian Leadership Conference, and this technique eventually brought over a million African-Americans to vote in the South. Amazingly, a simple technique used by adult literacy educators for teaching adults to write their names was instrumental in forging the civil rights movement, which has empowered millions more Americans with a voice in the governance of their nation.

From 1966 to the present, annual enrollments in the adult literacy education programs sponsored by the Adult Education Act of 1966 grew from some 375,000 in 1966 to around 3.5 million at the turn of the millennium (Sticht, 2002). During this time, hundreds of thousands of teachers, many working as unpaid volunteers, have brought over 100 million adults from the dim light of low literacy to a brighter light of improved literacy, increased belief in their self-worth, greater ability to read with their children, and a greater ability to find and hold a better job. To this day, tens of thousands of lamplighters are still at work in adult literacy education in the United States of America.

References

Arnaz, D. (1976). *A book*. New York: William Morrow.

Ayres, D. (1988). *Let my people learn: The biography of Dr. Wil Lou Gray*. Greenwood, SC: Attic Press.

Blassingame, J. (1965). The Union army as an educational institution for negroes, 1862–1865. *Journal of Negro Education*, 34: 152–159.

Brown-Nagin, T. (1999). The transformation of a social movement into law? The SCLC and NAACP's campaigns for civil rights reconsidered in light of the educational activism of Septima Clark. *Women's History Review*, *8*, 81–138.

Chall, J. (1967). *Learning to read: The great debate*. New York: McGraw-Hill.

Clark, S. (1962). *Echo in my soul*. New York: E.P. Dutton & Co.

Clark, S. (1986). *Ready from within: Septima Clark and the civil rights movement*. Navarro, CA: Wild Trees Press.

Cook, W. (1977). *Adult literacy education in the United States*. Newark, DE: International Reading Association.

Cornish, D. (1952). The Union army as a school for negros. *Journal of Negro History*, 37: 368–382.

Freire, P. (1970). *Pedagogy of the oppressed.* New York: The Seabury Press.

Goldberg, S. (1951). *Army training of illiterates in World War II.* New York: Teachers College, Columbia University.

Huey, E.B. (1968/1908). *Psychology and pedagogy of reading.* Boston, MA: MIT Press.

Jacobs, H. (2005/1861). *Incidents in the life of a slave girl: Written by herself.* New York: Barnes & Noble Classics.

Klapper, P. (1914). *Teaching children to read.* New York: D. Appleton & Co.

Lerner, G. (Ed.) (1972). *Black women in white America: A documentary history.* New York: Pantheon Books-Random House.

Morris, R. (1981). *Reading, 'riting, and reconstruction: The education of freedmen in the South, 1861–1870.* Chicago, IL: The University of Chicago Press.

Nelms, W. (1997). *Cora Wilson Stewart: Crusader against illiteracy.* London: McFarland & Company.

Spaeth, J. (1918). *Camp reader for American soldiers.* Atlanta, GA: National War Work Council, Y.M.C.A.

Spaeth, J. (1919). *Camp reader for American soldiers.* New York: The International Committee of Young Men's Christian Association.

Stewart, C. (1915). *Country Life Readers: First Book.* Atlanta, GA: B.F. Johnson Publishing Co. (pp. 36–37).

Stewart, C. (1917). *Soldier's first book.* Kentucky Illiteracy Commission.

Stewart, C. (1922). *Moonlight schools for the emancipation of adult illiterates.* New York: E.P. Dutton & Co.

Sticht, T. (2002). The rise of the adult education and literacy system in the United States: 1600–2000. In J. Comings, B. Garner, & C. Smith (Eds.), *Annual review of adult learning and literacy. Vol. 3.* (pp. 10–43). San Francisco, CA: Jossey-Bass.

Taylor, S. (1902). *Reminiscences of my life in camp with the 33rd U.S. Colored Troops, Late 1st South Carolina Volunteers.* Downloaded February 10, 2008 at http://www.digilib.nypl.org/dynaweb/digs/wwm97267/@Generic_BookView

U.S. Department of Education (2005). *State-administered adult education program: Program year 2004–2005 personnel.* Washington, DC: Office of Adult Education and Literacy.

Wildes, H. (1938). *Valley Forge.* New York: The Macmillan Co.

Witty, P. (1947, June). Principles of learning derived from the results of the Army's program for illiterate and non-English-speaking men. *Adult Education Bulletin, XI,* 131–136.

Witty, P. & Goldberg, S. (1943, December). The Army's training program for illiterate, non-English-speaking, and educationally retarded men. *The Elementary English Review, 20,* 306–311.

Part III

Foundational Issues in the Teaching of Reading

Chapter 9

Revisiting the Concept of "Natural Learning"

Brian Cambourne
University of Wollongong, Australia

For most of my professional life, the concept of *natural learning* has intrigued me. For most of this time it seems to have been part of the education background, seemingly regarded by the profession as a somewhat romantic nonrigorous, nonscientific notion which should not be taken too seriously (Collier & Iran-Nejad, 1995). When asked to contribute a chapter for this volume, I considered it timely to ask these questions.

1   Is natural learning a valid concept for the twenty-first century?
2   If so, what are its basic defining theoretical components?
3   What (if any) would be the pedagogical implications of such a theory?

Is Natural Learning a Valid Concept for the Twenty-first Century?

In terms of *face*[1] validity the answer is simple. When Googled, the term generates 133 MILLION links! This strongly suggests a general consensus that something called natural learning exists. In terms of *construct* validity,[2] the answer is not so simple. Despite the interest reflected by 133,000,000 links on the web, a close analysis indicates natural learning means different things to different people. There is an eclectic range of terms and/or pedagogies associated with the concept. Wikipedia links natural learning with this range of synonyms.

> . . . informal learning, incidental learning, child-led learning, discovery learning, delight-led learning, child-directed learning, home schooling, home education, self-directed learning, non-traditional learning, alternate-education, free-school (spelled "free-skool" to make the point), open learning, Summerhill-model, de-schooling, TCS (Taking-Children Seriously),

1 In the context of this chapter, *face validity* means "a general consensus that the concept exists".
2 In the context of this chapter *construct validity* means there is a theoretically consistent operationalization of the concept which adequately represents it.

non-coercive schooling, experiential education, brain-based learning, anarchic-schooling.

(Wikipedia, 2008)

These synonyms suggest a divergent range of theoretically inconsistent operational definitions for natural learning. For construct validity to be established it needs to be shown that the concept can be operationally defined in theoretically consistent ways. One way of doing this is to explore, at a deeper level, the various discourses associated with natural learning.[3]

Discourse Associated with the Concept Natural Learning

I found three categories of discourse within the literature of natural learning:

- discourse which contrasts *inside school* and *outside school* learning
- discourse which advocates learning to talk as a model for pedagogy
- the discourse of *brain-based learning/education.*

Discourses Contrasting Inside School and Outside School Learning

This category frames natural learning as the contrast between formal, academic learning which takes place *inside* traditional schools and the complex learning observed *outside* schools. Collier and Iran-Nejad capture the essence of this discourse thus: "Natural Learning represents the wealth of learning that occurs outside of school, especially during the years before formal instruction begins." They contrast this with *academic learning*, which "takes place within the formal learning environment of today's schools" (Collier & Iran-Nejad, 1995, p. (i) Abstract). While the terminology they use may be slightly different, this way of framing natural learning has wide currency.

Gardner (1991) for example contrasts "intuitive learning" with "scholastic learning" and describes how very young children "who develop complex theories of the universe or intricate theories of the mind, often experience the greatest difficulties upon entry to their school" (Gardner, 1991, p. 2). Resnick (1987) contrasts "learning in school" with "learning outside of school". She goes on to specify four distinct categories of difference between *in-school* and *outside-school* learning:

- individual cognition *in school* versus shared cognition *outside school*
- pure mentation *in school* versus tool manipulation *outside school*

---

3 By *discourses* I mean the way members of discourse communities communicate, think about, behave toward, feel about, and use language about certain topics and/or domains of interest.

- symbol manipulation *in school* versus contextualized reasoning *outside school*
- generalized learning *in school* versus situation-specific competencies *outside school*.

Schank and Cleary (1995) introduce another minor variation on this theme. They contrast "formal education" with "childhood learning" (Schank & Cleary, 1995), describing how:

> Children are little learning machines. Before they ever reach school, they manage to progress from newborns with innate abilities and minimal knowledge to children with an enormous amount of knowledge about the physical, social, and mental worlds in which they live. They accomplish this feat without classrooms, lessons, curricula, examinations, or grades. They are set up for learning before they enter this world.
>
> (Schank & Cleary, 1995, p. 45)

Yet another variation emerges from the *home school (ing)*, *home education*, *deschooling* movement(s). While these also contrast *in- school* learning with *outside-school* learning, the motivation seems different. Advocates of home schooling want to replace school learning with learning as a member of a loving family unit. Unlike Gardner (1991), Schank & Cleary (1995), and Resnick (1987), who argue that school learning should change to accommodate the amazing learning potential of young children, advocates of home schooling don't agree. Instead, while implicitly acknowledging that the human species is a learning species, they seem to be more concerned with the potential of compulsory schooling to damage their children, citing John Holt's claim that:

> . . . the human animal is a learning animal; we like to learn; we are good at it; we don't need to be shown how or made to do it. What kills the processes are the people interfering with it or trying to regulate it or control it.
>
> (Holt, 1980, cited by Baumgartner, 1980)

James Gee's work into the learning principles built into the architecture of bestselling video games (Gee, 2003) offers a slightly different perspective between in-school and out-of-school learning. Gee compares in-school learning with a special case of outside-school learning, i.e., bestselling video games. After describing how he learned to play a complex, bestselling video game, he poses this rhetorical question and proceeds to answer it: "How in heaven's name do they sell so many of these games when they are so long and hard?" His response is revealing:

> So here we have something that is long, hard, and challenging. However you cannot play a game if you cannot learn it. If no one plays a game then

it does not sell, and the company that makes it goes broke. Of course designers could keep making the games shorter and simpler to facilitate learning. That's often what schools do. But no, in this case, game designers keep making the games longer and more challenging (and introduce new things in new ones), and still manage to get them learned. How? If you think about it you see a Darwinian sort of thing going on here. If a game for whatever reason, has good principles of learning built into its design— that is if it facilitates, it gets played and can sell lots of copies.

(Gee, 2003, p. 6)

Unlike Gardner (1991), Schank and Cleary (1995), and Collier and Iran-Nejad (1995), Gee seems to place more emphasis on something he calls *the principles of learning* built into the context of the task (the game's architecture) and less on the natural learning potential of the human species. Instead of explicitly arguing (as they do) that out-of-school learning works better because it meshes with the way the human nervous system functions, he seems content to argue that there is a "theory of human learning" comprising 36 principles which designers of bestselling video games have discovered, and which the educators need to discover and apply to classrooms (Gee, 2003).

What Does the Discourse of "Inside/Outside School" Reveal about the Construct Validity of Natural Learning?

Not much. The examples discussed in this category loosely define natural learning as any learning which occurs "outside of a traditional, formal school setting." Furthermore, although all seem to agree that natural learning is an inbuilt characteristic of the human species, the definitional emphasis seems to be on location. Despite this emphasis, the variation between the examples suggests that a simple binary choice doesn't help identify an internally consistent operationalization of natural learning.

That more defining criteria than just *in school/out of school* are required is signaled in each of the exemplars reviewed. Gardner (1991) and Schank and Cleary (1995) explicitly add *developmental stage of learner* to the mix. Resnick (1987) thinks that it's her *four contrasting forms of cognition* inside and outside traditional schools which differentiates natural learning from what happens in traditional classrooms (Resnick, 1987). Gee's example of popular computer games (Gee, 2003) further suggests that more criteria are needed to achieve an adequate operational definition. A close reading of Gee's examples indicates that location is irrelevant. For Gee, natural learning is best defined in terms of principles embedded in the architecture of popular computer games. By implication these should be in close alignment with the pedagogical structures and processes applied in classrooms. Finally the home school movement seems to regard the emotional relationships between teacher and learner more significant than location.

Though they view natural learning from quite different assumptive para-meters and criteria, Schank and Cleary (1995), Gee (2003), Gardner (1991), and Resnick (1987) each imply that traditional learning practices in schools should at least be modeled on, and at best be replaced by, the kinds of natural learning which they describe. The different mixes of location and extra defining criteria used by each to explicate their particular versions of natural learning suggest a constructivist epistemology underpins their views of natural learning. Without explicitly mentioning *constructivism* they imply that differences between the learning (and therefore the pedagogy) which occur inside and outside formal school settings is akin to the differences between a constructivist and objectivist epistemology.

The home school/deschooling movement has little in common with the other exemplars in this category except the location of the learning. Its advo-cates appear to have no qualms with the model(s) of learning which is/are used in traditional formal schools. Rather their main concern seems to be who does the teaching.

Discourses Which Advocate Learning to Talk as a Model for Pedagogy

This category is *not* substantially different from the first. Learning to talk is typically completed before formal schooling begins. From this perspective it is merely another form of learning that occurs outside the context and pedag-ogical climate of formal schooling. Despite this I consider it a different category of discourse, mainly because of the diversity of perspectives adopted by those who have advocated learning to talk as *the* model for natural learning. I've identified at least three variations on this theme in the literature:

- learning to talk as the model for a pedagogy of reading
- learning to talk as the model for a pedagogy of learning a second language
- learning to talk as the model for pedagogy per se.

Learning to Talk as the Model for a Pedagogy of Reading

In 1976 Goodman and Goodman were among the first modern reading edu-cators to suggest that learning to talk and learning to read were analogous. They argued that psycholinguistic theory which informed their research and theory building strongly indicated that the oral and written versions of a lan-guage were merely "parallel versions of the same thing, namely language" (Goodman & Goodman, 1976). Their psycholinguistic theory emerged from research into speech perception in the 1960s. This clearly showed that the perception of sounds in human speech was contingent upon the human mind first working out the meaning of that speech (Miller & Isard, 1963; Miller, Heise, & Lichten, 1951; Obusek & Warren, 1973; Pollack & Pickett,

1964; Wanner, 1973; Warren, 1970; Warren & Obusek, 1971; Warren & Warren, 1970).

In the 1960s these results were considered counterintuitive. In a review of the literature of the time Wanner commented:

> In the past twenty years of psycholinguistic investigation into what the listener does when he (sic) understands a sentence, we have come to understand that there is no simple correlation between the properties of the acoustic stimulus and the listener's interpretation of the sentence. The listener makes a contribution which makes the problem of comprehension both difficult and interesting.
>
> (Wanner, 1973, p. 180)

Wanner concluded that the end result of the experimental results he'd reviewed showed clearly that comprehension of speech had a significant "inside-out" component and that such:

> . . . inside-out processing posed a thorny problem for the field because it served to rule out any model of comprehension based exclusively on outside-in mechanisms . . . we know we cannot build a satisfactory model of comprehension out of simple stimulus response connections in which a given stimulus uniformly triggers an invariant response.
>
> (Wanner, 1973, p. 181)

Given that the Goodmans' miscue research was converging to similar conclusions for written language, their assertion that the oral and written forms of language were merely "parallel versions of the same thing" made sense. Their miscue research revealed a written language analogue of the "thorny problem" Wanner had identified for oral language. Like Wanner, the Goodmans' conclusions from their miscue research strongly suggested that the human mind sought meaning before it sought anything else. If this was true it meant that once the different signals (sound or light) got through the different receptor organs (ears or eyes), they were processed in the same way by the same neural machinery.

It's not such a huge intellectual jump to assert that if these two forms of language are, "parallel versions of the same thing" then the same conditions that made learning the oral form of one's native language so successful could (and should) be applied to learning to control the written version of this language.

Learning to Talk as the Model for a Pedagogy of Learning a Second Language

Stephen Krashen's work exemplifies the discourse associated with natural learning in the second language learning field. While he strongly supports the

Goodmans' assertions about the relationship between learning to talk and learning to read, it is important to understand that Krashen came to this view via his research into second language teaching and learning (Krashen 1985a, 1985b, 1987, 1988).

Krashen's theory distinguishes two forms of learning associated with second language learning: *acquisition learning*, and learning that is the product of *formal instruction*, which he simply refers to as *learning* (see Table 9.1).

Krashen's concept of acquisition learning thus seems to equate with the broader concept of natural learning discussed above. For Krashen, acquisition learning is the product of a subconscious process very similar to the process children undergo when they acquire their first language. It requires meaningful interaction in the target language—what Krashen refers to as *natural communication*—in which speakers are concentrated not on the form of their utterances, but in the communicative act. His concept of learning is quite different. Learning is what happens in formal classrooms and results in what Krashen refers to as "the learned system." Unlike acquisition learning, his concept of learning is the product of formal instruction and it comprises a conscious process that results in conscious knowledge *about* the language, for example knowledge of grammar rules. Krashen strongly argues that learning is less important in learning to speak a second language than acquisition.

It might seem that Krashen's distinction between *acquisition* and *learning* would be more appropriately located in the *inside/outside school* category of discourse. While a valid perception, there is a significant difference between Krashen's views of natural learning and those described in the discourse associated with the inside/outside category. Krashen's concept of acquisition is theoretically located within a Chomskyan transformational linguistic framework (Chomsky, 1993). He relies heavily on Chomsky's notion of an innate *language acquisition device* (LAD) to support his Five Hypothesis Theory of second language learning (Krashen, 1985a, 1985b). Chomsky posits that because of the "poverty of stimulus" (Tomasello, 1999, 2003) in children's environments, first language learning cannot be explained by any known learning theory. Therefore it can only be explained if the brain comes pre-wired with all the knowledge needed to learn all past, present, and future human languages.

Krashen relies on this pre-wiring theory to argue that acquisition is triggered

Table 9.1 Krashen's two kinds of learning

Acquisition Learning	(Formal) Learning
Implicit, subconscious	Explicit, conscious
Informal situations	Formal situation
Uses grammatical *feel* (intuitions)	Uses grammatical rules
Depends on attitude	Depends on aptitude
Stable order of acquisition	Simple to complex order of learning

when this LAD is allowed to operate. In Krashen's theory, his other kind of learning kicks in when this LAD is prevented from operating naturally by "a mental block, caused by affective factors . . . that prevents input from reaching the language acquisition device" (Krashen, 1985a, 1985b).

Learning to Talk as the Model for Pedagogy Per Se

Although the Suzuki method (also referred to as *talent education* and *the mother-tongue* method) is best known as an educational philosophy-cum-pedagogy for teaching violin to young children, it indirectly hints at the possibility that learning to talk could be a model for pedagogy per se. The original theory quite explicitly states that the pedagogy on which it is based has been modeled on the assumption that the ecological, social, and emotional factors that are present when a toddler learns to talk can be used to support learning the violin (Suzuki, 1983).

Howard Gardner describes the Suzuki method of learning the violin as ". . . an intriguing experiment" (1985, p. 4) which makes it possible for "an individual with apparent modest genetic promise [to] make remarkable strides in a short time" (1985, p. 35). The program allows children as young as two to participate. According to Gardner, it has produced thousands of children who have "mastered the essential of a stringed instrument by the time they enter school" (1985, p. 99). He also claims that "even the less remarkable pupils will perform at a level that astonishes Western observers" (1985, p. 375).

The Suzuki pedagogy is based on a common-sense observation that learning to talk is easy and successful for most children. The method assumes this success is due to the mix of ecological, social, and emotional factors and processes which seem to support learning to talk, including immersion in the medium, repetition which produces mastery, small achievable steps, positive rather than negative reinforcement, focus on one thing at a time in a creative and enjoyable environment.

While Suzuki indirectly hinted at the link between learning to talk and learning per se, Cambourne (1988, 1995) was one of the first literacy educators to argue explicitly that learning to talk was a valid example of natural learning in action. Cambourne's interest in natural learning was motivated by a desire to develop an "educationally relevant, grounded, theory of learning" (Cambourne, 1995).

Cambourne spent several years "bugging" and "spying" on urban and rural toddlers as they interacted with parents, siblings, peers, neighbors, relatives, teachers, and strangers over the course of a day (Cambourne, 1972). His data comprised hundreds of hours of audio transcripts of the verbal inter-actions in which these children participated, as well as all the language of others they overheard. These were transcribed into thousands of pages of "raw" language used by the focal children and their interlocutors. This corpus of language was complemented by "specimen records" (rich field notes, see

Heft, 2001), which described both the behavior and the contexts in which the linguistic behavior took place. Ecological psychologists describe these kinds of data as *rich archival lodes* which can be "mined" again and again for different purposes (Heft, 2001).

Cambourne re-mined "this archival lode" from the perspective of the role which the ecological environment played in learning to use language. He used these data to identify examples of language use which occurred in experimenter-free contexts, seeking insights into the role which ecological and social conditions played in supporting the complex learning which was taking place. He identified a set of ecological conditions that supported language learning (see Figure 9.1).

While Cambourne's and Krashen's pedagogies would look similar at the classroom level, and while they would both support the Goodmans' assertion that "oral and written language are parallel versions of the same thing—language," at a theoretical level they rely on quite different theoretical frameworks. Unlike Krashen, Cambourne does not accept the *poverty of stimulus* or nativist theories of Chomsky (1993) and Pinker (2000), which argue for a brain pre-wired for language learning. Instead he argues for a theory based on

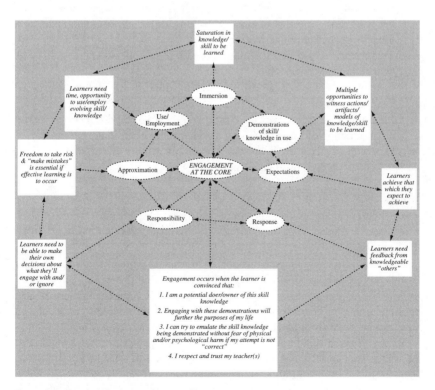

Figure 9.1 Cambourne's conditions of learning.

biological and cultural evolution, which does *not* support Chomsky's "black box Language Acquisition Device" or Pinker's "language as instinct" points of view (Chomsky, 1993; Pinker, 2000).

Cambourne argues that evolution theory clearly shows that there is more to language learning than a simplistic, innate language acquisition device. He argues that the notion that some miraculous genetic mutation at some time in the distant past, fortuitously produced a gene containing the grammatical blueprint of all past, present, and future human languages simply doesn't stand up to evolutionary scrutiny (Cambourne, 2009). Furthermore Cambourne claims that evolutionary neurobiologists and others interested in the evolutionary aspects of human cognition argue that oral language per se is actually an exemplar of a higher-order, more pervasive ability to construct complex meanings using abstract symbols, and this in turn is the result of a process of natural selection (Deacon, 1997; Donald, 1991, 2001). It makes much more sense (according to Cambourne, 2009) to argue that what *is* hardwired is the neurological equipment necessary for the construction of meaning using a wide range of different symbol systems (not just oral language).

In support of this claim Cambourne argues thus:

- Biological and cultural evolution *selected* homo sapiens' ability to construct meaning using a range of symbol systems (especially oral language) as a species-survival characteristic.
- This in turn meant that learning to use these symbol systems should be as near to fail-safe as possible.
- Learning and knowledge are the end product of internally constructed meanings.
- Meaning-making involves the continual construction, deconstruction and reconstruction of meanings using a wide range of semiotic systems.
- Learning to talk is the prototypical example of how this ability is as close to fail-safe as possible (Cambourne, 2009).

Cambourne argues that Deacon's concept of *co-evolution* (Deacon, 1997) has more theoretical and evidential support than Chomksy's innate *language acquisition device* or Pinker's *language instinct* (Cambourne, 2009; Chomsky, 1993; Pinker, 2000).

Deacon argues that language is not an instinct and there is no linguistically installed black box in our brains. Rather he asserts that the evolutionary record shows that meaning-making using abstract symbol systems tied to gesture, art, tool-making, and vocal sounds arose slowly through cognitive and cultural inventiveness. Anthropological evidence clearly shows that some 2 million years ago, one of our hominid ancestors (australopithecine), "equipped with non-linguistic, ape-like mental abilities, struggled to assemble by fits and starts, an extremely crude symbolic system" (cited in Fauconnier & Turner 2002, p. 173). According to Deacon, this symbolic system was fragile, difficult to learn given their neural equipment, inefficient, slow, inflexible, and tied to the rituals of social living (Deacon, 1997).

Deacon's thesis gets support from modern cognitive science. Fauconnier and Turner (2002) came to similar conclusions as Deacon from a quite different theoretical base, some five years after Deacon's challenge to the nativist view. In 2002 they commented thus:

> Two million years ago, australopithecines, equipped with non-linguistic ape-like mental abilities, struggled to assemble by fits and starts, an extremely crude symbolic system—fragile, difficult to learn, inefficient, slow, inflexible, and tied to ritual representation of social contracts like marriage. We would not have recognised it as language. But language then improved by two means. First invented linguistic forms were subjected to a long process of selection. Generation after generation, the newborn brain deflected linguistic inventions it found uncongenial. The guessing abilities and intricate nonlinguistic biases of the newborn brain acted as filters on the products of linguistic invention. Today's languages are systems of linguistic forms that have survived. The child's mind does not embody innate language structures. Rather the language has come to embody the predispositions of the child's mind.
>
> (Fauconnier & Turner, 2002, p. 173)

These crude and difficult language forms imposed evolutionary selection pressures on neural architecture. This evolving neurological hardware both shaped, and was shaped by, the culturally appropriate social conditions which nurtured our species' meaning-making behavior. The end product of this process is a species (us), which despite its puny body, its lack of speed, teeth, and claws, is currently the most powerful species on the planet.

What Does the Discourse "Learning to Talk" Reveal about the Construct Validity of the Concept Natural Learning?

The insights into natural learning provided by this category of discourse are significantly richer than those provided by the inside/outside category. In particular, six features of this discourse provide insights into the concept of natural learning:

1   This category of discourse coincides with other contemporaneous research and theory-building, which centered on the nature of language and its role in cognition. Researchers and theory-builders from reading and literacy education, deaf education, psycholinguistic research, cognitive science, linguistics, artificial intelligence, philosophy of language, began to show increased interest in intersection of language and cognition. This created

a convergence of theoretical interest in the relationship between three overlapping domains of concern:

- the nature of language as a meaning-making system
- the role of language in teaching and learning
- the learning of language(s) per se.

Research into these domains of concern has played a significant role in increasing our awareness of natural learning as a viable, valid concept worthy of further investigation.

2   This category of discourse also heightened awareness that learning to talk could be an exemplar of natural learning in action (Suzuki, 1983; Cambourne, 1995, 2009).

3   This heightened awareness in turn generated strong reaction against the thesis that learning to talk could be a model for pedagogy. For example:

- "... the idea that learning to read is just like learning to speak is accepted by no responsible linguist, psychologist, or cognitive scientist in the research community" (Stanovich, 1995; see also Wolf, 2008; Moats 2000).

4   This reaction provides a background for understanding the reluctance of much of mainstream education/psychology to acknowledge natural learning as a scientifically respectable model for classroom pedagogy. Chomsky's status as linguistic scholar and philosopher convinced many in mainstream education that theories which argued that the pedagogy of reading, literacy (or any domain of knowledge or skill) might be based on learning to talk should be summarily rejected.

5   The assertion that the *poverty of stimulus-LAD* explanation does not stand up to the scrutiny of evolution theory, and the emergence of an alternate *co-evolution neuro-cognitive* theoretical explanation provides insights which strengthen the possibility that learning to talk is a valid, evidence-based, theoretically sound model of natural learning which should inform classroom pedagogy.

6   Finally each of the exemplars discussed in this category of discourse explicitly reflect a constructivist epistemology of learning. Meaning-making lies at the core of each exemplar. Not only can the reactions against *learning to talk* as a viable and valid model of pedagogy be explained in terms of a conflict between constructivist and objectivist views of knowledge, but by equating meaning construction with knowledge (Cambourne, 2009) explicitly reframes knowledge as something which is internally constructed by the learner, rather than something which exists independently and has to be transmitted to the learner's mind.

The Discourse of Brain-Based Education/Learning (Neuroscience)

Irrespective of which term is used (brain-based *education* or brain-based *learning*), those who work in this area generally locate themselves under the broad umbrella of neuroscience. The discourse around neuroscience's relationship with education, learning, and pedagogy is diverse and sometimes conflicting.

There are two contested theoretical issues at the core of these conflicting points of view.

1   Can neuroscience, with so many possible layers of organization (from molecules to cells to circuits to larger and larger-scale systems) ever be a science in its own right, i.e., a unitary domain of concern that stands or falls by its own unique canons of evidence?

2   When might it be possible to take research from neuroscience and "derive unequivocal educational implications from it" (Sternberg, 2008)?

Let us examine each of these issues.

1. Can neuroscience, with so many possible layers of organization (from molecules to cells to circuits to larger and larger-scale systems) ever be a science in its own right, i.e., a unitary domain of concern that stands or falls by its own unique canons of evidence?

Some express the belief that while it is not yet currently developed to this stage, ultimately it will be (Jensen 2008a, 2008b). Others suggest that such a state of theoretical nirvana is neither possible nor necessary (Sternberg, 2008; Willingham, 2008). Feldman's attempt to develop a "neural theory of language" (Feldman, 2008) provides an exemplar of this issue in action. Feldman set out to develop a theory that treats language not as an abstract symbol system but as a human biological ability that can be studied as a function of the brain in the same way that vision and/or motor control can. His title *From Molecule to Metaphor* (Feldman, 2008) captures the essence of this issue—can one take two ends of a causal chain and explicate the links between them with a unified theory? Feldman found that there were no available methodologies for attempting such a task, so he was forced to use computer modeling to develop a *bridging theory* which "suggested"[4] how language and thought were realized in the brain.

2. When might it be possible to take research from neuroscience (such as Feldman's) and "derive unequivocal educational implications from it" (Sternberg, 2008)?

Sternberg's point is that research methodologies which would enable scientists like Feldman to develop a single unitary theory accounts for how the brain understands metaphors, or masters complex knowledge and/or skills, will not

---

4 Note that Feldman chose the term *suggested* rather than *unequivocally explained*.

be available in the foreseeable future and therefore it may be better use of time and resources to leave "the brain issue as one to be dealt with later, in the longer term" (Sternberg, 2008).

Fortunately there is a middle ground of opinion which argues that contributions that neuroscience might potentially make to classroom practice would need to be based on a "comprehensive blend of theories and facts" ranging across levels of organization of the nervous system "from molecules, and cells and circuits, to large-scale systems and physical and social environments" warning us against "explanations that rely on data from one single level, whatever the level may be" (Liston, 2001, p. 2).

The Natural Learning Research Institute: Synthesizing the Discourses of Neuroscience, Cognitive Psychology, Pedagogy, Constructivism, and Systems Theory

Caine and Caine's Natural Learning Research Institute (NLRI) (Caine & Caine, n.d.) is an exemplar of how this middle ground can inform an understanding of natural learning. Caine and Caine state that they "conduct research into natural learning, [by synthesizing] research from neuroscience, cognitive psychology and elsewhere." As a consequence of this synthesis they argue that humans are "whole biological systems" and that it is "the entire system which learns." Accordingly they claim that "the best way to grasp how people learn, therefore, is to adopt a systems perspective, *and to integrate research from all the different fields of knowledge that deal with learning*" (emphasis added) (Caine & Caine, n.d.).

What's interesting about the Caines' approach is that while they faced a similar problem to that faced by Feldman (Feldman, 2008), their solution was quite different. Like Feldman they needed to develop a theory which holistically "joined both ends of a causal chain". In Feldman's case the two ends of the chain were the molecules which made up the neuronal cells at one end and metaphorical meaning at the other (Feldman, 2008). In the Caines' case the two ends of their causal chain were findings from neuroscience and effective classroom practice.

Whereas Feldman used computer simulation to develop what he called *bridging* theories between the various layers of biological and cognitive systems he was trying to unify, the Caines used a quite different strategy—they adopted a systems theory model to frame their developing understanding of human physiology and cognition, and constructivist epistemology to frame the natural learning theory they developed. By *synthesizing and integrating* the theoretical principles underpinning systems theory and constructivism with findings from neuroscience, the Caines constructed what they call the "twelve principles of natural learning" (see Figure 9.2).

These principles become a (metaphorical) "bridge" between neuroscience and pedagogy. They also serve as a scientific justification-cum-rationale for the

1. All learning is physiological.
2. The Brain-Mind is social.
3. The search for meaning is innate.
4. The search for meaning occurs through patterning.
5. Emotions are critical to patterning.
6. The Brain-Mind processes parts and wholes simultaneously.
7. Learning involves both focused attention and peripheral perception.
8. Learning always involves conscious and unconscious processes.
9. There are at least two approaches to memory: archiving individual facts or skills or making sense of experience.
10. Learning is developmental.
11. Complex learning is enhanced by challenge and inhibited by threat associated with helplessness.
12. Each brain is uniquely organized.
    (Caine & Caine 2004 http://www.naturallearninginstitute.org/index.html)

Figure 9.2 Caine & Caine's twelve principles of natural learning.

pedagogies which they recommend. In essence they become a kind of "meta"-framework which defines their view of natural learning.

An example of how this meta-framework works to link a systems theory view of human physiology and cognition to a constructivist pedagogy, and then link both of these to scientifically respectable research from neuroscience can be illustrated by how they explicate the 12 principles. Here's the explication of Principle 6 (see Figure 9.3).

Note how they:

- State the principle.
- Present a real-world example of what the principle means.
- Link the principle to research in cognitive science.
- Then introduce "recent brain research" which clearly and obviously relates to the principle and the real-world example.
- Then finally link all this to a form of in-built cognitive potential which they label a *capacity* (thus implying there is an in-built natural capacity waiting to be triggered to support learning). The Caines seem to have few problems in linking pedagogy to neuroscience using these frameworks and models.

What Does the Discourse Neuroscience Reveal About the Construct Validity of the Concept Natural Learning?

The insights into natural learning provided by this category of discourse add to those which emerged from the discourse of learning to talk. Despite the concerns that neuroscience and pedagogy could not be theoretically linked, the

---

Principle #6: *The brain/mind processes parts and wholes simultaneously.*
Making sense of experience requires both a big picture and paying attention to
the individual parts. The experience of the whole provides a story, a model, or a
fascinating example of what can be achieved. Gestalt psychology (Sternberg,
2006) explicitly shows how the mind connects parts to make these wholes. And
some of the most recent brain research is now exploring the integrative role of
the prefrontal cortex (Fuster, 2003).

Capacity #6: All students can comprehend more effectively when details
(specific facts and information) are embedded in wholes that they understand
such as a real life event, a meaningful story, or a project that they create or
witness.

(Caine & Caine, n.d.)

Figure 9.3

Caines' multidisciplinary approach of synthesizing and integrating principles
from a range of theoretical domains seems to be one successful way of resolving this concern. Their 12 principles of natural learning provide a method for
linking at least these specific findings from neuroscience to pedagogy:

- research on neural plasticity, which shows that the brain is extraordinarily
  malleable and that many areas of the cortex are literally shaped by
  experience (Begley, 2007; Doige, 2007; Conlan, 1999; Diamond, 1988)
- research on the degree of interconnectedness between different regions
  of the brain, which shows that academic learning and comprehension
  are never separate from emotions, meaning, motivation, past experience,
  recognition, and memory (Fuster, 2003)
- research on what are called *mirror neurons*, which shows that children continuously (and largely unconsciously) learn from what is modeled by events
  and others around them (Rizzolatti & Craighero, 2004; Iacoboni, Woods,
  Brass, et al., 1999)
- research on emotions and the brain, which shows that some types of
  comprehending are inhibited by fear and helplessness and that the
  more positive emotions can affect and enhance certain types of learning
  (LeDoux, 1996; Paanksep, 1998).

Conclusions

Is Natural Learning a Valid Concept for the Twenty-first Century?

The answer to this question is an emphatic "Yes!" Natural learning is a viable,
valid concept. An analysis and evaluation of the three dominant discourses

associated with the concept indicate that there is a convergence towards a theoretically consistent operationalization of it. While the first category of discourse (the *inside/outside formal school* frame) suggested that natural learning would turn out to be a rather messy eclectic concept with little construct validity, a significant convergence of theories emerged from the analysis of the other two categories of discourse. This convergence drew from a range of theoretical domains including cultural and biological evolution, neurobiology, neuroscience, systems theory, constructivism, cognitive science, cognitive linguistics, psychology, education.

What are the Basic Defining Theoretical Components of a Theory of Natural Learning?

Natural learning is not a single *thing* or *entity* that can be described by listing sets of physical, cognitive, emotional, social, behavioral, etc. attributes. I have argued elsewhere that if we want to improve pedagogy then we must engage in reframing the concept of learning per se by "thinking about 'learning' in quite different, non-traditional ways" (Cambourne, 2009). The research and theory-building examined in addressing Question 1 is a de facto reframing exercise in that it involves evaluating the theoretical rationale and research underpinning some of the "quite different non-traditional ways of thinking about learning."

Here is a summary list of these "quite different non-traditional ways of thinking about learning." Any operational definition of the concept *natural learning* would need to take them into account.

A Theory of Natural Learning

- **equates** the term *learning* and its cognates (e.g. knowledge, understanding, comprehension, knowledge-building, etc.) with meaning, meaning-making
- **defines** *meaning* as "an unpredictable mix of personally constructed, internal, pictures, sounds, feelings, which seem to be unleashed by, and closely related to, the range of symbol systems humans are constantly using and manipulating to create new topical, and contextually relevant meanings which allow them make sense of the world" (Cambourne, 2009)
- **assumes that:**
    - meaning is an internal cognitive construction of the human mind which serves to make sense of the world
    - making sense of the world is essential for survival of the individual and the species
    - the human mind is capable of constructing meaning using a range of symbol systems

- biological and cultural evolution has *selected* the construction of meaning using a range of symbol systems as a species-survival trait for homo sapiens
- learning to create and communicate meaning using a range of symbol systems needs to be a fail-safe procedure in human society
- learning to control the oral form of language of the culture into which one is born is the primary and predominant symbol system which members of a culture need to learn.

- **concludes that:**

  - the ecological, social, physical, emotional conditions that support learning to talk are proto-typical of the way natural learning works.

- **looks like:**

  - Cambourne's Model of Learning (see Figure 9.1).

What are the Pedagogical Implications of a Valid Theory of Natural Learning?

- Nature, as represented by the processes underlying evolution, has already worked out what social, cultural, and physical factors need to be present in an effective learning setting.
- The conditions that support learning to talk (see Figure 9.1) should provide a framework for a theory of pedagogy which is truly evidence-based.
- The findings from neuroscience provide further evidential support for a pedagogy based on the principles of natural learning.
- Policy and pedagogy which are based on what evolution tells us about these conditions would be truly scientifically based.

End Point

Think of it. A theory of pedagogy is based on the strongest scientific theory ever proposed. A theory which has withstood more than 100 years of concerted attempts to disprove it, find it flawed, and dismiss its validity. 3.8 billion years of evolution together with the fundamental processes of social organization which characterizes all human society is a pretty strong evidence base for informing literacy policy and pedagogy.

References

Baumgartner, M. (1980). A *conversation with John Holt*. On the Natural Child Project Website. Accessed October 2008. (http://www.naturalchild.org/guest/marlene_bumgarner.html)

Begley, S. (2007). Brain training: How it works. *Newsweek*, November 2007. Accessed

October 2008. (http://www.blog.newsweek.com/blogs/labnotes/archive/2007/11/17/brain-training-how-it-works.aspx)

Caine & Caine's Natural Learning Research Institute (NLRI) (n.d.) (http://www.naturallearninginstitute.org/index.html)

Cambourne, B.L. (1972). A naturalistic study of the linguistic performance of rural and urban children in Australia. Unpublished Ph.D. thesis, James Cook University North Queensland, Australia.

Cambourne, B.L. (1988). *The whole story: Natural learning and the acquisition of literacy.* Auckland, New Zealand: Ashton-Scholastic.

Cambourne, B.L. (1995). Towards an educationally relevant theory of literacy learning: Twenty years of inquiry. *The Reading Teacher, 49*, 3, 182–192.

Cambourne, B.L. (2009). *Nature as mentor: Revisiting the concept of learning: Implications for the pedagogy of literacy.* In R. Meyer & K. Whitmore (Eds.), *Reviving reading in the post NCLB world.* Centre For Expansion of Language and Thinking (CELT). (Submitted to Urbana, IL: National Council of Teachers of English 2008).

Chomsky, N. (1993). *Language and thought.* Rhode Island: Moyer Bell Ltd.

Collier, S. & Iran-Nejad, A. (1995). *Natural and academic learning.* Paper presented at the Annual Meeting of the Mid-South Educational Research Association November 8–10, Biloxi, MS. (ERIC ED 393–891).

Conlan, R. (Ed.), (1999). *State of mind: New discoveries about how our brains make us who we are.* New York: John Wiley.

Deacon, T. (1997). *The symbolic species: The co-evolution of language and the brain.* New York: W.H. Norton.

Diamond, M. (1988). *Responses of the brain to enrichment.* New Horizons for Learning website. Accessed October 2008 (http://www.newhorizons.org/neuro/diamond_brain_response.htm).

Doige, N. (2007). *The brain that changes itself.* London: Penguin Books.

Donald, M. (1991). *The origins of the human mind.* Cambridge, MA: Harvard University Press.

Donald, M. (2001). *A mind so rare: The evolution of human consciousness.* New York: W.H. Norton.

Fauconnier, G. & Turner, M. (2002). *The way we think: Conceptual blending and the mind's hidden complexities.* NY: Basic Books.

Feldman, J.A. (2008). *From molecule to metaphor: A neural theory of language.* Cambridge, MA: MIT Press.

Fuster, J.M. (2003). *Cortex and mind. Unifying cognition.* New York: OUP.

Gardner, H. (1985). *Frames of mind: The theory of multiple intelligences.* London: Paladin Books.

Gardner, H. (1991). The tensions between education and development. *Journal of Moral Education, 20*, 2, 113–125.

Gee, J.P. (2003). *What video games have to teach us about learning and literacy.* New York: Palgrave (MacMillan).

Goodman, K.S. & Goodman, Y.M. (1976). *Learning to read is natural.* Paper presented at the Conference on Theory and Practice of Beginning Reading Instruction, University of Pittsburgh, Learning Research and Development Center, April 1976; (ERIC ED 125 315 and ED 145 399).

Heft, H. (2001). *Ecological psychology in context.* New Jersey: Lawrence Erlbaum.

Iacoboni, M., Woods, R., Brass, M., et al. (1999). Cortical mechanisms of human imitation. *Science, 286*, 5449, 2526–2528.

Jensen, E.P. (2008a). A fresh look at brain-based education. *Phi Delta Kappan, 89*, 6, 408–417.

Jensen, E.P. (2008b). Exciting times call for collaboration. *Phi Delta Kappan, 89*, 6, 428–431.

Krashen, S. (1985a). *The input hypothesis: issues and implications.* Harlow, UK: Longman.

Krashen, S. (1985b). *Language acquisition and language education.* Englewood Cliffs, NJ: Alemany Press.

Krashen, S.D. (1987). *Principles and practice in second language acquisition.* NJ: Prentice-Hall International.

Krashen, S.D. (1988). *Second language acquisition and second language learning.* NJ: Prentice-Hall International.

Krashen, S. & Terrell, T.D. (1983). *The natural approach.* Oxford: Pergamon.

LeDoux, J.E. (1996). Emotion circuits in the brain. *Annual Review of Neuroscience, 23*, 155–184 (volume publication date March 2000).

Lieberman, P. (1967). *Intonation, perception, and language.* Cambridge, MA: MIT Press.

Liston, C. (2001). An interview with Antonio R. Damasio. *The Harvard Brain*, Spring, p. 2.

Miller, G. & Isard, S. (1963). Some perceptual consequences of linguistic rules. *Journal of Verbal Learning and Learning Behaviour, 2*, 217–228.

Miller, G.A., Heise, G., & Lichten, W. (1951). The intelligibility of speech as a function of the context of the test material. *Journal of Experimental Psychology, 41*, 329–335.

Moats, L.C. (2000) *Whole language lives on: The illusion of "balanced" reading instruction.* Washington, D.C.: Thomas Fordham Foundation.

Natural Learning. Accessed October 2008 from http://en.wikipedia.org/wiki/Natural_learning

Obusek, C.J. & Warren, R.M. (1973). Relation of the verbal transformation and phonemic restoration effects. *Cognitive Psychology, 5*, 97–107.

Paanksep, J. (1998). *Affective neuroscience: The foundations of human and animal emotions.* USA: Oxford University Press.

Pinker, S. (2000). *The language instinct.* NY: Perennial Classics (HarperCollins).

Pollack, I. & Pickett, J.M. (1964). Intelligibility of excerpts from fluent speech: Auditory vs. structural context. *Journal of Verbal Learning and Learning Behaviour, 3*, 79–84.

Resnick, L.B. (1987). Learning in school and out. *Educational Researcher*, 16(9).

Rizzolatti, G. & Craighero, L. (2004). The mirror neuron system. *Annual Review Neuroscience, 27*, 169–192.

Schank, R.C. & Cleary, C. (1995). *Engines for education.* NJ: Lawrence Erlbaum Associates. Also accessed October 2008 on http://www.engines4ed.org/hyperbook/

Sousa, D. (2006). *How the brain learns* (with learning manual). Thousand Oaks, CA: Corwin Press Incorporated.

Stanovich, K. (1995). Editorial, American Educator. *Journal of American Federation of Teachers*, Summer, p. 4.

Sternberg, R.J. (2008). The answer depends on the question: A reply to Eric Jensen. *Phi Delta Kappan*, 89(6), 418–420.

Suzuki, S. (1983). *Nurtured by love* (trans. by Waltraud Suzuki). Miami: Warner Bros.

Tomasello, M. (1999). *The cultural origins of human cognition.* Harvard, MA: Harvard University Press.

Tomasello, M. (2003). *Constructing a language: A usage-based theory of language acquisition.* Cambridge, MA: Harvard University Press.

Wanner, E. (1973) Do we understand sentences from the outside-in or from the inside-out? *Daedalus* (Issued as *Language as a Human Problem*), Vol. 102, No. 3, Summer, pp. 163–184, of the Proceedings of the American Academy of the Arts and Sciences.

Warren, R.M. (1970). Perceptual restoration of missing speech sounds. *Science, 167,* 392–393.

Warren, R.M. & Obusek, C.J. (1971). Speech perception and phonemic restoration. *Perception and Psychophysics, 9,* 358–362.

Warren, R.M. & Warren, R.P. (1970). Auditory illusions and confusions. *Scientific American, 223,* 30–36.

Willingham, D. (2008). When and how neuroscience applies to education. *Phi Delta Kappan, 89,* 6, 421–423.

Willis, J. (2008). Building a bridge from neuroscience to the classroom. *Phi Delta Kappan, 89,* 6, 424–427.

Wolf, M. (2008). Proust and the squid: the story and science of the reading brain (cited from a review published in *Financial Times Magazine* 5 April 2008).

Chapter 10

Beyond Word Recognition

How Retrospective and Future Perspectives on Miscue Analysis Can Inform Our Teaching

Ken Goodman
Professor Emeritus, University of Arizona

Yetta Goodman
Regents Professor Emerita, University of Arizona

Eric J. Paulson
Associate Professor, University of Cincinnati

Over five decades, miscue analysis has contributed to an understanding of the reading process, how people learn to read, and how teaching reading supports learning to read. In this chapter Ken Goodman discusses the role of miscue analysis in the development of his theory of reading, Yetta Goodman follows with an overview of the influences of miscue analysis on reading instruction, and Eric Paulson discusses the future of miscue analysis focusing on the development of a new research methodology: *eye-movement/miscue analysis*.

Both miscue analysis and the model of reading based on it are in continuous refinement helped by new research methodologies and technologies.

Theory: Ken Goodman on Miscue Analysis and the Development of a Reading Theory

All readers, regardless of proficiency, make miscues, unexpected responses to a text during oral reading as they focus on making sense of print. Miscues result from the same cues and processes as non-miscued parts of the text. Analyzing the differences and similarities of the observed and expected responses in miscue analysis provides a window on the reading process and on language processes in general. Oral reading is unique in this respect because there is a continuous comparison between the published text the reader is transacting with and the personal text the reader is constructing. Miscues also occur in speaking, listening, and writing.

Miscue Analysis Theory

Theory-driven

Most scholars understand that all research is based in theory; however, the theory is often left unexamined. So miscue analysis, with its constant interplay between data analysis and theory, differs profoundly from other *error analysis* traditions. Long before I began the development of miscue analysis in 1963, there were studies of reading errors, notably by Marion Monroe (1932) and others, but these studies started with unexamined theoretical premises:

- that "good" reading is error-free
- that errors in reading are evidence of inadequacies and weakness and should be eliminated through instruction in order to improve reading.

The aim of these studies was to determine the nature of errors so that they could be removed through remediation. Yet none of these scholars ever examined how or why reading could be expected to be error-free.

Scientific Realism

Years after I began miscue research I discovered that miscue analysis is an example of scientific realism (Goodman, 2008). Research based in scientific realism is not designed to examine cause–effect hypotheses; rather its purpose is to build a theory of the structures and processes that exist in the aspect of reality being studied. My research met two major requirements of scientific realism:

1   The need to keep my study of reading in its real-world social context—I wanted to study real acts of reading, not responses to letters, words, and short, contrived sentences or paragraphs.
2   The need to develop a coherent theory of the reading process I was studying.

Underlying Theory and Process of Miscue Analysis

In miscue analysis, readers are asked to read whole texts (stories or articles) that they have not seen before. We originally assumed that reading could be studied through the methodology of linguistics, although it soon became evident that the analysis required psycholinguistic concepts since making sense of print involves both thought and language. Additionally, it was necessary to use sociolinguistic insights to fully understand the dialect and cultural backgrounds of different readers.

It quickly became obvious in this early research that readers' errors reflected their strengths in making sense of language as well as any weaknesses or difficulties. Their miscues showed their knowledge of language and of the content of what they were reading. The theoretical expectation that readers were actively trying to make sense of reading was easily verified in their miscues.

The term *miscue* was chosen deliberately as it became clear that the phenomenon reflected the readers' use of the reading process. *Error* wouldn't do because it was an inaccurate characterization of these unexpected responses—they were clearly more than errors. The term miscue was appropriate since it carries with it the notion of a response to language cues and the notion of being unexpected. Also, since the term had no history with language teachers, there were no existing connotations that might get in the way of their coming to understand the significance of miscues.

An early version of the theory is found in the article "Reading: A psycholinguistic guessing game" (Goodman, 1967) and a later, more complete version is in "Reading, writing and written texts: A sociopsycholinguistic transactional view" (Goodman, 1994). The most complete representation of miscue analysis is in *The Reading Miscue Inventory* by Yetta Goodman, Dorothy Watson, and Carolyn Burke (1987, 2005).

An Example of Miscue Analysis

Building on this brief introduction to miscue analysis, here's an excerpt to explicate both miscue analysis and the view of reading that underlies it. The reader, Tim, is a sixth grader in Appalachian Tennessee. His miscues are represented directly above the text item affected and explained below. The discussion of his reading of the passage follows the miscue markings (see Figure 10.1).

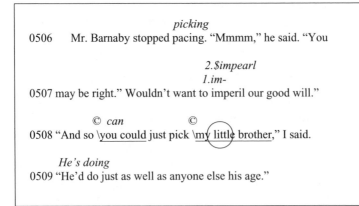

Figure 10.1 Excerpt of Tim's reading miscues.

Following usual miscue procedures, Tim's oral reading was tape recorded and his miscues were marked on a transcript of the text. The numbers on the left tell us that these are lines 6–9 of page five of the story he read. The lines break just as they did in the book he was reading.

On line 0506, Tim substituted *picking* for *pacing* and did not self-correct. His substitution is a real English word, a verb like the expected response. It keeps the *-ing* ending, and by listening to his intonation, we confirm that he intended a verb. Though the observed response (OR) and the expected response (ER) mean different things, the resulting sentence is both syntactically and semantically acceptable in the text (for example, people *pick* as well as *pace* when they are thinking). The sound and look of the ER and OR are both similar. They start and end in the same way, though *picking* looks a little more similar to *pacing* than it sounds. This is a relatively high-quality miscue that shows Tim's active use of all cuing systems in his meaning construction.

On line 0507, Tim makes two attempts at *imperil*. He produces a partial miscue, so called because he stops himself so that we can't tell what he intended to say. Then he produces a nonword, indicated by the symbol $, *$impearl*. Since he produced a nonword and didn't succeed in correcting himself he lost some of the meaning. The intonation helps us decide that his nonword has verb intonation and the miscue is syntactically acceptable in the sentence. The OR has high correspondence with the ER both graphically (how it looks) and phonemically (how it sounds). That is often true of nonwords readers produce, indicating that they are making use of phonics. Though Tim didn't ever say the word correctly, it is quite possible that he has some sense of its negative meaning from the context.

The next miscue, *can* for *could*, is corrected. It was both syntactically and semantically acceptable as Tim read it. Both the ER and the OR are modals—in fact they are present and past tense of the same word—but the shift makes the sentence less intense in probability. The ER and OR have only the beginnings in common graphically and phonemically.

Tim omits *little* on the same line, again correcting his miscue. The sentence is still syntactically and semantically acceptable without *little*; this far into the story it is well established that this is a baby brother. Nevertheless Tim corrected. He is self-monitoring his reading, perhaps too carefully.

His final miscue is *He's doing* for *He'd do* which is acceptable in meaning and in grammar. The full form is *He is doing* for *He would do*. Modals are involved and the meaning shifts slightly to be less a prediction than a description. Though Tim is using the words and word parts, he is operating at a phrase level: he could not have said *He's do* or *He'd doing* and still produce acceptable language. He does not correct—but then again, did he need to?

As part of every miscue analysis, we ask the reader to retell the story as a measure of comprehension. The retelling helps us understand the patterns of the miscues. The miscues are examined on three language levels: semantic, syntactic, and graphophonic. As Tim's reading shows, readers integrate the use of all three levels (cuing systems) in making sense of print.

Contributions to Understanding Reading

This short sequence from a single reader illustrates several important concepts:

1   Reading is constructive. It is not a series of word recognitions. Tim constructs meaning to make sense of the text. In the process he constructs his own text parallel to the published text.
2   It is his own constructed text that he is comprehending. He continuously monitors this self-constructed text, attempting to correct when it doesn't make sense, and using the published text as a check against what he has constructed. His comprehending across the text results in the comprehension represented by his retelling.
3   Readers make predictions and inferences on the basis of what they have already read. They use the cue systems of the text to confirm or disconfirm their predictions.
4   Context is used continuously in making sense of the text. It is not simply the wording that is aided by the context. In fact readers assign a grammatical structure to each sentence and use the developing meaning to make efficient minimal use of the graphic information from the text to be effective in making sense.
5   That means that readers are purposefully sampling from the print. *Exact* reading is neither efficient nor effective.

Both Qualitative and Quantitative

Miscue analysis is both qualitative and quantitative. Each reader produces many miscues in reading a complete text. The miscue taxonomy (Goodman, 1969) provides as many as 30 data points for each miscue so that miscue researchers can look at patterns and profiles of miscues. The patterns of miscues provide a profile of the reading. And the theory makes it possible to analyze the quality of the reading. In this excerpt, though there are several miscues, Tim shows himself as an effective and relatively efficient reader.

Miscue analysis began as a research procedure. It has been used with native readers of many languages (including American Sign Language), with second language learners, and with special populations at all ages and levels of proficiency (Brown, Goodman & Marek, 1996). *The Reading Miscue Inventory* (Goodman et al., 2005) makes miscue analysis available for teachers and reading specialists to use in diagnostic situations and in classrooms to identify strengths and weaknesses of readers. It is also used in teacher education as a means of helping teachers understand and revalue the reading process.

Instruction: Yetta Goodman on the Influence of Miscue Analysis on Instruction

Beginnings

Ken Goodman and I recently began archiving our research and writings. I have documented thousands of readings analyzed through miscue analysis methodology since 1963. Many of the studies had readers read more than one text so that we are able to study the same readers reading texts of varying difficulty to demonstrate changes in the reading process developmentally and over time. We analyzed the readings of populations with different abilities, languages, dialects, and ages. These are now available in the Goodman Archive, Special Collections at the University of Arizona library.

The first miscue dissertations were completed in the late 1960s at Wayne State University (WSU), and since then many more studies have contributed to Ken's transactional sociopsycholinguistic reading model and miscue analysis methodology.

The researchers at WSU were also involved with teacher education and professional development. We were doctoral students who had recently come out of elementary and secondary classrooms. We taught language arts, children's literature, and reading courses in school sites for preservice teachers in Detroit and its suburbs. That work turned our attention to the influences the model could have in classrooms and reading clinics.

Carolyn Burke, who was coordinating the Miscue Research Center, and I decided to document what teachers could learn from miscue analysis and the ways this knowledge of the reading process could help them develop reading curricula and instruction. We were invited to be part of a professional development project, The Psycholinguistic Approach to Reading (PAR), with elementary and middle school teachers in schools near San Diego, California, in the early 1970s. The state of California designated the project for dissemination as exemplary research.

At Wayne State we were exploring the spiral curricula, the role of inquiry in learning, the power of integration of subject matter with reading and writing, and the influences of children's literature in learning to read. We studied issues concerning language, thinking, and curriculum and their impact on schooling (Goodman et al., 1987). Our growing understandings and knowledge of the processes of literacy and learning and our work with practicing teachers helped us develop a philosophy later known as *whole language*. Many holistic practices were being successfully used in the field supported by our research and theory.

Miscue Analysis and Whole Language Instruction

Miscue analysis research played a role in the emergence of whole language as a philosophy. Whole language involves reading and writing for real purposes across the whole curriculum; using children's and adolescent literature as authentic materials in learning to read; engaging learners in inquiry through theme cycles; reading strategy lessons involving readers in discussions about reading; and establishing the construction of meaning as the major focus for reading and reading instruction. The concept of whole language developed over time from the late 1970s (Goodman, 1991). We formed the Center for the Expansion of Language and Thinking as a professional support group for ourselves as we moved to different institutions and continued to expand on holistic curricular practices.

Whole Language Philosophy

Those of us studying at WSU were already committed to progressive education. We found that many teachers were already engaged in language experience (Lamoreaux & Lee, 1963; Lee & Allen, 1963), individualized reading (Veatch, 1978), and sustained silent reading. We developed a language-centered view of curriculum as we worked with teachers to understand reading and writing as tools to be used by students in all their learning.

There were parallel influences on the developing concepts of whole language from other fields. Halliday (1979) taught us that whenever humans use language the result is learning *language*, learning *through* language about the concepts and ideas in the world, and learning *about* language as teachers and kids talk and think about language as a cultural object.

Other researchers emphasized the joint relationships between reading and writing processes. James Britton, with colleagues Margaret Meek Spencer, Harold Rosen, and Nancy Martin (Martin & Lightfoot, 1988) and others at the London Institute of Education, established the importance of using written language across the curriculum. Donald Graves (1991) established the focus on process writing in elementary school classrooms. Those of us involved in literacy education began to use the term *literacy* to recognize the uses of written language as culturally and socially constructed influenced by political control and access to literacy.

Teachers found their voices and began to articulate to parents the power of integrating reading and writing and using authentic literature. They developed inquiry curricula inviting students to raise questions and solve problems in social studies, science, music, art, and technology. Whole language is not a reading or writing methodology, but a set of principles to help teachers develop curriculum with students.

Whole language principles were used to established policies in some schools. Today there are many courageous teachers and administrators who continue to develop instructional programs that keep curricula integrated and whole even as No Child Left Behind (NCLB) and the states are mandating scripted and controlled commercial reading programs.

The Concept of Strategy Lessons and Reading Instruction

Those engaged in understanding whole language curricula were also considering what reading instruction should look like informed by miscue analysis and a model of reading. Teacher educators discussed reading and writing as a process of making sense. They engaged readers at all levels in predicting and confirming activities and developed artifacts that illuminated for teachers and readers that making miscues was an essential part of the reading process (Whitmore, Goodman, & Center for the Expansion of Language and Thinking, 1996).

They developed strategy lessons to use with individual students in small reading groups or in whole class settings. Exploring reading as an object of study became part of reading strategy lessons (Goodman, Watson, & Burke, 1996) and eventually this concept informed the development of retrospective miscue analysis (Goodman & Marek, 1996) that involved readers in examining their own miscues.

In the first edition of the *Reading Miscue Inventory* Carolyn Burke and I (Goodman & Burke, 1972) included examples of *reading strategy lessons*, which we believe is the first use of the term *strategy* in reading. We purposely used the term *strategy lessons* as opposed to *teaching strategies*, since all readers use strategies as they read. Readers select only the necessary cues that are most useful to them, they monitor their reading, they self-correct when necessary, they make sense as they read, and they solve the problems that result from their transactions with the text. We wanted to be clear that teachers do not teach the reading strategies which students develop as a result of learning to read. Rather, strategy lessons are organized to help readers use their developing strategies in the most efficient and effective ways.

We knew from miscue analysis research that readers sometimes use strategies that disrupt comprehension. This happens when readers focus too much on sounding out and on slow and too careful attention to surface text features such as spelling patterns, word analysis, and grammatical information. Sometimes students do not have the content knowledge that helps them understand the ideas being presented in a text. In such cases readers use strategies that lead to short circuits in the reading process.

Through our teaching, we help kids respect and value the proficient strategies that they use and to minimize the use of strategies that get in their way of making sense. The strategy lessons include careful observation, or *kidwatching* (Owocki & Goodman, 2002) on the part of teachers. The more teachers know miscue analysis, the more they are able to listen to readers in any context. As teachers read with their students, they listen to students' miscues and gain insight into their use of reading strategies. By talking about miscues with readers, teachers help them use their most proficient strategies and diminish their disruptive strategies.

Miscue analysis also provides insight into the knowledge students have about language. For example, an ESL reader who substitutes *the* for *he* in the phrase *he went to the well for some water* followed by a quick self-correction indicates that she was going to say *the man* or *the woodman* instead of *he*. With such evidence, the teacher notes that the reader is developing knowledge of English because only an English speaker makes this kind of miscue. Or, when more than 80% of a reader's substitution miscues serve the same grammatical functions as the text items, it reveals the reader's knowledge of English grammar. And if the substitutions are synonyms, the teacher also has insights into the reader's use of semantic knowledge.

Instructional strategies focus on helping students predict what is coming up in a text, to substitute appropriately related known names for unfamiliar ones, to decide what is important in reading and what can be skipped without concern that meaning will be lost, and to know when it is appropriate to stop reading.

Retrospective miscue analysis involves conversations with readers to bring to conscious awareness what they know about their strategy use and knowledge of their language (Goodman & Marek, 1996). Readers come to understand the reading process from a holistic perspective. The teacher and the student discuss the quality of miscues so they see themselves as readers in control of their reading and not readers who "mess up."

We realized the importance of using predictable texts for readers through miscue research that showed the predictions readers made when they read predictable content and text structures.

Miscue research on reading a range of texts by the same reader shows that the readers miscue differentially on different texts. The most effective kind of literacy materials in classrooms are books, magazines, and other written materials that are related to students' interests and familiarity. This is different for each reader and highlights the importance of classroom and school librar-ies as part of a rich literacy instructional environment. Each reading of a text by an individual reader is unique, so readers need many opportunities to access authentic literature: non-fiction, fiction, and the range of reading materials beyond books (newspapers, magazines, and the Internet). Through holistic practices readers demystify the reading process and realize that surface accur-acy of word reading is not the most important factor in reading.

Teachers, parents, and students need to realize that learning to read occurs in every context in which students are using reading and writing. Teachers are teachers of reading whenever they organize the school environment and whenever they engage readers in learning experiences.

Ken Goodman and I continue to be involved in miscue analysis research and our work continues to be enriched by doctoral students and colleagues. One of those former students, Eric Paulson, questioned and critiqued miscue analysis and moved us into understanding how our work might be enhanced by relating eye-movement research to miscue analysis. He ends this chapter by exploring the roads that miscue analysis research takes into the future.

Future: Eric Paulson on the Combination of Eye Movements and Miscue Analysis (EMMA)

The book *Studies in Miscue Analysis: An annotated bibliography* (Brown, Goodman, & Marek, 1996) includes more than 2,000 miscue studies. Miscue research shows no signs of slowing down; dozens of miscue analysis studies appear in a wide variety of journals and conference presentations every year. How will miscue analysis continue to shape the field of literacy education and meet the challenges of changing literacies?

Instruction and Assessment

Miscue analysis has been enormously effective in the areas of instruction and assessment, and it will continue to be effective in those areas. By *assessment* I mean diagnostic assessment, where the result is not a number or a placement, but a map of student strengths and challenges. By *instruction* I include uses of miscue analysis to help teachers understand what they should focus on with their readers, but also uses of miscue analysis as the basis of the instruction itself, such as retrospective miscue analysis where the readers are included in conversations about their reading (Goodman & Marek, 1996). The need for diagnostic assessment and instruction never ends, and so miscue analysis continues to provide a powerful tool in literacy education.

Research

In addition miscue analysis will continue to lead to new approaches in research. Miscue data-collection procedures provide as close to an authentic reading experience for the reader as possible. That means the data that are collected are those of a normal reading experience, not one that involves timed responses, nonreading-related decision-making, altered texts, or other tricks and tasks that are sometimes used to see how readers "respond." This authenticity makes miscue analysis a valid and powerful research tool. It also enables miscue analysis to be combined with other research tools to provide even more information about the reading process—and this combination is likely what the future holds for miscue analysis research.

Combining Miscue Analysis with Eye-movement Research

One such productive combination we are calling eye-movement/miscue analysis, or EMMA.

Eye-movement/Miscue Analysis: EMMA

Eye-movement research has a long and fruitful tradition of contributing to understanding the reading processes, dating back to the nineteenth century (Huey, 1908/1968). During reading, the eyes must pause, or fixate, at a point in the line of print in order to provide usable visual information to the brain, as no information is gained while the eye is in motion (Rayner, 1997), and only about 3–6 letter spaces—essentially a word-length amount of text information—are in focus during each fixation (Just & Carpenter, 1987; Paulson & Goodman, 2008).

As eye movements are reliable and valid indicators of ongoing attentional processes, researchers are able to make inferences about reading processes using three basic types of information: where the eyes stop, for how long they stop, and where they go next. If the participants are reading a whole authentic text aloud, doing miscue analysis simultaneously with the eye-movement study is an ecologically valid extension, and this is the approach used in EMMA studies. We understand reading as a language system, including social, transactive, sociocognitive, perceptual, and psycholinguistic processes, and EMMA acts as an unobtrusive reflection of those reading processes while they are unfolding, in real time.

Figure 10.2 shows the eye movements and miscues of a teenager reading "Wide-O," by Elsin Ann Graffam (1968); two paragraphs are excerpted here. The dots represent the reader's fixations, the numbers under the dots indicate the order of the fixations, and the miscue notations represent the reader's miscues. When analyzed together, there is a large amount of information about this reading, and about this reader's reading processes.

Figure 10.2 Eye movements and miscues.

This combination of eye-movement data with oral reading data provides powerful insights into this reader's reading processes about what text elements the reader attended to and what he read aloud, in real time, during the reading of a complete, authentic text. Here are some of the highlights.

Non-linear, non-sequential processing. The second sentence of the second line was read aloud with no miscues: "So I feel like an idiot, trying to stay up all night." But while the sentence was read verbatim, only some of the words were fixated, and in a very different order than they appear in the published text: SO-SO-LIKE-LIKE-AN-TRYING-STAY-ALL. There is an interesting difference between the text that the reader *read* orally and the text that the reader *looked at* in order to construct that oral reading. In fact, it seems impossible to get from SO-SO-LIKE-LIKE-AN-TRYING-STAY-ALL to "So I feel like an idiot, trying to stay up all night." Nevertheless, that is what happened: the combination of reader expectation, background knowledge, text information, the situated context of the reading task, and the reader's strategies and stance produced an oral reading that matched the written text.

That it is possible to skip words and still read a text verbatim provides important insights to the reading process in general and the *reader* side of the reader–text equation. While the reader perceived and produced the text in the same linear, sequential way that it is presented on paper, the text was accessed—visually acquired—in a nonlinear, nonsequential manner. Even where miscues are not involved, there is no isomorphic, one-to-one "what-I-see-is-what-I-read" limitation of the reading process.

Looking at miscues. The above excerpt is even more interesting when considering the eight miscues the reader produced in this section. While common sense might dictate that the words the reader miscued are probably also words that the reader did not look at, an examination of this reader's EMMA record shows otherwise. Three of his miscues were omissions; all were directly fixated. Similarly, two of his miscues were substitutions—*we're* for WELL and *it* for THAT—and the word THAT was fixated. The reader also made three insertions—inserting *all* after the word READ in two different places and inserting *in* between STAYING and THERE. Each time this reader inserted a word, he looked directly at at least one of the words adjacent to the insertion, and in one instance—with the insertion of the word *in*—looked right at the space between the words where the insertion was made.

So with the substitutions and omissions, and even insertions, there is a copious amount of graphic information available to the reader. Given this large amount of text data, one may wonder: if the reader has so much visual information, why not use it all? But the reader *is* using information selectively in the transaction between text and reader and miscues are places where the reader's expectations control use of text information in construction of meaning.

In all the examples in this excerpt, the reader integrated his knowledge of social, pragmatic, syntactic, semantic, and graphophonic information as well as his understanding of how texts work in combination with the visual information he found in the text itself. This is not an idiosyncratic trait of just this reader; the types of EMMA patterns this reader exhibits are statistically significant across many readers (Paulson, 2008; Paulson & Freeman, 2003). EMMA shows reading to be a social, transactive, language-based process on every level, from perception of small linguistic text units to comprehension of the author's intended message on a whole-text level.

Other Research Directions

Eye-movement/miscue analysis is one direction in which miscue analysis continues to prosper and develop. Other combinations abound. For example, Flurkey's (2008) work with fine-grained analyses of readers' oral reading combined with miscue analysis has resulted in dynamic changes in our understanding the concept of fluent reading. Flurkey used a readily available computer timing program to monitor the speed of readers as they read texts during miscue analysis.

He then demonstrated how they speed up and slow down in response to what is happening in the text and the readers' miscues in transacting with the text. He found that more proficient readers actually show more variations in speed of reading over the text than less proficient readers. Flurkey showed that reading *flows* more like water over a river bed than like water through a smooth pipe.

In short, the future of miscue analysis is as promising as its past has been influential. Its nature as an ecologically valid, unobtrusive data collection and analysis instrument makes it an invaluable tool for researching authentic reading. As NCLB has brought discredit to both norm and criterion referenced mass tests, miscue analysis will continue to gain respect as a tool to fairly represent reading competence in a wide range of readers.

Important Concepts that Grow Out of Miscue Research

Miscue analysis has led to important generalizations for understanding reading and reading instruction:

- All readers make miscues.
- Comprehension is central to the reading process.
- Absolute accuracy in reading is not necessary for comprehension.
- Readers do not process meaningful text letter by letter, word by word, or character by character.
- There is a single reading process, affected by social, cultural, economic, perceptual, linguistic, and emotional factors.
- Prediction and confirmation are strategies employed by readers to comprehend text.

- Syntactic, semantic, and graphophonic knowledge are used by readers selectively and simultaneously.
- Text complexity affects the quality of miscues.
- Proficient readers are more flexible in their use of language knowledge and reading strategies than less proficient readers.
- For purposes of instruction, teachers should focus readers on making sense and encourage lots of reading and prediction or informed guessing.

Miscue analysis plays a key role in changing our understanding of reading from a primitive view of reading as rapid recognition of words to understanding it as a transactional, sociopsycholinguistic process of constructing meaning—making sense of print (Goodman, 1994). This understanding highlights the importance of reading strategies: predicting, confirming, sampling, and inferencing. It also makes clear the importance of the use of authentic texts so readers are able to use their knowledge of language and concepts about the world as they comprehend. Readers develop flexibility by using a variety of literature, including both fiction and nonfiction (Flurkey & Goodman, 2004; Goodman, Goodman, & Martens, 2002; Paulson et al., 2003). When readers face real texts with potential meaning for them, they construct meaning "to wonder and to wander around this curious world" (Merriam, 1991).

References

Brown, J., Goodman, K., & Marek, A.M. (1996). *Studies in miscue analysis: An annotated bibliography*. Newark, DE: International Reading Association.

Flurkey, A. (2008). Reading flow. In A. Flurkey, E. Paulson, & K. Goodman (Eds.), *Scientific realism in studies of reading* (pp. 267–304). Mahwah, NJ: Lawrence Erlbaum Associates.

Flurkey, A. & Goodman, Y. (2004). The role of genre in a text: Reading through the Waterworks. *Language Arts, 81*(3), 232–245.

Goodman, K. (1967). Reading: A psycholinguistic guessing game. *Journal of the Reading Specialist, 6*, 126–135.

Goodman, K. (Fall, 1969). Analysis of oral reading miscues: Applied psycholinguistics. *Reading Research Quarterly*, 9–30.

Goodman, K. (1994). Reading, writing, and written texts: A transactional sociopsycholinguistic model. In R.B. Ruddell, M.R. Ruddell & H. Singer (Eds.), *Theoretical models and processes of reading* (4th ed., pp. 1093–1130). Newark, DE: International Reading Association.

Goodman, K. (2004). Reading, writing, and written texts: A transactional sociopsycholinguistic view. In R.B. Ruddell & N.J. Unrau (Eds.), *Theoretical models and processes of reading* (5th ed., CD supplementary article ed.). Newark, DE: International Reading Association.

Goodman, K. (2008). Miscue analysis as scientific realism. In A.D. Flurkey, E.J. Paulson, & K. Goodman (Eds.), *Scientific realism in studies of reading* (pp. 7–21). Mahwah, NJ: Lawrence Erlbaum Associates.

Goodman, K., Smith, E.B., Meredith, R., & Goodman, Y. (1987). *Language and thinking in school* (3rd ed.). New York: Richard C. Owen.

Goodman, K. & Smith, F. (January, 1971). On the psycholinguistic method of teaching reading. *Elementary School Journal*, pp. 171–181.

Goodman, Y. (March, 1991) Roots of the whole-language movement. *The Elementary School Journal*, pp. 113–127.

Goodman, Y. & Burke, C. (1972). *Reading miscue inventory manual: Procedures for diagnosis and evaluation.* New York: Richard C. Owen.

Goodman, Y. & Marek, A. (1996). *Retrospective miscue analysis: Revaluing readers and reading.* New York: R.C. Owen Publishers.

Goodman, Y., Goodman, K., & Martens, P. (2002). *Text matters: Readers who learn with decodable texts.* Oak Creek, WI: National Reading Conference.

Goodman, Y.M., Watson, D.J., & Burke, C.L. (1987). *Reading miscue inventory: Alternative procedures.* New York: R.C. Owen Publishers.

Goodman, Y.M., Watson, D.J., & Burke, C.L. (1996). *Reading strategies: Focus on comprehension* (2nd ed.). New York: R.C. Owen Publishers.

Goodman, Y.M., Watson, D.J., & Burke, C.L. (2005). *Reading miscue inventory: From evaluation to instruction* (2nd ed.). New York: Richard C. Owen Publishers.

Graffam, E.A. (1968). Wide O. In A. Asimov, *100 Malicious Little Mysteries.*

Graves, D.H. (1991). All children can write. In S. Stires (Ed.), *With promise: Redefining reading and writing for "special" students* (pp. 115–126). Portsmouth, NH: Heinemann.

Halliday, M. (1979). Three aspects of children's language development: Learning language, learning through language, learning about language. In Y. Goodman, M. Matlin, & D. Strickland (Eds.), *Oral and written language development research: Impact on schools.* Newark, DE and Urbana, IL: International Reading Association and National Council of Teachers and English.

Huey, E.B. (1908/1968). *The psychology and pedagogy of reading.* Cambridge, MA: The MIT Press.

Just, M.A. & Carpenter, P.A. (1987). *The psychology of reading and language comprehension.* Newton, MA: Allyn and Bacon Inc.

Lamoreaux, L. & Lee, D.M. (1963). *Learning to read through experience.* New York: D. Appleton-Century, Inc.

Lee, D. & Allen, R.V. (1963). *Learning to read through experience.* New York: Appleton-Century-Crofts.

Martin, N. & Lightfoot, M. (1988). *The word for teaching is learning: Essays for James Britton.* Portsmouth, NH: Heinemann.

Merriam, E. (1991). *The wise woman and her secret.* New York: Simon and Shuster.

Monroe, M. (1932). *Children who cannot read: The analysis of reading disabilities and the use of diagnostic tests in the instruction of retarded readers.* Chicago, IL: University of Chicago Press.

Owocki, G. & Goodman, Y. (2002). *Kidwatching: Documenting children's literacy development.* Portsmouth, NH: Heinemann.

Paulson, E. (2008). Miscue and eye movements: Functions of comprehension. In A.D. Flurkey, E.J. Paulson, & K.S. Goodman (Eds.), *Scientific realism in studies of reading* (pp. 247–264). Mahwah, NJ: Lawrence Erlbaum Associates.

Paulson, E., Flurkey, A., Goodman, Y., & Goodman, K. (2003). Eye movements and miscue analysis: Reading from a constructivist perspective. In C. Fairbanks, J. Worthy, B. Maloch, J.V. Hoffman, & D.L. Schallert (Eds.), *52nd Yearbook of the National Reading Conference* (pp. 345–355). Oak Creek, WI: National Reading Conference.

Paulson, E. & Goodman, K. (2008). Re-reading eye-movement research: Support for transactional models of reading. In A. Flurkey, E. Paulson, & K. Goodman (Eds.), *Scientific realism in studies of reading*. Mahwah, NJ: Lawrence Erlbaum Associates.

Paulson, E.J. & Freeman, A.E. (2003). *Insight from the eyes: The science of effective reading instruction*. Portsmouth, NH: Heinemann.

Rayner, K. (1997). Understanding eye movements in reading. *Scientific Studies of Reading*, *1*, 317–339.

Smith, F. & Goodman, K. (September, 2008). "On the psycholinguistic Method of Teaching Reading" revisited. *Language Arts*, *86*, 1, 61–65.

Veatch, J. (1978). *Reading in the elementary school*. New York: Richard C. Owen Publishers.

Whitmore, K.F., Goodman, Y.M., & Center for the Expansion of Language and Thinking. (1996). *Whole language voices in teacher education*. York, ME: Stenhouse Publishers.

Authors' Note: We would like to thank Sonya Armstrong and Perpie Liwanag for reading an early version of this manuscript and help with the bibliography.

Chapter 11

Spelling and Its Role in Literacy Education

An Historical Perspective

Richard E. Hodges
University of Puget Sound

There are numerous "literacies" being evoked in these contemporary times. *The Literacy Dictionary* (Harris & Hodges, 1995, p. 141), for example, defines nearly 40 literacies, ranging from *academic literacy* to *workplace literacy*. The common historical understanding for *literacy*, however, is defined in the *Oxford English Dictionary* (2004) as "The quality or state of being literate; knowledge of letters; condition in respect to education, esp. ability to read and write."[1]

Literacy in this definition is dependent upon a functional knowledge of the letters and their sequences that spell words in an alphabetic writing system. All of the words in the English language, for example, are contained in the keys of a typewriter or computer keyboard, *if* their respective letters are typed in conventional order.

Aristotle, in the third century BC, observed that "spoken words are the symbols of mental experience and written words are the symbols of spoken words" (cited in Cummings, 1988, p. 16). Several hundred years later, Isadore, the learned Bishop of Seville, reiterated Aristotle's observation when he wrote that "letters have the power to convey to us *silently* [italics added] the sayings of those who are absent" (cited in Manguel, 1996, p. 49). Charles Sainte-Beuve, an eighteenth-century French literary historian and critic, further declared that "orthography is the beginning of literature" (Matthews, 1892, p. 36). Such is the power of orthography to make it possible to preserve and distribute the thoughts of writers through time and across space to present and future readers.

The connection between orthography and literacy is the enterprise of *spelling* —the process of forming words from letters according to conventional usage. This is the role that spelling instruction performs in literacy education—that of

---

1 *Letter, literate. Literacy, literature, literary* have a common parent, the Latin word *littera* ("letter"). People who are illiterate are "unlettered," while literate people are "lettered;" and scholarly people are "well-lettered."

developing *orthographic literacy*, a knowledge of orthography underlying the processes of reading and writing.[2]

Spelling instruction not only performs a communicative function, it also plays a cultural one. As Paul Olson, an eminent literacy scholar, points out:

> . . . belief in the importance of literacy has come to so dominate our common consciousness that even a small decline in spelling-test scores is seen as a threat to the welfare of society. We see literacy, as do most other literate peoples, as central to our conceptions of ourselves as cultured, indeed civilized, people.
>
> (Olson, 1994, p. 6)

The history of orthographic literacy in the English-speaking world emerged from the arrival of Augustine and other missionaries to Britain in 597AD intent upon converting indigenous Anglo-Saxons to Christianity (Scragg, 1974, p. 1). In order to do so, they produced an alphabet consisting of Roman and some Runic letters—the Old English alphabet—with which to prepare religious texts and other materials for use in their conversion efforts.

There were considerable variations over the next several centuries in the spellings of Old English words as the orthography was adapted to the pronunciations of speakers of the various Anglo-Saxon dialects. The matter was further complicated with the Norman invasion of Britain in 1066 and the influence of the French language on the vernacular of the land. French became the language of the ruling class and of official papers of government. Later, with the centralization of Chancery record keeping and the placement in 1476 of Caxton's printing press in Westminster, a return to English as an official language emerged and a limited form of orthographic standardization began to fall into place.

As London became England's center of commerce, government, and printing, an educated prestige dialect—Received Pronunciation—developed as an oral standard upon which to base English orthography. Standard pronunciations, in turn, promoted a visual bias toward pronouncing printed words according to their spellings.[3] For the general English-speaking population, however, conformity to the standard spellings of common words was generally not the rule. People who could read but not write usually did so orally, and in their own dialects. For those who could write, correct spelling really

---

2 *Letteracy* is a recent coinage of various meanings that is intended to encompass a working knowledge of the letters and letter combinations that are used to spell words; and, conversely to pronounce words in print.

3 As English orthography stabilized, strict pronunciations were required of words in keeping with their spellings. Holofernes, a school master in Shakespeare's *Love Labours Lost* (Act 5, Scene 1) abhorred ". . . such rackers of orthography, as to speak dout . . . when he should say doubt; det when he should pronounce debt—d,e,b,t, not d,e,t . . . This is *adhominable*,—which he would call *adbominable* . . ."

didn't matter very much as long as the spoken forms of written words were recognizable.

The advent of printing inevitably had a profound effect on English society and on the advancement of literacy. Books and other printed materials could now be broadly distributed in the vernacular, thus making possible the transmission of religious and secular material to a larger and broader audience.

The principal agents of literacy instruction were "petty" schools where basic literacy skills—reading and sometimes "casting up accounts" or basic arithmetic—were taught to young scholars, mostly boys. Petty schools were usually attached to local churches and taught by hired instructors capable of teaching the "petties" to their young students. In some communities, the petties were sometimes taught by private teachers (often women) to children whose parents could afford their services.[4]

The first spelling book for children was *An A.B.C. for children.*[5] It was printed in England sometime between 1551 and 1661 and employed the "ABC method" used by teachers in ancient Rome and Greece (Bonner, 1977) and by their successors well into the eighteenth century. With this method, students were taught the alphabet letters and their names, how to combine them orally to form syllables with two or more letters (*ab eb ib bab beb bib*), then using syllables to form one-syllable words followed by multi-syllable words of increasing complexity.[6] This reading method was called *spelling* (also *true spelling*) and engaged young scholars in orally constructing and deconstructing words by their syllables.[7] Reading words aloud with their correct pronunciations according to their spellings constituted the skill of *orthoepy*.

The instructional materials used with young scholars began with the *Hornbook* from which they learned their letters. Once the letters were mastered,

---

4 Petty school masters were in many situations minimally educated themselves. Well-educated schoolmasters, those who had attended university, found their positions in grammar schools where classical education formed the curriculum and in which Latin was the principal of language or reading and writing. As one schoolmaster put it, "a good scholar will not come down so low, as the first elementary, and to so low a recompense also; it shall be left to the meanest and therefore to the worse" (Hezekiah Woodward. *A Light to Grammar*, 1641).

5 The complete title of this textbook was *An A.B.C. for Chyldren: Here is an A.B.C. devised with syllable, with the Pater Noster, the Ave Maria, and the Crede, both in Latin and in Englishe.* . . . It was actually an introductory reading book to be used by a petty master to guide instruction.

6 *Supererogatoriously* in *The English Primrose*, London, 1644, by Richard Hodges, Schoolmaster dwelling in Southwark, at the middle-gate within Mountague-Close.

7 This instructional method was first defined in print by William Bullokar, *Booke at Large*, 1580, as follows, "To divide syllable in a word [is] called spelling." Sixteen years later another writer elaborated the definition this way: "Thou has but two principall things to learne, to spell truly any word of one syllable, and to divide truly any word of many." Edmond Coote. *The English Schoole-maister*, 1596. The practice continued well into the nineteenth century, and defined by Samuel Oliver in 1825: "The division of words into syllables and letters into syllables is called 'spelling'."

instruction advanced to the *Absey* book[8] followed by a *Primer* and *Catechism*. These instructional materials ended formal schooling for many children (Bennett, 1965, p. 168). For those staying on, religious texts such as the *Psalter* and the *Testaments* provided new reading matter. In some instances, students also learned to write, if the schoolmaster was able to write as well as to read. Otherwise, writing instruction was usually provided by private teachers for a fee; for it was not uncommon in those times to find many adults in towns and villages throughout England who were able to read but unable to write (Cressy, 1977, p. 23).

In 1620, a group of English citizens set sail from Rotherhithe in the London borough of Southwark on the south bank of the Thames, bound for Plymouth Colony in the New World. They took with them their basic belongings and their culture and customs. Since the ABC method was the only instructional practice known at the time (Smith, 1986, p. 14), it readily found its place in the colonies, along with the *Hornbook*, *ABCs*, *Primer*, and *Catechism*.

While there was general agreement among the colonists of the need for catechetical materials, there were also strong disagreements over the religious teachings they provided. Between 1641 and 1684, nearly a dozen catechisms were used that expressed divergent religious views. From these materials emerged *The New England Primer* in the latter decades of the seventeenth century.[9] Early in the eighteenth century, spelling books from England were brought to the Colonies and four of them dominated colonial literacy education well into the 1800s—*A Guide to the English Tongue* (Thomas Dyche, 1707); *A New Guide to the English Tongue* (Thomas Dilworth, 1740); *Universal Spelling Book* (Daniel Fenning, 1756); and *The Only Sure Guide to the English Tongue* (William Perry, 1776).

The "English Tongue" used in the titles of three of the spellers illustrated that *orthoepy* (correct pronunciation) was a primary goal; meaning, of course, a London pronunciation that was represented by the Motherland's orthography. The spelling books, especially Dilworth's and Perry's, had widespread usage and ultimately became driving forces behind Noah Webster's aim to prepare an *American* spelling book (1783) and a dictionary (1828).[10]

---

8 The *Absey* book had the fuller title: *ABC with Catechism* [that is to say, A instruction to be learned by every person before he be brought to be confirmed by the Bishop.] It included basic religious instruction and some prayers.

9 *The New England Primer* was introduced into the Colonies in an advertisement in Newman's *News of the Stars*, Boston, 1690 (Smith, p. 19). It had the title *The New England Primer enlarged*, to which is added, more *Directions for spelling* . . . Sold by *Benjamin Harris*, at the *London Coffee House* in *Boston*. The primer contained an alphabet, syllabarium, alphabet lessons. The Lord's Prayer, Creed, Ten Commandments, figures and numeral letters, and the names of all of the books of *The Bible*.

10 Webster's speller, *The American Spelling Book; containing an Easy Standard of Pronunciation, Being the First Part of a Grammatical Institute of the English Language. In three parts*, was published in 1783. His *The American Dictionary of the English Language* appeared 45 years later in 1828. Both books led to a transformation from colonial English to an American English, represented in an American-English orthography.

Webster's *The American Spelling Book* (the famed *Blue-backed Speller*) quickly spawned numerous rival spelling books in the closing years of the eighteenth century as it gained popularity. But it was Webster's speller, subsequently revised and renamed *The Elementary Spelling Book*, that dominated sales as the nation spread westward and along with his dictionary became major forces in shaping American literacy education through much of the nineteenth century.[11]

Although the alphabet method retained its primacy in literacy instruction well into the nineteenth century, traditional views of the purposes and practices of spelling instruction as the platform to reading were being reexamined and challenged. Earlier in the eighteenth century, Robert Lowth, a British cleric and English language scholar, had pointed out that spelling had *two* functions, "spelling as the art of reading by naming the letters singly, and rightly dividing words into their syllables;" and "in writing, it is the expressing of a word by its proper letters" (Lowth, 1762). It was in this direction that literacy education now began to encompass spelling as a *writing* tool and using an *American* orthography.

Other forces were also at work that would shape the role of spelling instruction in literacy education in America. On the Continent, studies of the human mind, once the province of philosophy, were gaining momentum from an emerging science, *phrenology*, founded by a Viennese physician, Franz Joseph Gall (1758–1828). To phrenologists, the brain was composed of 27 organs, or *faculties*, each having a specific function, one of them the faculty of *language*. Believed to be located behind the eyes,[12] the language faculty contained a *verbal memory* component where words and their relationship were stored; and which with mental discipline could be strengthened by such exercises as repetition and drill that was thought to be required in learning to spell.[13]

11 The supremacy of the *Blue-backed Speller* influenced the content of competitors' spelling books, adding to its impact on literacy education. In this regard, *The Elementary Spelling Book, Revised and Adapted to the Youth of the Southern Confederacy's, Interspersed with Bible Readings on Domestic Slavery*, was published by Reverend Robert Fleming in Atlanta, Georgia in 1863. Fleming acknowledged that "no better spelling book than Dr. Webster's has ever been presented to the American people." He then explained that, because of the Union's blockade on the Confederacy had shut down supplies of the *Blue-backed Speller*, he felt compelled to produce a version for the Southern States. In it, Webster's moral lessons were replaced with Biblical quotations that Fleming believed supported domestic slavery. Fleming's speller became known as the Confederacy's "Gray-backed speller."

12 Some phrenologists contended that bulging eyes indicated a special strength of the language faculty. Although phrenology ultimately descended into a pseudo-psychology because of spurious claims by some of its proponents, aspects of the theory held steady in the early 1800s.

13 One nineteenth century spelling book author, William Adams, carried the notion of mental discipline to its limits in *A Spelling Book for Advanced Classes* (n.d.). The text contained 163 lessons, with 30 words per lesson (4,890 words), none of which provided any reference to meaning, pronunciation, and syllabication because, said Adams, "The dictionary will always be available to supply deficiencies" (Hodges, 1980, p. 15).

The traditional ABC method that was the mainstay of spelling instruction in the new nation also faced a new challenge in the form of a *whole word* approach introduced by Horace Mann, Secretary of the Massachusetts State Board of Education (1837–1848). Mann had become interested in reports from Germany of successful educational practices in reading instruction. So, in 1843 he visited Germany to study its educational system. There Mann observed a method of reading instruction which convinced him that spelling words aloud by their letters only confused young learners. He maintained, for example, that LEG spelled orally (*el'- e - jee*) L-E-G, generates ELEGY (a poem, or song, written to lament a deceased person). Words, he argued, should first be learned and studied as *whole* words before examining their parts. In keeping with the *law of association*, a tenet of *phrenology*, Mann proposed that spelling study should provide opportunities for students to make associations among similarly formed words listed in a common table, so that the spelling of any word would trigger the spellings of the others.

Spelling instruction in the nineteenth century provided more than lessons on how to spell words; it also affected students' social standing in classrooms where they were judged, ranked, and classified according to their proficiency in spelling classes. As one noted grammarian bluntly observed, "a bad speller should not pretend to scholarship" (Brown, 1823). Clara Barton (1821–1912), founder of the American Red Cross, recalled in her autobiography that, in the primary grades, she was placed in the "Artichoke" class in spelling (*artichoke* being the leading word in the three-syllable section of her spelling book), a prestigious ranking for a young girl (Finkelstein, 1989, p. 42).

Spelling books moved west with settlers along with their belongings and were readily available for purchase in country stores well into the late 1800s. The *Blue-backed Speller* was a runaway bestseller. "We sell them in cases of seventy-two dozen, and they are bought by all the large dry-good houses and supply houses, and furnished by them to every cross-roads store," a bookman reported in an 1880 issue of *Youth's Companion* (Sullivan, 1927, p. 128). Following the Emancipation at the close of the Civil War, one-and-a-half million copies of Webster's speller were sold to freed slaves who believed it necessary to have in order to learn to read (Sullivan, 1927, p. 18).

The literacy level of teachers in frontier and country schools was, like many settlers, often modest at best, due in part because the demand for teachers often exceeded the available supply. Abraham Lincoln's mother, for example, knew how to read but not to write, signing her name with an **X**. Lincoln's teacher in the frontier school he attended, "could perhaps teach spelling, reading, and indifferent writing, (and maybe) could cipher to the rule of three" (Donald, 1995, p. 16).[14]

---

14 The *rule of three* was a common arithmetic tool taught as early as the seventeenth century. Using proportion, the rule states that a fourth number of a proportion can be found if the other three numbers are known; for example "3 is to 4 as 6 is to ?"

Qualified teachers were also a rare commodity in the California mining camps of the mid-1800s. One young miner, Prentice Mulford, hard on his luck, applied for a teaching job for which he was examined by three school trustees, a doctor, a miner, and a saloonkeeper. Mulford recalled that he expected "a searching examination and trembled (because) it was years since I had seen a schoolbook." Before the doctor lay a spelling book from which Mulford was asked to spell *cat, hat, rat,* and *mat,* which he did successfully. The doctor responded, "Young man, you're hired!" (Freedman, 1984, p. 65).

Bishop L.J. Coppin, a son of slaves, recalled that his mother kept a clan-destine school in their Fredericktown, Maryland, house where she taught her children and those of neighborhood parents who could be trusted. The only text she used was *Comly's Spelling and Reading Book* (1850); and it was with this book that Coppin learned his "ABCs forward and backward." "The fact is," Coppin recollected, "that by the time you knew Comly from lid to lid, the spelling and the reading, as stories with moral lessons, and definitions, multiplication tables and all, and could teach it to others, you knew more than some present-day country teachers holding first grade certificates" (Coppin, 1919, p. 70).

English orthography readily lent itself to the mental gymnastics required to compete in the spelling bees and spelldowns held in the schoolhouses of nineteenth-century towns and countryside (Hodges, 1980).[15] Spelling contests have been memorialized in poetry and fiction, and in a recent popular film documentary *Spellbound* (Blitz & Welch, 2003). "Spelling," a retired university professor remembered, "was the *piece de resistance* and test of scholarship in the district school" (Sullivan, 1927, p. 122).[16]

As the nineteenth century neared an end, traditional views of the purposes and content of spelling instruction were challenged when Edgar Singer, a speaker at the 1880 meeting of the National Education Association, observed that:

> . . . to write the word, or to recognize it when written, constitutes the art of which oral spelling is but the theory. Written exercises are of greater worth than oral exercises. While both are necessary to insure a thorough mastery of [orthography] words which have become familiar in the pupil's speech or in his lessons should be made the basis of instruction . . .
>
> (Singer, 1880, p. 120)

15 Spelling contests are not nineteenth century inventions. Edmund Coote, in his spelling book *The English Schoole-maister* (1596), described a spelldown (also termed *opposing* or *apposing*) in the following dialogue between two students, John and Robert. John: "Do your worst, I wil prouide likewise for you, and never give you over until I have gotten the victorie: for I take no sum pleasure in any things els all day." Robert: "I am of your mind: for I haue heard our maister say, that his apposing doeth very much sharpen our wits, help our memories, and many other commodities."

16 See, for example, John Greenleaf Whittier's poem *In School days;* Brett Hart's poem *The Spelling Bee at Angels;* and Edward Eggleston's book *The Hoosier Schoolmaster.*

A few years later, Joseph Rice, a pediatrician and advocate of using education as an instrument for social improvement, conducted one of the first scientific investigations of instructional practices in spelling classes. Based on findings from his study (1897), Rice recommended several steps to take that would improve effectiveness of spelling study, including among them: using a variety of teaching methods; devoting no more than 15 minutes per day to instruction; giving preference to common words and omitting words that are easily spelled from their sounds; stressing drills on rules for adding suffixes and on small words with difficult spellings (Venezky, 1980, p. 24).[17]

Early on in the twentieth century, one of the staunchest advocates for the application of scientific principles to curriculum development was a University of Iowa professor, Ernest Horn. His influence on spelling and its role in literacy education began with a published review of the application of scientific principles and methods that should be applied to spelling instruction (Horn, 1919). It was here that he laid out specific findings and steps that were needed to develop a scientifically valid spelling curriculum; how words should be selected, grouped, studied, and tested to achieve optimum outcomes in a spelling program. Horn's recommendations impacted spelling research and curricular practice for nearly the next 40 years.[18]

Horn vigorously opposed the practice of organizing study lists with spelling-related words because, he argued, the vagaries of English orthography did not support doing so. For example, he argued that *circumference* could be spelled 396,900,000 different ways based on the various spellings of the respective sounds of the word (Horn, 1929). Words selected for spelling study, Horn declared, should only be those that are useful in daily writing (Horn, 1938).

There the matter largely rested until mid-century when, in 1953, an article in *The Elementary Journal* reported a doctoral study in which 3,000 words in an elementary spelling program were analyzed for possibly useful spelling generalizations (Hanna & Moore, 1953). Counter to Horn's contention, Moore's analysis revealed sufficient relationships between spoken and written words to lay a foundation for spelling instruction. The study foreshadowed the work of

---

17 Rice produced a speller in 1898, *The Rational Speller*, which he claimed included "a careful grading of the work in accordance with the natural growth of the child's comprehension." His speller presented common words, a small number at a time, with ample provision for drill and frequent reviews.

18 I was privileged to serve for several years as editor of *The Elementary School Journal*, a publication started in 1900 by John Dewey during his tenure as founder and director of the University of Chicago's Laboratory School. Having at hand a complete set of the *Journal* to 1975, I traced the treatment of spelling in all of the articles it included on the topic to that time. A listing of spelling issues that covered a 75-year span clearly illustrates the topics of concern to spelling curriculum researchers and practitioners throughout this period. The topics centered on: *sources of word selection* (child vs. adult needs); *organization of lists* (word frequency; thematic content; spelling difficulty of words); *grade placement and number of words for weekly study; testing* (study then test; test-study test); *study techniques* (hard spots in words; spelling by syllables in words; study of words missed on tests).

linguists and others who, a few years later, entered the debate with linguistic evidence supporting the development of spelling (and reading) programs that explicitly presented instruction on the relationship between spoken English and its written representation.[19]

Also, from a linguistic perspective, a major investigation was launched in 1962 using computer technology to examine spelling patterns in 17,310 words selected from a collegiate dictionary (Hanna, Hanna, Hodges, & Rudorf, 1966). Although aspects of the study were criticized, the main findings revealed a complex structure of American English orthography which merited the inclusion of sound–letter relationships as a basis for study in spelling programs.

Contemporary linguistic analysis also served as a basis for Richard Venezky's landmark study *The Structure of English Orthography* (Venezky, 1970) in which he documented the historical development of the writing system and its integral relationship to English speech from the vantage point of reading. Twenty-nine years later, a second book by Venezky, *The American Way of Spelling* (1999), was published which provided comprehensive coverage of the origins and development of American English orthography and its important position in literacy education.

The introduction to orthographic literacy for most children usually begins with the onset of schooling. But, in 1970, Charles Read, a doctoral student at Harvard University, challenged traditional assumptions about the origins of orthographic literacy with a report of his seminal research into the informal onset of writing and reading among preschool children (1970). Read applied "phonetics, phonology, and the study of writing systems to the understanding of how spelling develops" (Read, 1986, p. vii) among young children who informally encountered environmental print (e.g., books, road signs, labels, packaging) and from these experiences devised *spelling systems* of their own with which to write. The "invented" spellings his subjects used in their writing attempts were remarkably alike, and revealed a sequence of stages in which primitive orthographic attempts develop toward the use of standard spelling.

Read's research generated a spate of further investigations of the development of orthographic literacy from its preschool beginnings through the elementary school years and beyond. From these studies of children's developmental spellings and the linguistic and psychological factors that contribute to the maturation of orthographic literacy have emerged new terminology for the literacy education field—*phonological awareness, phonemic awareness, emergent literacy,* and more. Contemporary spelling books are far removed in purpose, content,

---

19 Two of the more influential early contributions by linguists to the debate were Leonard Bloomfield's and Clarence Barnhart's *Let's Read—A Linguistic Analysis* (1961) and Charles Fries' *Linguistics and Reading* (1962), the first an analysis of relations between speech and writing and also a beginning reading program, the latter a nontechnical survey of structural linguistic principles relevant to reading instruction.

and method from their sixteenth- and seventeenth-century ancestors. Despite differences, spelling book authors through the centuries have drawn their beliefs from shared wellsprings that have formed their beliefs and guided their writings: the role and purposes of spelling in literacy education, the nature of learning, learners, and orthography; and the kinds of instructional experiences thought to guide students to orthographic literacy.

Two insights can be gained from this brief historical glimpse into the purposes and practices of spelling instruction. First, that the acquisition of orthographic literacy is more profound than simply mastering the spellings of words. Second, that spelling instruction and reading instruction provide the warp and woof of the intellectual fabric from which orthographic literacy is formed, thus playing a crucial role in literacy education.

Orthography *is* the beginning of literature.

A Postscript

We are now well into the twenty-first century and orthographic literacy and literacy education seems for the present to be on a steady course. There are, however, rapid advances in electronic and digital technology that raise an interesting question posed by David Crystal, author of *The Cambridge Encyclopedia of the English Language* (Crystal, 1995). In a recent book, *Language and the Internet* (Crystal, 2001), Crystal asks, "Do the relaxed standards of e-mail augur an end of literacy and spelling as we know it?"

The ubiquitous *spam* and unedited email that daily fill our email boxes are samples of evidence that validate Crystal's concern. Other recent additions such as *text messaging* (short messages in which abbreviated spellings of words and phrases are used to transmit information between miniaturized communication devices) add further support to Crystal's observation.

Such concerns, however, are perhaps irrelevant. It is reasonable to predict a future in which handheld mini computers, by means of voice recognition, will record, transcribe, and print out dictation in standard orthography, properly punctuated, and grammatically correct for everyday use. Whether the resulting content is *literature* is another matter.

References

Adams, W.T. (n.d.). *A spelling-book for advanced classes*. Boston: Brewer & Tileston.

Anon. (1541). *An ABC for children. Here is an ABC. Deysied with syllables, with the Pater Noster, the Ave Maria, and the Crede, both in Latin and in Englishe*. . . . (British Library LR 419.a.7).

Bennett, H.S. (1965). *English books and readers, 1558–1603, being a study of the English book trade in the reign of Elizabeth I*. Cambridge, UK: Cambridge University Press.

Blitz, J. & Welch, S. (Producers). (2003). *Spellbound*. United States: ThinkFilm.

Bloomfield, L. & Barnhardt, C.L. (1961). *Let's read: A linguistic approach*. Detroit: Wayne State University Press.

Bonner, S.F. (1977). *Education in ancient Rome.* Berkeley & Los Angeles: University of California Press.

Brown, G. (1823). *The institutes of English grammar.* Delmar, NY: Scholars Facsimiles & Reprints, 1982.

Bullokar, W. (1580). *Bullokar's book at large, for the amendment of orthographie for English speech.* (Microfilm EEB 1475–1640; 951:4).

Comly, J. (1850). *Comly's spelling and reading book.* Philadelphia: Thomas L. Bonsal.

Coote, E. (1596). *The English schoole-maister....* (Microfilm EEB 1475–1640; A9600 736:04; Scolar Press facsimile edition, 1968).

Coppin, L.J. (1919). *Unwritten history.* Philadelphia: Book Concern.

Cressy, D. (1977). Levels of illiteracy in England, 1530–1730. *Historical Journal, 20,* 1–23.

Crystal, D. (1995). *The Cambridge encyclopedia of the English language.* Cambridge, UK: Cambridge University Press.

Crystal, D. (2001). *Language and the internet.* Cambridge, UK: Cambridge University Press.

Cummings, D.W. (1988). *American English spelling.* Baltimore & London: Johns Hopkins University Press.

Dilworth, T. (1740). *A new guide to the English tongue.* Delmar, NY: Scolar Press Facsimile, 1968.

Donald, D.H. (1995). *Lincoln.* New York: Simon & Schuster.

Dyche, T. (1707). *A new guide to the English tongue.* Delmar, NY: Scolar Press Facsimile, 1968.

Eggleston, E. (1895). *The Hoosier schoolmaster: A story of backwoods life in Indiana.* Revised edition. New York: Grosset & Dunlap.

Fenning, D. (1756). *The universal spelling book....* London, Boston (1769).

Finkelstein, B. (1989). *Governing the young: Teacher behavior in popular primary schools in nineteenth-century United States.* New York: The Falmer Press.

Fleming, R. (1863). *The elementary spelling book: Revised and adapted to the youth of the Southern Confederacy.* Atlanta, GA: J.J. Toon & Co., Publishers.

Freedman, R. (1984). *Children of the wild west.* New York: Clarion Books.

Fries, C. (1963). *Linguistics and reading.* New York: Holt, Rinehart and Winston.

Hanna, P.R, Hanna, J.S., Hodges, R.E., & Rudorf, E.H. (1966). *Phoneme-grapheme correspondences as cues to spelling improvement.* Washington, D.C.: U.S. Government Printing Office.

Hanna, P.R. & Moore, J.T. Jr. (1953). Spelling—from spoken word to written symbol. *The Elementary School Journal, 53,* 329–337.

Harris, B. (Printer) (1688) *The New England Primer.* Boston, MA.

Harris, T.L. & Hodges, R.E. (Eds.), (1995). *The literacy dictionary: The vocabulary of reading and writing.* Newark, Delaware: International Reading Association.

Hodges, R. (1644). *The English primrose....* London (Microfilm EEB 1640–1700; A2791 107:5; Scolar Press facsimile edition, 1969).

Hodges, R.E. (1980). *Early American spellers, 1775–1900.* A catalog of the titles held by the Educational Research Library, National Institute of Education.

Horn, E. (1919). Principles of method in teaching spelling, as derived from scientific investigation. In G.M. Whipple (Ed.), *The eighteenth yearbook of the National Society for the study of Education.* Part II. Fourth Report of the Committee on Economy of Time in Education. (H.P. Wilson, Chairman). Bloomington, IL, pp. 52–77.

Horn, E. (1929). A source of confusion in spelling. *Journal of Educational Research, 19,* 47–55.

Horn, E. (1938). Contributions of research to special methods in spelling. In *Thirty-seventh yearbook of the National Society for the Study of Education.* Part II. The scientific movement in education.

Lowth, R. (1762). *A short introduction to English grammar, with critical notes.* Scolar Press facsimile, 1969 (cited In Michael (1987), p. 94).

Manguel, A. (1996). *A history of reading.* New York: Viking.

Mann, H. (1827). *American Journal of Education, II.*

Mann, H. (1840). Lecture on the best mode of preparing and using spelling-books. In H. Mann, *Lectures on education.* Boston, MA: Marsh, Cape, Lyon, and Webb.

Matthews, B. (1892). *Americanisms and Briticisms, with other essays and other isms.* New York: Harper and Brothers.

Michael, I. (1987). *The teaching of English; from the sixteenth century to 1870.* Cambridge: Cambridge University Press.

Oliver, S. (1825). *A general, critical grammar of the Inglish. . . .* (In I. Michael. *The Teaching of English* (1987), p. 90.).

Olson, D. (1994). *The world on paper: The conceptual and cognitive implications of reading and writing.* New York: Cambridge University Press.

———. *Oxford English Dictionary,* second edition (1989–1997) (CD-ROM version 3.0, 2004). Oxford: Oxford University Press.

Perry, W. (1776). *The only sure guide to the English tongue.* Edinburgh: Scotland.

Read, C. (1970). *Children's perceptions of the sounds of English: Phonology from three to six.* Unpublished doctoral dissertation, Harvard University.

Read, C. (1986). *Children's creative spelling.* London, Boston & Henley: Routledge & Kegan Paul.

Rice, J.M. (1897, March & August). The futility of the spelling grind. *The Forum,* 163–172, 409–419.

Scragg, D.E. (1974). *A history of English spelling.* Manchester: Manchester University Press.

Shakespeare, W. (1995). *Love's labour's lost.* Ware, UK: Wordsworth Editions.

Singer, E.A. (1880).What constitutes a practical course of study. In *National Education Association Proceedings.* Philadelphia, Pennsylvania.

Smith, N.B. (1986). *American reading instruction.* Newark, DE: International Reading Association.

Sullivan, M. (1927). *Our Times,* Volume II. New York: Charles Scribners Sons.

Venezky, R.L. (1970). *The structure of English spelling.* The Hague: Mouton.

Venezky, R.L. (1980). From Webster, to Rice, to Roosevelt. In U. Frith (Ed.), *Cognitive processes in reading.* London, New York: Academic Press. pp. 9–30.

Venezky, R.L. (1999). *The American way of spelling: The structure and origins of American English Orthography.* New York & London: The Guilford Press.

Webster, N. (1783). *Grammatical Institute of the English Language.* Part I. Hartford, CT: Hudson & Goodwin.

Webster, N. (1817). *The American spelling book.* Boston, MA: West & Richardson.

Webster, N. (1828). *An American dictionary of the English language.* New York: S. Converse.

Woodward, H. (1641). *A light to grammar.* (Microfilm EEB 1641–1700; A2791:14).

Chapter 12

Readability

Insights, Sidelights, and Hindsights

Edward Fry
Rutgers University

Once upon a time many years ago in the middle of Africa (Uganda, 1961) I found a need for readability. I was assigned by the university to improve the reading of a group of community college instructors who were in turn going to improve the reading skills of their students. The practical problem was that the students had difficulty reading manuals for autos and other machinery. I knew, from some years running a reading clinic in the United States, that you can make more progress if you start the students out in relatively easy reading material so the students can read the materials with some comprehension and success. But how do you tell these African instructors how to select "relatively easy" reading materials in technical English? The answer, I deduced, was to use a readability formula. There not being any easily accessible readability formulas lying around in Uganda, I decided to make one. It worked for the Uganda context and, with modification and much more supporting research, it has served many thousands of teachers removed in both time and distance from that small group of community college instructors in the early 1960s.

Readability Defined

Harris and Hodges (1995) defined readability in *The Literacy Dictionary* as "the ease of comprehension because of style of writing." For the purposes of this chapter, I will focus on readability formulas that objectively assign difficulty levels to books and other written passages. Brenda Weaver, in another International Reading Association (IRA) publication *Leveling Books K–6* (2000), defines *leveling* as "selecting books to match the competencies of a reader or writer." Both definitions are correct.

At a very practical level, readability usually means the application of readability formulas. True readability does have a more general meaning found in popular dictionaries such as "easy or interesting to read—capable of being read" (The Random House Dictionary of the English Language, 1983). But in classrooms and publishing houses readability is often thought of as an objective numerical score obtained by applying a readability formula. Leveling, on the other hand, also yields a score of difficulty, but it is less objective and takes into account additional subjective factors not included in traditional readability formula. Readability formulas typically assign a grade level or some other numerical designation to a book. Readability designations have been applied to almost every kind of prose including laws, newspaper articles, test passages, military manuals, and advertising. It is not surprising that readability scores are most often found for textbooks and literature books used in the schools since most of the early research was done by university-based educational psychologists and much of the later work by or for educational publishers.

To put it in broad prospective, readability is really part of the scientific movement in education, which began in the 1920s when schools started using standardized tests to measure students' achievement and word counts to aid in curriculum development. Before that and continuing to the present, many educators use more subjective judgment with statements such as, "I think this book would be about right for my third graders." Most readability formulas, on the other hand, are so objective that they can be done by computers—simply type in a passage or scan in a whole book and a computer software program will give you an estimate of the difficulty level of the text's score (e.g, 3.0 grade level).

Most computer formulas are based on two inputs, which have been verified by many research studies (see Klare, 1988): (1) a measure of syntactic difficulty (grammatical complexity), usually measured by sentence length; and, (2) a measure of semantic difficulty (meaning or word meaning). A common measure of semantic difficulty is word length measured in syllables or number of letters. Alternatively, semantic difficulty is judged by frequency, either an actual frequency count of the word or the fact that the word does or does not appear on a list of familiar words. These two basic factors have been supplemented, and occasionally replaced, by a number of other input factors such as book length and other forms of subjective judgment of difficulty.

In fact, any readability formula must be used along with subjective judgment because formulas do not take many important factors into account, such as:

- **Motivation**—is the student really interested in the subject and/or are there other incentives?
- **Appropriateness**—adult novels might not be appropriate for junior high, though some of them have eighth grade readability scores.
- **Reader's background**—readers all have different cultural background and educative experiences (e.g., membership in some ethnic group, some social class, some geographical region).

To further clarify the nature and use of readability formula, it is helpful to consider some basic questions that surround readability.

What Is the Purpose of a Readability Formula?

Certainly one of readability formulas' most common purposes is to help students learn to read better. Teachers have long known that giving the student a book at the right level will both cause him or her (1) to really read it, (2) to comprehend it, and (3) to enjoy it. Give the student a book that has too high a readability level, and one or all of those three things is apt to be missing.

Aiding comprehensibility, or the transfer of information, is certainly one of the major purposes of readability. A readability formula attempts to predict the reader's understanding of the written passage. This is certainly important in selecting textbooks. Much education is expected to take place by reading the textbook in many subjects at every level from elementary school through college. Comprehensibility is also very important in many areas outside of school; it is no accident that General Motors, the Army, and the Navy have all done extensive work in readability as have all major publishing organizations whose output of manuals, correspondence, directives, and advertisements rival many traditional publishing houses.

An interesting use of readability can be found in the field of law. A number of states have Plain Language Laws, which state that various documents such as loan contracts or insurance policies must be readable. At least 27 states required plain language in insurance policies sold in their state. In practice this often means written at about the eighth grade level. President Carter signed a directive to federal government agencies that they should produce readable documents, but there is some doubt if this well-intentioned order has had much effect on such agencies as the IRS or the Department of Justice.

Readability formulas have fared rather well when tested in court. I was an expert witness in a class action suit brought against the Medicare system for informing users of their appeal rights in a difficult-to-read letter (Readability Grade Level 16). Judge Weinstein in the New York federal appellate court case found readability formulas appropriate and ordered the U.S. Dept. of Health and Welfare to rewrite a Medicare appeal letter (David v. Heckler 1984).

Some law professors have tried to get their students and the legal profession to write more clearly and drop "legalese." But considering how many lawsuits pivot on the understanding of a written document, readability has barely scratched the legal surface.

How Do We Know If Readability Formulas Are Any Good?

Readability is one of the most widely researched areas in education. Klare (1988) stated that there are over 1,000 published articles on readability. A more recent look (2006) in the ERIC system under the entry term *readability* yielded 2,692 documents. The overwhelming majority say readability works in fields as diverse as adult basic education and horticulture. The demonstration of validity is most often found in the correlation with a comprehension test. The student understands less as the readability score increases. The proof of student comprehension is often a multiple choice comprehension test but sometimes it is a written or oral response.

A somewhat unique comprehension proof is the use of a *cloze test* in which the student is asked to fill in blanks where words were omitted. One advantage of a cloze score is that it is very objective; for example, every fifth word can be omitted and only exact word replacement is counted. Cloze thus eliminates the subjectiveness of writing or selecting comprehension test items.

Another demonstration of the validity of readability formulas is the correlation with oral reading errors. As readability score increases so do oral reading errors. This interestingly enough substantiates the three levels, *frustration, instructional,* and *basic,* suggested by Emmett Betts in 1946. He proposed that a student read a passage and that one oral reading error in every 20 words would place that reading material on the student's *instructional level,* more errors would place the material on the student's *frustrational level,* and fewer errors on the *independent level.* But teachers have long known that too difficult material shouldn't be used. Readability formulas simply refine and objectify this concept.

Readership is a concept borrowed from library science and journalism. Basically it is concerned with how many people are reading their materials. Studies have shown that by lowering the readability score, readership increases.

Readability can also be shown by eye–voice span. Turn off the light in the middle of a student reading aloud and see how many words he continues to say. The more words he continues the easier the readability of the passage. In other words, the greater the distance between where the eye is fixating and where the voice is saying them, the easier the reading material.

A similar objective demonstration, or proof, is found in levels of subvocalization. *Subvocalization* is often thought of as the little voice you hear inside your head while reading silently. More objectively it can be measured by electrodes placed on the lips to monitor tiny muscle movements. The greater the subtle muscle movement the more difficult the passage.

Subjective judgment has also been used to validate formulas. A group simply reads a number of passages then ranks them. This ranking is greatly facilitated (made more reliable) if judgment is aided by comparisons with a set passage of known standard difficulty. This is the basis of the Singer (1975) readability procedure. Singer assigned readability grade levels by having the teacher or editor compare graded paragraphs with the text sample. Subjective judgment is part of the Reading Recovery book leveling procedure.

Finally, most formulas agree fairly well on ranking a set of books. We could say they have concurrent validity or good correlation. However, there is less agreement on giving the level. For example, one formula might place a book at fifth grade and another place the same book at sixth grade. Grade level scores are usually within a year difference. Lately readability measures have used a variety of types of scores, such as Level K or Lexile 370. See Table 12.1 for some comparisons of different types of scores.

Table 12.1 Comparison of reading levels among systems

Grade Level	Reading Recovery	DRP	Lexile	Fountas Pinnell*	Wright Group*
.5	3–5	27	70	B	B
1	10–11	35	170	F	G
2	16–17	42	370	K	L
3		46	508	)	Q

ATOS = Advantage TASA Open Standard (Similar to Flesch Kincaid); DRP = Degrees of Reading Power (TASA, 1999); Reading Recovery (Clay, 1991); Lexile (Meta Metrics, 1995); Fountas & Pinnell (1999); Wright Group (publishers Bothel, WA).
* Indicates scores from *leveling*. The others are readability formulas.

Are Readability Formulas Criticized?

Yes, they certainly are. Some of the major criticisms are partly philosophical; namely, there are still many educators who oppose the scientific method. To them classifying literature prose into a numerical score of difficulty is abhorrent. These same people frequently oppose standardized test scores. They prefer subjective judgment to objective scores. Flying under such banners as *whole language, literature based,* or earlier *progressive education,* they point out the flaws of readability formulas. Here are some of them:

Formulas and tests are sometimes wrong. Correct, there is a *standard error of measurement* in all prediction or assessment scores. There is no standard error of measurement in subjective judgment because there is no way of quantifying it. To take it out of measurement terms, readability formulas are sometimes wrong, but subjective judgment is sometimes "wronger." It is difficult to have a standard error if you don't use objective measures or understand or don't wish to use the applications of probability inherent in the normal distribution curve.

Readability formulas are also criticized for causing bad writing, sometimes called *formula writing* or "dumbing down" textbooks. The criticism goes something like this: "The reason many elementary textbooks and some children's trade books are so bad is because the writer had to write them to a certain grade level." While there is some truth in this, the formula didn't cause the bad writing, the formula is meant to estimate (predict) readability after a piece is already written. It is not the formula's fault if the publisher has a bad editor and a bad writer. For some comments on how to simplify and clarify writing, see Fry's article on writeability (in Zakaluk & Samuels, 1988, or ERIC ED 220 799). In brief, readability formulas are not writers' guides; there is much more to good writing than two simple inputs such as word and sentence length.

The critics are correct in pointing out that readability formulas do not take into account all of the more cognitive factors that make reading difficult. The formula-makers simply point out that the formulas are useful in doing what they are supposed to do, and that is in predicting comprehension and reading ease by a number of traditional and experimental measures.

Readability is not the same thing as *legibility*. Legibility has to do with type size, spacing, and the quality of letter formation (in handwriting for example). Publishers sometimes take an old children's story and set it in large type. This might increase sales to parents but it really does not change the true readability much and the readability score not at all.

How Old Is the Readability Field?

The first readability formula was published in 1923 by Lively and Pressey. However, before that there have been numerous discussions of literary criticism, rhetoric, and writing style and they date back to Aristotle and continue to the present. William Holmes McGuffey is credited with writing the first series of graded readers in the mid-1800s. The McGuffey Readers sold over 130 million copies between the 1850s and the early 1900s. Considering that the total population of the United States was 23 million in 1850 and only 76 million in 1900, that means a very high percentage of the school population used McGuffey's graded readers. This is interesting proof that graded reading textbooks had wide acceptance.

There are several rather detailed histories of readability (Chall, 1958; Klare, 1984; Gilliland, 1972; Harris & Jacobson, 1979). Discussions of readability also occur in many major reading methods textbooks used in teacher training, such as Harris and Sipay (1985), Ruddell (1999), Manzo and Manzo (1995), and Vacca, Vacca, and Gove (1995).

The most widely used formula in schools and with educational publishers in the 1950s, 1960s and 1970s was the Dale Chall formula (Dale & Chall, 1948). Businesses tended to use the Flesch formula (1948), or its slight modification known as the *Flesch Kincaid*.

The original Dale Chall formula graded books from grade 4–12, so for grades 1–4 in the 1960s, the Spache formula (1953) became popular for grading books below fourth grade. Both used a list of familiar words, sentence length, and required a numerical calculation.

In the 1980s popularity shifted, as Klare (1988) writes:

> Another significant move toward the ease of usage is the Readability Graph developed by Fry (1963). The Graph permits a direct estimate of reading grade level on entering with syllable length and number of sentences per 100 word sample, thus providing another way of avoiding the manual use of a formula. It seems safe to say that in its most recent version (1977), Fry's Graph is the most widely used of all readability methods.

By 2000, readability had become less dependent on one or a few formulas and much more diverse. The readability grading of books is now largely done by publishers and large companies often using formulas which require their computers. For example, Advantage Learning Systems has a graded list of 25,000 books, which contains most of the trade books used in schools. They use their own formula, known as *ATOS* (Advantage TASA Open Standard), which uses the inputs of sentence length, average grade level of words, and length of book. This formula uses a computer and the entire content of the book, not just samples of text. The formula yields grade-level scores that are coordinated with their own STAR reading achievement test (Standardized Test for Achievement of Reading).

Another company that has analyzed 15,000 books is TASA (Touchstone Applied Science Associates) using their own computerized readability formula, which yields DRP units (Degrees of Reading Power). Their inputs are sentence length, word length, and proportion of common words. These readability levels coordinate with their own reading test, which yields DRP units.

A third company that is doing computerized readability on large amounts of materials (26,000 trade books) is Meta Metrics. This program output is in units called *Lexiles*. Lexiles can be translated into grade levels. A student can take their achievement test that yields Lexiles, or any well-known standardized test like the Stanford 9 Achievement Test.

Traditional readability formulas like the Dale Chall and Fry Graph are also available in computer format for individual use. One company providing these is Micro Power & Light Co. Lexiles, DRP, and ATOS are not available for individual computers.

What Is "Leveling"?

Leveling refers to various systems of grading books for difficulty using a larger number of subjective and objective factors than most readability formulas. Leveling sometimes incorporates more traditional readability formulas or the inputs of traditional formulas. It is used much more at the primary levels than upper levels. The goal of leveling is often fluency, rather than strictly comprehension. Some of the factors taken into account by some of the leveling procedures are:

*   **Content**—is it appropriate or familiar to that age group?
*   **Illustrations**—do pictures tell the story or explain vocabulary?
*   **Length**—are there two words on a page? how many pages in the book?
*   **Levels**—(scores) are not necessarily grade levels, often finer grading.
*   **Curriculum**—levels related to teaching methods and/or framework.
*   **Language structure**—includes repetitious words or phrases, flow.
*   **Experience**—levels can be adjusted using subjective judgment from teaching experience.
*   **Format**—type size, spacing, page layout.

The modern use of leveling is due in no small part to the work of the New Zealand Department of Education. It was partly popularized in the United States by Marie Clay (1991) and her Reading Recovery system, which used early intervention of reading tutoring for children who had a high probability of failure. The Reading Recovery system found a need to find books with closely spaced difficulty level, particularly at the first and second grade levels. Most traditional readability formulas are not particularly sensitive at those levels. Traditional wide range readability formulas such as the Dale Chall and Fry Graph only give whole grade designations at grades 1 and 2. Large company book readability formulas such as Lexiles, DRP, and ATOS do have finer unit designations but usually lack the more subjective text support factors.

Readability formulas aimed at the primary level, grades 1–4, like the Spache (1953) and Gunning (1998) do give tenths of a year designations. However, the Spache and Gunning, like the other traditional formulas, still use only the two traditional inputs of sentence length and vocabulary.

Several leveling systems have book lists of a number of leveled books. Fountas and Pinnell (1999) have over 7,000 books, Weaver (2000) has over 2,000 books and Gunning (1998) over 1,000 books. Gunning's leveling incorporates his own primary readability formula, and Weaver's leveling incorporates the Fry Graph, Dale Chall formula, or DRP. Book leveling can be done by classroom teachers.

Book leveling is also a major part of the Reading Recovery system of reading teaching (Clay, 1991). She discusses *text support*, which includes text features that are predictive, repetitive, and close to a student's natural language.

Are Readability Formulas Available for Other Languages?

Klare (1988) reported that there are readability formulas for 14 languages ranging from Afrikaans to Vietnamese. Most of the languages are alphabetic and use the two major inputs of syntax and semantics, which in practice is sentence length and vocabulary. An interesting problem occurs in nonalphabetic languages like Chinese, which is written in ideographs (characters). The inputs for Chinese are vocabulary (proportion of words on a 5,600-word list) and brush strokes per character. Other languages have unique problems; for example, Spanish has many longer polysyllabic words than English. Gilliam, Pena, and Mountain (1980) found that in using the Fry Graph for the first three grades you need to subtract 67 from the average syllable count.

A readability formula developed in Sweden and that is used in Europe is the *lix*, which is short for "lasbarhetsindex" (which translated means readability index), and is simply sentence length plus word length. A later modification is called *Rix* and it is the number of long words divided by sentence length.

What Do Readability Formulas Actually Look Like?

Since there are over 100 readability formulas it would be difficult to show them all, but here are a few to give you a more concrete idea of what they look like. The original readability formula developed by Lively and Pressey (1923) used five inputs and six numerical constants in their formula to yield an average comprehension score:

x1 = .01029x2 + .009012x5 − .02094x6 − .03313x7 − .01485x8 + 3.77
x1 = average comprehension score
x2 = number of hard words not on Dale List of 769
x5 = number of personal pronouns
x6 = average number of words per sentence
x7 = percentage of different words
x8 = number of prepositional phrases

Readability formulas have since been greatly simplified. The New Dale Chall Readability Formula (Chall & Dale, 1995) has only two inputs to get grade level but is necessary to have the manual, which includes a 3,000-word vocabulary of familiar words and tables to yield grade level or cloze scores.

The Fry Graph, used widely in schools and by educational publishers, requires two inputs: sentence length and word length in number of syllables. These are entered into a graph to yield grade level.

To get Lexiles, DRP units, or ATOS Grade level you pretty well need a large computer—which in practice means that it is usually done by the company which developed those formulas.

The Flesch Kincaid Reading Ease Formula is used widely in industry and is fairly easy to calculate:

$$Grade\ Level = .4\ (words/sentence) + 12\ (syllables/word) - 16$$

Leveling requires specific directions according to which leveling system you wish to use. As was mentioned earlier, leveling often requires a number of subjective judgment factors such as content appropriateness, format, language structure, and illustration use.

What Are Some Other Applications of Readability Formula (Outside of Education)?

The concept of readability, and more specifically readability formulas, has had an important influence on American education and the selection of school reading materials. To a lesser extent readability has influenced written communication in the armed services, industry, government, and law. Some important practical uses of readability outside of textbooks are:

- **Newspapers**—Rudolf Flesch was hired by the Associated Press to bring down the readability of front page news stories—he did (from Grade 16 to Grade 12).
- **Public health**—schools of nursing found the need for materials on illness prevention and correction so they include readability formulas in some of their textbooks.
- **Insurance**—a number of state insurance commissioners demand that policies issued in their state be readable. In practice that means about Grade 8.
- **Banks**—in some states, such as New York, plain language laws state that consumer loan documents be readable. The banks resisted, saying that the legal language was necessary because it had been tested in the courts. Yet when the banks rewrote the loan documents in plain language they had fewer lawsuits—maybe because the customers understood what they were signing.

Conclusion

The fundamental purpose of readability is to improve reading comprehension. This is particularly important in selecting textbooks and trade books for school use, but it is important to consider readability in any type of written communication. Other important uses of readability are in selecting materials for successful reading instruction and for increasing the readership of library books and periodicals. Leveling is a variation of readability more often used along with instruction methods at the primary levels. It uses a number of subjective factors and has the related goals of fluency and teachability

Research has shown that most readability formulas are based on the two factors of syntax (often sentence length) and semantics (word difficulty). Furthermore, most formulas will rank a set of materials in the same difficulty order but there is less agreement on obtaining the same grade level for any one piece of writing. There is even less agreement on the way the readability score is reported. A grade level score is widely used, but difficulty is also reported in a variety of scores, such as alphabet (A, B, C, etc.), Lexiles, and DRP units. Readability is an active field under continuous development. The more than 2,500 references to readability in the ERIC system testify to its widespread uses and interest.

References

Anderson, J. (1983). Lix and Rix: Variations on a little known readability index. *Journal of Reading, 26,* 490–496.

Benson, R.W. (1985). The end of legalese: The game is over. *New York University Review of Law and Social Change, 13,* 519–573.

Betts, E.A. (1946). *Foundations of reading instruction.* New York: American Book Co.

Chall, J. (1958). *Readability: An appraisal of research and application.* Columbus, OH: Bureau of Educational Research, Ohio State University.

Chall, J., Bissex, C., Conrad, S.S., & Harris-Sharples, S.H. (1996). *Holistic assessment of texts, scales for estimating the difficulty of literature, social studies and science materials.* Cambridge MA: Brookline.

Chall, J.S. & Dale, E. (1995). *Manual for the new Dale-Chall Readability Formula.* Cambridge, MA: Brookline Books.

Clay, M. (1991). *Becoming literate: The construction of inner control.* Portsmith, NH: Heinemann.

Dale, E. & Chall, J.S. (1948). A formula for predicting readability. *Educational Research Bulletin*, Ohio State University, 27, 11–20.

David v. Heckler (1984), Appellate Court Case No. 79C2813, U.S. District Court, E.D. New York.

DRP Program: The Readability Standard. (1999). Brewster, NY: Touchstone Applied Science Associates (TASA).

Flesch, R.F. (1948). A new readability yardstick. *Journal of Applied Psychology, 32,* 221–233.

Fountas, I. & Pinnell, G.S. (1999). *Matching books to readers: Using leveled books in guided reading.* Portsmith, NH: Heinemann.

Fry, E.B. (1977). Fry's readability graph: Clarifications, validity, and extensions to Level 17. *Journal of Reading, 21,* 242–252.

Fry, E.B. (1988). Writeability: The principles of writing for increased comprehension. In B. Zakaluk & S.J. Samuels (Eds.), *Readability It's past, present, and future,* pp. 77–97. Newark, DE: International Reading Association. (ERIC ED 220 799).

Fry, E.B. (1989). *Legal aspects of readability.* ERIC System No. ED 322 489.

Fry, E.B. (2001). Readability. In B. Guzzetti (Ed.), *Literacy in America: An encyclopedia.* Denver, CO: ABC-CLIO.

Fry, E.B. (2002). Readability versus leveling. *The Reading Teacher, 56,* 3, 286–291.

Gilliam, B., Pena, S.C., & Mountain, L. (1980). The Fry Graph applied to Spanish readability. *The Reading Teacher, 33,* 426–430.

Gilliland, J. (1972). *Readability.* London: University of London Press.

Gunning, T.G. (1998). *Best books for beginning readers.* Boston, MA: Allyn & Bacon.

Harris, A.J. & Jacobson, M.D. (1979). A framework for readability research: Moving beyond Herbert Spencer, *Journal of Reading, 22,* 390–398.

Harris, A.J. & Sipay, E. (1985). *How to increase reading ability* (8th ed.). New York & London: Longman.

Harris, T.L. & Hodges, R.E. (1995). *The literacy dictionary: The vocabulary of reading and writing.* Newark, DE: International Reading Association.

Klare, G.R. (1984) "Readability." In Pearson, P.D. (Ed.) Handbook of reading research. New York: Longman.

Klare, G.R. (1988). The formative years. In B. Zakaluk & S.J. Samuels (Eds.), *Readability: It's past, present, and future* (pp. 14–35). Newark, DE: International Reading Association. (ERIC ED 220 799).

The Lexile framework for reading. (1995). Durham, NC: Meta Metrics Inc.

Lively, B.A. & Pressey, S.L. (1923). A method of measuring vocabulary burden of textbooks. *Educational Administration and Supervision, 9,* 389–398.

Manzo, A.V. & Manzo, U.C. (1995). *Teaching children to be literate.* Fort Worth, TX: Harcourt Brace.

New Breakthrough in Measuring Readability: the ATOS Readability Formula for Books. (2000). Wisconsin Rapids, WI: Advantage Learning Systems Inc.

Rabin, A.T. (1988). Determining difficulty levels in test written in languages other than English. In B. Zakaluk & S.J. Samuels (Eds.), *Readability: It's past, present, and future* (pp. 46–76). Newark, DE: International Reading Association. (ERIC ED 220 799).

Readability calculations. (1999). (Manual for computer disk). Dallas, TX: Micro Power & Light Co.

Ruddell, R.B. (1999). *Teaching children to read and write.* Boston, MA: Allyn and Bacon.

Simply Stated. (1983). Washington, DC: American Institute for Research.

Singer, H. (1975). A non-computational procedure for quickly estimating readability level. *Journal of Reading Behavior, 7,* 255–267.

Spache, G. (1953). A new readability formula for primary grade reading material. *Elementary School Journal, 53,* 410–413.

Thorndyke, E.L. (1921) *The teachers wordbook.* New York: Teachers College, Columbia University.

Vacca, J.A., Vacca, R., & Gove, M.K. (1995). *Reading and learning to read.* New York: Harper Collins.

Venezky, R.L (1984). The history of reading. In P.D. Pearson (Ed.), *The Handbook of Reading Research* (pp. 3–38). New York and London: Longman.

Vygotsky, L. (1978). *Mind and society.* Cambridge, MA: Harvard University Press.

Weaver, B.M. (2000). *Leveling books K–8: Matching readers to text.* Newark, DE: International Reading Association.

Zakaluk, B. & Samuels, S.J. (1988). *Readability: It's past, present, and future.* Newark, DE: International Reading Association (ERIC ED 292 058).

Part IV

Teaching, Teacher Education, and Professional Development

Chapter 13

Literacy Education at a Crossroad

Can We Counter the Trend to Marginalize Quality Teacher Education?

Gerald G. Duffy, Sandra M. Webb, and Stephanie Davis
University of North Carolina-Greensboro

Old saying: "The main thing is to keep the main thing the main thing."

The main thing for literacy education has long been development of professional teachers—that is, teachers who make informed decisions:

- when assessing student strengths and needs
- when responding appropriately to student misunderstandings during lessons
- when designing problem-solving tasks in literacy
- when determining how to reteach when things go wrong
- when adapting instruction for students whose background and language may be quite different from the teachers', and
- when developing excited, engaged, and inspired readers.

Futurists and various educational experts continue to support this goal (National Center on Education and the Economy, 2007; Forum for Education and Democracy, April, 2008; Shulman, 2004). But it is now being challenged by current policy, and the result is a trend to marginalize quality teacher education. Two examples are illustrative.

First, emphasis on test scores as the *only* measure of accountability is growing (for instance, Grier and Holcombe [2008] say the criterion for success in their school district is "students' projected and actual test scores and data about gains and losses in student achievement relative to a district-wide mean" [p. 27]). This emphasis threatens quality teacher education because, in order to raise test scores, more and more schools demand fidelity to program designs and require teacher candidates to teach with highly prescriptive materials. As a result, our student teachers neglect higher-level thinking (Correnti & Rowan, 2007), self-regulated learning (Paris, Byrnes, & Paris, 2001; Randi, 2004; Zimmerman & Schunk, 2001), and high-challenge, authentic tasks (Duke et al., 2006; Miller & Faircloth, in press; Parsons, 2008), and the thoughtful, informed, pedagogical decision-making associated with professionalism is minimized (see, for instance, Valli & Buese, 2007). Pearson (2007) calls this the "McDonaldization of teaching" (p. 154) because teachers are trained to follow a routine that forces them to be less thoughtful rather than more thoughtful. As such, quality teacher education is threatened by policy emphasis on test scores and technical means for increasing test scores.

Another illustration of the move to marginalize quality teacher education is the trend of universities and schools of education to put more and more courses online as a means for producing more teachers at less cost. The issue here is not "distance learning versus no distance learning." Distance learning is here to stay because it is an economical way to disseminate declarative and procedural knowledge and because it gives distant students equal access. What *is* at issue is whether online courses can develop professional teachers. Two problems are illustrative: First, while distance learning can convey declarative and procedural knowledge, can it develop teacher candidates' ability to deal thoughtfully and adaptively with the tentative, problematic nature of class-room life and with deeper issues associated with teaching? While electronic discussion boards and some websites provide opportunity for limited discussion of such issues, they do not meet the higher standards of discourse and argument associated with face-to-face collaborative groupwork, in-class discussions of teaching dilemmas, group analysis of cases, and guided analysis of difficult teaching decisions. Second, can we be sure electronic students are actually doing the coursework? One acquaintance of ours, for instance, reports he is enrolled in an online reading methods course at a major university, but that his mother is doing the coursework. He told us, "It's easy. Just give her your password and she can log on, do the assignments and do the discussion board stuff, and I get the credit." In short, without careful thinking and quality control safeguards, online courses may not foster an informed, reasoned, and passionate corps of teachers and, as such, quality teacher education is marginalized.

In sum, when it is test scores that count, smart policymakers turn to cheaper and quicker alternatives to teacher education because technicians can increase scores by limiting teaching to procedural drill and practice. So the policy goal becomes training rather than educating, and professionalism in teaching is marginalized.

What Can Literacy Educators Do?

One could blame policymakers for this situation. But we focus here on *our* share of the responsibility. Specifically, we have not generated enough research data to convince policymakers that *educating* teachers is essential and that training is inadequate.

This is not to say that there have been no teacher education research efforts.

To the contrary, two recent studies are exemplary: the three-year study of graduates of teacher education programs nominated as *excellent* (Hoffman et al., 2005; Hoffman, Sailors, Duffy, & Beretvas, 2004), and a study of what happens to graduates when they become beginning teachers (Valencia, Place, Martin, & Grossman, 2006). On the whole, however, and as Risko et al. (2008) recently reported, there are relatively few studies validating the effectiveness of teacher education. For instance, Risko et al. could find only 82 empirical studies that met their criteria and, of those, only a small number showed an effect on actual practice, with even fewer demonstrating an impact on student achievement. Other studies report similar findings. For instance, one noted that preservice teachers seldom adapted their instruction even though they were enrolled in a teacher education program having as its primary mission development of thoughtfully adaptive teachers (Duffy et al., 2008), while a second noted that fully one-third of the teacher candidates enrolled in a reform-based mathematics program rejected reform-based math practices throughout their field experiences (Stein, 2008).

Such findings convince us that we must follow up on the Risko et al. (2008) recommendation ". . . to form research collaboratives that can shape the public and policy discourse on teacher education" (p. 283). That is, we must study our own work at our own sites as a means for establishing that educating professionally thoughtful teachers is worth the time, effort, and expense.

Specifically, we propose a three-step strategy. First, when carrying out our research agendas, we must not only answer our particular research questions but also note implications for teacher education. While we sometimes do this now, we seldom follow up. That is, we seldom follow our graduates into the field to document that they do what we taught them to do (and, of course, to document that what we taught them to do positively impacts student learning), and we seldom make systematic attempts to change our teacher education practices based on what we learn about our graduates. Hence, our suggested second step is that we commit (1) to engaging in systematic follow-up studies of our graduates to determine their effectiveness, (2) to making program changes to correct revealed flaws or to strengthen weak areas, and (3) to collecting data designed to determine whether those changes are effective. The final step is to look across small studies conducted at various institutions as a means for disseminating findings about the effects of teacher education practices and how to improve them. A collectively created website, under the auspices of a professional organization such as the International Reading Association and modeled after the Project on the Next Generation of Teachers at the Harvard Graduate School of Education (http://www.gse.harvard.edu/%Engt/) would provide a growing data set that, over time, would validate quality teacher education.

Examples of How Literacy Educators Can Study Their Own Practice

As we note above, we believe we must accumulate data at our own teacher education sites to disabuse policymakers of the belief that literacy instruction can be "technicized." But what kind of things can literacy educators study?

We suggest below five possibilities. They are illustrative only. The important point is that teacher educators must take proactive research action if teacher education as we know it is to survive.

Suggestion 1: Continuing to Press for Quality Practicum Experiences

A priority suggestion is to empirically establish, by studying our own programs and our own graduates, the necessity of quality practicum experiences. At some point, all teacher candidates are assigned field placements in classroom settings. However, as we note above, school districts often require student teachers to implement practices that contradict university courses (Smagorinsky, Cook, Moore, Jackson, & Fry, 2004).

So how can we study practicum experiences and make the point that some field experiences are better than others?

One strategy is to redefine practicum sites as research sites that engage all stakeholders in inquiry (Graham, 2006; Rodgers & Keil, 2007; Tsui & Law, 2007). That is, teacher educators collect data regarding the impact of different kinds of field experiences, student teachers study the effectiveness of applying their course assignments in real situations similar to the concept of "learning in and from practice" (Ball & Cohen, 1999), and classroom teachers examine questions relating to the challenges of their practice. By collecting data on how different field experience impact student teachers, we would establish the need for practicum experiences in which schools are committed to modeling professional thinking and teacher educators are committed to being active agents in schools. As a result, we would (1) minimize the current problem of student teachers shifting their allegiance from practices emphasized in university courses to practices emphasized in the school, and (2) generate data to combat the current trend to "technicize" teachers.

Suggestion 2: Developing Knowledge Beyond Declarative and Procedural

Most of the knowledge dispensed in teacher education courses is declarative (i.e., knowing what to teach) and procedural (i.e., knowing how to teach). But as Greene (1991) points out, declarative and procedural knowledge is often of limited use in real classrooms because "general principles never fully apply to new and special situations . . ." (p. 7). When teachers are asked about their instruction, they often say, "it depends," rather than referring to a particular declarative or procedural rule or to a particular research-based finding.

So what is this additional kind of knowledge? Schepens, Aelterman, and Van Keer (2007) recently referred to it as situational knowledge, particularly situations relating to teacher–pupil interaction. Other instructional studies similarly describe teachers making decisions based on situational knowledge. For instance, effective teachers are often described as making independent, "against the grain" decisions when they feel it is necessary (see, for instance, Roehler, Duffy & Warren, 1988); or as "taking charge" of knowledge by orchestrating together a wide variety of techniques and strategies that fit the situation but may not be theoretically or ideologically pure (Wharton-McDonald, Pressley, & Hampston, 1998). One first grade teacher we observed noted that students repeatedly called the main story character a boy during a picture walk, so she used that as an opportunity to spontaneously present a mini lesson about stereotyping and its negative effects. This was a situationally appropriate addition that added depth and vitality to the lesson without jeopardizing basic reading content.

Or, teachers may be employing conceptual knowledge that allows them to "see the forest for the trees"—that is, when engaged in the day-to-day tasks of managing kids, teaching skills and strategies, and prepping for tests of accountability, they keep the big picture in mind, and in the minds of their students as well. Bransford, Darling-Hammond and LePage (2005) liken it to an orchestra where the conductor oversees all the various components but does not lose sight of producing a symphony. Professional teachers, like conductors, understand that declarative and procedural knowledge is crucial but they use their understanding of large conceptual purposes for literacy to rethink ideas and practices, to transform knowledge to fit situations, and to change what they are doing when, in their judgment, there is a need to do so.

We know little about such knowledge or how to develop it. Studying such teacher knowledge in the context of our own teacher education programs can help validate its role in quality teacher education programs.

Suggestion 3: Teacher Vision

A third suggestion is to study teacher vision and whether it plays a role in professional thinking. Educators frequently note that the best teachers develop an internal "sense of self" (Paris et al., 2001) representative of ". . . the eternal human yearning to be connected to something larger than our own egos" (Palmer, 2003, p. 377). It is a heightened self-knowledge, particularly self-knowledge regarding one's purpose and intent as a teacher.

This aspect of teaching is described using various labels. While many call it *vision* (Bransford et al., 2005; Duffy, 2002; Feiman-Nemser, 2001), others refer to it as *volitional control* (Randi, 2004) or as *agency* (Alsup, 2006). It is assumed that vision (or volitional control, or agency) explains why professional teachers are comfortable with the idea that there are few hard and fast answers in teaching, why good teachers embrace the inherent ambiguity of classroom life, why they have no illusions that everything they do will be scientifically based, and why they are disposed to use research findings in combination with their own judgment. It is a teacher's vision, it is assumed, that drives a commitment to keep the main thing the main thing in spite of the weight of policy and program requirements.

While we *think* vision is part of professional teaching, we have little data. Literacy educators can combat the trend to marginalize quality teacher education by studying the role of vision in their own graduates' pedagogical thinking.

Suggestion 4: Assessment Practices

A fourth potential research focus is the assessment practices we employ in teacher education. For instance, in an attempt to be explicit about course requirements, we provide objectives or rubrics or scales. Teacher candidates know that to get an "A" in our courses they must complete each objective or meet the criterion on each rubric or achieve a certain level on the scale. So that is what they do. They learn each separate entity piece by piece without making coherent connections to how one engages in professional thinking.

This is an old problem. We tested it thoroughly in the late 1960s and early 1970s, when it was called *competency-based teacher education* (one major example was Michigan State University's federally funded Behavioral Science Teacher Education Program). Now it reappears as standards, benchmarks, and competencies that are intended to raise standards but, instead, encourage teacher candidates to learn individual competencies as disconnected entities. It threatens quality teacher education because the sum of the parts do not necessarily add up to the desired whole. In short, it promotes technical rather than thoughtful learning.

We have long understood that what students *do*—that is, their assessments—are experiences they use to transform difficult tasks into simpler tasks, thereby increasing chances of getting a good grade (Doyle, 1983). As teacher educators, we need to use our own programs as sites for studying how to assess teacher candidates in ways that promote professional, as opposed to technical, actions.

Suggestion 5: Preparing Teachers for the Reality of Commercial Materials

As noted earlier, school districts purchase and use commercially packaged reading programs and require student teachers to use them. We know that without help student teachers are buried under the weight of commercial program requirements (see, for instance, Rohr & Qualls, 2007, December).

Once they graduate, as Kauffman et al. (2002) report, many are "lost at sea" among the complex and competing demands of their teaching situations, and actually favor commercial materials because they need guidance in what to teach and how to teach it (see also Valencia et al., 2006). So another research-able question for literacy educators is how to help our teacher candidates become critical users of commercial literacy materials.

For the most part, teacher education has addressed this issue much like the ostrich reacting to a threat. But ignoring or excoriating the use of commercial reading programs does not help our graduates respond to the realities they face during student teaching or induction. Consequently, we need studies documenting how to help our graduates do the pedagogical thinking required to be critical consumers of commercial programs.

For instance, we could use lesson observations as a site for studying what happens when postlesson conferences emphasize both (1) the principle that professional teachers *do* adapt program suggestions and (2) strategies for ana-lyzing and evaluating how to keep student learning the main thing. That is, we need to collect data on whether what we do to help student teachers modify and adapt commercial materials has the intended impact, and whether that impact endures.

In sum, helping teachers become critical users of commercial reading materials, and studying the effects of doing so, can preserve professional think-ing in teaching. While some literacy educators may view this suggestion as teaching to the programs, we believe that we have a responsibility to study our own teachers and their ability to be professional in the reality of the world in which they will work.

Conclusion

The above suggestions for countering the move to marginalize quality literacy education are not exhaustive. Nor do we suggest that our proposal to use our own programs as research sites is new. But there have been few past efforts to validate what we do in teacher education, and those few have been little noted. Policymakers have used this relative lack of data as justification for instituting policies that marginalize quality teacher education. For preparation of profes-sional teachers to prevail, we must accumulate data policymakers cannot ignore. Amassing those data is our responsibility.

Note: The authors wish to thank Dr. Richard Allington of the University of Tennessee, Dr. Michael Kamil of Stanford University, Dr. Sheila Valencia of the University of Washington, and their UNCG colleagues in the Curriculum and Instruction Department for their helpful responses to earlier versions of this chapter.

References

Alsup, J. (2006). *Teacher identity discourses: Negotiating personal and professional spaces.* Mahwah, NJ: National Council of Teachers of English (NCTE)/Lawrence Erlbaum Association (LEA) Presses.

Ball, D.L. & Cohen, D.K. (1999). Developing practice, developing practitioners: Toward a practice-based theory of professional education. In L. Darling-Hammond & G. Sykes (Eds.), *Teaching as the learning profession: Handbook of policy and practice* (pp. 3–32). San Francisco, CA: Jossey-Bass.

Bransford, J., Darling-Hammond, L., & LePage, P. (2005). Introduction. In L. Darling-Hammond & J. Bransford (Eds.), *Preparing teachers for a changing world: What teachers should learn and be able to do* (pp. 1–39). San Francisco, CA: Jossey-Bass.

Correnti, R. & Rowan, B. (2007). Opening up the black box: Literacy instruction in schools participating in three comprehensive school reform programs. *American Educational Research Journal, 44*, 298–338.

Doyle, W. (1983). Academic work. *Review of Educational Research, 53*, 159–199.

Duffy, G. (2002). Visioning and the development of outstanding teachers. *Reading Research and Instruction, 41*, 331–344.

Duffy, G., Kear, K., Miller, S., Parsons, S., Davis, S., & Williams, B. (2008). Teachers' instructional adaptations during literacy instruction. In V. Risko et al. (Eds.), *57ᵗʰ Yearbook of the National Reading Conference.* National Reading Conference.

Duke, N., Purcell-Gates, V., Hall, L., & Tower, C. (2006). Authentic literacy activities for developing comprehension and writing. *The Reading Teacher, 60*(4), 344–355.

Feiman-Nemser, S. (2001). From preparation to practice: Designing a continuum to strengthen and sustain teaching. *Teachers College Record, 103*, 1013–1055.

Forum for Education and Democracy. (2008, April). *Democracy at risk: The need for new federal policy in education.* Washington, D.C.: The Forum for Education and Democracy.

Graham, B. (2006). Conditions for successful field experiences: Perceptions of cooperating teachers. *Teaching and Teacher Education, 22*, 1118–1129.

Greene, M. (1991). Teaching: the question of personal reality. In A. Lieberman & L. Miller (Eds.), *Staff development for education in the 90s: New demands, new realities, new perspectives* (p. 7). New York: Teachers College Press.

Grier, T. & Holcombe, A. (2008). Mission possible. *Educational Leadership, 65*, 25–31.

Hoffman, J., Roller, C., Maloch, B., Sailors, M., Duffy, G., Beretvas, S., & The National Commission on Excellence in Elementary Teacher Preparation for Reading. (2005). Teachers' preparation to teach reading and their experiences and practices in the first three years of teaching. *Elementary School Journal, 105*, 267–288.

Hoffman, J., Sailors, M., Duffy, G., & Beretvas, S. (2004). Effective elementary classroom literacy environment: Examining the validity of the TEX-IN3 observation system. *Journal of Literacy Research, 36*, 303–334.

Kauffman, D., Johnson, S.M., Kardos, S.M., Liu, E., & Peske, H.G. (2002). "Lost at sea": New teachers' experiences with curriculum and assessment. *Teachers College Record, 104*, 273–300.

Miller, S. & Faircloth. B. (in press). Motivation and reading comprehension. In S. Israel and G. Duffy (Eds.), *Handbook of Research on Reading Comprehension.* New York: Routledge.

National Center on Education and the Economy. (2007). *Tough choices, tough times: The report of the New Commission on the Skills of the American Workforce.* San Francisco, CA: Jossey Bass.

Palmer, P.J. (2003). Teaching with heart and soul: Reflections on spirituality in teacher education. *Journal of Teacher Education, 54*, 377.

Paris, S.G., Byrnes, J.P., & Paris, A.H. (2001). Constructing theories, identities, and actions of self-regulated learners. In B.J. Zimmerman & D.H. Schunk (Eds.), *Self-regulated learning and academic achievement: Theoretical perspectives* (2nd ed.) (pp. 253–287). Mahwah, NJ: Lawrence Erlbaum.

Parsons, S. (2008). Providing all students ACCESS to self-regulated literacy learning. *The Reading Teacher, 61*, 628–635.

Pearson, P.D. (2007). An endangered species act for literacy education. *Journal of Literacy Research, 39*, 145–162.

Randi, J. (2004). Teachers as self-regulated learners. *Teachers College Record, 106* (9), 1825–1853.

Risko, V., Roller, C., Cummins, C., Bean, R., Block, C., Anders, P., et al. (2008). A critical analysis of research on reading teacher education. *Reading Research Quarterly, 43*(3), 252–288.

Rodgers, A. & Keil, V.L. (2007). Restructuring a traditional student teacher supervision model: Fostering enhanced professional development and mentoring within a professional development school context. *Teaching and Teacher Education, 23*, 63–80.

Roehler, L., Duffy, G., & Warren, S. (1988). Adaptive explanatory actions associated with teaching of reading strategies. In J. Readance & S. Baldwin (Eds.), *Dialogues in literacy research* (pp. 339–346). 37th Yearbook of the National Reading Conference. Chicago: National Reading Conference.

Rohr, J. & Qualls, R (2007, December). *Teachers' visions: Are they sustained on the job?* A paper presented at the National Reading Conference, Austin, TX.

Schepens, A., Aelterman, A., & Van Keer, H. (2007). Studying learning processes of student teachers with stimulated recall interviews through changes in interactive cognitions. *Teaching and Teacher Education, 23*, 457–472.

Shulman, L. (2004). *Wisdom of practice: Essays on teaching, learning and learning to teach.* San Francisco, CA: Jossey-Bass.

Smagorinsky, P., Cook, L.S., Moore, C., Jackson, A.Y., & Fry, P.G. (2004). Tensions in learning to teach: Accommodation and the development of a teaching identity. *Journal of Teacher Education, 55*(8), 8–24.

Stein, K. (2008). *A study of preservice teachers' beliefs about reform-based teacher education.* A doctoral dissertation completed at the University of North Carolina-Greensboro.

Tsui, A.B.M. & Law, D.Y.K. (2007). Learning as boundary-crossing in school-university partnership. *Teaching and Teacher Education, 23*, 1289–1301.

Valencia, S., Place, N., Martin, S., & Grossman, P. (2006). Curriculum materials for elementary reading: Shackles and scaffolds for four beginning teachers. *Elementary School Journal, 107*, 93–120.

Valli, L. & Buese, D. (2007) The changing roles of teachers in an era of high-stakes accountability. *American Educational Research Journal, 44*, 519–558.

Wharton-McDonald, R., Pressley, M., & Hampston, J.M. (1998). Literacy instruction in nine first-grade classrooms: Teacher characteristics and student achievement. *Elementary School Journal, 99*, 101–128.

Zimmerman, B. & Schunk, D. (2001). *Self-regulated learning and academic achievement.* New York: Springer-Verlag.

Chapter 14

Whole School Instructional Improvement through the Standards-based Change Process

A Developmental Model

Taffy E. Raphael
University of Illinois at Chicago

Kathryn H. Au
SchoolRise LLC

Susan R. Goldman
University of Illinois at Chicago

For the past six years, the coauthors of this chapter—Taffy, Kathy, and Susan—have collaborated in researching the Standards-based Change (SBC) Process (Au, 2005) to improve students' literacy achievement. We have engaged in this work in the midst of a political climate defined by both a commitment to school reform and a wide array of positions on what form such efforts should take. From scholars (e.g., Berliner, 2006; Darling-Hammond, 2007) to the federal government (e.g., No Child Left Behind [NCLB], 2002) to the popular press (e.g., Tough, 2008), the very definition of the problem and the solutions offered represent quite disparate positions. Some reformers (e.g., Berliner, 2006) point to the challenges, if not the futility, of school reform without changing the very real impact on student learning that living in poverty creates. Some (e.g., the architects of NCLB, the 2001 reauthorization of the U.S. Elementary and Secondary Education Act) argue that increasing standards and accountability for teaching all students is the way to school reform. Others argue that NCLB reflects problems from "unintended consequences and conspiracies of good intentions . . . (to the) principles and practices we have compromised" (Pearson, 2007, p. 145). And some argue for fundamental changes to the very nature of schools that essentially are still organized and teach curriculum designed by nineteenth and early twentieth century educators who could only imagine life in the twenty-first century (Heckman & Montera, 2009).

As literacy researchers and educators, we are well aware of the challenges ahead for reforming schools such that teachers and students engage together in powerful ways that prepare students to live, work, and seek personal fulfillment in the global society in which they live and will compete. And while we are painfully aware of the limitations that we face, we believe that literacy researchers can make a difference—that there is much that we can do to guide and support schools on a path to reforming their curriculum and instructional practices to more successfully meet the needs of all of their students. Our goal in this research line was to construct, enact, and evaluate the SBC Process as an alternative to prevailing models of school change that are based on faithful implementation of externally developed and monitored programs. Instead, we envisioned a process that could insure rigor and accountability in literacy instruction and assessment practices, while simultaneously helping schools devise and enact curriculum, instruction, and assessment tailored to the needs of their diverse learners. Simultaneously, the process builds capacity at the school level and ensures continuity of change over the longer term. During our individual careers as both literacy researchers and consumers of literacy research, we had developed a vision of what excellent classrooms and literacy instruction should look like. The logical next step in our work, individually and collectively, was determining how to make this vision a reality in a substantial number of schools, particularly in low-income communities.

Efforts to improve schools certainly aren't new—they have long been a part of the educational agenda in general, and literacy improvement more specifically. By the late 1950s, a body of literature on research and practice on educational change and reform had emerged (Passow, 1984) and the decades of research since then have left no doubt about the fact that districts and schools are complex systems in which to work, that effective teaching in these systems demands a deep understanding of the school subjects to be taught, and that there is an array of elements that must be addressed to improve and sustain improvements in literacy achievement across all students in a school (e.g., Duffy, 1993; Giles & Hargreaves, 2006; Taylor, Pearson, Peterson, & Rodriguez, 2003, 2005; Walpole, Justice, & Invernizzi, 2004). In this chapter, we describe how—through our different disciplinary lenses and our individual lines of research—the timing, the political climate in which we are working, our own interests, and a funding opportunity in Chicago led to this collaboration and sustained improvements in diverse schools committed to improving the quality of literacy instruction and their students' achievement levels.

We have organized the chapter into two main sections: (a) the knowledge base from which we were building—knowledge generated through our individual lines of research, as well as that of other scholars of literacy and literacy school reform, and (b) a description of our six-year collaboration, leading to the development and testing of the SBC Process Developmental Model of School Change.

What We Have Learned to Guide School Literacy Improvement

We divide the knowledge base for the Standards-based Change Process into the three broad topics, shown in the pyramid in Figure 14.1: learner outcomes, classroom practices, and school infrastructure. We trace how our individual lines of research, embedded in the research traditions of the time, served to highlight the importance of each of these topics and to lay the foundation for the developmental model.

Learner Outcomes

From our perspective, a sound model of school change in literacy starts with a vision of the excellent reader and writer, and all three of us have devoted many years to developing such a vision. Both Taffy and Kathy began their careers as classroom teachers, Taffy in intermediate grades in Illinois and North Carolina and Kathy in primary grades in Hawaii. In the 1970s, Taffy and Kathy taught directly from basal reading programs, like most teachers. They found themselves questioning when and how students would learn to construct meaning, interpret texts from different perspectives, question, or think critically about what they were reading.

Meanwhile, Susan began her career as a researcher during what has been called the *cognitive revolution*, an exciting time in psychology when the study of mind took center stage after decades in which studies of behavior had dominated the field. Susan was interested in understanding the kinds of thinking people had to do to understand information they read and strategies successful readers used to make sense of new information, as well as the ways that text structure and content domain knowledge facilitate or impede readers' understanding. In this line of research, she explored influences on readers'

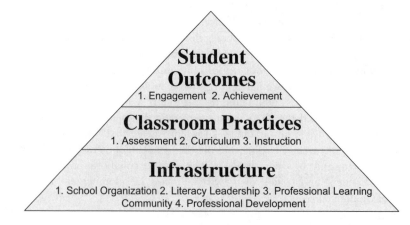

Figure 14.1 Knowledge base for the standards-based change process.

comprehension, such as the relationship between the context in which a text is read and the readers' ability to remember individual sentences (Perfetti & Goldman, 1974) or the interpretation readers create (Goldman, 1976).

In the late 1970s, while in graduate school at the University of Illinois, Urbana-Champaign, with assistantships at the Center for the Study of Reading, Taffy and Kathy also became part of the cognitive revolution. They were introduced to the exciting new perspectives of schema theory (Anderson, Spiro, & Montague, 1977; Anderson & Pearson, 1984) and metacognition (Brown et al., 1983; Flavell, 1979). Like other researchers at the time, Taffy, Kathy, and Susan focused on documenting comprehension processes and factors related to successful comprehension.

Susan, for example, studied the strategies used by adults and children when learning new information from text. Her research indicated that individuals who learned more demonstrated greater flexibility in strategy use, with skilled readers changing their strategies in response to the ease or difficulty they were having understanding the text (Goldman & Durán, 1988; Goldman & Saul, 1990). Further, Susan's research questioned some longstanding assumptions about how texts should be structured to facilitate comprehension (Goldman, Saul, & Coté, 1995; Goldman & Murray, 1992). Studies such as those conducted by Susan and her colleagues provided the field with many specifics about what capable readers must know and be able to do to comprehend text.

Taffy and Kathy contributed to this vision of excellent readers through their work with elementary students. Taffy explored comprehension strategies in her work with question-answer relationships (QAR), expanding into the area of writing and diverse students' interpretation and appreciation of fiction during student-led book club discussions (Goatley, Brock, & Raphael, 1995; Raphael et al., 2008). Kathy, with a career-long interest in issues of equity, particularly as faced by students of native Hawaiian ancestry, evolved a vision of excellent readers and writers through her work at the Kamehameha Elementary Education Program (KEEP). She and her colleagues demonstrated the importance of elementary school students using the writing process to communicate their ideas effectively, and, similarly, using reading comprehension processes to interpret and see the relevance of texts to their own lives (Au, 2003). Both Taffy and Kathy came to understand that ownership, or valuing of literacy, played a large part in students' growth as readers and writers, and that students must want to read and write for purposes they see as meaningful (cf., Guthrie & Ozgungor, 2002; Taylor et al., 2003).

Classroom Practices

Like many literacy researchers (e.g., Duffy et al., 1987; Palincsar, Brown, & Martin, 1987; Paris, Saarnio, & Cross, 1986; Pearson & Gallagher, 1983), all three of us realized that it was not enough to have a vision of excellent readers and writers. We needed to understand the classroom practices teachers could employ to make this vision a reality.

In her QAR line of research, Taffy created and tested this intervention as a means to help students and teachers develop a schema for questioning practices—an understanding of the relationships among the question, the readers' knowledge, and the text read and how information sources are used to respond to and construct questions successfully (Gavelek & Raphael, 1985; Raphael & Pearson, 1985; Raphael & Wonnacott, 1985; Raphael & McKinney, 1983). The findings showed that armed with a language for instruction, teachers were better able to teach about questioning practices; and armed with this language and knowledge, students were better able to handle the task of answering questions.

Continuing her research on instructional practices, Taffy worked with Carol Sue Englert on Cognitive Strategy Instruction in Writing (CSIW), designed to improve metacognitive knowledge about text organization for students diverse in academic abilities (Englert, Raphael, & Anderson, 1992; Englert et al., 1991; Raphael, Englert, & Kirschner, 1989). The research line expanded on Taffy's earlier work by explicitly integrating reading and writing and involving teachers over a period of years, rather than weeks or months.

Kathy had become interested in studying teachers who were effective in developing their native Hawaiian students' text comprehension. As she studied videotaped reading lessons, she discovered a pattern, which she labeled Experience-Text-Relationship (ETR; Au, 1979). Consistent with the tenets of schema theory (Anderson & Pearson, 1984), teachers began by drawing on children's experiences with the story's topic or theme. Next they had students read sections of the text, engaging in responsive questioning to make sure that they had understood key ideas. Then they helped students draw relationships between text ideas and their own prior knowledge.

In her analyses of the reading lessons with native Hawaiian students, Kathy noticed that comprehension discussions showed a high degree of overlapping speech, not just among the students but also between the teacher and students. With guidance from colleagues in anthropology, including Fred Erickson, Kathy learned to identify the participation structures in these lessons, or the rules governing speaking, listening, and turn-taking (e.g., Erickson & Shultz, 1982). Talk story, a common speech event in the Hawaiian community, is characterized by conarration and overlapping speech (Watson, 1974). Kathy found that during talk story-like reading lessons, students spent more time on task, discussed more text ideas, and made more logical inferences than in lessons taught following conventional classroom recitation rules (Au & Mason, 1981). ETR and talk story-like reading lessons became a staple of the professional development provided by KEEP to the teachers in 10 public schools in native Hawaiian communities.

Susan believed that it was important to connect the knowledge base on cognitive processes to the problems of practice that teachers typically face in their classrooms. In the early 1990s, she became a leader in a multi-site collaboration among three teams of researchers concerned with student learning: The Cognition and Technology Group at Vanderbilt (CTGV), Ann Brown and Joe Campione at Berkeley, and, at OISE, Marlene Scardamalia and Carl Bereiter. The goal of the collaboration, known as *Schools for Thought* (Lamon et al., 1996; Secules et al., 1997) was to create a middle-school program that built upon work that each of three teams had been doing independently, in the case of Susan's Vanderbilt team, on mathematical problem-solving (CTGV, 1997). The three programs shared a focus on creating and ultimately enacting and testing curriculum that promoted communities of learners in problem-solving within school content domains.

School Infrastructure

Successful school change in literacy must address issues of infrastructure, such as leadership, school organization, and a consistent direction for curriculum improvement (Fullan, 2005; Giles & Hargreaves, 2006; McLaughlin, 1990; McLaughlin & Mitra, 2001). Through our research experiences, the three of us realized that infrastructure was foundational to the success and sustainability of our efforts to bring about improvements in schools, although prior to our collaboration, it had not been central to our individual work.

In terms of sustainability, we learned the hard way about the importance of teacher ownership over innovative forms of instruction and participation as a member of a functional professional community (Mosenthal et al., 2003; Strike, 2004). About a year following the end of a two-year study (Raphael, Kirschner, & Englert, 1988), a precursor to the CSIW work, Taffy saw one of the teacher participants in the grocery store. During their conversation, Taffy asked about her literacy instruction, and the teacher volunteered that despite having enjoyed working together, she was no longer using "your writing program." Her comment surprised Taffy since the teacher had volunteered for the study, had been a willing and successful participant, and had seen her students' literacy skills improve during the course of the study. With hindsight, Taffy saw that what had been entirely missing was any teacher ownership of the intervention (i.e., the reference to "your writing program"). When the external support of the university partners went away, so too did the innovative practices.

After this incident, Taffy shifted to a collaborative approach of working with networks of teachers from the initial design of the intervention through implementation, data collection, and analysis. Examples were the Teacher Research Group (Goatley et al., 1994) and the Teachers Learning Collaborative (Florio-Ruane, Berne, & Raphael, 2001; Raphael et al., 2001). Teachers in these networks worked with Book Club, an approach in which Taffy emphasized ownership by both teachers and students (Brock & Raphael, 2005; McMahon & Raphael, 1997). However, Taffy also learned that while collaborative networks of teachers could sustain good practices, the excellent practices of an individual teacher rarely spread beyond her own classroom or grade level. She saw the lack of uptake of innovative practices, like Book Club, as a particular disadvantage in urban schools, where many students may need consecutive years of high-quality instruction to progress well as readers and writers.

Like Taffy, Kathy had the experience of seeing innovative practices vanish, once external support was discontinued. After KEEP closed in 1995, Kathy found that teachers did not continue with most of the practices associated with its literacy curriculum. Some practices, such as the consistent monitoring of student progress, had relied on the assistance of KEEP consultants and paraprofessional aides. Teachers could have continued other practices, such as small-group ETR lessons, but they generally did not, turning instead to the practices endorsed by the external programs that replaced KEEP. The quick disappearance of almost all traces of the teaching approaches recommended by KEEP suggested to Kathy that most teachers had never felt ownership over these approaches.

Susan reached conclusions similar to those of Taffy and Kathy as a result of her work with the Nashville Public School District, which received a Technology Innovations Challenge Grant to expand the *Schools for Thought* model (Goldman, 2005). The goals of that grant included expanding the middle-school model to the whole school and, over five years, increasing the numbers of teachers and schools. Susan and colleagues worked with groups of elementary and middle-school teachers throughout that project to create literacy units that brought together the realities of classrooms and the findings from the empirical research—her own and others. Even as teachers and researchers worked side by side to further the *Schools for Thought* model, and even with data indicating that it was an effective program, changes at the district and community level left it highly vulnerable. Ultimately, like Kathy's experience with KEEP and Taffy's experience with externally driven programs of research, it did not survive (see for details Goldman, 2005).

In summary, typical of many literacy researchers, the three of us had paid relatively little attention to issues of infrastructure, while attending extensively to issues of learner outcomes and classroom practice. We were part of an active literacy research community that had conducted numerous studies of literacy teaching (e.g., Duffy, 1993) and learning (see Barr, Kamil, Mosenthal, & Pearson, 1991; Kamil, Mosenthal, Pearson, & Barr, 2000), detailing features differentiating successful and struggling readers and the classroom practices that support students' progress. As we began our collaboration, we committed to thinking more deeply about infrastructure issues and making links to research on school reform—the decades of individual studies that identify features distinguishing successful and less successful schools and the forces that potentially facilitate or impede a school's reform effort. We designed our work to bring together our prior research on learner outcomes and classroom practices with other research on school reform. Emerging out of these efforts are the following principles that are key to schools moving forward in their improvement efforts.

1   Provide opportunities to produce "deep and consequential change in classroom practice . . . change that goes beyond surface structures or procedures through changes in underlying pedagogical principles" (Coburn, 2003, pp. 4–5; cf. Brown & Campione, 1996; Duffy, 1993; Florio-Ruane & Raphael, 2004).

2   Encompass features that lead to sustainability, including professional learning communities, links to other teachers and schools engaged in similar reform efforts, supportive school leadership, and alignment with other district policies (Borman & Associates, 2005; DuFour, 2004; Goldman, 2005; Strike, 2004).

3   Convey a means by which individuals enhance and deepen their understanding of the reform (McLaughlin & Mitra, 2001) in anticipation of sustaining the work within their school settings.

4   Have a strong structure with clear targets for students' literacy achievement (Rowan, Camburn, & Barnes, 2004).

5   Explicate the mechanisms through which a reform can be scaled up, or deliberately expanded to new settings (Datnow, Hubbard, & Mehan, 2002).

6   Provide a means for shifting ownership from external support systems to support systems internal to the school (Coburn, 2003; McLaughlin & Mitra, 2001).

We see our work with the SBC Process as contributing to a second generation of school literacy reform research focusing on the *processes* by which schools *become* successful (e.g., Mosenthal et al., 2003; Taylor et al., 2005; Timperley & Parr, 2007). This research broadens the criteria for defining successful schools from a narrow focus on student achievement test scores to a more inclusive focus on the factors, processes, and conditions needed to sustain improvements in student achievement (e.g., Borko, Wolf, Simone, & Uchiyama, 2003; Strike, 2004). These include a stable and respectful environment for students, teachers, administrators and the community; a strong infrastructure—including leadership that is both centralized (e.g., in the principal) and distributed (e.g., among teachers)—to support teachers working together within a professional learning community; exemplary classroom practices that promote students' engagement with interesting and challenging materials; and knowledgeable staff with the disposition to move students to high levels of achievement on a variety of measures.

Guided by the SBC Process and with these criteria in mind, we designed our research agenda to construct a developmental model that can both explain and guide school progress or lack thereof on the road to reform. The model provides a series of developmental benchmarks that assist in evaluating the impact of using the SBC Process on school infrastructure, including leadership and professional learning communities; quality classroom practices; and students' engagement and achievement in literacy.

Collaborating on the SBC Process: 2002–2006

In our three-phase research process, we drew on the methods of the design experiment (Brown, 1992; Collins, 1992) and design-based research (Design-based Research Collective, 2003) to document and inform the use of the SBC Process in a broad array of schools, beginning in Hawaii, the tenth largest district in the United States, and expanding to Chicago, the third largest district. The first phase of the research drew upon Kathy's work in Hawaii between 1997 and 2001. During this time she created and piloted the SBC Process, identified its core components (Au, Hirata, & Raphael, 2005) and proposed an initial iteration of a model of school change (Au, 2005). The second phase of the research focused on scaling the SBC Process to Chicago by Taffy and Susan, with extensive documentation of its implementation that allowed us to test both the process and Kathy's first iteration of the change model. The third phase of the research brought together the experiences in Hawaii and Chicago. During this phase we created a second iteration of the change model, forming the more explicit SBC developmental model and we fine-tuned the SBC Process as it was enacted in new schools in both districts.

Phase I: Constructing the SBC Process and the Model for School Change

Through research conducted within the KEEP laboratory and public schools over a period of 24 years, Kathy learned a great deal about the conditions under which Hawaiian students could become excellent readers and writers. However, despite the extraordinary level of support the KEEP program provided to public school teachers in its attempts to replicate these conditions, KEEP had difficulty showing consistent gains on standardized tests of reading achievement. In retrospect, Kathy was able to identify three factors that had contributed to the challenges encountered by KEEP. First, a reading improvement effort should address all the grades and classrooms in an elementary school, not solely K–3. It was the rare case that struggling readers did not require high-quality instruction beyond grade 3 to support their continued progress. Second, Kathy realized the importance of involving all the grades in the school, right from the very start of the change effort. When KEEP consultants sought to extend their services beyond grade 3, the upper-grade teachers were often reluctant to participate, viewing KEEP's attention to them to be an afterthought. Third, given the relatively quick disappearance of the initiative from the schools when funding ended, Kathy hypothesized that to be sustained, long-term change efforts needed to be owned by insiders to the school and designed to be carried out with the resources available to the typical public school.

In 1997, following the end of KEEP, Kathy received an invitation to work on the reading curriculum at Kipapa Elementary School. The school's curriculum leader, Kitty Aihara, believed that all the teachers in the school should work together on improving the reading curriculum. Kipapa offered Kathy the opportunity to create a reading improvement effort that would address what she had hypothesized to be core weaknesses in KEEP's work. The Kipapa effort was built on the premises that teachers would take ownership of innovative practices; that innovative practices would be manageable by the teachers themselves, without requiring additional resources; and that all grades and all teachers, including those in special education, would be involved from the start. In contrast to KEEP, there was no preset program; instead Kathy would guide the teachers as they developed their school's own reading curriculum. In 1999, the approach developed at Kipapa became known as the Standards-based Change (SBC) Process and was adopted by Holomua Elementary School. By 2002, spreading from the base of these two schools, the SBC Process was being implemented at over 20 schools in Hawaii.

The SBC Process guides a school's administrators and faculty to come together as a schoolwide professional learning community, with the purpose of developing a staircase or coherent literacy curriculum. The intellectual challenge and complexity of collaborative activities increase over time, as teachers work through the nine components of the processes depicted in Figure 14.2 (see Au, Raphael, & Mooney, 2008a, 2008b).

The process starts with faculty members in a whole-school setting surfacing philosophical differences or tensions in their beliefs about teaching, learning, and literacy, "to legitimize critique and controversy within organizational life" (Uline, Tschannen-Moran, & Perez, 2003, p. 782) and use conflicting perspectives in constructive ways. Through small- and large-group discussion, teachers work through their differences to construct a common vision of the excellent readers and writers who comprise the graduates from their school. Subsequent work within each grade level and school subject team encourages each team to consider how their instructional efforts contribute to achieving the community's vision of the graduate.

The next set of components involves grade level and department teams identifying the goals their students must achieve to insure their progress toward the shared vision of the graduate. Each team describes their step on the staircase leading up to that vision. The within-grade and within-subject area teams begin by constructing benchmarks and aligning them with state and national standards. They then meet with teachers at adjacent grade levels to compare their goals, revising until they are confident that each step in the staircase is high enough to reach the vision and that there are no gaps that could derail

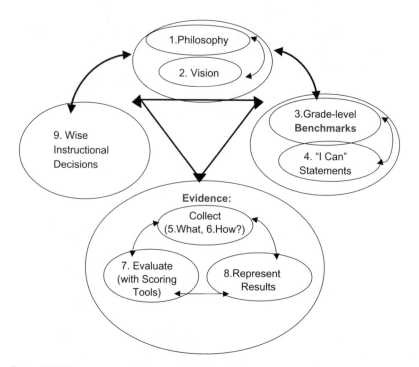

Figure 14.2 Components of the standards-based change process. The "To Do List."

students' progress. Teacher teams then translate the end-of-year goals into student-friendly "I Can" statements, worded in ways that make the goals understandable to students and their families.

The third set of components addressed by the schoolwide professional learning community focuses on the evidence system each grade level and department creates to monitor students' progress and inform instructional decisions. The evidence system includes (1) tasks that yield data on students' progress toward meeting benchmarks, (2) directions to be followed to promote consistency in evidence collection procedures across classrooms within grade levels, (3) rubrics or scoring procedures for collaborative analysis of student work, and (4) bar graphs that provide an overview of students' progress, to be shared with the whole school.

The final component focuses on the instructional decisions teachers make individually and in consultation with their team members, based on the evidence system. Teachers use assessment results to identify students' strengths and weaknesses in literacy, and they differentiate instruction to build on strengths while remedying weaknesses (Au et al., 2005; Au et al., 2008a). In the SBC Process, workshops on instructional strategies are conducted after students' strengths and weaknesses have been documented through the evidence system, and after it has been determined that teachers see the need for these instructional strategies.

By 2002, when Taffy and Susan began to discuss scaling the SBC Process to Chicago, Kathy had introduced the process to almost 100 public schools in Hawaii. About 25% of these schools appeared willing and able to sustain the work over time with resulting positive impact on student learning. A hierarchical linear modeling analysis showed that where the SBC Process had become established, students in Title I schools had significantly higher grade 5 scores on the state reading test than in Title I schools that had not implemented the process (Au, 2005). Kathy's observations of these successful schools indicated the presence of a key curriculum leader who could play the role that Kitty Aihara had fulfilled at Kipapa. These schools successfully engaged in curriculum improvement following the *To Do List* process.

Through the work with the schools that did not stick with the SBC Process, Kathy discovered that schools wrestled with competing initiatives and had difficulty maintaining the single-minded focus the SBC Process requires. In contrast to the "Kipapa-like" schools, they needed a much higher level of customized support to enact curriculum improvement through the To Do List process. In the absence of customized support, these schools soon gave up on the process.

Drawing on her observations of successful schools, artifacts from professional development sessions, videotaped interviews, and photo documentation of site-based activities, Kathy constructed an initial Four-Level Model of school development to provide a sense of how teachers at schools successful in the SBC Process took on more challenging curriculum tasks over time. The model pointed out that the central task the school needed to accomplish evolved over the years (Au et al., 2008b):

- Level 1: Pulling Together as a Whole School. Teachers develop an initial understanding of the components of the SBC Process; learning about goal-setting, progress monitoring, analysis and presentation of evidence, and implementation of instructional improvements.
- Level 2: Sharing Results within a Professional Learning Community. With the framework of the SBC Process, the school establishes *evidence windows* at the beginning, middle, and end of the year to collect data on student progress toward meeting benchmarks, and teachers share their results at whole-school meetings.
- Level 3: Constructing the Staircase Curriculum. Teachers document their school's literacy curriculum, collaborating to create curriculum guides. Each grade level or department team pulls together a binder that includes their schoolwide vision as well as their grade-level benchmarks; their evidence system, including procedures for collecting evidence, rubrics, and anchor pieces; instructional strategies needed to move students forward in response to the evidence, and instructional materials for use by students

(e.g., peer editing checklists) or teachers (e.g., a list of read alouds to illustrate voice).

- Level 4: Engaging Students and Families. Through student portfolios, teachers engage their students in participating actively in setting their own learning targets and having a voice in selecting evidence that reflects their progress toward their goals.

Kathy found that Level 2 was a turning point for schools as teachers began "teaching to students' needs as literacy learners" (Au, 2005, p. 280), rather than assuming that following curriculum materials and the teachers' guide would meet the needs of their students. Engaging in the Level 2 activities required a school to commit time and resources and the discipline to stay the course in the face of new initiatives and competing agendas from the district.

Phase II: Scaling the SBC Process to Chicago and Testing the Four-Level Model

In the second phase of the work, Susan and Taffy—with Kathy's advice and informed by her Phase I work—brought the process to Chicago through Partnership READ, the University of Illinois at Chicago team of the Advanced Reading Development Demonstration Project (ARDDP, 2008). ARDDP was an initiative designed to improve literacy achievement in Chicago Public Schools through a partnership among the district, six Chicago area universities, and the Chicago Community Trust, funded through the Searle Funds of the Trust. Scaling to Chicago was mutually beneficial. From Taffy and Susan's perspective, the SBC Process aligned well with the goals of ARDDP— building capacity to sustain literacy improvement within the schools rather than creating dependency on an external partner—so it made sense to adapt that process rather than start from scratch. From Kathy's perspective, bringing the process to a new site offered an opportunity to test her hypotheses about the course followed by successful schools and to elaborate on the existing model. Scaling to Chicago would force us to make explicit the processes underlying this particular reform initiative and test Kathy's Four-Level Model.

The Chicago schools were located in high poverty areas; had high transience of administrators, teachers, and students; supplied little existing infrastructure for teachers' collaborative teamwork; and showed fewer than 30% of students meeting basic standards on the state reading tests. Partnership READ included Taffy, Susan, and a team of support staff who could spend up to one day a week in each participating school, in addition to a network of professional development sessions (e.g., for literacy leadership teams or literacy coordinators from all participating schools). This allowed us to balance professional development for school leaders with customized support tailored to individual schools' needs. Thus, the Chicago adaptation of the SBC Process included the higher levels of customization to individual school needs based on Kathy's findings in Hawaii.

We documented our work using data sources typical of qualitative methods (e.g., interviews, observations, artifact collections). We gathered artifacts of school-based work (e.g., professional development activities, grade level and staff meetings) using videotapes, fieldnotes, photos, and work products; as well as information about participants' beliefs and experiences of the activities through interviews and questionnaires. Analyses provided information about conditions that appeared to facilitate or impede school progress and surfaced what were often implicit but critically important details in enacting the SBC Process successfully. What we were learning helped contribute to ARDDP's effort to develop a set of indicators of school progress (Hanson et al., 2006) and it surfaced the need to expand the SBC Process model from four to seven levels.

We analyzed the situation in 10 Chicago schools in fall 2004 using constant comparative methods (Strauss & Corbin, 1994), as the research team read through the data sources to describe school progress. Building on Kathy's hypotheses about key factors for success we examined their progress in terms of:

- participation levels and progress on the SBC Process To Do List
- challenges identified by the school and/or READ staff members
- participants' understandings of the SBC Process revealed through interviews, actions (e.g., presentations during whole-school sharing sessions, instructional decisions), and artifacts (e.g., benchmarks, evidence systems)
- in-school activity formats and content through which the SBC Process was enacted
- goals and activities of literacy coordinators, principals, and READ leadership and school support staff.

Based on the evidence of progress, we assigned each school to one of four groups. Schools in Group 4 (those showing the most progress) had begun implementing the SBC Process components or were showing promise of progress based on planned activities. Schools in Group 3 were cognizant of problems and planned to reintroduce the SBC Process the following school year to create a fresh start. Some were making changes in key leadership personnel, others in teaching staff. Schools in Group 2 had implemented isolated components of the SBC Process and encountered major barriers (e.g., unsupportive principal, dysfunctional infrastructure). They showed few signs of concern or plans to change their approach. Schools in Group 1 were frustrated with little to no progress. Their problems were beyond those addressed through the SBC Process (e.g., severe discipline issues, high student/teacher turnover, threats of school closure, related low morale). The findings from these four groups of schools were consistent with Kathy's initial hypotheses as expressed in the Four-Level Model: Only the Group 4 Chicago schools showed any evidence of the characteristics of Level 1 in the model, with some evidence of Level 2. The other three groups of Chicago schools lacked the characteristics of Level 1.

Nevertheless, it was also evident that the Four-Level Model failed to capture key areas of work that were critical to making progress with the SBC Process and on which Chicago schools had indeed made progress over the 30 months that Partnership READ had been in operation. READ staff and school leaders could point to areas of progress in their schools. Yet, the Four-Level Model seemed insensitive to them. For example, the progress we saw in the Group 4 schools related to improvements on a cluster of variables related to how a school organized to do the work, the knowledge and skills of those leading the process, the coherence of the school's professional community, and the planning and enactment of professional development activities. Group 4 schools had put in place a literacy leadership team that had a representative from each grade level and had block scheduling that allowed grade-level teachers to meet during a common planning time. In contrast, Group 3 and 2 schools had leadership teams that did not meet regularly and varied in terms of whether there was common planning time for grade-level teachers. In all the schools, responsibility for creating the structural conditions for initiating the SBC Process resided with the administration and curriculum leaders, especially the literacy coordinator, a mandated staff position that was a condition for participation in Partnership READ. But opportunities to become knowledgeable about organizing for improvement and specifically for a change process focused on literacy had typically not been provided to the administrators and literacy coordinators charged with leading the process.

In other words, many of the schools needed guidance in how to develop the organization necessary to engage in the process. Organizing for productive change included providing time and resources for administrators, curriculum leaders, and a team of teachers representing grade levels, subject areas, and special populations (e.g., ELL, gifted and talented, special education) to deepen their own knowledge of literacy, the change process, and leadership. As well, the school needed to organize as a professional community with effective means for communicating information, ideas, challenges, and concerns so that everyone had a voice in the process. Such a community created a context for highly functional working teams and productive use of time together—from whole staff to grade level to subject area department meetings. The work toward development of these capacities constituted levels of school improvement that had to occur prior to Kathy's Level 1.

In sum, the comparisons and contrasts we saw among the initial group of a dozen Chicago READ schools indicated that there were critical *readiness* characteristics prior to Level 1 of Kathy's model (Au, 2005). Thus Phase II of the research met Kathy's initial goal of testing the process and the Four-Level Model and fulfilled Taffy and Susan's goal of bringing an already-tested process for building capacity to the ARDDP initiative. During Phase II we identified the aspects of the process that could be scaled and those that required adaptation to be successful in a new context. Our Phase II findings provided insights and confirmation of what all the participants in ARDDP had learned were needed for successful school reform (indicators citation).

As a result of what we learned in Phase II, we expanded the original Four-Level Model to seven levels and we developed or refined the descriptions of schools at each level (see Table 14.1).

In the new iteration of the model, what had been Level 1 in the Au (2005) version was now Level 4. Levels 1 through 3, all focused on infrastructure, were added to capture the type of work involved in becoming a school where staff members can work together within a professional learning community. The descriptions reflect the synthesis of the analyses we reported above. Schools at Level 1 have a key person or a small but influential group of staff members who verbalize a general dissatisfaction with the status quo and note that something needs to be done to change their practices. Schools at Level 2 have begun to engage in reorganizing to support the SBC Process activities—creating functional leadership teams, new and more effective forms of communication, and time/space/resources to support the work. Schools at Level 3 introduce the SBC Process to the whole school as building blocks for change—as something the school staff believes to be critical to the way they want to function as a professional learning community.

The work of the first three levels leads to schools being able to begin the work of the SBC Process successfully—with structures in place and time scheduled to engage in the work and with staff members who can describe the work to colleagues in ways that indicate it is their choice to participate, not an external mandate. When administrators and teachers see the need, are organized for the work, and introduce the SBC Process as *their* approach to improving their literacy curriculum and students' achievement, they are ready to come together as a professional learning community to do the work. With the levels of development identified in a general way, we began Phase III of our collaboration.

Phase III: Finalizing the Seven-level Model

The major task in Phase III was intensive documentation and analysis of data from Chicago and Hawaii to identify the specific dimensions that constituted the areas of development as schools worked on the increasingly complex activities required of the SBC Process, and how those dimensions changed over time. Coincident with the SBC-specific effort, we were engaged in conversations with the partners in the ARDDP work to identify indicators of schools' progress on instructional improvement. Thus, the identification of dimensions of change drew on work taking place in Hawaii and in approximately 75 schools in Chicago, about 18 of which had been engaged with READ. The others were using several different models for literacy improvement (ARDDP,

Table 14.1 Core Dimensions of the Standards-based Change Process Developmental Model

Cluster Names	Dimensions	Definition
Infrastructure	School Organization	The material and physical resources (e.g., time, money, space allocation) that support structures (e.g., whole-school, grade-level team, and small-group meeting time) and settings (e.g., grade level/department meetings, vertical meetings, gallery walks) critical to the work of the SBC Process.
	Literacy Leadership	The actions taken by formal (e.g., principal/administrators, curriculum coordinators) and informal school leaders that support enactment of the SBC Process, and ensure continuous deepening of participants' knowledge and understanding of literacy, standards, and evidence-based teaching.
	Professional Learning Community (PLC)	The creation of a whole-school environment that supports professional collaboration and curricular cohesion within and across grade levels to improve teaching and student learning. Attributes of the PLC include shared language, vision, and norms for collaboration and inquiry.
	Professional Development	The plans and/or implementation of plans internal or external to the school that support ongoing learning by personnel. Professional development includes school-wide, grade-level specific, or small group formal and/or informal events.
Classroom Practices	Assessment	The thinking and actions of school personnel with respect to evidence of student learning, emphasizing the use of assessments—formative and summative—to inform instructional practices.
	Curriculum	The thinking and actions of school personnel with respect to a coherent framework of end-of-year goals for all grades (the staircase curriculum), including the strategic use of resources to support differentiated instruction and insure students' progress toward meeting or exceeding these goals.
	Instruction	The thinking and actions of school personnel with respect to instructional decision-making—methods/approaches, materials, student participation—that address students' identified needs and work toward end-of-year goals.
Student Outcomes	Student Engagement and Involvement	The degree to which students demonstrate motivation to learn through awareness, understanding, and valuing of learning goals, and through active participation in achieving these goals.
	Student Achievement	The progress of students (i.e., trends across data points) as indicated by both classroom and standardized measures that reveal students' comprehension and critical thinking, and their understandings of skills, strategies, and concepts.

2008). Despite the different models in use and the geographic dispersion, the conversations converged on a set of indicators that seemed key to tracking the progress of schools attempting to improve their instruction. These conversations were also informed by ARDDP annual reports in which a team of external evaluators summarized themes regarding facilitators and impediments to change (e.g., DeStefano & Hansen, 2005, 2006). By spring 2006, we had converged on nine candidate dimensions for use in the SBC Process Seven-level Developmental Model, as listed and defined in Table 14.2 (Raphael et al., 2006). The nine dimensions constitute three clusters. Infrastructure dimensions are school organization, literacy leadership, professional learning community, and professional development. Classroom practices dimensions are assessment, curriculum, and instruction. Student outcomes dimensions are student engagement/involvement and achievement.

During Phase III we embarked on an intensive process of defining and validating these dimensions in terms of what development on each dimension looked like, and the utility of these dimensions and the Seven-Level Model more generally to contribute to the knowledge base about change over time in school improvement and on a practical level to guide the change process itself. We saw potential for the SBC Developmental Model to serve as a roadmap that would help schools set proximal goals for moving forward with an improvement process. This struck a responsive chord with all of us based on our past work with teachers and schools in which the question "How do we get there?" had frequently been raised. While there are a number of descriptions of what successful schools look like and how they function (e.g., Langer, 2004; Mosenthal et al., 2003; Rowan et al, 2004), the stories of how they got there are often too specific and unique to be of much guidance to other schools attempting to improve. Thus, we sought to create a model that could help schools locate themselves in the SBC Process and provide *next steps* that were at an actionable grain size along the different dimensions.

Our strategy for specifying and refining the dimensions across levels involved thematic analysis of several data streams from Chicago and Hawaii schools gathered between fall 2002 and spring 2006: annual interviews with literacy coordinators, school administrators, and teachers; schoolwide sharing of progress (i.e., Gallery Walks); fieldnotes, video, and audio records of meetings of grade levels, schoolwide staff, literacy coordinators, and administrators; and photo archives of products from professional development sessions, school-based work sessions, and network meetings of principals and/or literacy coordinators. We coupled this process with validity studies conducted with the schools. In this process, we also compared and contrasted our dimensions with the work of others engaged in school literacy reform (e.g., ARDDP, 2008; Mosenthal et al., 2004; Taylor et al., 2005).

Partnership READ staff reviewed and coded the data streams in four passes through the data. Four questions guided the analyses: (1) What is the content of the data and how does it help us reflect on the events

Table 14.2 The Seven Levels of the SBC Process Developmental Model

Level	Major Task	School Activity
1 Recognizing a Need	Gain knowledge of the SBC Process and learn the steps leaders must take to support progress.	Leaders and teachers participate in the needs assessment. Leaders attend leadership seminars to build their knowledge of how to work successfully with the SBC Process.
2 Organizing for Change	Build infrastructure to support school improvement with the SBC Process.	Leaders work to strengthen the school's infrastructure to support improvement efforts centered on the SBC Process. Grade-level or department liaisons work to strengthen their knowledge of the SBC Process and the target content or focus area.
3 Working on the Building Blocks	Introduce the SBC Process components to the whole school.	Grade-level or department liaisons continue professional development on SBC Process leadership. Teachers work together as a whole school to develop the school's philosophy and vision statement. Within grade levels or departments, teachers begin to think about how the philosophy and vision apply to their curriculum, assessment, and instruction.
4 Pulling the Whole School Together	Complete all the components of the SBC Process To Do List.	Teachers work with their grade-level or department to construct: (1) grade-level or course benchmarks, (2) "I Can" statements, (3) evidence to show that students are making progress, (4) procedures for collecting evidence, (5) scoring tools (rubrics), (6) bar graphs, and (7) instructional improvements. At each step along the way, grade levels and departments share their products with the whole school.
5 Sharing Results within a Professional Learning Community	Establish three times per year sharing of student results.	Teachers score student work according to rubrics within grade-level or department teams. The teams share the results with the whole school three times per year: pretest, midyear check, posttest.
6 Constructing Your School's Staircase Curriculum	Create grade-level or department guides to document the staircase curriculum.	Teachers work within grade levels or departments to develop their own curriculum guides with the following sections: (1) goals for student learning, (2) instructional strategies, (3) instructional materials, (4) assessment. Teachers participate in a carousel where they share their team's guide and review the guides of others.
7 Engaging Students and Families	Develop portfolios and involve students in self-assessment.	Teachers learn a manageable approach to portfolios, based on the student evidence they are already collecting, and foster student self-assessment and goal-setting.

within each school? (2) What were the key activities reflected in the content examples identified within each year, and what patterns of themes or topics appear to emerge within and across the years? (3) How reliably do the clusters of dimensions in the model capture factors, conditions, and activities, and do they have face validity when applied developmentally to the data from a school over time? (4) Within and across schools, what appear to be influential turning points for a school's movement from level to level? These analyses yielded initial versions of the descriptions of the dimensions provided in Table 14.2.

Following these analyses, case studies of schools' development were created using the model in an explanatory way to describe key features and activities of progress. For example, Cosner (2006) presented data demonstrating how one school's growth in organization and literacy leadership contributed to its progress. Positive steps included hiring a supportive principal committed to using the SBC Process as a means to introduce evidence-based teaching to his staff, creating an administrative team to begin moving the school toward shared leadership, supporting two literacy coordinators to work together to cover the primary and the upper grades, and strengthening communication practices among administrative staff and faculty. Mooney and Raphael (2006) and Madda and McMahon (2006) described turning points in schools' progress from initial work on school infrastructure to focusing on using their infrastructure to reform classroom practices—and the factors that supported or impeded their progress.

With each dimension in the model elaborated with characterizations of the school and its activity at each level, we began to engage practitioners and other researchers in tests of both the face validity of the model (in this case, its ability to describe a school's progress through the SBC Process) and its consequential validity (in this case, its value as a tool for planning and guiding school change). To assess the model's face validity, we asked participants in both Chicago and Hawaii (n=146, including administrators, curriculum coordinators, classroom teachers) to identify their school's progress by level on each of the nine dimensions. Participants were asked to provide at least one reason why they believed their choice to be reasonable and, if possible, to identify evidence to support their choice (for example, classroom observations, student portfolios, test results). Participants were also asked to suggest revisions to the wording of descriptors for levels within the various dimensions.

In Chicago, administrators who had previously tried unsuccessfully to use the Four-Level Model to describe their schools' level of progress found the Seven-Level Model more tractable. Principals' school analyses aligned more closely with those of the READ staff and with literacy coordinators and fellows within their school, despite the greater number of levels from which to choose. Across nine schools where at least two school participants and one READ staff member completed surveys asking them to use the Seven-Level Model to describe their school, six of the schools had standard deviations of less than one level (0.44–0.88). The remaining three had standard deviations less than two levels (1.23–1.82).

In Hawaii the face validity of the model was tested with 90 educators representing 19 schools: seven administrators, 20 curriculum coordinators or resource teachers, and 63 classroom teachers. All but four were from schools that had been following the SBC Process from one to nine years. At two schools, all teachers met by grade levels to complete the forms. All participants, including those whose schools did not use the SBC Process, stated that the Seven-Level Model helped them gain new insights about their school, and several noted that they understood better why their school had (or had not) been able to make good progress.

Following testing for face validity at both sites, the consequential validity of the Seven-Level Model was tested in Hawaii in needs assessments conducted at five elementary schools beginning in September 2006. During the needs assessments, evidence was collected to document each school's level on the nine dimensions. Two forms of self-report evidence were gathered: (1) school self-assessment surveys completed by teachers, working in grade levels and departments, and by the school's leadership team, and (2) in-depth interviews conducted with six individuals representing different perspectives (for example, a teacher new to the school and a teacher who had been there 10 years or more). The three other forms of evidence were documentary, observational, or online. An example of documentary evidence for professional development was the school's yearlong schedule indicating the topic for each waiver day. An example of observational evidence for instructional practices was photographs of charts created during lessons. An example of online evidence for student achievement involved test scores available in school status reports posted on the district's website. Evidence for each dimension had to include documentary, observational, or online items in addition to self-report. Each school received a written report of about 50 pages, including conclusions drawn about the school's overall level on the Seven-Level Model, as well as its level on each of the nine dimensions. Each report included 5–7 specific recommendations aimed at moving the school from its present level to the next higher level. A half-day debriefing and planning meeting based on the needs assessment was conducted with each school's leadership team. School leaders' responses to the needs assessments were uniformly positive. All leadership teams made plans to implement the recommendations, including excerpts from the reports in their annual academic and financial plans, and followed through accordingly.

Following this pilot phase, needs assessments were conducted at an additional 20 Hawaii schools between January 2007 and July 2008. During this time, adjustments were made to accommodate middle and high schools, and school leaders continued to vouch for the benefits of the needs assessment results, which made it clear what their schools needed to do to progress through the Seven-Level Model. Analysis of email messages documenting schools' feedback on the needs assessment drafts indicated, with one exception, no disagreements with the recommendations presented. The vast majority of feedback concerned corrections to specific details in the reports, such as the date when a new teacher meeting schedule had been introduced. Following the consequential validity testing of the Seven-Level Model in Hawaii, an abbreviated version of the needs assessment was carried out in Chicago. When this work showed promising results, in fall 2007 a full version of the needs assessment process was carried out with five Chicago schools, using the procedures developed in Hawaii. These were shared with the individual schools. Like Hawaii, the Chicago schools found the assessment to yield useful information, and most of the schools had, by the start of the 2008–2009 school year, acted upon many of the recommendations.

Despite contextual differences, schools in both Hawaii and Chicago appeared to benefit in similar ways from participation in the needs assessment process based on the Seven-Level Model. We provide two examples to illustrate these reactions.

Malama Elementary School

In Hawaii, we conducted a needs assessment at Malama Elementary School, a suburban K–5 Title I school, in spring 2007, shortly after the arrival of a principal who had worked successfully with the SBC Process at his previous school. The school decided on writing as the first subject to be tackled with the SBC Process. The needs assessment showed that the school was at Level 2 overall on the Seven-Level Model. Dimensions of strength included the school's professional learning community and previous work with assessment. As is typical with schools that have not previously worked with the SBC Process, most of the recommendations had to do with infrastructure. The recommendations were (1) to build a strong school infrastructure to support curriculum improvement in writing, (2) to spell out the role and responsibilities of the curriculum coordinator in a written job description, (3) to make sure that there was a strong support group for the curriculum coordinator, and (4) to develop both a yearlong and a multiyear plan for the SBC Process work (necessary to keep a clear focus in professional development). A final recommendation had to do with introducing the To Do List by having the teachers engage in a discussion of philosophy and draft a vision of the excellent writer who graduates from Malama Elementary School.

School leaders found that the recommendations matched their own sense of what needed to be done to move the school forward, and they worked conscientiously to implement the infrastructure recommendations. The SBC Process To Do List was introduced in the fall of 2007. By spring 2008, teachers all had To Do List items in place and had shared both their midyear check and posttest assessment results during whole-school meetings, signaling the school's accomplishment of Level 4 and entry into Level 5. With the guidance provided by the needs assessment, the school leaders strengthened the infrastructure, and teachers were given the support needed to move their school from Level 2 to Level 5 on the Seven-Level Model in little more than a year's time. This rapid progress was made possible by the teachers' willingness to build a schoolwide professional learning community, by the provision of time for teachers to work together on the To Do List and share their results, and by the clear direction provided by the principal and curriculum coordinator. The goal for 2008–09 was to establish Level 5, three times per year reporting of results, and possibly enter Level 6, documentation of the writing curriculum, either in spring or fall 2009.

Marquette Elementary School

In fall 2007 we conducted a needs assessment with Marquette Elementary School, a preK–8 Chicago school that serves students living in a low-income neighborhood. The student population is half African-American and half Latino. Though the school leaders were fairly certain that the focus of the needs assessment would be reading, they were still debating the relative advantages and disadvantages of beginning their work with the SBC Process in reading or writing. The needs assessment showed the school to be between Levels 1 and 2, with strengths in three areas. The school leaders—both the principal and assistant principal (AP)—were committed to improving literacy instruction at Marquette and believed in the value of evidence-based teaching. Time had already been designated for grade-level meetings and for a weekly leadership team meeting. The teachers were highly qualified, with 55% of the staff members having graduate degrees.

At the debriefing session in early December, recommendations similar to those for Malama Elementary School focused on building a strong infrastructure to support implementation of the SBC Process. The first recommendation was to identify a literacy coordinator (LC) to lead improvement efforts and serve as the point of contact for the external partner. The job description for the LC was to be rewritten to include these responsibilities and insure the person had adequate time to fulfill them. The second recommendation was to identify an existing group, or possibly create a new group, to serve as the literacy leadership team supporting the LC. This group was to include the LC, AP, and a teacher from each grade level, and it too was to have a write-up detailing its role and responsibilities. The third recommendation was to have the LC and members of the literacy leadership team participate in professional development to deepen their knowledge of the SBC Process so they could lead from within and not become overly dependent on the external SBC Process liaison.

Between January and the end of the 2007–08 school year, Marquette had addressed all these recommendations successfully, ending the year with a highly successful whole-school event for all returning teachers. Members of the literacy leadership team led the event. They emphasized that it had been the team's decision to adopt the SBC Process for their school's literacy improvement plan, and that a major reason was that they believed it would help them "take back their professionalism." They emphasized that no one knows their students better than they do, that they are tired of just being handed new programs without any choice in the matter, and that they thought it was a fair tradeoff if more public accountability about their students' progress meant freedom to teach in ways they each valued. The team devised a professional development plan that made use of weekly grade-level meetings, monthly staff meetings, and monthly *restructured days* that gave them a half-day each month to work together guided by the SBC Process. The team's willingness to step forward led to consensus that the teachers make a three-year commitment to achieve visible improvements in their professional learning community, their classroom practices, and their students' achievement levels.

Marquette began its work for 2008–09 with a focus on reading, especially comprehension. The faculty members were beginning at Level 3 and intended to move seamlessly into Level 4 work during the fall semester. By the end of the academic year, they plan to have their school's vision of the excellent graduating reader in place, grade-level and subject area department benchmarks constructed and aligned, and "I Can" statements as a basis for increasing students' engagement in their own learning to read. Looking ahead, during 2009–10, they plan to complete Level 4 and move into Level 5, which requires that they construct, pilot, and refine their evidence system and begin three times per year schoolwide sharing of assessment results. During 2010–11, the goal is to move into Level 6 with the goal of documenting the Marquette Literacy Curriculum.

As these examples suggest, the value of the Seven-Level Model lies in providing a roadmap for school improvement over the years. Work with practical applications of the Seven-Level Model through needs assessments, along with yearlong and multiyear planning, is continuing at schools in both Hawaii and Chicago. We are also currently engaged in retrospective analyses of schools that did not or are not making progress to determine the utility of the model for understanding why schools fail to make progress in a more nuanced way than has been possible in the past.

Concluding Comments

In common with many others in the field of literacy, we have sought to contribute to the improvement of literacy achievement, especially in schools in diverse low-income communities, through both research and practical action. We began the chapter describing major themes in our work prior to beginning our collaboration on school change—developing our visions of literacy, literacy learners, and classrooms where students could attain high levels of literacy—as well as our frustration at seeing promising projects end with few if any lasting effects. We recognized the importance of teacher ownership and a supportive school infrastructure in sustaining change over a period of years, features we emphasized in our collaboration.

The second and third phases of our joint work with the SBC Process occurred at the very time when schools all over America experienced the often chilling effects of NCLB. Despite that climate, we were able to develop and evaluate the SBC Process in a broad array of schools. The SBC Process permits teachers to enable their students to meet rigorous standards for academic achievement. In the tradition of scholars such as Bullough and Gitlin (1985) and Darling-Hammond (1997), we placed our confidence in teachers and their professional knowledge and judgment, rather than in packaged programs and other practices encouraged by NCLB. We found that the SBC Process provided a roadmap for schools to move forward without resorting to one-size-fits-all or cookie-cutter solutions. We were able to customize our approach to take into account differences in school histories, faculties' professional backgrounds and experiences, and students' needs as learners. The narrow focus on raising test scores promoted by NCLB proved to be both a blessing and curse in our work with schools: a blessing because NCLB created an urgency for school improvement in many settings, and a curse because it created a quick-fix mindset, a mindset that fosters the wholesale adoption of packaged programs on their promise of effectiveness with all students. This mindset is in direct contradiction to the view of teacher-developed staircase curricula that we sought to promote through the SBC Process. In retrospect, given the circumstances, we stand amazed and impressed that leaders at so many schools had the courage to undertake the SBC Process.

Because of the number and range of schools that undertook the SBC Process, our combined work in Hawaii and Chicago provided verification that all three clusters in the developmental model pyramid—infrastructure, classroom practices, and learner outcomes—had to be addressed for school improvement efforts to succeed. At the same time, no two schools were exactly alike in the support needed to successfully address each cluster. Further, we found that while having a strong school infrastructure was necessary, it alone was not sufficient for improving students' literacy achievement. For example, in addition to time to meet as grade levels or subject area departments, teachers needed knowledge of literacy and the SBC Process to progress on their school's staircase curriculum in literacy.

We see our work with the SBC Process as contributing to a second generation of research on school improvement. We believe this second generation of research is moving the field forward on the basis of advancement in three areas, highlighted in our work as well as that of others. First, the new generation of research on school improvement is verifying that definitions of success include more than achievement test gains. Promoting student learning, especially higher-level thinking, and creating student ownership of their literacy learning requires far more than teaching to the test. Thus as educators we must hold ourselves responsible for pushing students toward higher standards for literacy achievement with an equal emphasis on student ownership. Second, teachers' experiences count: The SBC Process involves teachers in constructing and implementing their staircase curriculum in literacy. This ambitious endeavor requires that teachers engage in continued, collaborative intellectual efforts over a period of years. They must own the change effort. In situations where teachers feel little or no ownership of their work with the SBC Process, the initiative cannot be maintained for the length of time necessary for real and sustainable change to take hold.

Third, this second generation of research on school improvement is marked by attention to processes of change, rather than a focus primarily on identifying the characteristics of successful versus unsuccessful schools or program implementations. In contrast to some widely used school reform models, such as America's Choice or Success for All (see Correnti & Rowan, 2007), we started with a view of school change based on fidelity to a process rather than a set program. This process has two key elements: the To Do List and the Seven-Level Model. Implementing the To Do List allows teachers to create their school's own basic system for improving student achievement through standards, while following the Seven-Level Model provides a school with a multi-year roadmap for change. By now we have presented the To Do List and Seven-Level Model, and the concepts and research underlying them, at numerous schools, and we know that they are quite easy to explain to our fellow educators. But we have learned from both research and experience with the SBC Process that the challenge at the school level lies less in knowing what steps to take next and more in actually executing those steps successfully. As external partners, we provide guidance and support, but real change must come from the administrators and teachers themselves. As seen in the examples of Malama and Marquette, educators at the school level must take ownership of the change effort and step forward to make things happen.

Our study of implementing the SBC Process culminated in the validation and practical application of the Seven-Level Model and nine dimensions vital to school improvement in literacy. We have confidence in the model and dimensions as descriptive of broad patterns as schools move forward. However, we have seen that each school follows its own individual path as it moves through the levels in the model, with its own unique pattern of strengths and challenges on the nine dimensions, as the examples of Malama and Marquette illustrate. Customization of the services and guidance we provide to schools as external partners is vital, because our research shows that one size does not fit all. We find a needs assessment based on the Seven-Level Model and nine dimensions to be a sound starting point in our customized work with schools, eliminating the need for guesswork about the strengths a school can build on, and the challenges it must address, to be successful in improving students' literacy achievement.

What about the scalability of a change process such as the one described here? This question remains unanswered. To date, the SBC Process has been successfully established at several dozen schools in both Hawaii and Chicago, but we do not have an implementation in either district involving more than about 25 schools. The central strengths of the SBC Process are at the same time the major obstacles to its quick and easy implementation. On one hand, fidelity to a process, rather than a program, allows administrators and teachers to devise their own, site-specific solutions for moving forward through the Seven-Level Model and sustaining literacy improvement over time. Sustainability is enhanced by the fact that educators within the school take control of the change process and tailor curriculum improvement efforts to address the needs of their students. Thus, the strengths of the SBC Process lie in the fact that it can be customized to schools and that it promotes ownership of the change process at the school level. On the other hand, scaling such a customized process is no simple thing. Although our knowledge of the Seven-Level Model and nine dimensions makes the patterns clear, the specific path to be taken at each school to implement the SBC Process successfully cannot be known in advance. Rather, this path must be co-constructed anew at each site through a close collaboration between insiders and outsiders. We argue that the SBC Process is not a quick fix, but a sure and steady one, and for this reason is well worth pursuing for the benefits it brings to willing schools.

References

Anderson, R.C. & Pearson, P.D. (1984). A schematic theoretic view of basic processes in reading comprehension. In P.D. Pearson (Ed.), *Handbook of reading research* (pp. 255–292). New York: Longman.

Anderson, R.C., Spiro, R.J., & Montague, W.E. (Eds.), (1977). *Schooling and the acquisition of knowledge*. Hillsdale, NJ: Lawrence Erlbaum.

ARDDP. (2008). Partnerships for improving literacy in urban schools: Advanced reading development demonstration project. *The Reading Teacher, 61*(8).

Au, K.H. (1979). Using the experience-text-relationship method with minority children. *The Reading Teacher, 32*(7), 677–679.

Au, K.H. (2003). Literacy research and students of diverse backgrounds: What does it take to improve achievement? In C.M. Fairbanks, J. Worthy, B. Maloch, & J. Hoffman (Eds.), *52nd yearbook of the National Reading Conference* (pp. 85–91). Oak Creak, WI: National Reading Conference.

Au, K.H. (2005). Negotiating the slippery slope: School change and literacy achievement. *Journal of Literacy Research, 37*(3), 267–288.

Au, K.H., Hirata, S., & Raphael, T.E. (2005). Improving literacy achievement through standards. *California Reader, 39*(1), 5–10.

Au, K.H. & Mason, J.M. (1981). Social organizational factors in learning to read: The balance of rights hypothesis. *Reading Research Quarterly, 17*(1), 115–152.

Au, K.H., Raphael, T.E., & Mooney, K. (2008a). Improving reading achievement in elementary schools: Guiding change in a time of standards. In S.B. Wepner & D.S. Strickland (Eds.), *Supervision of reading programs* (4th ed., pp. 71–89). New York: Teachers College Press.

Au, K.H., Raphael, T.E., & Mooney, K. (2008b). What we have learned about teacher education to improve literacy achievement in urban schools. In V. Chou, L. Morrow & L. Wilkinson (Eds.), *Improving the preparation of teachers of reading in urban settings: Policy, practice, pedagogy* (pp. 159–184). Newark, DE: International Reading Association.

Barr, R., Kamil, M.L., Mosenthal, P., & Pearson, P.D. (Eds.), (1991). *Handbook of reading research* (Vol. II). New York: Longman.

Berliner, D.C. (2006). Our impoverished view of educational research. *Teachers College Record, 108*(6), 949–995.

Borko, H., Wolf, S.A., Simone, G., & Uchiyama, K.P. (2003). Schools in transition: Reform efforts and school capacity in Washington State. *Educational Evaluation and Policy Analysis, 25*(2), 171–201.

Borman, L.M. & Associates. (2005). *Meaningful urban educational reform: Confronting the learning crisis in mathematics and science*. Albany, NY: SUNY.

Brock, C. & Raphael, T.E. (2003). Guiding three middle school students in learning written academic discourse. *The Elementary School Journal, 103*(5), 481–502.

Brown, A.L. (1992). Design experiments: Theoretical and methodological challenges in creating complex interventions in classroom settings. *The Journal of the Learning Sciences, 2*(2), 141–178.

Brown, A.L., Bransford, J.D., Ferrara, R.A., & Campione, J.C. (1983). Learning, remembering, and understanding. In P.H. Mussen & W. Essen (Eds.), *Handbook of child psychology* (Vol. 3, pp. 77–166): New York: Wiley & Sons.

Brown, A.L. & Campione, J.C. (1996). Psychological theory and the design of innovative learning environments: On procedures, principles, and systems. In L. Shauble & R. Glaser (Eds.), *Innovations in learning: New environments for education* (pp. 289–325). Mahwah, NJ: Erlbaum.

Bullough, Jr., Robert V., & Gitlin, A.D. (1985). Schooling and change: A view from the lower rung. *Teachers College Record, 87*(2), 219–237.

Coburn, C.E. (2003). Rethinking scale: Moving beyond numbers to deep and lasting change. *Educational Researcher, 32*(6), 3–12.

Cognition and Technology Group at Vanderbilt. (1997). *The Jasper project: Lessons in curriculum, instruction, assessment, and professional development*. Mahwah, NJ: Erlbaum.

Collins, A. (1992). Toward a design science of education. In E. Scanlon & T. O'Shea (Eds.), *New directions in educational technology* (pp. 15–22).

Correnti, R. & Rowan, B. (2007). Opening up the black box: Literacy instruction in schools participating in three comprehensive school reform programs. *American Educational Research Journal, 44*(2), 298–338.

Cosner, S. (2006, December). *Elementary principals and Standards-Based Change: Early work and next steps*. Paper presented at the annual meeting of the National Reading Conference. Los Angeles, CA.

Darling-Hammond, L. (1997). *The right to learn: A blueprint for creating schools that work*. San Francisco, CA: Jossey-Bass.

Darling-Hammond, L. (2007). The flat earth and education: How America's commitment to equity will determine our future. *Educational Researcher, 36*(6), 318–334.

Datnow, A., Hubbard, L. & Mehan, H. (2002). *Extending educational reform: From one school to many*. New York: RoutledgeFalmer.

Design-based Research Collective. (2003). Design-based research: An emerging paradigm for educational inquiry. *Educational Researcher, 32*, 5–8.

DeStefano, L. & Hanson, M. (2005). *Annual evaluation of the ARDDP initiative.* Champaign-Urbana: University of Illinois.

DeStefano, L. & Hanson, M. (2006). *Annual evaluation of the ARDDP initiative.* Champaign-Urbana: University of Illinois.

Duffy, G.G. (1993). Teachers' progress toward becoming expert strategy teachers. *Elementary School Journal, 94*(2), 109–120.

Duffy, G.G., Roehler, L.R., Sivan, E., Rackliffe, G., Book, C., Meloth, M.S., et al. (1987). Effects of explaining the reasoning associated with using reading strategies. *Reading Research Quarterly, 22,* 347–268.

DuFour, R. (2004). What is a "professional learning community?" *Educational Leadership, 61*(8), 6–11.

Englert, C.S., Raphael, T.E., & Anderson, L.M. (1992). Socially-mediated instruction: Improving students' knowledge and talk about writing. *Elementary School Journal, 92*(4), 411–449.

Englert, C.S., Raphael, T.E., Anderson, L.M., Stevens, D.D., & Anthony, H.M. (1991). Making writing strategies and self-talk visible: Cognitive strategy instruction in writing. *American Educational Research Journal, 28,* 337–372.

Erickson, F. & Shultz, J. (1982). *The counselor as gatekeeper: Social interaction in interviews.* New York: Academic Press.

Flavell, J.H. (1979). Metacognition and cognitive monitoring: A new area of cognitive-developmental inquiry. *American Psychologist, 34*(10), 906–911.

Florio-Ruane, S., Berne, J., & Raphael, T.E. (2001). Teaching literature and literacy in the eye of reform: A dilemma in three acts. *The New Advocate, 14*(3), 197–210.

Florio-Ruane, S. & Raphael, T.E. (2004). Reconsidering our research: Collaboration, complexity, design, and the problem of "scaling up what works." *National Reading Conference Yearbook, 54,* 170–189.

Fullan, M. (2005). *Leadership sustainability: System thinkers in action.* Thousand Oaks, CA: Corwin Press.

Gavelek, J.R. & Raphael, T.E. (1985). Metacognition, instruction and the role of questioning activities. In G.E. MacKinnon & T.G.W.D.L. Forrest-Pressley (Eds.), *Metacognition, cognition and human performance* (Vol. II, pp. 103–132). Orlando: Academic Press.

Giles, C. & Hargreaves, A. (2006). The sustainability of innovative schools as learning organizations and professional learning communities during standardized reform. *Education Administration Quarterly, 42*(1), 124–156.

Goatley, V.J., Brock, C.H., & Raphael, T.E. (1995). Diverse learners participating in regular education "Book Clubs." *Reading Research Quarterly, 30*(3), 352–380.

Goatley, V., Highfield, K., Bentley, J., Pardo, L.S., Folkert, J., Scherer, P., et al. (1994). Empowering teachers to be researchers: A collaborative approach. *Teacher Research: The Journal of Classroom Inquiry, 1*(2), 128–144.

Goldman, S.R. (1976). Reading skill and the minimum distance principle: A comparison of listening and reading comprehension. *Journal of Experimental Child Psychology, 22,* 123–142.

Goldman, S.R. (2005). Designing for scalable educational improvement. In C. Dede, J.P. Honan, & L.C. Peters (Eds.), *Scaling up success: Lessons learned from technology-based educational improvement* (pp. 67–96). San Francisco, CA: Jossey Bass.

Goldman, S.R. & Durán, R.P. (1988). Answering questions from oceanography texts: Learner, task and text characteristics. *Discourse Processes, 11,* 373–412.

Goldman, S.R. & Murray, J.D. (1992). Knowledge of connectors as cohesion devices in text: A comparative study of native-English and English-as-a-second-language speakers. *Journal of Educational Psychology, 84*, 504–519.

Goldman, S.R. & Saul, E.U. (1990). Flexibility in text processing: A strategy competition model. *Learning and Individual Differences,* 2, 181–219.

Goldman, S.R., Saul, E.U., & Coté, N. (1995). Paragraphing, reader, and task effects on discourse comprehension. *Discourse Processes,* 20, 273–305.

Guthrie, J.T. & Ozgungor, S. (2002). Instructional contexts for reading engagement. In C.C. Block & M. Pressley (Eds.), *Comprehension instruction: Research-based best practices* (pp. 275–288). New York: Guilford.

Hanson, M.R., DeStefano, L., Mueller, P., Blachowicz, C., & Eason-Watkins, B. (2006). *Development, validation, and use of "The Indicators of High Literacy Performance": A framework for improving school literacy programs.* San Francisco, CA: American Educational Research Association.

Heckman, P.E. & Montera, V.L. (2009). School reform: The flatworm in a flat world: From entropy to renewal through indigenous invention. *Teachers College Record, 111*(1). Retrieved 1/13/2008 12:04:26pm from http://www.tcrecord.org, pp. 1–12.

Kamil, M.L., Mosenthal, P.B., Pearson, P.D., & Barr, R. (Eds.), (2000). *Handbook of reading research* (Vol. III). New York: Erlbaum.

Lamon, M., Secules, T., Petrosino, A., Hackett, R., Bransford, J., & Goldman, S. (1996). Schools for thought: Overview of the project and lessons learned from one of the sites. In L. Schauble & R. Glaser (Eds.), *Innovations in learning: New environments for education* (pp. 243–288). Mahwah, NJ: Erlbaum.

Langer, J.A. (2004). *Getting to excellent: How to create better schools.* New York: Teachers College Press.

Madda, C. & McMahon, S.I. (2006, December). *Turning points in school reform: A case study of changes in discourse and action.* Paper presented at the National Reading Conference, Los Angeles, CA.

McLaughlin, M.W. (1990). The RAND Change Agent Study revisited: Macro perspectives and micro realities. *Educational Researcher, 19*(9), 11–16.

McLaughlin, M.W. & Mitra, D. (2001). Theory-based change and change-based theory: Going deeper, going broader. *Journal of Educational Change,* 2, 301–323.

McMahon, S.I. & Raphael, T.E., with V.J. Goatley & L.S. Pardo (1997). *The Book Club connection: Literacy learning and classroom talk.* New York: Teachers College Press.

Mooney, K. & Raphael, T.E. (2006). *Turning points in school reform: One school's journey through the Standards-Based Change Process.* Paper presented at the National Reading Conference, Los Angeles, CA.

Mosenthal, J., Lipson, M., Mekkelsen, J., & Thompson, E. (2003). The dynamic environment of success: Representing school improvement in literacy learning and instruction. *Yearbook of the National Reading Conference, 52*, 308–320.

Mosenthal, J., Lipson, M., Torncello, S., Russ, B., & Mekkelsen, J. (2004). Contexts and practices of six schools successful in obtaining reading achievement. *The Elementary School Journal, 104*(5), 343–367.

No Child Left Behind Act of 2001, Pub. L. No. 107–110, 115 Stat. 1425. (2002). Retrieved April 10, 2003, from http://www.ed.gov/offices/OESE/esea

Palincsar, A.S., Brown, A.L., & Martin, S.M. (1987). Peer interaction in reading comprehension instruction. *Educational Psychology, 22*(3 & 4), 132–252.

Paris, S.G., Saarnio, D.A., & Cross, D.R. (1986). A metacognitive curriculum to promote children's reading and learning. *Australian Journal of Psychology*, *38*(2), 107–123.

Passow, A.H. (1984). Educational change and school improvement: Three perspectives. *Teachers College Record*, *86*(1), 238–247.

Pearson, D.P. (2007). An endangered species act for literacy education. *Journal of Literacy Research*, *39*(2), 145–162.

Pearson, D.P. & Gallagher, M.C. (1983). The instruction of reading comprehension. *Contemporary Educational Psychology*, *8*, 317–344.

Perfetti, C.A. & Goldman, S.R. (1974). Thematization and sentence retrieval. *Journal of Verbal Learning and Verbal Behavior*, 13, 70–79.

Raphael, T.E., Englert, C.S., & Kirschner, B.W. (1989). Students' metacognitive knowledge about writing. *Research in the Teaching of English*, *23*(4), 343–379.

Raphael, T.E., Florio-Ruane, S., Kehus, M., George, M., Hasty, N.L., & Highfield, K. (2001). Thinking for ourselves: Literacy learning in a diverse teacher inquiry network. *The Reading Teacher*, *54*(6), 596–607.

Raphael, T.E., George, M.A., Weber, C.M., & Nies, A. (2008). Approaches to teaching reading comprehension. In G.G. Duffy & S.E. Israel (Eds.), *Handbook of research on reading comprehension* (pp. 449–469).

Raphael, T., Goldman, S.R., Au, K, & Hirata, S. (2006, April). *A developmental model of the Standards-Based Change Process: A case study of learning in a school change project.* American Educational Research Association annual meeting, San Diego, CA.

Raphael, T.E., Kirschner, B.W., & Englert, C.S. (1988). The expository writing program: Making connections between reading and writing. *The Reading Teacher*, *41*, 790–795.

Raphael, T.E. & McKinney, J. (1983). An examination of 5th and 8th grade children's question answering behavior: An instructional study in metacognition. *Journal of Reading Behavior (now Journal of Literacy Research)*, *15*, 67–86.

Raphael, T.E. & Pearson, P.D. (1985). Increasing students' awareness of sources of information for answering questions. *American Educational Research Journal*, *22*, 217–236.

Raphael, T.E. & Wonnacott, C.A. (1985). Heightening 4th grade students' sensitivity to sources of information for answering comprehension questions. *Reading Research Quarterly*, *20*, 282–296.

Rowan, B., Camburn, E., & Barnes, C. (2004). Benefiting from comprehensive school reform: A review of research on CSR implementation. In C. Cross (Ed.), *Putting the pieces together: Lessons from comprehensive school reform research* (pp. 1–52). Washington, DC: National Clearinghouse for Comprehensive School Reform.

Secules, T., Cottom, C., Bray, M., & Miller, L. (1997). How children learn. *Educational Leadership*, *54(6)*, 54–60.

Strauss, A.L. & Corbin, J. (1994). *Basics of qualitative research: Grounded theory procedures and techniques*. Newbury Park, CA: Sage.

Strike, K.A. (2004). Community, the missing element of school reform: Why schools should be more like congregations than banks. *American Journal of Education*, *110*, 215–232.

Taylor, B.M., Pearson, P.D., Peterson, D.P., & Rodriguez, M.C. (2003). Reading growth in high-poverty classrooms: The influence of teacher practices that encourage cognitive engagement in literacy learning. *The Elementary School Journal*, *104*, 3–28.

Taylor, B.M., Pearson, P.D., Peterson, D.P., & Rodriguez, M.C. (2005). The CIERA

School Change Framework: An evidenced-based approach to professional development and school reading improvement. *Reading Research Quarterly, 40*(1), 40–69.

Timperley, H.S. & Parr, J.M. (2007). Closing the achievement gap through evidence-based inquiry at multiple levels of the education system. *Journal of Advanced Academics, 19*(1), 90–115.

Tough, P. (2008). 24/7 school reform: An analysis. *The New York Times*, Retrieved October 5, 2008, pp. 1–4 from http://www.nytimes.com/2008/09/07/magazine/07wwIn-lede-t

Uline, C.L., Tschannen-Moran, M., & Perez, L. (2003). Constructive conflict: How controversy can contribute to school improvement. *Teachers College Record, 105*(5), 782–816.

Walpole, S., Justice, L.M., & Invernizzi, M.A. (2004). Closing the gap between research and practice: Case study of school-wide literacy reform. *Reading & Writing Quarterly, 29*, 261–284.

Watson, K.A. (1974). Transferable communicative routines: Strategies and group identity in two speech events. *Language in Society, 4*, 53–72.

Part V

Policy and Practice in Literacy Education

Chapter 15

Language Policy and Literacy Instruction

The View from South Africa to South Texas

James V. Hoffman
University of Texas at Austin, U.S.A.

Misty Sailors
University of Texas at San Antonio, U.S.A.

Leketi Makalela
University of Limpopo, South Africa

Bertus Matthee
READ Educational Trust, South Africa

> Most plurilingual societies have developed an ethos which balances and respects the use of different languages in daily life. From the perspective of these societies and of the language communities themselves, multilingualism is more a way of life than a problem to be solved. The challenge is for education systems to adapt to these complex realities and provide a quality education that takes into consideration learners' needs, whilst balancing these at the same time with social, cultural, and political demands. While uniform solutions for plural societies, may be both administratively and managerially simpler, they disregard the risks involved both in terms of learning achievement and loss of linguistic and cultural diversity.
>
> (UNESCO, 2003, p. 12)

Language is at the very heart of personal and collective identity. Our language community is our safe cultural space that affirms our importance. Our language community often reflects whom we stand with and what we stand for. Stepping outside of *our* personal perspective we discover the existence of many different language communities. Some of these other language communities may be found no further than a neighbor next door. Thousands of other language communities are to be found at far greater distances. As the world becomes "flatter" (Friedman, 2005) these multiple language communities come into increasing contact. When languages come into contact, they compete for status and, in some cases, for survival. Sometimes it becomes a case of win or lose (with languages disappearing entirely). Just as often, it is a case of languages changing and adapting through this process. There is a kind of Darwinian survival of the fittest struggle within and between language communities. However, these are not the *natural* processes described by Darwin but socially mediated processes of assimilation and adaptation. The language struggles may involve quite conscious and purposeful efforts by some to manipulate the outcomes of language competition. In this way, language policy at the societal level can become a tool of oppression or liberation.

We situate our discussion of language change, language policy, and literacy instruction inside of two contexts: South Africa and South Texas. We acknowledge, from the start, that South Africa and South Texas are far apart in more than just distance. There are significant historical, social, and political contrasts as well. Nonetheless, we feel there is much to learn in looking across these two contexts for an understanding of language in education, literacy practices in schools, and the influence of public policy. Our experiences (as teachers, teacher educators and researchers) have stimulated our thinking to examine important links between the two contexts that can potentially inform each other and other areas of the world where language diversity manifests itself. In this chapter, we first describe the ways in which language policy has evolved in South Africa, from two perspectives: historical and contemporary. We consider how policy shapes instructional practices in schools serving low-income communities. Second, we turn these understandings back on schools that serve low-income communities in the United States—with a particular focus on schools serving low-income Hispanic communities in South Texas. We begin this chapter with a brief overview of language policy in education in South Africa. Next, we offer a summary of some our recent research into language policy and language use in South African schools. Finally, we return to discuss issues in the United States with respect to language policy and practice with a particular focus on both problems and promising practices in South Texas.

Background: The South African Context for Language in Education

South Africa has experienced more than its share of oppressive practices, whether one examines the early practices of colonizers from Europe or the more recent era of Apartheid. Control over the education of the youth has been one of the chief modes of policy control over language. Under Bantu education policies the indigenous cultural groups in South Africa were schooled in home languages through the primary grades restricting access to the more socially powerful languages of Afrikaans and English (Hartshorne, 1995). With the end of Apartheid in 1993 and the passing of the new Constitution in 1996, the political focus on language and language in education has accelerated, especially for foundation phase students (students in Grades 1–3). The government has exerted efforts to remove the oppressive language policies of the former regime and replace them with policies that serve to liberate, enrich and empower all communities. As a result, literacy learning is beginning to take on a more democratic look, differing greatly from past literacy learning, especially for African language-speaking learners. (Here we offer a brief sketch of the past and present as a background for our report. For a more complete presentation of the issues, in particular with respect to the historical context, we recommend several important books on the topic: *The Mind of South Africa* (Sparks, 1990); *Changing Class* (Chisholm, 2004); *The State, Education and Equity in Post-Apartheid South Africa* (Motala & Pampallis, 2002); *Elusive Equity* (Fiske & Ladd, 2004); and *Language Policy and National Unity in South Africa/Azania* (Alexander, 1989).

Education under Apartheid

Under the Apartheid Regime, the Bantu Educational Act of 1953 spelled out the kinds of educational experiences African-language-speaking learners were to receive. Under this act, school was to prepare African students for a subservient role in society—in contrast to the more academic curriculum in "white," "coloured" and "Indian" schools (Hartshorne, 1995). To that end, schools provided mother tongue instruction until the end of the primary phase (8 years) to further separate development and, in the eyes of most observers, to prevent African-language-speaking learners from developing ambitions outside their own communities (Alexander, 1989; Hartshorne, 1995). Teachers introduced learners to Afrikaans (the official language of the country and the language of the Apartheid regime) and English as subjects separate from mother tongue instruction in primary schools. During this time, the matriculation rates of African-speaking learners steadily improved from 43.5% in 1955 to 83.4% in 1976 (Heugh, 1995, 1999). Outside of the politics of Bantu Education, the language of instruction that allowed learners to be schooled in languages that they understood may be attributed to mother tongue instruction.

However, African-language-speakers, both parents and learners, resented "Bantu Education" and interpreted it as a mechanism to prevent access to power, social equity, and international ideas. The active political liberation movements of the 1950s, the African National Congress and the Pan African Congress, launched several campaigns directed against the Bantu Education system, and by implications, to using languages for ethnolinguistic divisions of the African majority population (Makalela, 2005). Beyond the first eight years of schooling, English and Afrikaans were used as dual media of instruction on a fifty-fifty basis. In order to increase the domination of Afrikaans language and the Afrikaner culture, the Apartheid government exerted its influence to use Afrikaans as the medium of instruction in primary schools in the early

1970s. This action was meted out with protests that culminated into the 1976 Soweto Uprising, where students fought not only against the introduction of Afrikaans in lower grades, but also against the whole system of Bantu Education. The government took notice and passed the Education and Training Act of 1979, which reduced the language in mother tongue to four years of primary school followed by either Afrikaans or English as the choice of instructional medium. This option was used by the missionary groups who controlled the education system, largely under the influence of the British education system, of the African learners until 1952. Regarding English as a neutral language and a language of the struggle for freedom, as expected, most Black schools opted for English. By the early 1990s, mother tongue instruction was further reduced and offered for a maximum of three years of primary education at the most.

Heugh (1999) attributed the "failure of black education in South Africa" to the reduction of instruction in mother tongue and the "resulting drop in matriculation rates to 44% by 1992" (pp. 303–304). This is, however, a controversial finding and a complex one because it would be difficult to single out language as the cause of high pass rates within a system that was illegitimate and bent on setting learners for failure. Other factors, as Young (1995) noted, may be teachers' lack of proficiency in English, excessively large classes, poor textbook resourcing, and inadequate teacher training to support the demands of using English as the medium for instruction. For our purpose, it is noteworthy that the whole idea of instruction in mother tongue under Apartheid was distorted and it fueled negative stereotypes toward African languages, which were associated with the Bantustan reserves and the whole apartheid concept of separate development.

Post-Apartheid Education

Education, like the rest of the country, underwent major changes with the passage of the Constitution in 1996. Section 29 of the Constitution asserts:

(1) Everyone has the right to a basic education, including adult basic education.
(2) Everyone has the right to receive education in the official language of their choice in public educational institutions where that education is reasonably practicable.

The move to provide all learners in South Africa an education in the official language of their choice remains a formidable task, at least in part due to the Constitution's recognition of 11 official languages: Sepedi; Sesotho; Setswana; SiSwati; Tshivenda; Xitsonga; Afrikaans; English; IsiNdebele; IsiXhosa; and IsiZulu.

The language-in-education policy of South Africa is based on the notion of additive multilingualism, and promotes the use of the home language along-side an additional language (which in most cases is English). This policy encourages, according to Desai (2001), a "multilanguage" society with the goal of elevating the status and advancing the use of indigenous languages. The language policy of the country calls for "parity of esteem and the equitable use of the official languages." To encourage a multilingual nation, the language-in-education policy calls for learners to:

- learn their home language and at least one additional official language
- become competent in their additional language while their home language is maintained and developed
- learn an African language for a minimum of three years by the end of the General Education and Training Band (Revised National Curriculum Statement Grades R–9, 2002).

Under the language policy of the country, learning in the Reception Year (Grade R) and Grade 1 is to occur in the learners' home language. Teachers are to introduce the additional language as a subject in Grade 1. Teachers are to use the home language alongside the additional language for "as long as possible" (National Curriculum Statement, p. 5). The National Curriculum gives "School Governing Bodies the responsibility of selecting school language policies that are appropriate for their circumstances and in line with the policy of additive multilingualism" (p. 4). The current language-in-education policy is a move, albeit a gradual one, toward a multilingual society (Brock-Utne & Holmardottir, 2001).

Other researchers (Alexander, 2001; Makalela, 2005; Kamwangamalu, 2001; Makoni, 2003; Phaswana, 2003) took a more critical stance over the 11 official language policy because it failed to address the real language struggle in South Africa: the present linguistic entities were a result of a colonial system of rule and divide and that its success will be limited (Makalela, 2005; Webb, 2002). These scholars hold that instead of appropriating the *disinventions* of the missionary linguists and *minsinventions* of the Apartheid regime (Makoni, 2003), attempts to redress past linguistic inequalities and to address the present sociolinguistic realities should begin with an exerted effort to harmonize mutually intelligible languages (Makalela, 2005; Prah 2002) in order to deal with the practical challenges of "artificial" multilingualism (see Makalela, 2005, for a full discussion). The policy provisions received further scathing criticism because the changes, if any, were slow, piecemeal, and largely reported as ineffective, with the old language practices carried over in the majority of the public schools and major official domains. According to Kamwangamalu (2001), the only visible change in post-Apartheid context is that English has taken more clout over Afrikaans, casting doubt on whether indigenous African languages would have "parity of esteem" as proscribed in the Constitution. It is against this background of predictions for failure and the rise of English-only linguistic ecology, as recently reported, that we needed to pay close attention to the evolution of actual language practices emanating from a multilingual policy for school and draw useful lessons for the U.S. public schools that operate within the aegis of a no-policy or English-only practice.

High-Performing South African Schools Serving Low-Income Communities

The Learning for Living Project was a large-scale intervention directed by the READ Educational Trust in close collaboration with the National and Provincial Departments of Education "to improve the communication, language, cognitive and literacy skills of learners from Grade 1 to 7." This five-year intervention, initiated in 1999, offered quality texts, teacher training, and school improvement initiatives. The intervention focused on just 1,000 schools, over 10,000 teachers, and close to 1 million learners over the course of the five-year project. All of the target schools served low-income communities in mostly rural settings. The schools were distributed across all nine South African provinces. The evaluation of the impact of this project, focusing on a sample of the intervention and control schools, indicated substantial impact on the quality of teaching and quality of learning in schools (Sailors, Hoffman & Matthee, 2007). At the end of the five-year intervention, seven of the 90 schools participating in the evaluation study stood out as consistently high-performing within the sample and across all of the measures of student achievement from the final evaluation. The analysis of the seven schools began with an inspection of the qualitative, descriptive data in the project files. These data included self-reports from the schools, demographic data on the schools, and monitoring reports from supervisors and coordinators (for a complete report on this high-performing study, see: Sailors et al., 2007). Additional data was gathered through site visits to these schools (interview and observational data).

In the analysis of the critical attributes of these seven high-performing schools, one theme emerged across schools—the language policy of these schools was critical to the success of the schools. These successes were due to the identity that the schools had created for themselves and this identity was formed largely because the schools capitalized on South Africa's language in education policy. Through this policy, the schools sought to maintain the culture of the community they served. As a result, the schools had a good reputation within their communities and were places in which learners were successful.

The high-performing schools we studied were located in four provinces and operated under similar language in education policies themselves. In keeping with the provincial policies of choice for schools and communities, the way in which schools offered instruction to learners was very different. Four of the high-performing schools offered the home language of the learners as the medium of instruction beginning at the Reception Grade and continuing until at least Grade 2, when English was introduced as a subject; two of these schools introduced a third language beginning in Grade 4. One school offered learners instruction in English beginning at the Reception Grade; the home language was introduced until Grade 4. Two other schools offered choices for learners and their parents upon entry into their schools—learners could choose Afrikaans or Sesotho, or English. While there was clearly a plan for language use moving from home language at the first grade to an emphasis on English in Grades 2 and above, there was flexibility everywhere. In some classrooms, we observed Foundation phase teachers using the home language of the learners for instruction but changing to English to give directions. There seemed to be two clear purposes for the language policies across these schools. One major theme was the maintenance of culture and the second was "getting the learners ready for the workplace." Each was unique to the language policy the school and community had set forth.

The underlying principles articulated in South Africa's national language policy are reflected in these high-performing schools. Multilingualism is valued as a primary outcome of education. Choice is offered within the school or at least in a neighboring school and there is significant involvement in each of these schools for the language policy. All of these schools provide for the teaching of two languages and in some cases three. In all cases there is the opportunity for the learners to study their home language. Due to its economic value and higher social status, learning English is an obvious priority in these schools. English is the medium of instruction or taught as a second language across these schools, while there is a high regard for local customs. There is no one size fits all. Patterns of language policy vary and all of these seem to lead to success in promoting literacy skills in English and maintaining local culture through the use of home languages in varying degrees.

While some have written about the limitations of the multilingualistic policy of South Africa (e.g., Brock-Utne & Holmardottir, 2001; Heugh, 1999, 2002) and the problems faced within that country as implementation becomes prag- matic (e.g., Webb, 1999, 2002), we see the power of the current language policy in literacy learning based on our work in these high-performing schools. The language in education policy in South Africa that allows for freedom of choice and implementation by the schools and the communities they serve is exciting for us. We do note however that the challenges of choice are huge, especially the parents' choice between English—a powerful language with resources and prestige, on the one hand—and African languages, which still need corpus planning and material development, on the other hand (Makalela, 2005). The issue at stake though is that parents have immediate needs to have their children get good education. It would also appear, unlike previously argued, that the boundaries of choosing between English and an African language are grad- ually becoming fluid, with multiple identities being nurtured in a pluricentric society (i.e., English accepted without rejecting local cultures through African languages) (see Canagarajah, 1999, on multiple identities and discourses of

English as an international language). We have found that the overwhelming response among the participants was that they needed both cultural mainten-ance and access to language of social upward mobility—a point showing their dual consciousness. This is truly so when English can no longer be viewed as the language of the colonizer, but the language that has been indigenized and locally owned (Kasanga, 2003; Kachru, 1986; Makalela, 2004).

We take a stance that development of multilingual policy creates the possi-bility for negotiation of new language identities as dictated by the socio-linguistic realities of the nation. As seen in this study of high-performing schools, the South African policy has created spaces where schools and com-munities are able to demonstrate their togetherness and gain grassroots control of the languages in school instead of the top-down policies of Apartheid. That is, the schools and the communities are able to come together for a common purpose—maintaining their culture and educating their young. In other places we have reported on the orderliness and structure that exists in these schools, the strong leadership, quality teaching, and the collaborative spirit that exists between the community and these schools (Sailors et al., 2007). Here, we need to add that a language policy crafted on the basis of community participation and input has the power to grant such confidence and ultimate success in the schools under investigation. We are inclined to claim that additive multilingual-ism has gradually taken root and its empowering nature promises even a brighter future for the country.

Language in Education Policy in the United States

The United States has no official language policy. Although English is the language that drives commerce, almost 18% of the population (5 years and older) speaks a language other than English (U.S. Census Bureau, 2000). While some states do have official languages (Hawaii, for example, has two official languages, Hawaiian and English), the majority of the 50 states either do not have an official policy that embraces bilingualism or explicitly prohibits it, as does Arizona and California. In the U.S., the 1990 and 1992 Native American Languages Act declared that the U.S. government's policy is to "preserve, protect, and promote the rights and freedom of Native Americans to use, practice, and develop Native American languages" (P.L. 101–477, Section 104[1]). It is not clear how much active support this provision has received in practice. It is clear, however, that the protection provided for in this Act does not apply to speakers of Spanish or other "non-native" languages. In fact, far from protection, most attention to the other languages in the United States is negative, as evidenced in the "English Only" initiatives in numerous states.

Richard Ruiz (1996; cited in Hornberger, 1998) points out that "movements toward the officialization of English in the United States are consistent with the tendency in large multinational states to promote a transethnified public culture." In the U.S., Ruiz argues, languages other than English are:

perfectly acceptable . . . [but only] as long as they are mediated through individuals and not communities; [however,] if they are community languages, they should be confined to the private sector and not make demands for public subsidy; [and] if there is to be public subsidy, their use should be for the common public good, and not signal competing allegiances.

Hornberger argues that in a language ideology built on the promotion of transethnification, instrumentalism, and nationism it is difficult to find room for state-supported programs of language education that would promote the full use and development of two or more languages in school, and that would lead to the kind of bilingual/biliterate/bicultural versatility encapsulated in the immigrants' twin plea to "learn the new and keep the old" (p. 447).

Hornberger (1998) believes that:

> . . . language minorities must be empowered to make choices about which languages and which literacies to promote for which purposes; and that, in making those choices, the guiding principles must be to balance the counterpoised dimensions of language rights for the mutual protection of all. Among the balances that must be struck across competing language rights are those between tolerance-oriented and promotion-oriented rights (Kloss 1977), between individual and communal freedoms (Skutnabb-Kangas 1994), between freedom to use one's language and freedom from being discriminated against for doing so (Macías 1979), and between "claims to something" and "claims against someone else" (Ruiz 1984). These are difficult ethical choices, but they must be made; I am arguing here that those best qualified to make them are the language minority speakers themselves.
>
> (pp. 454–455)

An Historical Perspective on United States Language Policy

Immigration has been a continuous force in shaping the social, political, and economic reality of the United States. Immigration has brought diversity to this nation. Immigrants adapted to their new environment but they shaped changes in the environment as well. The struggles and contentions around linguistic diversity have resulted in various formations of policy and practice—in particular within the educational system. Carlos Ovando (2003) has identified four stages of response to linguistic diversity.

The Permissive Period (1700–1880s)

There was a fair amount of tolerance during this period with many immigrant communities holding on to their identity through the protection and promotion of their maternal languages. This promotion and protection included the creation of schools that used maternal languages as the medium of instruction. Ovando, for example, cites Kloss (1977/1998) claim that in 1900, approximately 600,000 (4% of the elementary population) were receiving all or part of their instruction in German.

The Restrictive Period (1880s–1960s)

There was increased attention during this period on the standardization of American schools—with a common language central to the effort. Nationalism took hold and the war with Germany sparked fear and suspicion of many immigrants from eastern Europe. Most of the German-speaking schools disappeared during this period. Kloss (1977/1998) reported that by 1923 34 states had initiated English-only instruction in schools.

The Opportunistic Period (1960s–1980s)

Various legislative and court actions spawned a shift in language policy in schools. The Bilingual Education Act (Title Seven of the Elementary and Secondary Education Act) was passed in 1968 as part of Lyndon B. Johnson's War on Poverty. This act was designed to support the education of language-minority students. School districts that received federal funds were required to meet the needs of English language learners in schools. The U.S. Supreme Court ruled in *Lau v. Nichols* (414 U.S. 5637) that equal treatment of English-speaking and non-English-speaking students did not constitute equal educational opportunity and, therefore, violated non-English-speaking students' civil rights (Ovando, 1977). While no specific curriculum approach was required by this ruling, the action of the court fueled a variety of approaches to meet the needs of linguistically diverse learners. Programs tended to adopt a range of approaches from:

- structured immersion (with no use of maternal language)
- partial immersion (with a small amount of time set aside each day for maternal language instruction)
- transitional bilingual programs (intensive instruction in maternal language and English with provisions for early exiting into the traditional curriculum)
- maintenance bilingual programs (with continuous attention to the growth of both maternal language and English)
- two-way immersion programs (with native speakers of both languages placed together for instruction in both languages).

The Dismissive Period (1980s–present)

The anti-bilingual education movement gained momentum during this period with funding cuts by the federal government during the Reagan era and a general shift to conservative values. Rising immigration, both legal and illegal, has fed public concerns for the preservation of the status of English in schools and in the country. For example, Hispanic students currently compose one-fifth of the population under eight years old and are projected to be a quarter of this population by 2030 (National Task Force on Early Childhood Education for Hispanics, 2007). State initiatives in California and Arizona that first led to limitations on the content of bilingual education programs were followed by the banning of all bilingual education programs in these states in favor of intensive ESL instruction.

Language Education in South Texas

As of 1998, the state of Texas had over 500,000 school-aged students identified as linguistically diverse (Texas Education Agency, 1998). Of these, over 90% spoke Spanish as their primary language. The state of Texas, in contrast to states like California and Arizona, has maintained a commitment to bilingual education in the form of support for programs. Though Texas has no formal state policy that reflects a vision for multilingualism, school districts within the state have considerable flexibility in designing language instruction to support English language learners (ELLs). Alanis (2000) reports that state-wide, 49% of these learners are being served in transitional bilingual programs and 38% are in ESL programs. The fact that both of these approaches fail to regard the maternal language as an asset worthy of development leads to what Angela Valenzuela has described as a state of "subtractive" schooling (Valenzuela, 1999). Additive bilingualism (as portrayed in dual language programs) are less common in Texas despite the fact that there is considerable research pointing to the merits of such an approach (Alanis, 2000).

Bertha Perez (2002) has carefully documented the evolution of two dual-language schools in the San Antonio area. These two schools are located in the inner-city area of San Antonio. Both schools serve a predominantly Mexican-American population. Perez describes the evolution of these schools from low performing academically to recognized status in the area through the cooperation of community members, local educators, and teacher educators. The program, in both schools, evolved to a fully developed dual-language model.

Despite this demonstrated success (and after the Perez report), they fell under increasing pressure from the school district to move back from a dual-language model to an ESL emphasis. Both schools resisted the pressure and, with community support, moved to charter status within the state of Texas and have thus been able to continue the emphasis on dual-language instruction.

These two elementary schools exemplify many of the qualities of language policy and language practice we found in the high-performing study in South Africa. There is not only community support but also community input into the curriculum. There is an explicit commitment to multilingualism and there is evidence of success.

Moving deeper into South Texas, we have encountered even more complex views of language policy as they interact with community values. Cameron County Texas is both the most southern and the poorest county in the continental United States. Over the past two years, we have been working in a federally funded project designed to upgrade the language and literacy teaching skills in private daycare centers serving low-income Hispanic families. More than 70% of the families using the daycares in the study receive subsidies for low-income families (Childcare Management Systems, 2005). Fifty percent of the children in the local school district are considered Limited English Proficient (Texas Education Agency, 2007), and the number is higher for children just entering kindergarten. Prior to the beginning of the study, early childhood educators in the area were surveyed. According to the survey responses, more than 65% of the educators had a high school education or less. The project has provided staff development to over 65 early childhood educators in the use of effective language and literacy instructional strategies. Educators could choose between professional development and mentoring in English or Spanish. Approximately one-fourth of the educators in the research study chose to receive their instruction and mentoring in Spanish and three-quarters in English. Professional development sessions included information, hands-on activities, and opportunities for early childhood educators to share ideas with their peers. Literacy topics included oral language development, teaching English language learners, reading aloud to children, print awareness, alphabet knowledge, phonological awareness, phonics, encouraging emergent writing, setting up reading and writing centers in the classroom, and how to use the materials provided through the program. In addition, instructional specialists explained to the early childhood educators how to incorporate literacy throughout the day and to include literacy materials at all centers.

Our evaluation data suggest that practically all of the daycare centers participating in this project use English as the primary medium of instruction despite the maternal language of the children and the maternal language for the vast majority of the early-childhood educators. The daycare centers are private and compete—often succeeding in this competitive environment—based on the promise of English instruction for the young children. There is no public policy shaping this decision. It is parental choice and market forces that are shaping language policy and practices in these schools. The data regarding the impact of the training of early childhood educators has demonstrated positive impact on teaching practices (e.g., enriched literacy environment) and significant positive impact on student acquisition of language skills (in English). The choice of English as the primary medium of instruction with some Spanish used to scaffold student engagement (e.g., through code-switching) in this predominantly Spanish-speaking community is familiar from our experiences in South Africa where parents have choices and schools that promise English language instruction from the start are attracting more students. In contrast with South Africa, there is no public policy or societal vision to insure attention to maintenance of home language. These are the poorest of the poor struggling to find a path out of poverty through education.

Conclusion

> Language is not only a tool for communication and knowledge but also a fundamental attribute of cultural identity and empowerment, both for the individual and the group. Respect for the languages of persons belonging to different linguistic communities therefore is essential to peaceful cohabitation. This applies both to majority groups, to minorities (whether traditionally residents in a country or more recent migrants) and to indigenous peoples.
>
> (UNESCO, 2003, p. 15)

This chapter sits inside of a book focused on change in literacy contexts, literacy policy, and literacy teaching. Here, we have focused on the changes that surround languages in two contexts. We have argued that in South Africa, the issues surrounding language policy are complex and that the risks of privilege—even hegemony—remain real. However, despite the weaknesses inherent in the policy provisions and in some cases continuation of the old subtractive language in education practices, there is demonstrated appreciation in South Africa for multilingualism and the strength it affords a society.

The vision of multilingualism, the respect and valuing of difference inspire us to think about the U.S. schools and the language challenges ahead. In our view, it is time (perhaps way past time) that U.S. policymakers begin to situate its national goals and interests within the broader global context of language diversity and language change. The fact that English is increasingly becoming the global language of commerce and communication should not be used to argue for an English-only language policy (tacit or otherwise). Rather, the U.S. should embrace multilingualism, additive bilingualism, and pluralism as national goals that are in its own political, economic, and social interests. Policy in the United States should encourage local decision-making, as in South Africa, to insure that the languages within a school meet community needs and resources. For South Africa, the journey through a policy that allows choice for communities on the language of instruction, as illustrated through the schools we studied, has just begun.

Within the United States, the dialogue must be opened. As in South Africa, we must find schools in the United States where a vision of multilingualism and a flexible policy to support and guide practices works for the benefit of all. The UNESCO appeals for attention to mother tongue instruction and the preservation of languages in the face of globalization remind us of the importance of high stakes for language policy at both the human and societal levels.

References

Alanis, I. (2000). A Texas two-way bilingual program: Its effects on linguistic and academic achievement. *Bilingual Research Journal, 24*(3).

Alexander, N. (1989). *Language policy and national unity in South Africa/Azania.* Cape Town: Buchu.

Alexander, N. (2001). Why the Nguni and the Sotho languages should be harmonized. In K. Deprez & T. Du Plessis (Eds.), *Multilingualism and government* (pp.171–175). Pretoria: Van Schaik Publishers.

Brock-Utne, B. & Holmardottir, H.B. (2001). The choice of English as medium of instruction and its effects on the African languages in Namibia. *International Review of Education, 47,* 293–322.

Canagarajah, S. (1999). *Resisting linguistic imperialism in English teaching.* Oxford: Oxford University Press.

Childcare Management Systems. (2005). *Report on the number of families receiving childcare subsidies in Cameron County, TX.* Unpublished raw data.

Chisholm, L. (Ed.), (2004). *Changing class. Education and social change in post-apartheid South Africa.* London: Zed Books.

Desai, Z. (2001). Multilingualism in South Africa with particular reference to the role of African languages in education. *International Review of Education, 47,* 323–339.

Fiske, E.B. & Ladd, H.F. (2004). *Elusive equity: Education reform in post-apartheid South Africa.* Washington, D.C.: Brookings Institution Press.

Friedman, T. (2005). *The world is flat: A brief history of the twenty-first century.* New York: Farrar, Straus & Giroux.

Hartshorne, K. (1995). Language policy in African education: A background to the future. In R. Mesthrie (Ed.), *Language and social history: Studies in South African sociolinguistics.* Cape Town: David Philip.

Heugh, K. (1999). Languages, development and reconstructing education in South Africa. *International Journal of Educational Development, 19,* 301–313.

Heugh, K. (2002). Recovering multilingualism: Recent language policy developments. In R. Mesthrie (Ed.), *Language in South Africa* (pp. 449–475). Cambridge: Cambridge University Press.

Hoffman, J. & Matthee, B. (2004). Improving literacy instruction in South African schools: The Business Trust's Learning for Living Project. *Thinking Classrooms, 5,* 27–33.

Hornberger, N.H. (1998). Language policy, language education, language rights: Indigenous, immigrant, and international perspectives. *Language in Society, 27,* 439–458.

Kachru, B.B. (1986). *The alchemy of English: the spread, functions and models of non-native Englishes.* Oxford: Pergamon.

Kamwangamalu, N.M. (2001). The language planning situation in South Africa. *Current Issues in Language Planning, 2*(4), 361–445.

Kasanga, L. (2003). "I am asking for a pen": Framing requests in Black South African English. In K. Jaszczolt & K. Turner (Eds.), *Meaning through language contrast* (pp. 213–235). Amsterdam: John Benjamins.

Kloss, H. (1977/1998). *The American bilingual tradition.* Rowley, MA: Newbury House.

Makalela, L. (2004). Making sense of Black South African English for linguistic democracy in South Africa. *World Englishes, 23*(3), 355–366.

Makalela, L. (2005). We speak eleven tongues: Reconstructing multilingualism in South Africa. In B. Brock-Utne & R.K. Hopson (Eds.), *Languages of instruction for African emancipation: Focus on postcolonial contexts and considerations* (pp. 147–174). Cape Town: CASAS.

Makoni, S. (2003) From misinvention to disinvention of language: Multilingualism and the South African constitution. In S. Makoni, G. Smitherman, A. Ball, & K. Spears (Eds.), *Black linguistics: Language, society and politics in Africa and the Americas* (pp. 132–149). London and New York: Routledge.

Motala, E. & Pampallis, J. (Eds.), (2002). *The state, education and equity in post-apartheid South Africa.* Aldershot: Ashgate.

National Task Force on Early Childhood Education for Hispanics. (2007) *Para nuestros ninos: Expanding and improving early education for Hispanics.* (Main report) Tempe, AZ: Arizona State University.

Nettle, D. & Romaine, S. (2000). *Vanishing voices: The extinction of the world's languages.* New York: Oxford University Press.

Ovando, C.J. (1977). School implications of the peaceful Latino invasion. *Phi Delta Kappan, 69*(4), 230–234.

Ovando, C.J. (2003). Bilingual education in the United States: Historical development and current issues. *Bilingual Research Journal, 27,* 1–23.

Pérez, B. (2004). *Becoming biliterate: A study of two-way immersion education in San Antonio.* Mahwah, NJ: Lawrence Erlbaum.

Phaswana, N. (2003). Contradiction or affirmation: The South African language policy and the South African Government. In S. Makoni, G. Smitherman, A. Ball, & A.K. Spears (Eds.), *Black linguistics: Language, society and politics in Africa and the Americas* (pp. 150–164). London and New York: Routledge.

Prah, K.K. (Ed.) (2002). *Speaking in unison: Harmonisation and standardisation of Southern African languages.* Cape Town: CASAS.

Ruiz, R. (1996). *English officialization and transethnification in the USA.* Paper presented at the Annual Meeting of the American Anthropological Association, San Francisco, November.

Sailors, M. (2004). The READ Educational Trust of South Africa. *Thinking Classrooms, 5,* 34–36.

Sailors, Hoffman, & Matthee. (2007). South African schools that promote literacy learning with students from low-income communities. *Reading Research Quarterly, 42,* 364–387.

Sparks, A. (1990). *The mind of South Africa.* New York: Knopf.

Texas Education Agency. (1998). *Enrollment trends in Texas public schools.* Policy Research Report No. 11 (Document No. GE8 600 05). Austin, TX: Author.

Texas Education Agency. (2007). *Academic Excellence Indicator System.* Retrieved February 29, 2008 from http://www.tea.state.tx.us/

UNESCO. (2003). *Education in a multilingual world.* Paris: France. The United Nations Educational, Scientific and Cultural Organization. www.unesco.org/education.

UNESCO. (2006). *Multilingualism in cyberspace: Safeguarding endangered languages*. Retrieved November 18, 2006 http://portal.unesco.org/ci/en/ev.php-URL_ID=7856& URL_DO=DO_TOPIC&URL_SECTION=201.html

U.S. Census Bureau. (2000). Language spoken at home. Census 2000 Summary File 3. QT P.16. Download available at http://factfinder.census.gov/. Downloaded on June 16, 2005.

U.S. Census Bureau. (2004). International data base. Retrieved March 22, 2004, from http://www.census.gov/ipc/www/idbnew.html.

Valenzuela, A. (1999). *Subtractive schooling: U.S.-Mexican youth and the politics of caring*. Albany, NY: State University of New York Press.

Webb, V. (1999) Multilingualsim in democratic South Africa: The overestimation of language policy. *International Journal of Educational Development, 19*, 351–366.

Webb, V. (2002) *Language in South Africa: The role of language in national transformation, reconstruction and development*. Amsterdam: John Benjamin.

Young, Y. (1995). Preparing teacher trainees to teach in multilingual classes. In K. Heugh, A. Siegruhn, & P. Pluddermann (Eds.), *Multilingual education for South Africa*. Johannesburg: Heinemann.

Chapter 16

Fifty Years of Federal Government Involvement in Reading Education

Patrick Shannon and Jacqueline Edmondson
Penn State University

Leticia Ortega
R.J. Hendley School

Susan Pitcher
Elizabethtown College

Christopher Robbins
Eastern Michigan University

For the last 50 years, sincere federal representatives and employees have worked diligently to influence the daily practices in American public schools. Since Brown *v.* the Board of Education Topeka, Kansas in 1954, the federal government has required states to ensure that all citizens receive equal opportunities to public schooling. Implementing and enforcing the Brown ruling has not been easy or straightforward because experts, politicians, judges, and educators have struggled to define what equal opportunity and treatment under the law could mean for education in general and reading education in particular. Depending upon one's perspective, federal actions in reading education could be considered progress, regress, or just a mess. In this chapter, we describe, analyze, and comment upon the federal legislation from Brown to the recent No Child Left Behind law, paying particular attention to their consequences.

Although the overall federal agenda for education over the past 50 years has been the general improvement of American citizens' literacy, all members of government have not agreed on how that might be accomplished, which citizens need more help, and why they need it. Remember that a 50-year retrospective considers the Eisenhower, Kennedy, Johnson, Nixon, Ford, Carter, Bush, Clinton, and now George W. Bush administrations, with their varying degrees of commitment to the Brown decision and their somewhat divergent views about public schooling. Across that time span and political spectrum, liberal optimism about the role of education and the best solutions rising to the top in the marketplace of ideas were replaced by a more deterministic pessimism concerning which educational values are most important, who is worthy of public education, and how those values might be achieved for the worthy.

Recent calls for a federal study of teacher education, the "what works" enthusiasm, zero tolerance policy, cancellation of the Bilingual Education Act (title VII), and the Education Science Law of 2002 appear to be attempts to direct public schools toward standardization and to discipline educators who continue to value the productive possibilities of diversity of views and practices. We engage in this review because we continue to be optimistic about public schooling as projects of possibility:

> ... the transformation of the relations between human capacities and social forms. More particularly the project requires both the expansion of forms to accommodate capacities and the expansion of capacities to make the realization of new forms possible. Such a project would reject the resolution of this contradiction between capacities and forms through narrowing of capacities to fit existing forms or through the narrowing of forms to fit preconceived, fixed, "naturalized" notions of capacities.
>
> (Simon, 2001, p. 145)

We organize the chapter around five themes or areas of federal initiatives— teacher education, elementary and secondary curriculum, race relations, language difference, and uses of science. In each, we trace the history of federal policy and some consequences. We provide a timeline for federal activity in Table 16.1 as a support for reading the analysis provided in this chapter.

We argue in this chapter that federal power has been both productive and restrictive—it has extended as well as limited the diversity among social forms within each of these areas. Although it might seem odd that federal policies could stimulate diversity, that conclusion is reasonable once you lose the notion that the government acts rationally or according to a centralized plan. It does not. Sometimes one branch of government's actions or policies counteracts those of another branch, without recognizing the contradiction. Consider Congress's history with the Head Start program, which began in the 1960s' War on Poverty. The program was originally intended to be the great equalizer, helping poor children to become as well prepared for schooling as their middle-class peers. Yet, Congress has not adequately funded Head Start even once since its inception. Moreover, the latest federal plans for Head Start ignore the original vision of multiple models for preschools and call for a single model in order to increase efficiency—but still sufficient funding for all eligible children is not provided.

Table 16.1 Timeline for Federal Government Involvement in Reading Education

1954: **Brown v. the Board of Education of Topeka** ruled that racial segregation was a violation of the equal protection clause of the fourteenth amendment.

1958: **National Defense Education Act** promoted science, math, and foreign language instruction in the wake of Sputnik and the Space race.

1964: **Civil Rights Act** outlawed segregation in U.S. public schools. The **Economic Opportunity Act,** central to President Johnson's War on Poverty, established several programs to promote health, education, and well-being for the poor, including Head Start.

1965: **Elementary and Secondary Education Act (ESEA)** provided federal funds for public schools, including Title I money for schools serving a high percentage of poor children. The **Higher Education Act** provided money to strengthen post-secondary education in the United States, including financial assistance for students.

1967: **Education Professions Development Act** amended the Higher Education Act to improve the education of poor rural and urban children through initiatives that included in-service teacher education.

1968: **Bilingual Education Act** (Title VII of ESEA) provided federal support encouraging public schools to use native language instruction.

1969: **National Assessment of Education Progress** (NAEP) established to conduct periodic evaluations of American students' reading, math, science, writing, and history skills.

1974: **Reauthorization of Bilingual Education Act** required bilingual and bicultural instruction. **Lau v. Nichols** case questioned meaning of equal treatment and required states to take steps to overcome language barriers children might face in school.

1975: **Individuals with Disabilities Education Act** (IDEA), originally called the **Education for All Handicapped Children Act,** established the federal government's role in providing education for individuals from birth to age 21 who have disabilities.

1978: Amendments to the **Bilingual Education Act** extended the definition of eligible students, but threatened some programs.

1979: **Department of Education Organization Act** established the U.S. Department of Education. Reagan promised to eliminate the cabinet position when he ran for office in 1980, but he was unsuccessful in doing so.

1981: **Education Consolidation and Improvement Act** (reauthorization of ESEA) consolidated federal education programs under the elementary and secondary education block grant authority.

1983: *A Nation At Risk* report released warning the public of the need for widespread improvements in public education in order to maintain a competitive workforce.

1984: Reauthorization of **Bilingual Education Act** shifted toward English language proficiency. The **Education for Economic Security Act** supported new science and mathematics education programs in public schools and universities and included magnet schools.

Continued

Table 16.1 Continued

1985: *Becoming a Nation of Readers*, the report of the National Commission on Reading, released. Noted the importance of reading aloud to children and contained cautious advocacy for phonics instruction.

1990: Marilyn Jager Adams publishes *Beginning to Read: Thinking and Learning about Print*, supporting the need for explicit code instruction for young readers.

1991: **National Literacy Act** established the National Institute for Literacy, the National Institute Board, and the Interagency Task Force on Literacy.

1994: **Goals 2000: Educate America Act** was established to promote standards and testing in American public schools. Formed the National Education Goals Panel and the National Education Standards and Improvement Counsel. **The Guns Free School Act** legislated zero tolerance. **Improving America's Schools Act** reauthorized ESEA and included provisions for charter schools, Title I, drug-free schools, and impact aid.

1997: **America Reads Challenge** initiative used federal money to support volunteer tutors to help children learn to read. **Proposition 227** dismantled bilingual education in California.

1998: **Reading Excellence Act** provides legislative definition of reading and reading research. *Preventing Reading Difficulties*, report from the Committee on the Prevention of Reading Difficulties, published.

2000: National Reading Panel report *Teaching Children to Read* released, providing a framework for the **Reading First Initiative** that would be incorporated into No Child Left Behind.

2001: No Child Left Behind (reauthorization of ESEA) established testing and eliminated the **Bilingual Education Act** (Title VII) as the law shifted to a focus on English-only instruction in U.S. public schools.

2002: **Education Sciences Reform Act** created the Institute of Education Science, a research arm of the U.S. Department of Education, and established guidelines for education research.

Critical Policy Analysis

We adopt a critical stance, for this chapter, on federal policymaking and policy. Rather than determining the functional consequences of whether a policy reached its goals or examining the language used among the negotiators, we concentrate on how the policies came into existence, why they were proposed, and who has benefited from their enactment (Shannon & Edmondson, 2005). Our analyses are based on four tenets:

1   Policy is the authoritative allocation of values to maintain the social, economic, and/or political status quo.
2   Policymaking is a political negotiation among groups possessing unequal power.
3   Policy is the product of historically conditioned social relations that are often hidden from view by common-sense understandings of "the way things are."

4   Policy change can come through self-reflective social action (Edmondson, 2004).

Under these conditions, we understand reading policy negotiations as taking place among groups with unequal power, and therefore, the benefits of reading education are distributed unequally among affected parties. Because the current reading education policies and negotiations are based on the social relations of the past, participants often understand the unequal power as "just the way things are" and outcomes are accepted as "the best we can do." Through critical policy research, we attempt to illuminate the past 50 years of federal reading education policies, to document their consequences for various groups, to identify the contradictions between the rhetoric of equity and the limits of their benefits, and to pose these contradictions as possible spaces for action in projects of possibility.

The reading education policies enacted within these five areas are expressions of dominant values within the federal government. They are reflections of their times, but also they have shaped their times as well. All policies position participants through the categories they invoke and the practices they advocate. For example, the original Head Start policy positioned community members in poor neighborhoods as unwilling or unable to prepare children properly for schools; it sanctioned school expectations as beyond reproach; and it categorized those who raised questions about the program as conservative, counterproductive, and perhaps racist. The current thrust in Head Start policy positions advocates of social models for preschool curricula as unproductive or soft on excellence. By approaching reading education policy critically, we make it vulnerable to reasoned analysis, which could confirm or disconfirm its values and value.

Teacher Education

Historically, the federal government has been a minor, primarily financial partner in the development of teacher education policy. State governments, colleges, professional organizations, and accrediting agencies have negotiated the shape and substance of teacher education throughout most of the professionalization of teachers during the twentieth century. Direct federal involvement began with the National Defense Education Act (1958) in which the government sought to improve students' knowledge of math and science by providing funding for curricular innovations and teacher training in these subjects. The Higher Education Act (1965) sought to address teacher shortages by offering financial incentives for college students to become teachers (federal loans forgiven, military deferments for math and science teachers), providing salaries for schools to hire returning Peace Corp volunteers, and establishing a teacher corps of college graduates without teacher training. The Education Professions Development Act (1967) targeted curricular disciplines and geographic regions to overcome teacher shortages.

After the many reports naming an educational crisis within America and calling for extensive school reform in the 1980s, the federal government passed several laws which indirectly affected teacher education programs. The failed Higher Education Act of 1992 proposed partnerships between schools, colleges, and state departments of education in order to align curricula. Goals 2000: Educate America Act (1994) provided grants to states in order to develop these partnerships and world class standards for school children to meet. The Elementary and Secondary Education Act: Improving America's Schools allotted funds to ensure that teachers were prepared to teach to these high standards. The Higher Education Act (1998) required that colleges of education make their teacher education candidates' scores on teacher exams public in order that students and their families could make informed choices about which teacher education programs are approaching teacher education in the manner that the federal government proposes. And finally, the Elementary and Secondary Education Act: No Child Left Behind (2001) requires that all schools will be taught by highly qualified teachers, applying pressure on teacher education programs to produce teachers in needed subject areas with appropriate certifications, but offering little funding to schools or teacher education programs to accomplish this goal.

Across the past 50 years, the federal government has increased its level of involvement, becoming more prescriptive not only in what it expects from teacher education, but also how it expects it to be accomplished. For example, the federal government remains concerned about shortages of teachers in specific subjects and geographic contexts, but it now ties its concern to particular ways that these teachers are to be trained. In the 1960s and 1970s, federal officials appeared to respect the authority of colleges, schools, professional organizations, and accrediting agencies to negotiate the best ways to educate teachers. Recently, the federal government connects this education to standards and requires public scrutiny of outcomes. In 2004, Congress asked the Institute of Education Sciences (IES) to conduct a study concerning the consistency of required coursework in teacher preparation, how reading and math are taught, and the degree to which programs are aligned with scientific evidence on the subjects. Grover Whitehurst, the Director of IES, will oversee the federal study. During a speech at the White House Conference on Preparing Tomorrow's Teachers, Whitehurst defined good teaching as having a positive effect on students' test scores and poor teaching as not increasing those scores. He found no differences between teachers who graduated from college-based teacher education programs and those who completed alternative programs. According to Whitehurst, only direct training on test-based instruction will improve teachers' performance (not certification, not graduate degrees, not teacher research, and not professional development). A national study, when directed by a leader with those convictions, negates the evaluative authority of professional organizations, accrediting agencies, colleges of education, and state departments of education altogether.

Elementary and Secondary Curriculum

According to the Tenth Amendment to the US Constitution, control of public schooling is a state's right. The federal government has no direct authority over schooling in America. According to its website, it has acted "as a kind of 'emergency response system,' a means of filling gaps in State and local support for education when critical national needs arise" (http://www.ed.gov/about/overview/fed/role.html). That support has most often translated into funding to meet designated goals defined by federal agencies. The Morrill Act in 1880, the Smith Hughes Act of 1917, and Lanham Act of 1941 had indirect impact on school curricula, providing land for colleges, skill training for workers, and supplemental funding for school districts affected by the war effort. The NDEA of 1958 was the first comprehensive federal effort to influence curriculum directly, promoting science, math, and foreign language in order to compete with the Soviets in space. The ESEA of 1965 provided substantial funding to organize additional instructional aid to disadvantaged children. Because federal officials feared that schools would not use the funding for the targeted populations, they required standardized tests of reading and math achievement be given annually and the results be communicated to parents. These test scores could be used to evaluate the quality of the programs.

The 1981 reauthorization of ESEA as the Education Consolidation and Improvement Act cut funding for schools considerably and pushed responsibilities for the renamed Chapter 1 remedial programs to the states. Fewer regulations were attached to how these funds could be used. Although at that time the U.S. Department of Education's evaluation of ESEA programs was positive ("a fifteen year decline in educational achievement is beginning to reverse, particularly among low-achieving groups" [White, 1982]), the evaluation was never released to the public. Rather in 1983, the federal government trumpeted the *A Nation At Risk* report, which declared that the public school system was in crisis and responsible for the declining status of the U.S. economy. This report and the many that followed pushed Reagan's conservative agenda for schools (choice, prayer, and less federal involvement) aside, and began the two-decade long campaign to reform schools. For example, Secretary of Education William Bennett's focus on moral literacy and traditional subject matter was overcome by state governors' enthusiasm for the report's suggestion that business principles be used to rationalize public schools.

Beginning with America 2000, successive presidential administrations have proposed solutions to the "school crisis." The first attempt was to develop world-class standards that all students would meet by the turn of the century. A more aggressive Secretary of Education proposed that the federal government fund *break the mold* schools, which would experiment with different organizational structures, staffing, curricula, and assessments in order to increase school productivity. However, none of these schools were built. A month into Clinton's first term, his administrators rewrote ESEA, returning Chapter 1 to

Title 1 and changing the mission of the program from its original charge to provide support for poor and minority students to a new charge to prepare all students to meet the demands of the national educational goals. In 1992, America 2000 became Goals 2000 with funding for professional organizations to write standards, and then assessments, for each subject. Those standards were to be in place by 1998 with assessment to be ready in 2000. Clinton's second-term project, America Reads, sent thousands of paid volunteers into schools to help all students learn to read a book by the end of third grade. A Republican-led Congress cut America Reads funding after one year and backed the Reading Excellence Act (REA), which required that only scientifically based reading instruction be used in schools receiving federal funding. Defining science as experimentation, the REA attempted to set a national curriculum for reading and the mode of instruction for each classroom.

Mired in political controversy, the Clinton Administration failed to pass the reauthorization of ESEA in 1999 when it was due. G.W. Bush's No Child Left Behind does not differ significantly from Clinton's proposal. G.W. Bush offered four principles for his educational agenda: teacher accountability through annual assessments in reading and math; identification of failing schools; flexibility in educational spending; and school choice options for parents. Bush explained his position on reading education, while visiting an elementary school:

> This is a school that focuses on a reading curriculum that works. I hope it's said that the Bush Administration is willing to ask the question, what works, and then help districts implement programs that do work. Phonics works. It's an important part of a good reading—balanced reading curriculum. The reason I know is because I have asked the question to folks at the National Institute of Health. They're not Republicans, they're not Democrats, they're not—they are scientists, who have spent a lot of time figuring out how to make sure all children have the capacity to learn.
> (http://whitehouse.gov/news/releases/2001/02/20010220-4.html)

Perhaps as no other federal education policy, the history of the ESEA demonstrates how political values resonate from Congress to classrooms. The original intention to provide additional services for disadvantaged students has now morphed into a law which insists that all students reach proficiency on world-class standards. In between, ESEA waded through the fairly benign neglect of the Nixon, Ford, and Carter Administrations, only to be turned back toward the states during the Reagan years. Those state governments insisted that the federal government provide support for the transition of schools from local prerogatives to national priorities. The new business of schooling requires accountability based solely on the bottom line of test scores and a pedagogy based on the means/ends analysis of methods that will increase that bottom line—defined as *what works*. What works is now the mantra in official educational circles, and government services to schools are honed according to those definitions.

Race Relations

Race relations are a primary focus of federal policy for education. The consequences of the Brown decision reverberate throughout all versions of ESEA from its original substitution of poverty for race as the primary criterion for eligibility in Title 1 programs to the rhetorical victory of leaving no child behind in its current version. According to officials within the Johnson Administration, that substitution was necessary to ensure the bill would pass through the House of Representatives. Some speculate that Brown, ESEA, and the Voting Rights Acts precipitated the two-decade transition of the Democratic South to the Red States of G.W. Bush's election. Certainly, Nixon's Southern strategy for his election in 1968 struck the racial chord that connected Democrats, integration, and equal opportunity in schooling. The trope of leaving no child behind performs two vital functions around race. First, it assures all minority parents that the federal government is insisting on equal opportunity (and perhaps outcome as they repeatedly reference the achievement gap between black and white students). At the same time, federal officials are reassuring white parents that their children are receiving government largess because federal funds will be used to bring all students (not just poor and black students) to proficiency.

Behind ESEA lurks an ambivalence concerning the abilities of racial minorities to sew themselves seamlessly into mainstream society—schools, business, and public life—because their culture does not prepare them adequately. While the courts insisted that states must follow the Constitution, government officials and many experts sought pedagogies that would teach minority families and communities how to perform up to middle-class white standards of deportment, caring, and academic achievement. Project Head Start and Follow Through, ESEA, and even the First Grade Studies in reading instruction can be read this way. Each policy was expected to set standards and provide rules to discipline families and communities to prepare their children for school properly. Each was judged a success or failure based on its ability to match minority students' dispositions and schools expectations. Lack of success according to this criterion has frustrated government officials, legislators, and business leaders, directing their efforts to tighten school accountability and to withdraw support for students, families, and communities that will not align their behaviors with expectations.

Zero tolerance, as legislated by the Gun Free Schools Act of 1994, emerged at a moment when the US was undergoing rapid economic, social, political, and demographic changes. Deregulation of industries, globalization, and immigration challenged the certainties upon which middle-class Americans understood their lives. Increasingly, public discourses circulated in news reports and talk radio and images promoted by the shock-and-sell tactics of Hollywood conveyed a belief that suburban (read *white*) communities and cultures were under siege from lazy Mexicans, dangerous African-Americans, and overachieving Asians and Asian-Americans. This threat could be observed most readily in the school violence, which it was argued (without statistical evidence) was at crisis levels. Although closing the achievement gap might prove elusive, the violence gap could be closed through legislation and consequent policy. The Zero Tolerance Act reads: No federal assistance will be provided to states and local educational agencies that do not have a policy "requiring the expulsion from school for a period of not less than one year of any student who is determined to have brought a weapon to a school under the jurisdiction of the agency" (Public Law 103–227, 1994).

Three problems arise from this federal policy about schooling. First, despite the racially neutral language of Zero Tolerance, the public translation is still racially stilted. The images of Hollywood films, nightly newscasts, policymaker discussions, talk radio, and the editorials in newspapers quite literally "color" the public's, including teachers', perceptions of who commits and who is subjected to school violence. Despite the fact that the most tragic acts of school violence—Columbine, West Paducah, Jonesboro, Santana High in San Diego—came after Zero Tolerance and were perpetuated by white suburban youth, community members lamented their disbelief during interviews with statements, "How could this happen here?" No such language followed the tragedy on the Chippewa Reservation in rural Red Lake, Minnesota.

Second, the legislation is distorted and misread, leaving wide policy variations among states and within states. For instance, Pennsylvania's law basically replicates the federal law, while Michigan's includes caveats for suspension in the event a student's speech is deemed disruptive or threatening. Some schools include dress code violations within their local Zero Tolerance policies. Other districts allow possession of firearms during hunting season, as long as they remain in the students' vehicles. Sixty-five percent of Zero Tolerance exclusions from school are for nonviolent behaviors and another 15% are for fighting without weapons. Therefore, 80% of Zero Tolerance exclusions are for infractions unaccounted for in the federal law. Moreover, African-American students are excluded from schools at over two times their representative population. Since the majority of these exclusions are for nonviolent or weaponless infractions and there is little evidence that African-American students are more violent then their white peers, racism seems to figure into the decisions surrounding Zero Tolerance in schools.

Third, Zero Tolerance addresses only the symptoms of school violence, actually hiding underlying issues of poverty, alienation, and racism, which seem to perpetuate violence in and out of schools. In this way, Zero Tolerance is yet another federal policy which positions African-American families and communities as failures in adequately preparing students to function in schools while it purports to help all students to succeed. Zero Tolerance provides a means to glimpse how federal policies reflect more than deflect societal biases concerning race.

Language Difference

Bilingual education demonstrates the shifts in federal educational policy over the last 50 years. From its inception within the 1968 Bilingual Education Act (Title VII of ESEA) to the beginning of the Reagan Administration, the federal government advanced the cause of simultaneous instruction in home language and English during school. Over the last 20 years, however, the federal government has been ambivalent at best and hostile at worst toward bilingual education. Children whose home language is not English represent an increasing percentage of the school population across the United States. According to the 2000 census, 18% of school-aged children speak a language other than English in their homes. Since research on bilingualism demonstrates that the best way to become literate in a second language is to develop literacy in the home language, the recent shift away from bilingual education within federal policy seems to be driven more by political considerations than by science.

The original bill in 1968 came on the heels of the civil rights movement and the liberalizing of immigration laws, which allowed more Latin-Americans and Asians to enter the United States. The 1968 revision of ESEA included a compensatory directive (Title VII) to provide supplemental instruction for students learning English as a second language. Because the language of the directive left pedagogical decisions to the state and local levels, maintenance and transitional bilingual programs developed across the country. Maintenance programs were intended to help individuals to become biliterate and bicultural. Transitional programs were temporary support to ease students' transition to a monolingual English-only program. The 1974 reauthorization required bilingual and bicultural instruction in funded programs, and provided funding for professional development in order to enable teachers to deliver such instruction.

Struggle for recognition among language minority groups drove the federal policy throughout the 1970s. Parents of Mexican-American, Puerto Rican, and Chinese-American children and community groups protested unequal treatment under the law. For example, the Lau v. Nichols case in 1974 questioned the value-neutral solution that treating all students the same necessarily constituted equal treatment. Rather the court ruled that English language learners were entitled to special assistance in order to be able to participate equally in school programs. In order to accommodate the ruling, the Office of Civil Rights issued Lau Remedies, which mandated transitional programs for limited English proficient students. In 1978, the reauthorization of Title VII set the exit criteria for the length of transition programs—until the child was competent. President Carter's attempt to include maintenance programs with Lau Remedies was soundly defeated by a growing English-only movement, which feared language segregation and valued the rapid assimilation of immigrants into American culture and language.

With the Reagan Administration, the focus of educational policy underwent a shift from issues of justice to issues of cost-effectiveness and state rights. Not only was federal spending on education reduced, federal oversight of schools was replaced by state and local self-inspection. Relying on the flawed American Institute for Research study which found no significant differences between maintenance bilingual programs and other transitional models, Secretary of Education Terrell Bell proposed that states and districts decide which methods and models to use to supplement ESL learners. In the 1984 reauthorization of Title VII, funding started to shift from bilingual programs to English-only—up to 10% of federal funds could be used for programs in which only English was spoken. When William Bennett was appointed to that office, he raised that limit to 25%, and English-only practices had a significant foothold within bilingual education. The Clinton Administration's battles to return bilingual education to the support in home language were met with stiff resistance from a Republican Congress.

Against significant evidence for the importance of the home language in the education of language minority populations, the new version of the ESEA, as it was reauthorized under No Child Left Behind, cancelled the Bilingual Education Act (Title VII) and replaced it with the Language Instruction for Limited English Proficient and Immigrant Students Act (Title III). Title III requires that English language learners exit from *remedial* programs within three years of schooling, and that they take standardized tests in English by that time. Krashen (2002) pointed to the contradictory nature of this legislation, which stresses the importance of scientifically based research to guide educational decisions, but which imposes regulations that are not based on any kind of scientific evidence. Krashen reasoned that schools with high percentages of limited English proficiency (LEP) students will experience a decline in average scores when they take standardized tests in English, pushing the school toward the NCLB label, *schools in need of improvement*. In this way, federal policy now positions LEP students as a problem for schools.

Use of Science

Prior to 1954, the federal government offered unsteady support for the Office of Education. Fearing federal involvement in states' rights, congressmen often failed to provide sufficient funding to enable federal officials to gather even accurate statistics on enrollments, graduations, and funding. Stimulated by the Cold War and the civil rights movement, however, the federal government began to establish an infrastructure for conducting basic research on education, believing that education was essential to national security and economic development. The Cooperative Research Program (1954) was originally charged with hiring outside contactors in order to provide a national assessment of the education of mentally retarded. It quickly expanded to other projects and by the middle 1960s, nine research and development centers were established to attract critical masses of researchers to address targeted issues. By design these centers were to be separate from colleges of education in order to coordinate interdisciplinary work. Shortly after the centers began to complete projects, Congress provided funding for educational laboratories and the Educational Resources Information Center in order to disseminate the results of federally funded research.

Specific funding for educational research was part of most educational bills after 1954: National Defense Education Act of 1958, the Head Start provisions of Economic Opportunity Act of 1964, the Civil Rights Act of 1964, and the Elementary and Secondary Education Act of 1965. The apparent successes of these research programs led officials in the Kennedy and then Johnson Administrations to debate and then establish the National Assessment of Educational Progress in 1969. During the Nixon Administration, the National Institute of Education (Silverman, 1972) published its four research goals:

1   to help solve or alleviate the problems and achieve the objectives of American education
2   to advance the practice of education as an art, science, and profession
3   to strengthen the scientific and technological foundation on which education rests, and
4   to build a vigorous and effective educational research and development system.

From these modest beginnings, the federal government built its presence into the primary force concerning research on teaching and learning across all school disciplines. Its power is derived through funding, with over 80% of research on reading and reading education being funded through federal agencies. Michael Opuda (2003) calls this the golden rule of educational research—the federal government has the money and therefore sets the rules, by defining the topics for and conditions of educational research. The early federal initiatives were somewhat open competitions to find the best methods for teaching reading to disadvantaged children (Head Start), primary students (First Grade Studies), or second language learners (Bilingual Education Act). Later efforts were more directed through centers (Center for the Study of Reading at University of Illinois) or networks (Learning Disability Research Networks). In these later cases, topics were identified, but the methods for addressing those topics through research were left to the discretion of the directors. Because federal officials selected directors through a process of competing proposals, the federal government had a directing hand in reading research even under these conditions. However, the federal government did not pursue a single agenda.

For example, during the 1980s and 1990s, the U.S. Office of Special Education and Rehabilitation Services and the National Institute for Child Health and Development funded the National Center for Improving Tools for Educators (NCITE) at the University of Oregon and the U.S. Office of Vocational and Adult Education provided funds for the National Center for Research on Vocational Education (NCRVE) at the University of California at Berkeley. Oregon's NCITE assumed that all basic questions about reading education had been answered and all that remained to complete were means/ends studies in order to find best methods of teaching children to read. Simultaneously, Berkeley's NCRVE funded studies such as Glynda Hull's critical ethnography about workplace literacy, probing the accusation of a mismatch between job demands on reading and writing and workers' capacities. Such variety in funding facilitated the growing diversity within the reading research community. Although in 1989 Shannon concluded that nearly all research published in the flagship professional reading research journals employed mean/ends assumptions and methodology, by 2004, less than two-thirds of the published articles could be so classified. The rest of the studies were based on alternative assumptions about the goals and means of education research. Over one-third of the official record of reading research (articles published in professional journals) pursued interpretive and critical goals using phenomenological, hermeneutic, critical, feminist, and poststructural theories.

The federal government has not welcomed this diversity within the reading research community. Beginning with the Reading Excellence Act in 1998, the federal government offered an official definition of education research—the only type of research that will be considered for government funding:

> Scientifically based reading research . . . shall include research that employs systematic, empirical methods that draw on observation or experiment; involves rigorous data analyses that are adequate to test the stated hypotheses and justify the general conclusions drawn; relies on measurements or observational methods that provide data across evaluators and observers and across multiple measurements and observations; and has been accepted by a peer-reviewed journal or approved by a panel of independent experts through a comparably rigorous, objective, and scientific review.
>
> (http://thomas.loc.gov)

After intervention from professional organizations, the language of means/ends approaches soften somewhat in the ESEA reauthorization of 2000 and the Education Sciences Reform Act of 2002, but the message to the reading research community remained clear.

Conclusion

The past 50 years of federal government involvement in reading education can be split into two movements (Shannon, 2007). From the 1960s to 1980, liberal enthusiasm sought to develop the possibilities of public schooling with other social agendas. From the 1980s to the present, with the Clinton Administration as a partial exception, federal officials have demonstrated a lack of confidence in the productive capacities of the government to address social problems and of teachers and researchers to develop a nation of readers. The promise of Head Start, Title 1 and Title VII have given way to restrictions of prescribed curricula, testing, and scientism. The Brown decision let black students in the front doors of public school while Zero Tolerance shows too many of them the backdoor out to the streets and into jails. The enthusiasm for world languages in order to engage the world of commerce and culture has turned into English-only programs and forced testing in English. And the official definition of educational science is captured by enthusiasm for pictures of chemical reactions in the brain and double-blind experiments. In each case, the federal government has lost hope that the best ideas will rise to the top, and as reported in the Department of Education Inspector General's Report on Reading First, federal officials have resorted to bullying school personnel to follow guidelines (Paley, 2007).

What are the consequences of this federal retreat from confidence in schools? At the very least, federal mandates have increased public school bureaucracies at the state and local levels, making all relationships among people into formal operations. As Max Weber (1978) explained, formal operations diminish the possible relationships among participants, stifling alternatives and commitment. Under formal bureaucratic operations, teacher education and public elementary school curricula work to narrow human capacities. In this way, recent federal policies narrow the social forms that were established in the 1960s to support the growth of human capacities. By following federal mandates, schools and teachers convey to minorities that many of them possess dangerous dispositions, substandard languages, and deficient cultures, which schools and teachers are eager to supplant with mainstream culture in the name of equality. Ignoring its own rules, none of these federal acts has scientific evidence to recommend its use as effective.

While imperfect in many ways at its inception, the original ESEA Act was intended to help poor and minority students as part of the War on Poverty. That war also included other acts that would support the efforts of schools and schooling of all children: the Economic Opportunities Act and the Social Security Act of 1965, which included VISTA, the Job Corp, Head Start, Legal Services, Community Action Programs, Medicaid and Medicare, and food stamps. In order to support these programs, people and businesses had to pay taxes. Poverty did decline and test scores for poor and minority students did rise. These were social projects of possibility that expanded social forms in order to extend human capacities and to accommodate those capacities with more flexible social forms. These positive trajectories were suppressed by the Vietnam War and the Oil Embargo of the 1970s, but they were only reversed in the 1980s when pessimism about the powers of government to influence the lives of citizens replaced the optimism of the 1930s through the 1960s (Orfield, 2006).

If we wish to return to positive trajectories of learning and schools as projects of possibility, then we must reject the pessimism of the past 25 years of federal involvement (Glass, 2008). Public schools cannot solve the problems of achievement gaps without support from other social programs. Healthcare, income, food, and housing gaps predict students' achievement gaps and the variability in reading levels. According to David Berliner (2006), research on closing those social gaps demonstrates positive results in schools. He points us in a good direction:

> In my estimation, we will get better public schools by requiring each other's participation in building a more equitable society. This is of equal or greater value to our nation's future well-being than a fight over whether phonics is scientifically based, whether standards are rigorous enough, or whether teachers have enough content knowledge.

References

Berliner, D. (2006). Our impoverished view of educational reform. *Teachers College Record*, *108*, 949–995.

Edmondson, J. (2004). *Understanding and applying critical policy study*. Newark, DE: International Reading Association.

Glass, G. (2008). *Fertilizer, pills, and magnetic strips: The fate of public schools in America*. New York: Information Age Publishing.

Krashen, S. (2002). Bilingual education works. *Rethinking Schools, 16*, 3, 4–6.

Opuda, M. (2003). NCLB—A threat or a challenge to public education? *Journal of Research in Rural Education, 18*, 35–38.

Orfield, G. (2006). Introduction. In J. Lee. *Tracking achievement gaps and assessing the impact of NCLB on the gaps*. Cambridge, MA: Civil Rights Project Harvard University.

Paley, A. (May 10, 2007) Four officials profited from publishers, report finds. *Washington Post*, A 11.

Shannon, P. (1989). Paradigmatic diversity in the reading research community. *Journal of Reading Behavior, 21*, 97–107.

Shannon, P. (2007). *Reading against democracy: The broken promises of reading instruction*. Portsmouth, NH: Heinemann.

Shannon, P. & Edmondson, J. (2005). *Reading education policy*. Newark, NJ: International Reading Association.

Silverman, H. (1972, July). *NIE planning status*. NIE Archives 1003. ERIC ED088162.

Simon, R. (2001). Empowerment as a pedagogy of possibility. In P. Shannon (Ed.), *Becoming political, too*. Portsmouth, NH: Heinemann.

Weber, M. (1978). *Economy and society*. Berkeley, CA: University of California Press.

White, E. (1982, January 26). Federal agency's unpublished study. *Education Week*. Retrieved April 1, 2004 from http://www.edweek.org/ew/articles/1982/01/26/01180092/h01.html.

Chapter 17

Literacy Policies That Are Needed

Thinking Beyond "No Child Left Behind"

Richard L. Allington, PhD
University of Tennessee

Let me begin with a short history of educational policymaking in the U.S. Basically, federal literacy policymaking commenced in 1966 with the passage of the Elementary and Secondary Education Act (ESEA). That bill, grounded in the then new national War on Poverty, targeted new federal money to schools serving large numbers of children who lived in economically disadvantaged homes. That program was viewed as a compensatory educational initiative in which these dollars would be used to purchase educational services that would supplement those funded through local and state education agencies' money. In other words, the new federal money was seen as making it possible for schools serving many students from low-income families to add new educational services that would compensate for their economic *disadvantagedness*. In actuality, the new funds largely narrowed the education funding gap between schools in lower- and higher-income communities (Cross, 2004). This legislative act, ESEA, set in motion a series of federal education policies, policymaking that continues to this day.

In the following section, I provide a brief historical summary of just how the original ESEA has been changed over the past 40 years since its passage. In the next section I discuss what we know about the effects of federal policymaking viewed through the lens of ESEA reauthorizations. I close with my recommendations for future federal policymaking in the area of literacy education.

A Brief History of the Elementary and Secondary Education Act of 1966

In many respects, ESEA created the profession of *reading specialist*. The bill provided financial incentives for teachers to engage in graduate study of the reading process, especially studying techniques for reading diagnosis and remediation. As a result new graduate programs in reading education emerged in colleges and universities across the United States and many states began to construct criteria for certification as a reading specialist. Some states made earning such a credential necessary for employment as a reading specialist under programs funded by ESEA funding (McGill-Franzen & Goatley, 2001).

The ESEA has been reauthorized by Congress consistently over the past four decades. It has also been criticized consistently, primarily for failing to reduce the achievement gap between poor and nonpoor children. As I write, the No Child Left Behind Act of 2001 (NCLB) represents the current version of the original ESEA. But much has changed over the years. The current NCLB has been characterized as representing a *new era* of federal involvement, an era that has dramatically altered the relationships between the states and the federal government. As Sunderman, Kim and Orfield (2005) note:

> The No Child Left Behind Act of 2001 (NCLB) was a startling departure from this [ESEA] history, both in terms of its requirements and its sponsors. It required specific large changes in the basic assessments systems of states, set requirements for progress in education in two specific subjects, contained unusual and large sanctions, and commanded many forms of specific state actions. It clearly moved to the heart of the educational process.
>
> (p. 2)

They also argue that NCLB shifted the role of state education agencies from one of collaborative distribution of federal resources to one of monitoring and regulating federal requirements in local educational agencies.

I will suggest, however, that these changes began earlier, though reaching culmination under NCLB, as federal officials continued to attempt to shape the ESEA into an educational effort that closed the rich/poor achievement gap. The 1978 reauthorization of ESEA, under President Carter, established *schoolwide projects* eligibility for the first time. Under this new rule schools where 75% of the students were identified as students from low-income families could use the funding under ESEA to provide services for all students, not just those who were economically disadvantaged. This was viewed as an attempt to expand the role of federal money into schoolwide reform, not just to provide supplemental services to eligible students. The most common uses of the federal dollars under this rule were reductions in class size and extending the school day or the school year (Winfield, 1991). Today over 90% of all eligible urban schools use the schoolwide option.

Then President Reagan attempted to reduce federal education expenditures and systematically trimmed the money available through the passage of the Educational Consolidation and Improvement Act (ECIA), the 1981 reauthorization of the original ESEA. The ECIA trimmed some 40 categorical programs that had been part of the ESEA and consolidated 20 programs into a single authorization. In addition, states were provided far greater latitude in decisions on how to spend the federal dollars they received under ECIA. However, for the first time in the history of the ESEA the budget shrank across every year of the eight years of the Reagan Administration, the federal share of school revenues also dropped from 9.9% of the total school expenditures to 6.9% by 1988 (Cross, 2004).

The 1988 reauthorization of ESEA added new requirements that states would be required to define the levels of reading proficiency that students benefiting from federal funding would achieve. This seemed to reflect a growing consensus among policymakers that setting curriculum standards in reading and other subjects and then testing students to see if they were meeting those standards was one path to improving educational outcomes. While states generally complied with this mandate, most created *minimum competency* reading assessments for use at two grade levels. The 1994 reauthorization under President Clinton retitled the ESEA to Improving America's Schools Act (IASA). This reauthorization required states to develop challenging academic standards and tests to measure student progress toward attaining those standards. However, the law also set the 2000 school year as the deadline for complying with the standards and testing requirements. One other major change was lowering the eligibility requirements for schoolwide projects from 75% to 50% of poor students enrolled in a school (Wong, 2003). The net effect of this change was a dramatic rise (U.S.D.E., 2007) in the number of Title I participants who attended a Title I school using the schoolwide projects option (between 1995 and 2005 the number of Title I students enrolled in schoolwide projects schools tripled from 6.7 million to 20.1 million).

However, only 17 states were in compliance with the federal curriculum standards and testing requirements by January 2001 when President Bush took office. He made passage of his version of the ESEA, the No Child Left Behind Act of 2001, his key legislative initiative. The lack of compliance with the 1994 accountability rules seemed to fuel the arguments for a more aggressive stance on accountability for schools receiving Title I monies (Cross, 2004; DeBray, 2006). And the NCLB delivered new accountability requirements as well as strong federal efforts to dictate how reading would be taught. The accountability fell under new rules for assuring all students, including pupils with disabilities, were making "adequate yearly progress" toward achieving the standards of reading proficiency set by each state, with 100% of the students achieving these standards no later than 2014. (Actually it is 97–98% of students who must achieve standards with the remaining 2–3% allowed for pupils with disabilities who would not be required to meet the standards but were required to be making progress in that direction.)

The NCLB required all states to have both standards and a testing system for grades 3–8 approved and in place by the 2005–2006 school year. All states, with the exception of Nebraska, met this requirement (Nebraska's legislature, against the advice of its commissioner of education, Doug Christianson, brought state testing to Nebraskans in the spring of 2008). However, there exist huge differences in how the states defined proficiency levels on their reading assessments. The differences in grade 3 proficiency standards, using national normative percentile ranks, are illustrated in Figure 17.1.

CO	7	IL	35
TX	12	SC	43
NJ	15	NV	46
WI	16	CA	61

Figure 17.1 Comparisons of several state grade 3 national percentile reading ranks proficiency criteria.

From: Cronin, Dahlin & Kingsbury, 2007

As easily observed in Figure 17.1, one might expect far greater numbers of California schools to fail to meet AYP than schools in Colorado. Additionally, there seems to be little comparability between grade 3 and grade 8 reading proficiency standards in many states. For instance, some states raise the bar: South Carolina goes from the 43rd percentile at grade 3 to the 71st percentile for proficiency at grade 8. Illinois moves the standard downward over the same grades with proficiency dropping from the 35th percentile in grade 3 to the 22nd percentile in grade 8 (Cronin et al., 2007). Further, about half of the states have backloaded their criteria such that almost all of the improvement is expected in the final four years of NCLB (2011–2014). In other words, each state set a percentage of students expected to meet the state reading proficiency standard for each year under the NCLB and not requiring 100% proficiency until 2014. But while some states gradually increased the proportion of students expected to meet the standards each year, other states left most of the improvement to be accomplished in the final years of the NCLB.

Thus, while NCLB included a far stronger accountability mechanism than earlier versions of the ESEA, in leaving standard-setting to the states it created a situation that some states took advantage of. Nonetheless, it is difficult to find any assessment scholar who believes that the 100% proficiency standard is attainable by 2014 as the NCLB requires (Linn, 2005).

The Effects of Federal Policymaking in Reading

Puma et al. (1997) note that Title 1 funds have long been spread broadly but thinly, "The level of instructional assistance Title 1 students generally received was in stark contrast to their levels of educational need" (p. iii). In other words, students who participated in some form of supplemental services funded by

Title I monies added between one and two months' growth per year to their reading development. However, this additional growth was not sufficient to close the reading achievement gap and, in fact, allowed the achievement gap to continue to widen over the years of services. Because funding from ESEA/ NCLB Title I goes to the vast majority of school districts in the United States, each high poverty school receives only enough funding to provide some services but not enough money to provide the sorts of research-based services that have been shown to accelerate students' reading development (Allington, 2009).

As for longer-term effects of Title I and other federal supplemental education programs (e.g., special education, bilingual education, migrant education), one can examine the trend data from the reading portion of the National Assessment Educational Progress (NAEP). These data are available on a common scale from 1971 through 2004. On the NAEP the fourth grade student scores show some growth, from a scale score of 208 in 1971 to 221 in 2007. But just over half of that growth occurred in the first decade of the assessment with the 1980 scaled score of 215. Over the remaining 27 years (1980 to 2007) NAEP fourth grade reading performance improved by almost the same amount (6 scaled score points). At the eighth and twelfth grade levels reading scores remained basically unchanged over the 30+ years represented by the NAEP data. Thus, while NAEP reading scores improved in elementary school students, the reading performances of older students remained unchanged.

When we examine the rich/poor reading achievement gap (at http:// nces.ed.gov/nationsreportcard/pdf/main2007/2007496_2.pdf) we find that the gap stands at 27 scale score points on the 2007 NAEP (232 vs. 205 for students ineligible for free or reduced-price meals and students eligible for free meals). The achievement gap is identical to what it was in 2002, the year NCLB was signed into law. Nonetheless, this 27-point gap is some improvement since the earlier NAEP comparisons where the gap was nearly twice as wide (gap was reduced from 44 points to 29 between 1971 and 1996). But almost all of the closing of the rich/poor achievement gap occurred prior to 1996. Since 1996 there has been little progress in closing the achievement gap or raising levels of reading achievement.

But the nation's schools did substantially close the rich/poor reading gap between 1971 and 1996. What has changed since 1996 that might account for the recent impotence of federal education legislation and funds to further close the rich/poor reading achievement gap? I see two distinct possibilities—insufficient funding coupled with crony capitalism and the expansion of the use of schoolwide projects as an option within the Title I program.

Insufficient Funding and Crony Capitalism

One of the largely untold aspects of federal policymaking is centered on just this fact—insufficient funding provides insufficient responses. Congress had been bombarded with expert testimony, much of this from G. Reid Lyon of the National Institutes for Health, indicating that if schools used *research-based* interventions we could expect that 98% of all beginning readers would be reading on grade level (Lyon, 1997). Thus, within the federal agencies managing NCLB the problem came to be viewed as one of following a *scientifically based* agenda versus allowing states and schools to follow whatever agenda they desired. But there was more to it than this.

What Lyon had not explained in his testimony was that the research he relied most heavily on, that funded by his agency, the National Institute of Child Health and Development (NICHD), had provided either one-to-one expert reading tutoring or very small group interventions to produce these results (Allington, 2004). He also did not mention that *on level* reading proficiency was any performance that was above the 16th or 23rd percentile (both within one standard deviation of the achievement mean and thus meeting a technical definition of on level). There are many reasons to praise these accomplishments, primarily accelerating the reading development of some of the nation's lowest-achieving students. But it remains unclear just what this evidence says about the nature of effective classroom instruction and who should fund the extraordinary costs associated with widespread one-to-one expert tutoring.

Instead of promoting easier access and funding for expanding the availability of expert tutoring, the U.S. Department of Education moved in the direction of promoting the use of scientifically based reading materials. To date, unfortunately, there exists not a single study supporting the use of any of the core reading programs on the market and only one program, Reading Recovery, is rated as having "strong evidence" it improves children's reading achievement (What Works Clearinghouse, 2007).

Nonetheless, the USDE pushed ahead with its agenda. As DeBray (2006) notes:

> At one of the winter Reading Leadership Academies, department officials listed three examples of acceptable reading programs: McGraw-Hill's Open Court reading, Harcourt's Trophies, and Houghton-Mifflin Reading. Federal officials at the workshop did not explicitly state that a district could put together its own overall strategy with multiple components that met the law's requirements as a whole. Nor did officials discuss the option of a district's using a "homegrown" program if it is designed with a basis in research findings.
>
> That the Department of Education did not clearly dispel these perceptions in the educational community about a narrow range of approvable programs only added to the early confusion.
>
> (p. 139)

Further, two of the technical assistance centers funded under NCLB provided a shortlisting of reading programs that came to be viewed as *approved* programs, even though little if any research backed their use. Finally, the USDE and the National Institute for Literacy (NIFL) provided funding for the preparation of a consumers' guide to core reading programs and a listing of commercial assessments that supposedly met rigorous criteria for use in NCLB programs. As became clear through the investigations of the department's Office of the Inspector General, neither of these products were actually based in much research and in both cases represented the views of a select few. As Michael Grunwald (2006), reporter for the *Washington Post*, put it:

> An accumulating mound of evidence from reports, interviews, and program documents suggests that Reading First has had little to do with science or rigor. Instead, the billions have gone to what is effectively a pilot project for untested programs with friends in high places.
>
> (p. B 1)

Likewise, the report on assessments was scorched by the Inspector General's review noting that the NIFL had refused to release the report based on potential financial conflicts of interest and the potential violation of Section 9526 of the NCLB law. As Andrew Brownstein (Brownstein & Hicks, 2006a) of the *Title I Monitor* noted:

> The audit [by the Office of the Inspector General] highlights e-mail exchanges between Ed Kameenui, University of Oregon professor Doug Carnine, and former Reading First director Chris Doherty that illustrate a campaign by federal officials to obscure NIFL's funding role and publish the report without going through the proper channels.
>
> (p. 3)

These folks were ultimately successful in linking the University of Oregon's website to the federal NCLB website in a way that most state officials assumed meant the document was an official federal guide. Thus, the listing of the Dynamic Indicators of Basic Early Literacy Skills (DIBELS) in that document, along with pressure from USDE officials, resulted in at least 37 states selecting that assessment to monitor progress in reading (Brownstein & Hicks, 2005).

On the other hand, research points to some aspects of reading instruction in Title I schools that do raise achievement—but no one seems to be paying any attention to that research. For instance, Puma et al. (1997), in their congressionally mandated study of Title I programs, found that:

> Instructional practices and content emphasis may also distinguish high-performing high-poverty schools. Several schools where teachers adopted a balanced view of remedial skills and higher-order thinking had high-performing disadvantaged students. Rather than viewing instruction

in basic skills as a prerequisite for higher-order and more challenging materials, teachers in these schools appeared to generally challenge their students with cognitively demanding material.

(p. 63)

Borman, Wong, Hedges, and D'Agostino (2003) analyzed the impact of coordination between the classroom and the Title I reading programs based on 4,228 Title I students and questionnaires completed by their Title I and classroom teachers based on a model for remediation that emphasized coordinated instructional programs (Johnston, Allington, & Afflerbach, 1985). They used a two-level hierarchical model analysis to predict reading achievement effects of curricular congruence and found that increases in congruence were:

> . . . associated with an increase of 4.7 to 7.1 normal curve equivalents in classroom mean reading achievement . . . and with a reduction of the Title I achievement gap by 0.2 to 0.3 standard deviation units. In other words, when Title I and regular teachers implement a curriculum that is similar or the same, they may increase the achievement levels of all students, and may reduce a substantial proportion of Title I students' achievement deficits.

(p. 112)

Curricular congruence was the only one of eight variables (e.g., Title I minutes per week, classroom minutes per week, regular instruction missed, location) that achieved statistical significance.

Knapp (1995), after studying 140 classrooms in 15 Title I schools in three states, also reports on the effects of different sorts of reading instruction on reading achievement. Comparing *skills-emphasis* and *meaning-emphasis* classrooms, meaning emphasis instruction produced 5.6 NCE higher on California Test of Basic Skills, which was statistically significant, the writing of Title I students was also significantly better in meaning-emphasis classrooms, all the while controlling for both poverty and achievement differences, gains for lower-achieving students as large or larger than gains for higher-achieving students. He concluded, "Meaning-oriented practices do not impede the mastery of discrete skills and may facilitate it" (p. 136)

His federally funded study of Title I depicted the reading instruction in meaning-emphasis classrooms this way:

—   maximum opportunities to read
—   integration of reading and writing with other subject areas
—   focus on meaning and means of constructing meaning
—   providing students the opportunity to discuss what was read.

These characteristics are similar to those identified in successful high-poverty schools by Taylor et al., (2003), Pressley et al., (2001), and by Allington and Johnston (2002). But this evidence, though generated by federally funded researchers, has been largely ignored by federal policymakers in the design of NCLB.

Ignoring much of the research on effective intervention for struggling readers may be related to the fact that so much of the education establishment and educational professional and advocacy groups had associated themselves with Democratic policies and politicians for so long, when Republicans gained control of the White House and both branches of Congress, conservatives sought other voices on education issues. Thus, "expertise itself became contingent on ideology" (DeBray, 2006, p. 78)

Traditional education advocacy groups (e.g., NEA, IRA, NCTE, NRC, AERA) were shut out of the negotiations on NCLB because they were largely seen as defending the status quo or big learning organizations' bureaucracies. DeBray (2006) suggests that the success of the "diverse coalitions that include business and civil rights interests (but not the teachers' unions or education professional organizations) are a harbinger of a likely new advocacy models in the DC educational policy subsystem" (p. 150) because the negotiation and passage of NCLB was truly a bipartisan affair. She suggests one sobering lesson from the NCLB process is "that the more heated the parties' competition over education becomes, the harder it is for empirical knowledge to enter the policy stream" (DeBray, 2006, p. 155). This we can observe from the rise of new voices in the design of NCLB. The Heritage and Fordham Foundations and the Business Roundtable carried far more weight than traditional educational groups in the design of NCLB as did the voices of G. Reid Lyon and Louisa Moats representing the National Institute of Child Health and Development and, of course, key Republican legislators like Bill Goodling of the House and Bob Sweet, who worked as a staffer for the education committee (Song, Coggshall, & Miskel, 2004). Lyon, in particular, provided Congress with a clear voice on the design of NCLB following closely the advice he had provided in Texas to then Governor Bush. Song et al. (2004) suggest that:

> He [Lyon] expresses his policy ideas and research findings in clear, unambiguous—even absolute—terms. One can speculate that this is why Lyon's message appeals to policymakers—they need a solution and data to support it, and he has this in spades.
>
> (p. 456)

Whether Lyon actually had convincing data on the policy path to pursue has been the subject of much debate (c.f., Allington, 2002; Hammill, 2004; Haney, 2000; Strauss, 2003; Taylor et al., 2000; Taylor, 1998) as has the advice given by the National Reading Panel (c.f., Camilli, Wolfe, & Smith, 2006; Cunningham, 2001; Garan, 2002; Goodman, 1998; Hammill & Swanson,

2006; Krashen, 2001; Pearson, 2004). Nonetheless, these criticisms came from members of the traditional educational advocacy and research community, and so were also largely ignored in Washington.

Finally, there is the current $71 billion funding gap between what the NCLB originally projected for funding the federal mandates and the actual funds allocated for 2008 (Kahlenberg, 2008). I am not sure that even had this original funding level been met that the plan inherent in NCLB could have produced the results demanded. Nevertheless, attempting to achieve the mandated results with $71 billion fewer dollars suggest one good reason that the Institute of Education Sciences study of the effects of the Reading First component of NCLB found no effects on reading achievement (Manzo, 2008).

The Growth of Schoolwide Projects and the Shrinking Effect of Title I Programs

The second possible cause for the slowing of closing the reading achievement gap is the enormous expansion of schoolwide projects in the highest poverty Title 1 schools. Reducing class size has some research supporting its use as one way to improve reading achievement (Achilles, 1999) but a recent reanalysis of the same data set (Tennessee STAR study) found that teacher effects were still more important than class size effects. In other words, as the authors of that study noted:

> The finding that teacher effects are larger than school effects has interesting implications for improving student achievement. Many policies attempt to improve achievement by substituting one school for another (e.g., school choice) or changing the schools themselves (e.g., whole school reform) . . . If teacher effects are larger than school effects, then policies focusing teacher effects as a larger source of variation may be more promising than policies focusing on school effects.
>
> (Nye, Konstanopoulos, & Hedges, 2004, p. 254)

While smaller classes to seem to allow many teachers to provide improved reading instruction, too many teachers have limited expertise in teaching reading whether their classes are large or small. By reducing class size with Title I funds schools largely eliminated reading specialist positions and the remediation they had typically provided prior to the advent of this policy shift. Thus, these highest poverty schools then were left with more limited faculty expertise on reading instruction and with reading remediation left to classroom teachers. In this case, then, struggling readers in the highest poverty schools may have been provided both less reading instruction with the elimination of remediation lessons and with less expert reading as reading specialists transferred to schools where poverty was low enough that schoolwide project adaptations were not allowed.

Federal Reading Policy after NCLB

I write this section somewhat skeptically. Skeptically because unless the new administration that will be coming in January 2009 alters the current state of affairs dramatically, it seems unlikely that anything written by me, or any other member of the traditional education establishment, will get much notice in Washington. Nonetheless, I offer my advice on future reading policy direction.

Eliminating Federal Educational Policymaking and the USDE

Future federal reading policymaking should be extremely limited, in my view, because of the demonstrated potential for ideological themes to dominate the negotiation of these policies (Allington, 2002; DeBray, 2006) and the 40 years of minimal effects of federal policy on closing the rich/poor achievement gap. It might be better to consider whether having a USDE is worth having, or whether we might be better off with no federal educational policymaking. In other words, leave reading policy and education policy generally up to the states and local school districts. The federation of states (United States) represents a geographical collection of governmental areas that are more different than similar on many levels including key industries, ethnic and religious affiliations, age, languages spoken, and views and practices concerning marriage, employment, immigration, education, religion, and such. As a nation we are a collection of states that are becoming more different from each other with every decade (Hodgkinson, 1993). No national curriculum or even a national assessment system will alter these trends. So why do we employ all those folks at the USDE?

The only real leverage Congress has in passing educational legislation is through the dollars it allocates for these programs. If states simply rejected the funding they could reject the federal education programs. Given the shrinking federal share of the national education budget it seems a likely time to seriously consider ignoring Washington, D.C. and boycotting all federal education initiatives.

My basic argument in this sense concerning reading is this: After 40 years of federal educational programs and policies there seems little improvement in student reading achievement. After hundreds of billions of dollars allocated through the big three federal education programs—Title I, special education, bilingual education—there has been little evidence that any of these federal programs have closed the reading achievement gap. In federal study after federal study (Berends, Bodilly, & Kirby, 2002; Bond & Dykstra, 1967; House et al., 1978; Kimbrough & Hill, 1981; McLaughlin, 1991; USDE, 2007) the results have always been the same: Local capacity, or the lack of it, trumps federal policies every time. The findings of these reports have another similar theme: More expert teachers of reading create more students who read better than fewer expert teachers of reading. Actually, these studies all said that differences in *local capacity* were the reason that federal education programs worked in some places and failed to work in just as many others. Differences in local capacity has been the *scientific* reason that no federal education programs have worked reliably or consistently.

However, at the root of the concept of local capacity is teacher quality, teacher capacity to teach reading well. Other local factors—financial support, planned professional development, strong building leadership, adequate buildings and supplies, and so on—all work for or against generating a large supply of high-quality teachers of reading and providing them with adequate resources to do their jobs well. And while NCLB has a paper requirement for ensuring all teachers are highly qualified, nothing in the law requires highly expert teachers of reading. In fact, the USDE report on high-quality teaching largely ignores the research that the USDE has funded on effective teachers. As Darling-Hammond and Youngs (2002) wrote, "Whatever the contributions of this report to the debates on teacher quality, an accurate rendering of the research base on these important topics is not one of them" (p. 13). Rather than building local expertise, NCLB provided a restricted set of options for purchasing new curriculum materials. Not that there is or has been any evidence that providing particular commercial curriculum materials has ever reliably produced higher reading achievement (What Works Clearinghouse, 2007).

So, given the failure of federal education programs to accomplish much good over a 40-year period, why continue them? Perhaps we could leave in place the Institute for Education Sciences with a dual function of monitoring the achievement in the nation's schools (through the NAEP and the Schools and Staffing Survey processes) and funding research to improve our knowledge base about teaching and learning.

Monitoring Federal Policymaking Rigorously

If the Congress and the USDE continue creating reading policy then I would suggest that any such policymaking be subjected to rigorous review by both advocates for the policies and opponents of the policies prior to any vote on such legislation. But accomplishing this seems extremely unlikely. The reading community, alternatively, could commission a group to study federal policies and release a report that provides a balanced critique of the policies, but I am not optimistic that any such report would likely be read by any of the policymakers, much less produce a shift in the policymaking that might be recommended by a commission.

Develop Comprehensive Policy Statements and Write Legislation

We could create a commission that would write its own review of the research on reading instruction. Then using that document we could write actual legislation that would enact policies indicated by that summary and then present both to federal policymakers. The problem here is one of accomplishing both tasks. Members of the reading research community served on the NRP and served in USDE offices all in the creation of NCLB. How to create a commission that would reflect the diversity of stances obvious in reading education and how that commission would actually write a consensus document and how legislation might be developed from the consensus report are issues filled with potential pitfalls and unanswered questions.

Allow States and School Districts Considerably More Leeway in Designing Their Own Policies for Reading Education

For me, this option holds the greatest promise. I would couple this with the elimination, or dramatic downsizing, of the USDE. What such an approach would do is allow a variety of reading policies to be implemented and their effects documented (perhaps by researchers funded through the Institute on Education Sciences) over time. Surely some states and some school districts would create powerful policies that worked to eliminate the existing achievement gaps and foster higher levels of literacy among all students. In fact, some states and some schools have already done this (though NCLB has caused some to undo good policies and replace them, by mandate, with far less effective policies). In some senses this model supports experimentation on a grand scale and with good monitoring procedures in place would allow states and schools to learn from each other about achieving the goals that federal policies have tried, but failed, to achieve.

Summary

We have had federal policymaking in U.S. literacy education for more than 40 years. The federal policymakers have passed law after law, created federal agency after agency, funded program after program, and spent billions of dollars while failing to achieve two basic goals: more equitable and improved reading outcomes (Allington, 2005).

Perhaps it is time to consider whether a federal approach to achieving these goals is a reasonable one. I have suggested it is not. Instead, I suggest that federal policymaking should be largely eliminated and that such activities be returned to the states and school districts. This would create opportunities for wide experimentation in policy development and implementation. Through such experimentation and documentation we might just arrive at far better solutions for creating more equitable and improved reading outcomes. If there is a role for the federal government it is one of monitoring educational outcomes across the nation and publicizing the findings to the public.

References

Achilles, C.M. (1999). *Let's put kids first, finally: Getting class size right.* Thousand Oaks, CA: Corwin Press.

Allington, R.L. (2001). Does state and federal reading policymaking matter? In T. Loveless (Ed.), *The great curriculum debate* (pp. 268–298). Washington, DC: Brookings.

Allington, R.L. (2002). *Big brother and the national reading curriculum: How ideology trumped evidence.* Portsmouth, NH: Heinemann.

Allington, R.L. (2004). Setting the record straight. *Educational Leadership, 61*(6), 22–25.

Allington, R.L. (2009). *What really matters in response to intervention: Research-based designs.* Boston, MA: AllynBacon.

Allington, R.L. & Johnston, P.H. (Eds.), (2002). *Reading to learn: Lessons from exemplary 4th grade classrooms.* New York: Guilford.

Berends, M., Bodilly, S., & Kirby, S.N. (2002). Looking back over a decade of whole-school reform: The experience of New American Schools. *Phi Delta Kappan, 84*(2), 168–175.

Bond, G.L. & Dykstra, R. (1967). The cooperative research program in first-grade reading instruction. *Reading Research Quarterly, 2*(4), 5–142.

Borman, G.D., Wong, K.K., Hedges, L.V., & D'Agostino, J.V. (2003). Coordinating categorical and regular programs: Effects on Title 1 students' educational opportunities and outcomes. In G.D. Borman, S.C. Stringfield, & R.E. Slavin (Eds.), *Title 1: Compensatory education at the crossroads* (pp. 79–116). Mahwah, NJ: Lawrence Erlbaum Associates.

Brownstein, A. & Hicks, T. (2005). When research goes to market, is it a good thing for education? *Title I Monitor, 10*(9), 1–2 & 14–18.

Brownstein, A. & Hicks, T. (2006a). Ed ignored early warnings on Reading First conflicts, report says: Officials obscure origins of influential assessment review. *Title 1 Monitor, 11*(11), 1–4 & 17–21.

Brownstein, A. & Hicks, T. (2006b). Former Reading First director draws fire—and defenders. *Title 1 Monitor, 11*(11), 1 & 11–16.

Camilli, G., Wolfe, P.M., & Smith, M.L. (2006). Meta-analysis and reading policy: Perspectives on teaching children to read. *Elementary School Journal, 107*(1), 27–36.

Cronin, J., Dahlin, D., & Kingsbury, G.G. (2007). *The proficiency illusion.* Washington, DC: Thomas B. Fordham Institute.

Cross, C.T. (2004). *Political education: National policy comes of age.* New York: Teachers College Press.

Cunningham, J.W. (2001). The National Reading Panel report. *Reading Research Quarterly, 30*(3), 326–335.

Darling-Hammond, L. & Youngs, P. (2002). Defining "highly qualified teachers": What does the "scientifically-based research" actually tell us? *Educational Researcher, 31*, 13–25.

DeBray, E.H. (2006). *Politics, ideology, and education: Federal policy during the Clinton and Bush administrations*. New York: Teachers College Press.

Garan, E. (2002). *Resisting reading mandates: How to triumph with the truth*. Portsmouth, NH: Heinemann.

Goodman, K.S. (Ed.), (1998). *In defense of good teaching: What teachers need to know about the "reading wars"*. York, ME: Stenhouse.

Grunwald, M. (2006, Sunday, October 1). Billions for an inside game on reading. *Washington Post*, p. B1.

Hammill, D.D. (2004). What we know about correlates of reading. *Exceptional Children*, *70*(4), 453–468.

Hammill, D.D. & Swanson, H.L. (2006). The National Reading Panel's meta-analysis of phonics instruction: Another point of view. *Elementary School Journal*, *107*(1), 17–26.

Haney, W. (2000). The myth of the Texas miracle in education. *Education Policy Analysis Archives*, *8*(41). Retrieved on July 17, 2002 from http://epaa.asu.edu/epaa/v8n41/.

Hodgkinson, H. (1993). American education: The good, the bad, and the task. *Phi Delta Kappan*, *74*(8, April), 619–623.

House, E.R., Glass, G.V., McLean, L., & Walker, D. (1978). No simple answers: Critique of the Follow Through evaluations. *Harvard Educational Review*, *48*, 128–160.

Johnston, P., Allington, R.L., & Afflerbach, P. (1985). The congruence of classroom and remedial reading instruction. *Elementary School Journal*, *85*, 465–478.

Kahlenberg, R.D. (2008). *Fixing No Child Left Behind*. New York: The Century Foundation. Retrieved from: http://www.tcf.org/publications/education/agenda_rk.pdf

Kimbrough, J. & Hill, P.T. (1981). *The aggregate effects of federal education programs*. Santa Monica, CA: Rand Corp.

Knapp, M.S. (1995). *Teaching for meaning in high-poverty classrooms*. New York: Teachers College Press.

Krashen, S. (2001). More smoke and mirrors: A critique of the National Reading Panel report on fluency. *Phi Delta Kappan*, October, 119–123.

Linn, R.L. (2005). Conflicting demands of No Child Left Behind and state systems: Mixed messages about school performance. *Education Policy Analysis Archives*, *13*(33).

Lyon, G.R. (1997). *Statement of G. Reid Lyon, Ph.D before the Committee on Education and the Workforce, U.S. House of Representatives*. National Institute of Child Health and Human Development, National Institutes of Health: Bethesda, MD.

Manzo, K.K. (October 18, 2008). Latest "Reading First" study reports limited benefits. *Education Week*, p. 12.

McGill-Franzen, A. & Goatley, V. (2001). Title I and special education: Support for children who struggle to learn to read. In S. Neuman & D. Dickinson (Eds.), *Handbook of early literacy research* (pp. 471–483). New York: Guilford.

McLaughlin, M.W. (1991). The Rand change agent study: Ten years later. In A. Odden (Ed.), *Education policy implementation* (pp. 143–155). Albany: SUNY Press.

Nye, B., Konstantopoulos, S., & Hedges, L.V. (2004). How large are teacher effects? *Educational Evaluation and Policy Analysis*, *26*(3), 237–257.

Pearson, P.D. (2004). The reading wars. *Educational Policy*, *18*(1), 216–252.

Pressley, M., Allington, R.L., Wharton-MacDonald, R., Collins-Block, C., & Morrow, L. (2001). *Learning to read: Lessons from exemplary first-grade classrooms*. New York: Guilford.

Puma, M.J., Karweit, N., Price, C., Ricciuti, A., Thompson, W., & Vaden-Kiernan, M. (1997). *Prospects: Final report on student outcomes*. Washington, DC: U. S. Department of Education, Office of Planning and Evaluation Services.

Song, M., Coggshall, J.G., & Miskel, C.G. (2004). Where does policy usually come from and why should we care? In P. McCardle, & V. Chhabra (Eds.), *The voice of evidence in reading research* (pp. 445–462). Baltimore, MN: Paul Brookes Publishing.

Strauss, S.L. (2002). Politics and reading at the National Institute of Child Health and Human Development. *Pediatrics, 109*(1), 143–144.

Strauss, S.L. (2003). Challenging the NICHD reading research agenda. *Phi Delta Kappan, 84*(6), 438–442.

Sunderman, G.L., Kim, J.S., & Orfield, G. (2005). *NCLB meets school realities: Lessons from the field*. Thousand Oaks, CA: Corwin Press.

Taylor, B.M., Anderson, R.C., Au, K.H., & Raphael, T.E. (2000). Discretion in the translation of research to policy: A case from beginning reading. *Educational Researcher, 29*(6), 16–26.

Taylor, B.M., Pearson, P.D., Peterson, D.S., & Rodriguez, M.C. (2003). Reading growth in high-poverty classrooms: The influences of teacher practices that encourage cognitive engagement in literacy learning. *Elementary School Journal, 104*(1), 4–28.

Taylor, D. (1998). *Beginning to read and the spin doctors of science: The political campaign to change America's mind about how children learn to read*. Urbana, IL: National Council of Teachers of English.

United States Department of Education (2007). *National assessment of Title I final report: Summary of key findings*. Institute of Education Sciences (Vol. NCEE 2007–4014): National Center for Education Evaluation and Regional Assistance.

What Works Clearinghouse (2007). *Beginning reading*. Washington, DC: U.S. Department of Education. Retrieved from http://ies.ed.gov/ncee/wwc/reports/beginning_reading/topic/

Winfield, L.F. (1991). Lessons from the field: Case studies of evolving schoolwide projects. *Educational Evaluation and Policy Analysis, 13*, 353–362.

Wong, K.K. (2003). Federal Title I as a reform strategy in urban schools. In L.F. Miron & E.P.S. John (Eds.), *Reinterpreting urban school reform* (pp. 55–76). Albany, NY: SUNY Press.

Chapter 18

Literacy Education 2.0

Looking through the Rear Vision Mirror as We Move Ahead

Robert J. Tierney
The University of British Columbia

I begin this chapter with a backward look at the developments that we have endured, the present issues and developments that we are confronting, and some comments on perceived needs. In the second half of the chapter, I shift to the road ahead and explore the possibilities around a new narrative tied to reprofessionalization of teaching, rethinking the nature of educational research, and its relationship to practice and visioning literacies anew.

We are now approaching 2010, the start of a new decade, and developments are afoot which seem to be dislodging, supplanting, or shifting the prescribed standards and testing-based school improvement models that have begun to be viewed as corrupted. With the discrediting of some of the major policy directions of the past 20 years, we are seeing the beginnings of a shift in orientation away from the federal controls and standardization to calls for collaborative engagement, the growth of learning communities and contemporary views of literacy. We see the road ahead as involving a re-envisioning of literacies and literacy education, shifting how we engage in educational research and development, reasserting teacher professionalism and recommitting to an ethical approach to our activities. My hopes are consistent with other authors in this volume. Shannon et al., for example, suggest a return to some values of the "social projects of possibility that expanded social forms in order to extend human capacities and to accommodate those capacities with more flexible social forms" prior to the reversals of the past 25 years. Allington argues for "opportunities for wide experimentation in policy development and implementation for creating more equitable and improved reading outcomes." To achieve such he questions whether ". . . federal policymaking should be largely eliminated and that such activities be returned to the states and school districts." Harste urges us to build upon social constructivist and critical traditions as well as notions of inquiry that honor the professional judgment of educators responsive to learners and the learners' communities.

Looking Through the Rear Vision Mirror at Literacy and School Reform Models

Today, if you visited schools in the U.S., U.K. and Australia, you would find yourself still embedded in a model of school improvement, especially literacy improvement, which emphasizes achievement gains on a subset of traditional reading skills as measured by selected tests. You would encounter a form of federalism involving national testing, common curricula, and a pursuit of ways to align what all students learn. Global competition, accountability, coordination, and mobility are often cited as the basis for these pursuits.

This *one size fits all* approach together with high-stakes testing represent a search for common denominators where consistency, common criteria, and proficiency levels became the mantra. The problem arises that one size may not fit all and standardization of measurement has contributed to the ends dictating the means. *The ends* becomes teachers teaching toward tests, which are unlikely to adequately represent reading and writing or the different ways literacy develops or literacy education should proceed. The measure of success is defined by a test score and not a fuller set of considerations. And, the measure of a school's commitment is its alignment with prescribed practices rather than practices connected with and building upon the resources and needs of those communities.

The historic nature of these shifts cannot be overstated. We have seen support for a limited definition of reading, a lessening of teachers' academic discretion, an imposition of prescriptive practices and a narrowing of what counts as research. The rich diversity of cutting-edge curricula and practices developed has been displaced by uniform standards and attempts to align assessment criteria. If you were interested in teachers and students engaged in site-based teaching and inquiry you may have been dismayed or gone underground or left the profession. If you were pursuing rich forms of literacies, you might do so in the margins. If, as a teacher, you were engaged in research and development or enlisting your own observations and decision-making, your voice was apt to be silenced as you were expected to assume the role of technician rather than reflective practitioner. And, if you were a beginning teacher, you might find yourself appreciative of the prescription, but unaware of what might or should be your goals. As a beginning teacher you might find yourself struggling to survive a system in which you were isolated, alone, and overwhelmed. If you were a curriculum developer you may or may not find yourself directed away from a rich view of literacy to approaches that teach to what is testable, and directed to develop curricula or teaching activities tied to a narrow band of skills rather than an expanded view of literacy. If you were a researcher or involved in professional development, you would find yourself being asked to identify best practice from traditional research rather than your ongoing site-based professional research and development efforts with teachers. Essentially, the U.S. and other countries which have resorted to testing and standards as a panacea have seen a massive teaching to the test and prescribed curriculum that flies in the face of diverse curriculum, teacher professionalism, consideration for language variability, teacher research, classroom-based assessment, etc. Too often the tests become the program. And, what counts as literacy falls much along the lines of what Campbell's law suggests:

> The more any quantitative social indicator is used for social decision-making, the more subject it will be to corruption pressures and the more apt it will be to distort and corrupt the social processes it is intended to monitor.
>
> (Campbell, 1975, p. 35)

The educator may lament what has occurred; the cynic might assign malevolent intent. Sharon Nichols and David Berliner (2007) have noted that across the major newspapers in the States and White House documents that there was a dramatic shift beginning in 1995 toward tying discussions of education improvement to achievement and a corresponding displacement or disappearance of discussions of equity or educational opportunity. Since 1995, newspapers and White House documents make very few mentions of equity matters while comments about achievement have ascended. A number of other countries seem to have followed suit. For example, a recent examination of discussions of education across the Canadian provinces by Chan, Fisher, and Rubenson (2007) found an emphasis upon neoliberal discussions of education emphasizing educational achievement devoid of discussions of social development. In Australia, accountability and standardization seem to have become the mantra of the federal and state governments over the last 10 years. Indeed, the Ministerial Council on Education, Employment, Training and Youth Affairs (MCEETYA) seems to have assumed an approach to educational development tied to similar sentiments. As Australia's Hon. Dr. David Kemp MP, Minister for Education, Training and Youth Affairs, suggested to the Curriculum Corporation 6th National Conference (6–7 May, 1999) in an extended discussion of these issues:

> We can't be sure that our education system is serving all young Australians as they deserve unless we have ways of measuring and reporting the outcomes of schooling nationally. The community has a reasonable expectation that the massive public and private investment in school education should lead to appropriate improvements in skill levels and general educational attainment of our young people. To determine the extent of improvement in broad terms, data has to be collected about how students are accessing schooling, the ways they are participating in it, how they are achieving, and where they are going after they leave school. Good

accountability relies on good reporting—at all levels, the school level, the systemic authority or State level, and nationally. If we are to have a school system for the next millennium, which meets the expectations and has the confidence of the Australian community, then we must have mechanisms in place that allow us to measure the key outcomes of all Australian schools and report these outcomes to the Australian community. We need to make clear our expectations for all schools—government and non-government schools alike.

In the U.S., the rhetoric was accompanied by mandates and funding incentives to ensure buy-in and implementation. Since school budgets are stretched to cope with ongoing expenses and are dependent upon funding from external sources, school boards mostly aligned with these mandates. Again, concerns over achievement gaps and a common curriculum for all supplanted an emphasis upon curriculum enlisting and building cultural resources and relevance. On first glance, these developments may seem worthwhile as they mandate that schools be accountable to all students and by requiring schools to report the achievement of various subgroups. On closer examination, these reform efforts may give the appearance of supporting minority interests, but achieve the opposite—at least in the long term.

Using South Africa as a case study, James Hoffman, Misty Sailors, Leketi Makalela, and Bertus Matthee (in this volume) discuss how educational developments on a global scale appear to be adopting expedient approaches to educational improvement devoid of a full and long-term consideration for the home language development needs of diverse groups of students and cultures. In Australia, we see parallel developments in the ways the government's educational agenda positions indigenous educational initiatives. Politicians override calls for equity with an emphasis upon test performance and the achievement gap as politicians. One must question if the approach isn't subversive. For example, in the state of New South Wales a recent aboriginal education document developed by indigenous educators includes powerful guidelines addressing areas of need and issues of support built upon culture resources and respect with scant mention of achievement. The letter included in the foreword by the Minister of Education does not address matters of community development and cultural resources as important; instead, the Minister of Education identifies increased achievement as the key. (See New South Wales Government, 2002.) I believe the NSW aboriginal documents may be symptomatic of the tension between what many educators understand and what politicians (with the support of some educators) presume—the view against and for achieving sustainable equity as well as educational reform/improvement by standardized monitoring of standards attainment by testing.

In this volume, Patrick Shannon, Jacqueline Edmondson, Leticia Ortega, Susan Pitcher, and Christopher Robbins argue the policies of the past 15 years are racist in nature and intent. In a similar vein, Kris Gutierrez (2004) offers a cautionary tale based upon her experiences with her own son after she moved to LA. As she stated:

> When my son, Scott, entered the second grade, he was a confident and fluent reader and writer. Several months after his entry to the school, I received an urgent call from his teacher requesting an immediate meeting with me. I sat nervously in his classroom trying to imagine what had prompted his urgency. I was concerned, as the school and its participants had had some difficulty adjusting to its first Latino (he is Chicano/African-American) to ever enroll in the school.
>
> Our meeting began. Leaning forward, her voice in a whisper as if not to embarrass me, the teacher shared her concern that Scott might not make it through the second grade: he didn't know phonics. I was puzzled and relieved. After all, he excelled in reading, and his literacy skills were sophisticated for his age, a fact verified by their own standardized tests. It turned out that what he didn't know how to do (or more likely didn't want to do) were the sets of repetitive phonics exercises that he had been assigned for the past several weeks . . . I asked how she would assess my son's ability to read and, without hesitation, she replied, "oh he's probably the best reader in the class."
>
> (pp. 101–102)

Kris Gutierrez suggests a number of concerns:

> What is implicated in this very brief narrative is a set of complex issues that defines schooling for so many students today. It is an account of the consequences of narrow views of literacy and how a teacher's understanding of literacy is complicated and constrained by mandated school curriculum that was conceptualized and implemented of the knowledge and practices of its students. It is an account of the ways that we understand the competence across racial, ethnic and class lines. It is an account of the consequences of the ways we measure what counts as literacy, especially, if we only see it in snapshots in discrete moments in time disconnected from the laminated, multimodal reality of literacy activity. And it is an account of how parents can mediate school policy and practices.
>
> The challenges my son faced are all too common, but they are particularly so from non-dominant groups, especially English learners. However, unlike poor and immigrant parents unfamiliar with the institutions of our country, I could mediate vigilantly and persistently the effects of discrimination and of policies gone awry. I knew that I was the school's worst nightmare: I was more than a meddling, middle-class mother, I was a meddling, middle-class, and Latina mother! This is no insignificant

point, however, it is a point misunderstood (or not taken up) by policy makers.

(p. 102)

Alfie Kohn (1998) in an article entitled "Only My Kid" discussed how accountability and tougher requirements tend to perpetuate the historic privilege of those who have learned to navigate the system well while excluding those who have not. Kohn (1998) contrasted the position of Dewey espoused in *School and Society* with the egocentric attitudes toward testing, grading, etc., of parents. As Kohn argues based upon Dewey's suggestion:

What the best and wisest parent wants for his own child, that must the community want for all of its children. Any other ideal for our schools is narrow and unlovely; acted upon, it destroys our democracy.

(John Dewey, *School and Society*)

In contrast, Kohn suggests that parents:

. . . are not concerned that all children learn; they are concerned that *their* children learn. There is no national organization called Rich Parents Against School Reform, in part because there doesn't have to be. But with unaffiliated individuals working on different issues in different parts of the country, the pattern is generally missed and the story is rarely told. Take a step back, however, and you begin to grasp the import of what is happening from Amherst, Massachusetts, where highly educated white parents have fought to preserve a tracking system that keeps virtually every child of color out of advanced classes, to Palo Alto, California, where a similarly elite constituency demands a return to a "skill and drill" math curriculum and fiercely opposes the more conceptual learning outlined in the National Council of Teachers of Mathematics (NCTM) standards; from an affluent suburb of Buffalo, where parents of honors students quashed an attempt to replace letter grades with standards-based progress reports, to San Diego, where a program to provide underachieving students with support that will help them succeed in higher-level courses has run 'head on into vigorous opposition from some of the community's more outspoken, influential members—the predominantly white, middle-class parents of high-achieving students.'

The apartheid-like character of these reforms is vexing. Complicity with these developments or support of them, for self-interest, extends beyond parents to educational policymakers and researchers with motives that are both ideological and economic. There has been institutional and individual complicity at times and at other times a disregard for the violation of the ethics involved. In the U.S., the Inspector General made visible via evidence from emails the unethical behavior of public representatives as they attempted to ensure that certain decisions would be made over others and moreover that these decisions carried with them certain assets (including position). It identified individuals in our field as instigators or perpetrators of actions to advantage some (including themselves) while disadvantaging others. They appeared to be operating in a manner which was covert, coercive, fraudulent—intended to misrepresent how decision-making was occurring. Certain parties were involved in a campaign motivated to mandate some programs and approaches to educational research and development to the exclusion over others—indeed, the exclusion of some programs, the exclusion of certain voices, and the maintenance of certain control of what counts as literacy, literacy progress, and literacy curriculum as well as personal financial gain. Despite admissions of conspiring secretly to gain advantage for selected programs, despite admissions of conflicts of interests, and despite financial disclosures of profiting, the implicated individuals seem interested in acting as if their behavior was warranted and the institutions deny that the program itself has been corrupted. Indeed, if we were to apply a broader lens to what has occurred, a number of institutions and individuals might be considered co-conspirators, collaborators, and beneficiaries of an initiative that was recognized as a form of apartheid in our field while others were the victims. At the same time, individuals could be identified as the whistleblowers (individuals and institutions) or as agitators. As I have analogized, the exclusionary mission reflected a form of apartheid and a desire to move an agenda forward. The agenda was not a democratic agenda; rather, almost a form of theocracy and control in the interests of some who have much to gain.

Those of us in the U.S. or Australia are not alone in terms of its past embrace of and current concerns with and criticism of the reform model. An evaluation of these initiatives has reached almost a consensus that the standards and testing regimen was unreliable and at times limiting as well as misdirected. Indeed, some countries seem set to abandon or soften the standards and testing regimen. In the U.K., for example, in a recent *Times Educational Supplement* report ("Test regime must change," *Times Educational Supplement*, November 2, 2007), Warren Mansell discussed the criticisms by various researchers and others around the emphasis upon testing and league tables as the vehicle for leveraging educational improvements (http://www.primaryreview.org.uk/Publications/Interimreports.html). Mansell noted: "In a strong critique of Labour's record, academics denounced the testing regime as 'inadequate': it provides unreliable information on Standards, encourages schools to neglect lower achievers, narrows the curriculum, and increases pupils' anxiety." Professor Robin Alexander, the project team leader, stated: "The consensus which these reports reinforce is now so commanding that it is hard to resist the view that sooner rather than later the apparatus of national testing must change radically." Interestingly, the U.K. Prime Minister Gordon Brown was reputed to have said: "We must keep assessment under review to ensure that it supports learning and achievement and does not dominate teaching."

Certainly there is growing disillusionment now with the reform program as a result of the disappointing returns, and the corruption and collateral damage of the school improvement models tied to standards and testing. In the U.S., there has been considerable debate around the renewal of the No Child Left Behind Act (NCLB), but only some of the features of the program faltered. There is now some recognition that the model of literacy extrapolated from the National Reading Panel report was limited to a narrow set of skills and areas, which perpetuated a reductionist and limited view of literacy and literacy teaching. Some query the motivations and ethics which led to certain findings of the National Reading Panel being overemphasized; and others ignored as policymakers appear to have cherry-picked the report to justify the approaches that they advocated and undermined support for others. As I have discussed, a U.S. Justice Department investigation revealed that the U.S. Department of Education staff and appointees conspired to support certain approaches over others, including approaches for which they had vested financial interests. The U.S. Department of Education personnel offered the retort that the means justified the ends, while expressing concern over some of the behavior of their staff. This is perplexing given the recent data on *the ends*.

In terms of the success of these efforts, many school boards seem to be on a trajectory which identifies them as failing at the same time as they are directed to set goals and adopt programs which may not meet their long-term needs. Indeed, the most comprehensive study to date of the practices derived from the NCLB and its offshoot Reading First are troubling to anyone who advocates these reforms. In particular, despite the insistence on the worth of the decisions, a study conducted under the auspices of the United States Department of Education of Reading First failed to support the very initiatives that they had advocated and prescribed. Reading First initiatives may have improved performance narrowly defined, but do not appear to be capable of achieving the broader goals, including its own prime goal of having more students reading "at their grade level." Further, in areas such as reading comprehension and interest or engagement in reading, students enrolled in Reading First initiatives fell behind students in non-Reading First initiatives. The report suggested that the longer students were in Reading First the poorer the students did as compared to others. Allington's discussion of the impact of federal legislation upon Title 1 in the current volume offers a number of similar observations or corollary evidence of the lack of effectiveness of these reform efforts. He traces how political and other influences contributed to prescribing certain suspect practices. He suggests that there is little evidence from the National Assessment of Educational Progress that the achievement gap has been reduced since 1992. Federal policymakers and media pundits appear to want to redirect the blame for the failure of the reform initiatives on teachers or teacher education and press for greater fidelity in what is taught and tested. Meanwhile, educators struggle with the pressure to teach toward the test and schools struggle with threats of withdrawal of funding or public disgrace unless they do so. They find themselves facing akin to a Hobson's choice or a take it or leave it situation as they struggle with having to sideline or displace their students' other key needs.

The Road Ahead

Over the next 10 years we are facing a major turnover in the teaching force and a massive global teacher shortage. By 2015, it is estimated that the majority of teachers will be new. I would hope that their preparation and induction supports them as *rich* collaborators and inquirers rather than the current positioning of teachers that mandate-driven prescriptions dictate. I would hope that we could align teacher development and preparation to a new ethical form of teamwork across schools, which respects and builds upon inquiry-driven possibilities. I would hope that we would develop programs that would support literacy development in a fashion which respects and builds upon the cultural resources of communities similar to what colleagues such as Victoria Purcell-Gates (2006, 2008) advocate. As she has charged, models of literacy teaching and learning need to acknowledge and build upon the significant ways in which families and cultural communities impact young children's language and literacy development. As Purcell-Gates states:

> Teachers must be aware of what the children come to school knowing, and not knowing, and then must be allowed to tailor beginning reading instruction that will make a difference for all children in the context of real reading and writing activities. Teaching models that strip down reading and writing to technical skills outside of meaningful practice may show what looks like good results on skills tests, but these gains are quickly lost after grade two. Children learn to read and write better when teachers respond to them based upon knowledge of them as individuals and as members of cultural communities.
>
> (2008, p. 5)

I would hope that we support educators with the digital, linguistic skills and cultural awarenesses to build upon indigenous resources, including language and the multicultural nature of our increasing cosmopolitan settings.

As the narrative shifts and we begin a new chapter, I would hope our ambitions move beyond an ideal that defines educational advances as improved test performance. There is much we should have learned and not done, much we have to learn and pursue differently in our schools and more broadly in our society in the interests of equity and opportunity. A call for or hope of a new narrative may not capture the full gravity of my concerns. Currently schools seem to have been placed in a situation where they can do the best to meet the mandates of governments in ways that compromise their professionalism and redirect them from what they know and observe and would deem as priorities. Unfortunately, schools seem to be forced to deal with mandates that have the potential to move us further back than forward as compliance to *best* and prescribed practices, setting improvements in test scores as the target and there is an insistence on fidelity between standards, legislation, and practice.

As I have argued, the standards- and testing-based reform efforts tend to perpetuate interesting paradoxes: while they claim to be bridging a gap in reading achievement, they limit what counts as literacy; while they blame teachers for school failures, they give only lip-service to teacher professionalism and teachers' engagement in site-based program development. First, let me discuss the growing gap between what students may be taught and what they might need to learn for today's digitally enhanced world.

Selfe and Hawisher (2004) have argued:

> If literacy educators continue to define literacy in terms of alphabetic practices only, in ways that ignore, exclude, or devalue new-media texts, they not only abdicate a professional responsibility to describe the ways in which humans are now communicating and making meaning, but they also run the risk of their curriculum no longer holding relevance for students who are communicating in increasingly expansive networked environments.
>
> (p. 233)

Over the past 15 years, literacy has remained quite narrowly defined and restricted to what literacy has been, rather than what literacy is or has become today. Some suggest that the lack of responsiveness of schools goes beyond intractable views of what counts as literacy. Some suggest that the institution of schooling may not support the transition of these new literacies to school settings in ways consistent with their potential and participatory, including the possible shifts in power dynamics that might occur (Sheehy, 2007). The contrast between school curriculum and the informal engagement via the internet, digital gaming, social software, and media production has become stark. What may be accessible outside of school appears to have surpassed what most students in schools may be given the opportunity to access within schools. And, what may cross over to school may involve a mutation, which may not have the same saliency or worth. As Street (2006) argued, outside of schools there is often an interest in global issues, networking, webs, multimodality, flexibility and so on, whereas inside schools there is often a tendency to stress stability and unity. Indeed, in some situations, these new literacies are framed as discrete skills such as programming, internet access, or presentation skills rather than as learning tools with complex palates of possibilities for students to access in a myriad of ways. It is as if learning with technology is being perceived as *learning the technology* rather than using a range of multimodal literacy tools (supported by these technologies) in the pursuit of learning. Similarly, Squire (2006) has argued that the approach to learning within most schools falls short of what digital-based games are already achieving—most notably, situated learning with an array of imageful resources plus an accessible network of others developing expertise and understanding through performance.

There is growing recognition of the need for spaces and the license to rethink literacy and redo learning so that it befits our changing digital literacies and the entrepreneurial, participatory, interactive, and multimodal experience akin to *Web 2.0* (e.g. in this volume: Harste as well as Lapp, Flood, Heath, and Langer). For example, just as the United Nations established functional reading and writing goals for the world over 50 years ago, the UN recognizes digital literacy as equivalent to those goals for today. Particularly notable are the Geneva principles on building the information society that were the focus of the world summit on the informational society in 2003 (United Nations, 2003). The summit began with:

> Principle 1: We, the representatives of the peoples of the world, assembled in Geneva from 10–12 December 2003 for the first phase of the World Summit on the Information Society, declare our common desire and commitment to build a people-centered, inclusive and development-oriented Information Society, where everyone can create, access, utilize and share information and knowledge, enabling individuals, communities and peoples to achieve their full potential in promoting their sustainable development and improving their quality of life, premised on the purposes and principles of the Charter of the United Nations and respecting fully and upholding the Universal Declaration of Human Rights.

The principles argued for participation "where human dignity is respected" and where we access these informational technologies to further development:

> ... to reduce many traditional obstacles, especially those of time and distance, for the first time in history makes it possible to use the potential of these technologies for the benefit of millions of people in all corners of the world ... as tools and not as an end in themselves. Under favorable conditions, these technologies can be a powerful instrument, increasing productivity, generating economic growth, job creation and employability and improving the quality of life of all. They can also promote dialogue among people, nations and civilizations.

They emphasize the use of a range of technologies as fundamental to local and global problem-solving and development as a tool for search, inquiry, exchange, and the expression of idea. They suggest that educators need to not just develop an environment for allowing students to participate in using a range of digital literacies but also develop learners who become:

- capable information technology users
- information-seekers, analyzers, and evaluators
- problem-solvers and decision-makers
- creative and effective users of productivity tools
- communicators, collaborators, publishers, and producers
- informed, responsible, and contributing citizens

Today's digital literacy requires appropriating skills in defining and refining goals, searching and selecting various documents, websites, and other sources for relevant material. Digital users need skill in gathering relevant material and considering how they connect or might be relevant compositions from these searches. They need a sense of agency as they engage in research and design as well as ongoing conversations which are complex, multilayered, virtual and face-to-face, global and local, identity-shaping as well as informing. Rather than the traditional triad of pre, during, and post, a different array of strategies and skills receive emphasis as one considers engaging with multiple literacies associated with project-based ventures incorporating web searches and other resources, multimedia and multilayered project development, and postings on the Internet for consumption and connections.

Without suggesting a rigid sequence or discrete categories, today's digital inquirers are engaged in ongoing and recursive research, development, design, dissemination, critique, refinement, etc. As they move across or within networks and web-like engagements, they are sifting, linking, sampling, following leads and paths, at the same time as they are doing forms of layering and affiliating as they pursue for themselves and others confirmations, understandings, plans, commitments, answers, directions, or acknowledgements. Those researchers examining the cognitive strategies involved in meaning-making online bring to the fore the importance of several strategies which may be somewhat nuanced in the networked environment—the importance of refining searches, forward inferencing (akin to predicting), making linkages and other integration in a fashion that coheres and is relevant, flexible, and recursive. It suggests that the meaning-maker(s) is/are engaged in simultaneous linking together of ideas (texts, images, and sounds) as the meaning-maker(s) refine(s) or expand(s) understandings at the same time as they evaluate them and assess coherence.

We are also aware that today's digital literacy requires a significant shift in the social bases of our models of literacy. Whereas traditional reading and writing models focus upon the individual and transacting with an author, digital meaning-makers encounter different forms of transactions (and co-constructions) daily as they engage with colleagues, collaborators, and others in various time zones. It is significant that digital meaning-makers are often engaged in a form of group meaning-making akin to a jazz ensemble. They play with different personae, move in and out of groups or operate in all manner of fashions—unified or dispersed. Even in solitude, today's digital meaning-makers may view themselves as operating in multiples, especially as they interact with texts of others and their own selves, including sometimes their playing out a range of roles. Building upon the work of Dyson (1995) and McEneaney (2006), the notion of participatory culture has been used by Jenkins and his colleagues to describe these engagements. As Jenkins, Clinton, Purushotma, Robison, and Weigel (2008) define participatory culture, they suggest that it involves:

> . . . a culture with relatively low barriers to artistic expression and civic engagement, strong support for creating and sharing one's creations, and some type of informal mentorship whereby what is known by the most experienced is passed along to novices . . . one in which members believe their contributions matter, and feel some degree of social connection with one another (at the least they care what other people think about what they have created).

> Affiliations—memberships, formal and informal, in online communities centered around various forms of media, such as Friendster, Facebook, message boards, metagaming, game clans, or MySpace).

> Expressions—producing new creative forms, such as digital sampling, skinning and modding, fan videomaking, fan fiction writing, zines, mash-ups).

> Collaborative Problem-solving—working together in teams, formal and informal, to complete tasks and develop new knowledge (such as through Wikipedia, alternative reality gaming, spoiling).

> Circulations—shaping the flow of media (such as podcasting, blogging).

As Jenkins et al. (2008) emphasize, "participatory culture shifts the focus of literacy from one of individual expression to community involvement. The new literacies almost all involve social skills developed through collaboration and networking."

Drawing from years of engagement in improving the professional practice of teachers intent on immersing students in digitally enhanced learning, Dwyer has offered advice that resonates with these views. As Dwyer (1996) indicated in his reflections of the advances and obstacles faced by the Apple Classroom of Tomorrow (ACOT), progress seemed to occur when the approach to teaching was authentic, interactive, and collaborative, resource rich, and inquiry driven. He observed that students were successful when they were afforded access to and support for multiple representations of ideas, shared, critiqued, and pursued innovatively by a community of students that see the possibility of re-imaging selves across digital spaces and other literacy fields or spaces.

The Growth of Support for "Rich" Collaborative Site-based Research and Development

Throughout this volume a number of authors call for leadership in order to develop a narrative that supports a definition of research and relationship to practice which builds upon social constructivist and critical traditions as well as notions of evidence-based practicing that honors the professional judgment and decision-making of teachers and their preparation.

In his 2007 NRC address, "An Historical Analysis of the Impact of Educational Research on Policy and Practice: Reading as an Illustrative Case," Pearson mounted a criticism of the method of research synthesis used to guide the educational policy and prescribe practice as orchestrated by NCLB and other mandates. Pearson argued that the approach to policy development represented an important shift in a number of ways. First, theory development was "replaced by synthesis" and in turn the synthesis began to define models of reading, not the reverse (see Figure 18.1). Second, the syntheses seem to be used to leverage a predetermined agenda—that is, selected findings of the syntheses became the basis of legislation to mandate certain curriculum elements and teaching practices to ensure predetermined agendas would be enacted. In other words, as Pearson stated, "monitoring tools (to ensure fidelity in standards-based reform) and sanctions (to motivate schools and teachers to higher achievement and stricter adherence to reforms) are added to keep the system moving." The end result was a narrowing both of the definition of research and in turn literacy via the selective enlistment of research findings to propel certain agendas over others. Again, a range of leverages were used to guarantee fidelity with an agenda of standards, testing, prescribed practices directed at addressing an achievement gap as measured by selected tests and a host of unethical (if not illegal) practices enlisted to ensure that: certain findings and approaches were supported and funded over others by key staff within the U.S. Department of Education selected committees to ensure certain agendas were maintained and not challenged; results were cherry-picked and decontextualized to achieve certain directions or emphasis; and personal financial gain seem to override the better judgment by and recusement of select individuals from decision-making roles.

Based upon his own research and review of other research on effective schools, David Pearson has argued that a more collaborative site-based approach to inquiry and teacher decision-making will more likely be successful than a model of research into practice which is prescriptive and scripted. He

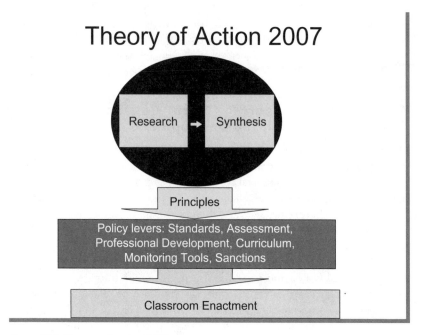

Figure 18.1 Theory of action 2007.

and his colleagues have stressed that most success occurred when teachers work together and use their observations to develop instructional plans along with customized ways to assess them to distinguish effective literacy programs (Taylor, Pressley, & Pearson, 2002). Consistent with their argument for a more dynamic interactive approach to educational research, policy and practice, Deb Butler (2008) has proposed a model for research into practice which re-establishes educational research as a joint collaborative enterprise between the research community, teachers, and other stakeholder groups. She argues for shifting to a model of knowledge generation which involves the collaborative engagement of teachers, researchers, and other stakeholders from the outset—from the inception of the issue or problem or question—to the formulation of interventions, pursuits, observational procedures, measurements, analyses, the interpretation of the results, and their use en route to shaping and reshaping policy (see Figure 18.2). She and her colleagues have argued for engaging multiple stakeholders "in parallel, coordinated, and/or collaborative inquiry" as a means to "simultaneously support teacher professional development, foster a constructive, progressive discourse in education, and enhance efforts towards educational reform" (Butler et al., 2008).

Both Butler's and Pearson's proposals re-establish the teacher as an

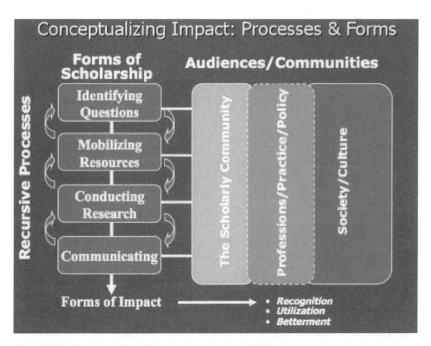

Figure 18.2 Conceptualizing impact: processes and forms.

experimenter, consistent with the notions espoused in the historic Bullock report. As Bullock proffered:

> In our view, teachers should be involved not only experimenting with the outcomes of research, but also in identifying the problems, setting up hypotheses and carrying out the collection and assessment of data. We should particularly like to see more action research . . . for we believe that this form of activity holds considerable promise for the development of new practices in school.
>
> (Bullock, 1975, p. 553)

The significance of these discussions of the nature and quality of educational research is profound. The typologies for describing educational research in terms of antecedent, purposes, values, processes and products may prescribe educational practices in ways that constrain or limit who, what, why and how inquiries are engaged. In universities it may privilege certain research traditions over others in ways that guide whether inquiry is exclusively detached from site based and collaborative inquiry. In the U.K., for example, the National Research Assessment Exercise has contributed to a type of social contract as applied and basic research distinctions are formulated and the quality indicators of such research are imposed (see Hammersley, 2008).

Whereas the U.S. universities have not experienced research assessment directly, we have witnessed the corollary narrowing of what counts as inquiry. In particular, developments such as the Reading Excellence Act have limited what can count and inform policy. In turn, these developments privilege some forms of research and researchers over others in ways that can, in turn, be corrupted by self-interest. In Canada, agencies seem to be addressing a similar question, but answering them differently. For example, Canada agencies seem to recognize the need for an approach to inquiry in the social sciences, which is embedded in communities, and tied to community engagement. Figures 18.3 and 18.4 reflect an attempt by the primary Canadian funding agency for educational research to render the nature of the dynamics of inquiry, especially the diversity of inputs that might spur research, the convergence at the point of inquiry and divergence of possibilities emerging from and with the inquiry in partnership with communities (Bennett & Bennet, 2007).

The notion of communities of inquiry is consistent with a return to Dewey's view of educational scholarship and recently touted by Bruce and Bishop in a recent article, entitled *New literacies and community inquiry* (Bruce and Bishop, 2008) As Bruce and Bishop state:

> Community inquiry provides a theoretical and action framework for thinking about and working on these issues. It emphasizes the need for

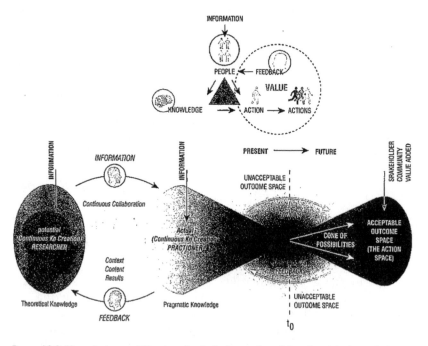

Figure 18.3 Knowledge mobilization. Assimilating and applying the right knowledge to solve problems, make decisions, and take effective actions.

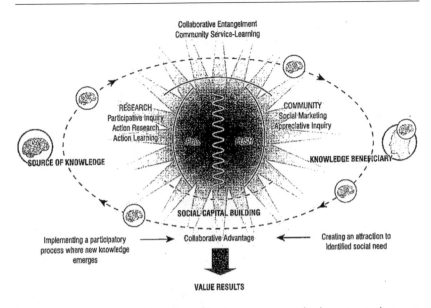

Figure 18.4 Developing collaborative advantage: as an organization, as a nation, as a connected world.

people to come together to develop shared capacity and work on common problems in an experimental and critical manner . . . respond to human needs by democratic and equitable processes . . . learn about community and its situation . . . recognize that every member of the community has knowledge which may be critical to solving a problem, but can be discovered only if that individual has a voice . . . communities become learning organizations.

(p. 711)

Within this Deweyian framework, inquiry situated within and derived from different communities' needs and goals; knowledge is negotiated, held and used in a reciprocal fashion by and with individuals and groups.

These discussions may be less visible in literacy journals, but are clearly and repeatedly addressed in current essays appearing for the broader educational research community such as through the Educational Researcher over the past two years and British Journal of Educational Research. In essays and book reviews in 2008–2009, matters of indeterminism of research findings, hybridization of research findings, site-based complexities, the social processes of knowing and the position of knower and knowledge, the merits and nature of research syntheses are among the topics discussed repeated. For example, in her recent book *Getting Lost* (Lather, 2008a) and her review essay in Educational Researcher (Lather, 2008), Lather troubled the return to positivism and determinism her recent review of an edited book by F. Hess (2008) entitled, "*When research matters: how scholarship influences educational policy.*" Drawing upon Canadian researchers, Pitt and Britzman (2003), Lather argues for "embracing constitutive unknowingness, generative undecidability, and what it means to document becoming" (Lather, 2008b p. 363). In her article and other articles, we have energetic discussions as to whether or not research can be viewed as deterministic versus indeterminate or transferable versus situation-specific.

Overall, we seem to be seeing a potential shift to realization or re-realization of an account of educational research which encompasses a fuller consideration of the complexities, scope and dynamics of participation as well as alternative conceptualizations of the generative character within and across the communities pursuing inquiries. I would suggest we might see a new generation of research models for educational research, which connects the research enterprise to ongoing collective and sustainable inquiry.

Closing Comments

The suggestion that the standards- and testing-based reform efforts may pass and shift to our rear vision mirror should not be considered farfetched. While Australia seems to be amidst a major struggle between its support for diversity and matters of equity and its initial embrace of a form of standards and some national testing practices as a means of achieving a new form of federalism in education, I am hopeful that developments both in North America and globally have seeded a shift toward teacher-based inquiry in all countries. Indeed, international comparisons on tests (especially the success of countries such as Finland) appear to warrant a shift away from standardization to a form of what Hargreaves and Shirley (2007) suggest is "post-standardization" where:

> . . . summative quality assurance is replaced by assessment *for learning*, where data are used to inform ongoing decisions to produce better outcomes. In this second theory of change, the teaching profession is a high-caliber resource for and responsible partner in modernization, not an obstacle to be undermined.

Whereas standards-based testing as a means of achieving school improvements may give the appearance of data-based decision-making by teachers, the high-stakes testing has become more often a stick rather than a support to teachers. The road ahead requires a more dynamic and robust form of assessment and inquiry. It demands a richer collaboration among teachers, researchers, other resource personnel, learners, and community stakeholders. The notion of *rich* collaborative communities of inquiry might represent a better fit with the nature of educational decision-making than the singularly positivistic orientation and translation models that seem to be trying to imitate the physical sciences and findings that simplify the connection between research and practice as well as objectify rather than humanize the differential support needs of all learners and reciprocal expectations of communities.

References

Bennett, A. & Bennet, A. (2007) *Knowledge mobilization in the social sciences and humanities: moving from research to action*. Frost, West Virginia; MQI Press.

Blair, J. (2004). Congress orders thorough study of teacher education programs. *Education Week*, *23*(25), 13.

Bruce B. & Bishop, A. (2008) New literacies and community inquiry. In J. Coiro, M. Knobel, C. Lankshear, & D. J. Leu (Eds.) *Handbook of research on new literacies*. New York: Routledge/Lawrence Erlbaum, pp. 699–741.

Bullock, A. (1975). *A language for life. Report of the Committee of Inquiry appointed by the Secretary of State for Education and Science*. London: Her Majesty's Stationery Office.

Butler, D.L. (2008). *Moving towards a research accord: Conceptualizing educational scholarship and its impact*. Presented on May 30, 2008 at the ACDE Research Accord working group meeting, at the annual meetings of the Canadian Society for Studies in Education. Vancouver, BC.

Butler, D.L., Schnellert, L., & Higginson, S. (2008). *Fostering agency and co-regulation: Teachers using formative assessment to calibrate practice in an age of accountability*. Paper presented at the American Educational Research Association, New York, April, 2008.

Campbell, D. (1975). Assessing the impact of planned social change. In G. Lyons (Ed.), *Social research and public policies; the Dartmouth/OECD conference*. Hanover, NH: Public Affairs Center, Dartmouth College.

Centre for Education Evaluation and Regional Assistance. (2008). *Reading First Impact Study: Interim Report*. Institute of Education Sciences/U.S. Department of Education.

Chan, A., Fisher, D., & Rubenson, K. (2007). *The evolution of professionalism: Educational policy in the provinces and territories of Canada*. New York: Peter Lang.

Dwyer, D. (1996). The imperative to change our schools. In C. Fisher, D. Dwyer & K. Yocam (Eds.), *Education and technology: Reflections on computing in classrooms* (pp. 15–34). San Francisco, CA: Jossey Bass.

Dyson, A. (1995). Writing children: Reinventing the development of childhood literacy. *Written Communication*, *12*(1), 4–46.

Gutierrez, K.D. (2004). Literacy as laminated activity: Rethinking literacy for English learners. In C.M. Fairbanks, J. Worthy, B. Maloch, J.V. Hoffman, & D.L. Schallert (Eds.), *53rd Yearbook of the National Reading Conference* (pp. 101–114). Oak Creek, WI: National Reading Conference.

Hammersley, M. (2008) Troubling criteria: a critical commentary on Furlong and Oancea's framework for assessing educational research. *British Educational Research Journal*, *34*,6, December, 2008, pp. 747–762.

Hargreaves, A. & Shirley, D. (2007). The coming age of post-standardization. *Education Week*, December 21, 27.

Hawisher, G. & Selfe, C. (Eds.), (2000). *Global literacies and the World-Wide Web*. London: Routledge.

Hess, F.M. (2008) When research matters: how scholarship influences educational policy. Cambridge, MA: Harvard University Press.

Jenkins, H., Clinton, K., Purushotma, R., Robison, A.J., & Weigel, M. (2008). *Confronting the Challenges of Participatory Culture: Media Education for the 21st Century*. An Occasional paper, Massachusetts Institute of Technology. http://www.digital learning.macfound.org/atf/cf/%7B7E45C7E0-A3E0-4B89-AC9C-E807E1B0AE4E%7D/JENKINS_WHITE_PAPER.PDF

Kohn, A. (1998). Only for my kid: How privileged parents undermine school reform. *Phi Delta Kappan*, April 1998.

Kress, G. (2003). *Literacy in the new media age*. London: Routledge.

Lather, P. (2008a) *Getting Lost*. Albany: State University of New York Press.

Lather, P. (2008b) New wave utilization research: (re) Imagining the research/policy nexus. *Educational Researcher*, 37,6, 361–364.

Mansell, W. (2007). Test regime must change. *Times Educational Supplement*, November 2, 2007. http://www.tes.co.uk/article.aspx?storycode=2456685

Manzo, K.K. (April 20, 2007). "Reading First" information sent to Justice Dept. *Education Week*, retrieved on August 20, 2007, from http://www.edweek.org/ew/articles/2007/04/25/34read_hear.h26.html.

McEneaney, J.E. (2006). Agent-based literacy theory. *Reading Research Quarterly*, *41*(3), 352–371.

National Reading Panel. (2000). *Teaching children to read: An evidence-based assessment of the scientific research literature on reading and its implications for reading instruction (Report of the Subgroups)*. Washington DC: U.S. Department of Health and Human Services, Public Health Service, National Institutes of Health and the National Institute of Child Health and Human Development.

National Research Council. (2002). *Scientific research in education*. Committee on Scientific Principles for Education Research (Shavelson, Richard J. and Towne, Lisa [Eds.]). Washington D.C.: National Academy Press.

New London Group. (1996). A pedagogy of multiliteracies: Designing social futures. *Harvard Educational Review*, *66*(1), 60–92

New South Wales Department of School Education. (2002). *Aboriginal education policy*. Retrieved from http://www.det.nsw.edu.au/policies/curriculum/schools/aborig_edu/pd02_35_aboriginal_education.pdf.

New South Wales Government. (2007). *Using A to E grades to report student achievement*. Retrieved from http://arc.boardofstudies.nsw.edu.au/go/home/.

Nichols, S.L. & Berliner, D.C. (2007). *Collateral damage: How high stakes testing corrupts America's schools*. Cambridge: Harvard Educational Press.

Office of the Inspector General. (2006). *The Reading First Program's Grant Application Process: Final Inspection Report* ED-016/113-F0017

Pearson, P.D. (2009). *An historical analysis of the impact of educational research on policy and practice: Reading as an illustrative case*. In Rowe, D.W. et al. (Eds.), *56th Yearbook of the National Reading Conference* (pp. 14–40). Oak Creek, WI: National Reading Conference Inc.

Pitt, A.J. & Britzman, D.P. (2007) Speculations on qualities of difficult knowledge in teaching and learning: an experiment in doing psycho-analytic research. In Kenneth George Tobin, K. Tobin, J. Kincheloe (Eds.) *Doing Educational Research explores a variety of important issues and methods in educational research*. Rotterdam: Sense Publishers, pp. 379–402.

Purcell-Gates, V. (2006). What does culture have to do with it? In J.M. Hoffman, D.L. Schallert, C.M. Fairbanks, J. Worthy, & B. Maloch (Eds.), *55th Yearbook of the National Reading Conference* (pp. 43–59). Oak Creek, WI: National Reading Conference, Inc.

Purcell-Gates, V. (2008). *Public policy brief: Increasing literacy levels of Canadian students.* Unpublished paper, University of British Columbia.

Reading Excellence Act of 1998, Pub. L. No. 105–227. Retrieved on December 1, 2006, from http://www.ed.gov/offices/OESE/REA/index.html.

Sheehy, M. (2007). *Can the literacy practices in an after-school program be practiced in school? A study of literacies from a spatial perspective.* Unpublished manuscript.

Squire, K. (2006). From content to context: Videogames as designed experiences. *Educational Researcher, 35*(8), 19–29.

Street, B.V. (2006). New literacies, new times: how do we describe and teach forms of literacy knowledge, skills, and values people need for new times? In J.M. Hoffman, D.L. Schallert, C.M. Fairbanks, J. Worthy, & B. Maloch (Eds.), *55th Yearbook of the National Reading Conference* (pp. 21–42). Oak Creek, WI: National Reading Conference, Inc.

Taylor, B., Pressley, M., & Pearson P.D. (2002). Research-supported characteristics of teachers and schools that promote teaching achievement. In B. Taylor, M. Pressley, & P.D. Pearson (Eds.), *Teaching reading. Effective schools, accomplished teachers* (pp. 361–373). NJ: Lawrence Erlbaum Associates.

The White House. (2001). *No Child Left Behind.* Washington, D.C.: The White House. Retrieved 2007, from http://www.ed.gov/policy/elsec/leg/esea02/index.html, No Child Left Behind Act of 2001. Pub. L. No. 107–110, 115 Stat. 1425 (2002).

United Nations. (2003). *Declaration of principles: a common vision of the information society. World Summit on the information society; building the information society; a global challenge for a new millennium.* December 12, 2003 Geneva. (http://www.itu.int/wsis/docs/geneva/official/dop.html).

United Nations Educational, Scientific and Cultural Organization. (2008). *The ICT Competency Standards for Teachers.* Paris: UNESCO. http://portal.unesco.org/ci/en/ev.phpURL_ID=25740&URL_DO=DO_TOPIC&URL_SECTION=2

United Nations Educational, Scientific and Cultural Organization Institute for Statistics. (2006). *Teacher and Educational Quality: Monitoring global needs for 2015.* Montreal, Quebec.

Index